BABY POOP

BABY POOP

What Your Pediatrician May Not Tell You

*... about Colic, Reflux, Constipation, Green Stools,
Food Allergies, and Your Child's Immune Health*

Linda F. Palmer, DC

Edited by Susan Markel, MD

SUNNY LANE PRESS
San Diego, California

Sunny Lane Press
San Diego, CA

www.BabyReference.com
ORDERS@BabyReference.com

While the author has taken great pains to bring the reader the most accurate information and interpret it wisely, no part of this text is a substitute for medical diagnosis or treatment prescription.

The author and publisher specifically disclaim any and all liability arising directly or indirectly from the use of any information contained in this book. A health care professional should be consulted regarding your specific medical situation. Any product mentioned in this book does not imply endorsement of that product by the author or publisher.

PRINTED IN THE UNITED STATES OF AMERICA

Copyediting and index by Coreen Boucher
Text design by Dana Martin
Cover design by Corlin Design
Back cover photo by Michele Ehlers Photography

Palmer, Linda Folden
    Baby poop : what your pediatrician may not tell you
    about colic, reflux, constipation, green stools, food allergies, and
    your child's immune health / Linda Folden Palmer. --
        p. cm.
    Includes bibliographical references, glossary, and index.
    ISBN 13: 978-0-9753170-2-0
    LCCN: 2015902598

Contents

Why the Poop

The Message in the Diaper

Why would anyone want to talk about baby poop? To many, it's offensive and something to be whisked into the trash or toilet without a second thought. It turns out, however, that this stuff coming out of otherwise adorable little bundles can provide us with worlds of information. Baby poop is a window into the functioning of the most vital systems in a child's body. We don't get baby's words or explanations: We get smiles or tears, and we get poop.

Yes—poop. Parents spend inordinate amounts of time worrying about what goes into their babies. All the while, what shows up in baby's diapers provides tremendous clues about baby's digestion, immune functioning, and overall wellness. The organs that house and produce this stuff are in great control of baby's immunity and nutrient absorption. The health of the digestive system also has tremendous impact on baby's lifelong risks of a wide variety of disorders from diabetes to heart disease to inflammatory bowel diseases. The symptoms that go along with disordered poops help to complete a highly informative picture—not only about what health issues may be presently going on inside baby—but about what future health risks may be threatening. A proactive response to such cues may serve to not only bring greater comfort to baby—and more sleep to those around her—but also to potentially improve the child's lifelong health.

Baby's Vulnerable Gut

The gastrointestinal (GI) tract is the chief means of contact between baby and the outside world. It not only receives food but is bombarded constantly with swallowed microbes from the world around. Because of this vulnerable position, the GI system comprises nearly 70% of the body's own immune system. There's much more, though, to the digestive system's immune forces.

You think of your baby as one organism, but actually trillions of organisms are intricately involved in protecting your child. Thousands of bacterial species inhabit baby's intestines, and they all play a central role in baby's ability to fight infections. Many of these bacteria are also vital to baby's digestion and absorption of nutrients. Some tough microorganisms are crucial for keeping the most dangerous bacteria in check.

Imbalances in baby's flora can lead to lack of tolerance to foods (food allergies), development of GI distresses and eventually GI diseases, and initiation of autoimmune diseases involving other parts of baby's body—such as asthma, diabetes, and arthritis. Certain bacteria, which result from poor gut health, play roles in causing obesity, which can lead to heart disease and can further increase baby's risk of developing health-impairing diabetes in later decades.

The health of the digestive system also has tremendous impact on baby's lifelong risks of a wide variety of disorders from diabetes to heart disease to inflammatory bowel diseases.

Floral balance has recently been discovered to even play a part in the development of autism—which has escalated to one in every 68 U.S. children. Food reactions have certain brain effects as well. These reactions often result from, and possibly contribute to, the development of disorders on the autism spectrum.

Even though allergies, autism, bowel diseases, and other autoimmune maladies all have genetic components, genetics are becoming less and less important to the development of these disorders that are growing at exploding rates. Early drug exposures—especially antibiotics, interferences in the birth process and in natural feeding, and a slew of other factors, from pesticides to plasticizers, have all been shown to play roles in the dramatically increased risks of chronic illnesses

Just because events may not have all gone entirely as planned, there are ways to help a child's gut recover and to reduce his future health risks.

in our children and the adults they will become. The modern child's restricted contact with dirt and sunshine also contributes to these consequences, as does regular use of highly sterilized water.

In this book, I will present how the seeds for all of these developments are planted in infancy—the most vulnerable and formative period—being driven chiefly by interruptions in intestinal health. I demonstrate that just because events may not have all gone entirely as planned, there are ways to help a child's gut recover and to reduce his future health risks.

Gut Beginnings

The mode of baby's birth—whether vaginal or surgical—and the place of birth—whether home, birth center, or hospital—have been found to yield tremendous impact on the establishment of baby's flora. Strongly measurable differences in long-term disease risks have been correlated to children's floral beginnings.

Newborns have little immune system functioning of their own. Breastmilk regularly coats the digestive track and provides a large portion of an infant's protection, in part by supporting a highly protective flora. Breastmilk also supplies factors that automatically wipe out various unwanted microbes and, through the broncho-entero-mammary pathway, supplies antibodies that are specifically tailored to defend against whatever microbes are currently challenging the child. Extra gut healing efforts can help mitigate the greater infection risks posed if infant formula has been introduced early.

In case of a preterm birth, it is highly valuable for expectant parents to learn about issues over which they may have some influence. Premature infants can face many critical health challenges. Most challenges have to do with feeding and with the digestive system. Even though premature infants are cared for in the hospital, with experienced medical staff performing life-saving measures, parents can take steps to increase their child's chances for optimal outcome. The value of human milk is unmatched in the health and development of premature infants, although a child born early can pose many challenges to breastfeeding. Some of the most valuable options are not standard practice in most preemie care units.

Problematic Poop

Orange, lime, black, purple, red, white; watery, seedy, mucusy, runny, pasty, hard—there's a huge spectrum of possible findings in babies' diapers. Before we can begin to talk about abnormal poop, we need to know what normal poop is. Infant stools are surprisingly different in appearance and frequency from what adults are used to, and changes in poop habits can be alarming to parents. Yet, these are the important signals that, if properly read, tell what's going on inside a child's body. Observed changes are cues to seek answers and to respond with good attention. *Baby Poop* helps parents to ascertain the options that are available for response to observed stool changes—from a need to alter baby's diet to a need to seek urgent medical care.

Many pediatricians are uninterested in most stool color or consistency changes. Generally, they'll assume these are from either a change in diet or a little stomach bug and usually this is the case. Yet, baby poop and a few other symptoms are all we have to go by in terms of determining the presence or absence of some disorder.

Diarrhea is the body's means of rushing anything unwanted quickly out of the body. This is particularly important in the case of food or chemical poisoning. It helps to rid a child of bacterial or viral infection as well. Our primary goal is not to stop the diarrhea; rather, our goal is to determine the cause and decide how best to prevent or treat it. Baby's doctor needs to be involved when baby is sick with infectious diarrhea or when the cause is not known, but it's still the parents' job to continue baby's care at home. Besides GI infections, a great deal of diarrhea in children results from hypersensitivity reactions to foods. Regardless of the cause, any significant amount of diarrhea can lead to dangerous dehydration. *Baby Poop* provides information for dealing with the home care of children who have diarrhea from various causes and for preventing future cases.

Baby Poop *helps parents to ascertain the options that are available for response to observed stool changes.*

Constipation can quickly turn into a serious problem, or can become a chronic problem for years. On the other hand, infants can go 10 days or more without presenting any poop and still not be constipated. This is rather common, but is it healthy? Baby will benefit greatly when caretakers vigilantly note the frequency with which a slow pooper moves his bowels and the consistency in which the poop arrives. Once problems are detected, early healing efforts can reduce lifelong stool challenges.

Food allergy and intolerance join the ranks of other rapidly growing disorders in children and are often the first signs of future GI ailments and autoimmune diseases. Food reactions are largely the cause of early colic, reflux, constipation, diarrhea, sleeplessness, rashes, and many more symptoms. Outside of genetic tendencies, which are becoming less and less necessary for food allergy develop-ment, challenges to infant gut health are at the root of such food reactions.

Industrialization and Disease

Infectious disease rates are high in many less developed parts of the world, with high infant and child mortality rates. Infectious diarrhea is second only to pneumonia as a cause of death among children in developing nations. Appropriate sanitation and hygiene, adequate food and financial resources, and available medical care bring infec-tious disease rates far lower in industrialized nations—but industrialization, medicine, and money are not the end-all answers to optimal child survival. Even though the United States

Even though the United States ranks Number 1 in health expenditures, 55 nations rank better than the United States in infant survival.

ranks Number 1 in health expenditures—with one third more money spent per person than the next highest country—55 nations rank better than the United States in infant survival. In terms of child survival rates before the age of five, 44 countries

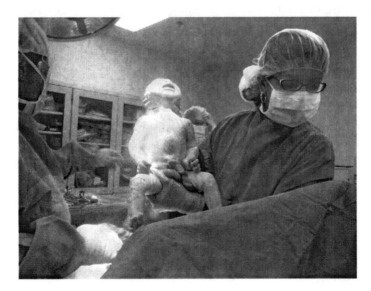

are better than the United States. The United States has the 10th highest rate of cesarean sections, at one third of all births. Although occasionally valuable, cesarean births can cause lasting impairments in children's floral balance, which is reflected in their overall health. Maybe this high cesarean rate saves more mothers? No. Forty-eight nations have better maternal survival rates than the United States, including some developing or recently developed countries such as Serbia, Bulgaria, and Kuwait—and the U.S. maternal death rate has recently been rising—a 50% increase from 1990 to 2013. The United States is the only industrialized nation with increasing maternal mortality, and anesthesia complications are a major cause of this increase.

The United States is the only industrialized nation with increasing maternal mortality, and anesthesia complications are a major cause of this increase.

Clearly there's more that can be done to protect our children and mothers. *Baby Poop* brings answers from science and medical studies and from the collective wisdoms of mothers, midwives, lactation consultants, and other infant care specialists—answers that are shown to optimize children's health.

Bacterial staph infections have long been an enemy in hospital patient care. Today's medical practices have not only created a super-strain of *Staphylococcus* that resists antibiotic drugs but also have altered the floral balance of whole populations, which has allowed this new strain—known as MRSA—to flourish in communities throughout Europe and the Americas. In 2011, the number of U.S. MRSA deaths per citizen was more than triple the rate of polio deaths during the peak of the polio epidemic.

It's common to blame the growing predominance of chronic diseases on our longer lifespans, but these diseases are appearing at ever younger ages.

Although MRSA commonly affects the skin and other areas, its chief reservoir is the gut, including the intestines of a large percentage of young children.

Even more recently, a bacterial GI infection, *Clostridium difficile*, has actually surpassed MRSA in its devastating impact—caused again by excess antibiotic use and allowed to flourish due to many other gut-damaging practices. An especially toxic new strain of C. *diff* is appearing frequently in young children, both in hospitals and in the community.

Dangerous strains of *E. coli* are currently making inroads as well—especially affecting premature infants. This occurrence is strongly linked to the provision of antibiotics to mothers during labor.

Infectious diseases are far more avoidable than they once were, and lifespans greatly lengthened, yet chronic, chiefly autoimmune illnesses have soared. It's common to blame the growing predominance of chronic diseases on our longer lifespans, but these diseases are appearing at ever younger ages. The percentage of children suffering from asthma has increased to 10%, up from 2% in the 1960s. Childhood obesity tripled between 1980 and 2002, now at 17%. Nearly 25% of children suffer from food hypersensitivities, up from negligible levels 50 years before. Lastly, 2 in 1,000 U.S. children have already developed diabetes by the age of nineteen, 5 times as many as in 1935.

Looking far down the road in a child's life—where there's chronic inflammation, there's a great risk of cancer. Colon and other digestive system cancers are strongly linked to the kinds of early GI assaults and maladies that are described throughout this book.

Although the life-threatening dangers were recognized in the 70s, it wasn't until 2005 that U.S. federal guidelines weakly recommended against the consumption of trans fats.

To help prevent your child from joining any of these statistics, gut healing and continued gut health efforts are worthwhile, especially if your child expresses any of the symptoms of concern discussed in this book, has been exposed early to antibiotic drugs, has had early exposure to formula feeding, or has experienced multiple GI infections.

Industrialized Nutrition

Another chapter in the story of industrialization's progression from widespread infectious diseases to a predominance of chronic illnesses is the tale of advancement from a low food supply to an excess of poorly nourishing and even toxic foods.

Economics, and later, bad science, led to vitamin D-filled (when animals lived outdoors) butter and lard being replaced with toxic trans fats from hydrogenated vegetable oils. Well known today for their serious heart-damaging effects, chronic inflammation caused by consumption of trans fats begins where they enter the body: the gut. Although the life-threatening dangers were recognized in the 70s, it wasn't until 2005 that U.S. federal guidelines weakly recommended against the consumption of trans fats.

Fish and liver consumption dropped throughout the 1900s, leaving everyone deficient in the important omega-3 fatty acids, DHA and EPA. This deficiency has largely contributed to the development of food allergies and to chronic inflammation in general. For unknown reasons, "meat by-products" became villainized and their consumption also decreased. As a result, consumption of the omega-3 fatty acids, which the by-products contain, dropped even more. Also found in these joint and organ tissues are joint-building and intestinal-healing factors such as glucosamine, hyaluronic acid, MSM, and chondroitin sulfate. These too vanished from our diets—these being already quite reduced when bone broths disappeared from common consumption during the 1800s.

Infant Guts in the Industrialized World

Baby Poop is about child health dilemmas faced in industrialized nations. These are distinctly different from the challenges in less developed countries as most of these challenges are caused directly by modernization. Below are some of the important issues that will be discussed in this book:

- 15 to 25% of U.S. babies suffer from colic and/or reflux.

Today, nearly the same number of babies who were once labeled with colic are now diagnosed with reflux—concordant with the emergence of expensive new reflux drugs. Other symptoms such as green stools, diarrhea, or constipation often go along with colic and spitting up, and they help to determine the true root causes of baby's discomfort.

- 4 to 8% of infants receive the newer, expensive reflux medicines today.

These drugs have not been proven to reduce the crying, spitting up, and other symptoms for which they are prescribed, yet they have some concerning side effects. Examining the symptoms and exploring more effective solutions can bring a happier, healthier baby.

- The most common cause of colic, reflux, non-infectious diarrhea, and constipation is food hypersensitivity—whether to formula, solid foods, or to foods in nursing mother's diet.

Food reactions and other allergies have grown immensely in the industrialized world, as a direct result of many modern practices. Finding and avoiding irritating foods and taking other steps to heal the gut not only bring greater comfort to baby but help prevent future diseases.

- 10% of infants who experience colic continue to have colic symptoms past a year.

Even more children continue other GI symptoms from infancy. Contrary to common medical lore, a large portion of babies don't just "grow out" of colic;

rather, they "grow in" to new symptoms that can haunt them into adulthood when not addressed early.

- 35% of Americans aged 20 years or older today have pre-diabetes.

This autoimmune disease is growing at an alarming rate in industrialized nations, as are other autoimmune diseases. Early gut health is the biggest factor, and efforts that move toward normalizing baby poop are the key to reducing a child's future health risks.

- Infectious diarrhea accounts for over 1.5 million outpatient visits for U.S. children.

Medications for these infections are seldom much help and often make matters worse. Good monitoring, consistent hydration, and support of the immune system will bring optimal results.

- Frequent, small amounts of soft or watery poops are generally a sign of constipation.

Potty training age is the most common time for a child to develop withholding. This can lead to stool blockage and uncontrollable leaking around the impaction.

- 20 to 30% of young children who have constipation problems continue to have significant constipation challenges into adulthood.

Constipation in young children is highly common, but greatly ignored, even though one simple case of constipation can quickly turn into a serious problem.

- Adults who had been exposed to antibiotics before the age of one are over 5 times more likely to develop irritable bowel syndrome than those with no childhood antibiotic use.

Researchers today are realizing that early antibiotic exposures can have large consequences for the lifelong health of children. These exposures are shown to increase a child's vulnerability to the later development of any one or combination of the following: inflammatory bowel disease, celiac disease, allergies, autism, diabetes, and obesity.

Healing Baby's Gut

The good news is that studies with probiotics and other healing measures are revealing that positive impacts can be made on baby's flora and intestinal health—thereby reducing later risks of many chronic diseases. The first step is to discover and remove any gut-irritating factors.

Baby Poop: Becoming a parent means becoming an expert not only on what goes into your baby but also on what comes out.

These pages will tell you how. I encourage parents to take charge of their own child's health while keeping healthcare professionals in the loop.

This book is designed to assist parents in making choices that are best suited to their own family's needs and priorities—and choices that can make a real difference. I believe that becoming a parent means becoming an expert not only on what goes *into* your baby but also on what comes *out*.

It's Alive

The Biggest Part of Your Baby's Immune System

Amazingly, 90% of the cells in your baby's body do not come from your genetic contributions; rather these cells come from bacteria and some fungi. These microorganisms are far smaller than human cells, though far greater in abundance. Starting from scratch, your baby will hopefully accommodate from 10 billion to over 10 trillion total microorganisms in his intestines, the majority of these within a few days after birth. These microbes are referred to as the intestinal **flora**. That's a lot of mouths to feed! So let's try to do it well.

Bacterial flora can be considered the most important part of a baby's immune protection. You may be surprised to learn about the huge impact that intestinal bacteria can have on your baby's health and the powerful effect very early floral development can have on your child's whole life. The establishment of healthy intestinal bacteria can go a long way toward ensuring an infant's overall health, yet pediatricians are only beginning to pay attention to this valuable system of microorganisms.

Intestinal flora aids in digestion, performs several kinds of immune functions, and provides various kinds of nutritional support. It helps to guide intestinal growth in infants, controls inflammation, and plays roles in the creation and absorption of gas. Most of our flora is made up of "good guys." Then there are "tough guys" who help to hold back overgrowth of the most undesirable bacteria. When out of balance, the flora plays a role in generating diseases such as inflammatory bowel disease, celiac disease, allergies, autism, diabetes, and even obesity. The stage for these can be set during infancy and, as we will discuss further, antibiotic drug treatments create the greatest assault on healthy flora.

With the advent of new DNA sequencing technology for recognizing specific strains of bacteria, research on infant intestinal flora is abundant today and offers promising findings. Science has gone even deeper than bacterial flora to learn that it, too, has its own natural flora of sorts. A huge spectrum of tiny viruses, known as **bacterio-phages**, lives among the gut bacteria and plays roles in supporting and maintaining the bacterial colonies. Russia is already using phage therapy to treat antibiotic resistant bacterial infections, with good success. Phage therapy research is just beginning in the West. Knowledge of this important viral support system for flora begs the question as to whether anti-viral medications, occasionally used in treating flus, could disrupt healthy bacterial flora by ruining its own submicroscopic support system.

Most of our flora is made up of "good guys." Then there are "tough guys" who help to hold back overgrowth of the most undesirable bacteria.

For a healthier and happier baby with a more vital future, a basic under-standing of the growth and actions of your baby's intestinal microbes can help you understand the benefits of maintaining healthy flora and recognize acces-sible options when things go awry.

Gut Flora Works to Complete Baby's Nutrition

Children and adults harbor upwards of 1,000 different bacterial species—of several thousand possible strains—throughout their bodies. Some 700 different species of bacteria are found in the gut and make up over half of the solids in poop. Although the small intestine has its own smaller assortment of florae, with their own duties, the flora in the large intestine, or **colon**, plays an important role in baby's nutrition.

Food is largely processed by digestive enzymes in the stomach and the small intestine and then is passed on to the large intestine. From the matter presented to the colon, various kinds of bacterial flora produce several essential vitamins that are absorbed and used by baby's body. Many B vitamins are created. The ones that are thought to be absorbed into the body include B2 (riboflavin), B5 (pantothenic acid), B7 (biotin), and B12 (cobalamin). Vitamin K2, used for blood clotting and bone growth, is also produced by the flora and absorbed.

Though all of these vitamins are also available in a child's diet, mild deficiencies of some of these vitamins are seen with various intestinal diseases, meaning that children's bodies rely somewhat on flora to complete their nutritional needs. Frequent antibiotic treatments may create mild temporary vitamin deficiencies in babies by wiping out much of the vitamin-forming flora.

In addition to creating vitamins, the colonic flora helps to digest many components of consumed food. Important for brain development, over 40% of calories in human milk and infant formula come from sugars, which are simple carbohydrates. The obliging flora helps to digest and absorb many of the various sugars that pass through the baby's own digestion. It also assists in the absorption of fats and proteins.

Lactose is a sugar that is not found in any food other than milks from mammals, such as breastmilk and cow milk, and left in many milk formulas. This baby sugar attracts some more beneficial flora to dinner, such as many kinds of **bifidobacteria**. As these types of flora break down (**ferment**) lactose and some other food components, they produce a variety of **fatty acids** that nourish the intestinal linings, help with the absorption of calcium and other minerals, and nourish baby's body in other ways.

The digestive assistance of intestinal flora is far greater in infants than in adults—another reason why disturbing healthy flora can shift the trajectory for health and wellness in early life.

Healthy bacterial flora increases the amount of calories an infant derives from his diet. This is a very important concept in a baby with weight gain challenges that has been on antibiotics, which wipe out much of the healthy flora. A study of rats raised without bacterial flora, known as germ-free rats, found they need to eat 18% more calories. It's possible that a baby who has been on antibiotics and diagnosed with "failure to thrive" would benefit from probiotic supplementation with bifidobacteria in order to obtain more calories from its diet. Just as the germ-free rats mentioned above require 18%

Supplementing a breast-fed infant with formula, when intending to boost weight gain, may actually raise the caloric requirement for the child, increasing the amount of milk needed.

more calories than those with full flora, human infants who receive any formula or foods besides breastmilk are known to consume 20% more calories. It's probable that the greater amount of the digestive-aiding friendly flora in exclusively breastfed infant intestines take partial responsibility for this discrepancy in caloric intake, as this flora increases the digestion and absorption of sugars, fats, and proteins, decreasing overall caloric needs. This means that supplementing a breastfed infant with formula, when intending to boost weight gain—a seldom successful effort—may actually raise the caloric requirement for the child, increasing the amount of milk needed or decreasing weight gain.

flora and fermentation

The term **fermentation** is used for microbial digestion of carbohydrates. We know from winemaking that fermentation of fruit by yeast creates alcohol—and gas. Well, besides valuable fatty acids and other end results of bacterial fermentation in the intestines, gas is created. All babies—all people, for that matter—create plenty of gas every day. A large portion of gas is absorbed into the bloodstream and handled nicely from there to be expelled by the lungs. Some gas comes up as burping, and some goes out the other end—quietly or loudly, odorless or odiferous—depending upon what's going on in the intestines at the time. With healthy flora, a good portion of gas can be handled by certain other kinds of friendly bacteria that consume gas. These are generally various kinds of **lactobacilli** and are handy to have around.

When gas is made chiefly from fermenting leftover complex carbohydrates from breastmilk and/or vegetable matter, it's generally hydrogen and carbon dioxide—the not-smelly kind. Unfriendly

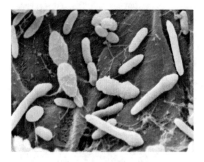

bacteria may dominate if good bacteria are wiped out by antibiotic use or if the flora is imbalanced from illness, food reactions, or other reasons. These unfriendly problem guys may gobble healthy sulfur compounds from the diet and turn them into smelly sulfur dioxide gas, rather than allowing the child to absorb the healthy sulfates. Sulfur gas is known to add insult to some digestive disorders in infants. Formula-fed babies may fall somewhere in-between these two examples. The flora in formula-fed babies makes methanethiol gas, which can cause some unpleasant odor. Soy formula-derived flora also produces extra hydrogen sulfide and methane gas, which also may carry extra odor. In a solid food eater, a high meat-protein diet can occasionally develop some extra odor as can a diet with excess sugars.

Detoxifying

When not wiped out by antibiotics, healthy flora performs many detoxifying tasks, turning unwanted chemicals into non-harmful substances. For instance, good flora will turn nitrates found in the diet into nitric oxide that helps keep the linings of arteries healthy. Beneficial flora also acts to see that toxic mercury entering the body orallay is carried away in the poop. When antibiotics have been used, undesirable flora causes mercury to be retained. This mercury is then detrimentally stored in the brain and other organs. Some toxins are even degraded to more harmful chemicals by unfriendly flora; however, the body can be an effective filter for unwanted toxins if a healthy dose of friendly flora is maintained in the intestines.

Flora Provides Valuable Immune Protection

Intestinal flora in the newborn plays a very valuable role in the development of the baby's immune system. The flora continues to be a very important part of a young child's immune protection in a multitude of ways. This immune role occurs in healthy bodies throughout life but is most powerful during exclusive breastfeeding.

As one example, friendly flora creates antibiotic-type factors, referred to as **bacteriocins**. When in healthy abundance and variety, bacteriocins kill off specific undesirable strains of bacteria—keeping it all friendly.

In a healthy intestine, a large portion of the beneficial bacteria attach themselves to the mucus that coats the intestinal walls, where they do the following:

- gobble up available nutrients in order to starve out undesirable bacteria
- produce fatty acids that help maintain the health of intestinal membranes
- tighten the junctions of cells that line the intestinal walls so inappropriate proteins or bacteria don't leak through the walls
- act as guards
- create communities that have greater strength in numbers
- dominate attachment sites preventing undesirable bacteria from being able to glom on
- rouse immune system responses when enemies are detected

Some types of the friendliest flora, chiefly certain strains of *Lactobacillus* and *Bifidobacterium*, are equipped to flourish when special immune-aiding carbohydrates (oligosaccharides) are provided by mother's milk. In turn, these strains of flora provide extra prevention against infections while the infant's own immune system matures.

Once formula or any other food is introduced to baby, other more challenging kinds of bacteria feed on the free iron now available from these foods. These new flora grow to overshadow some of the protective abilities of bifidobacteria and lactobacilli. Of course, eventually every baby will consume some other food besides breastmilk. Thus, at some point, every child's flora will grow to be more and more like adult flora, which has its own purposes and benefits.

This "mature" flora, depending upon its quality, continues to protect against intestinal infections and to temper inflammatory processes elsewhere in the body. German researchers recently showed that intestinal flora is even involved in the initiation of the body's immune responses against viruses, such as colds and the flu.

Gut-Brain Axis: Flora Influences Baby's Brain

The ability of the brain to influence gut health has long been studied. We know that stress can create diarrhea, and depression can create constipation, though these are seen more in adults than in young children. Impressive new studies are finding that the reverse can also be true—gut flora actually plays quite a role in regulating mood and other brain functions. More studies confirm this every day and indicate that it happens more significantly in infants than in adults.

Studies on mice suggest that certain permanent beneficial brain effects from the establishment of good flora seem to be initiated only during infancy.

Studies on mice are suggesting that certain permanent beneficial brain effects from the establishment of good flora seem to be initiated only during infancy.

In one study, researchers fed mice a strain of *Lactobacillus* known as *L. rhamnosus*. This strain is common in healthy guts, found in many yogurts, and is found in high numbers in the majority of breastfed babies. Mice fed *L. rhamnosus* demonstrated lower anxiety and stress hormone levels and were not prone to show the depression symptoms seen in other test mice. Researchers then cut the vagus nerve in these mice, which is a long nerve that connects the gut to the brain. The mice's hormone levels returned to prior levels once this neurological connection between brain and gut was gone, confirming that the flora was influencing brain functions. Although *L. rhamnosus* was used in this one study, *Bifidobacterium infantis* and other lactobacilli and bifidobacteria are used in similar studies. A large part of the friendly flora appears to have these early brain-enriching abilities.

Some of these studies used germ-free mice. These are mice that have been raised in a perfectly sterile environment and thus have no gut flora. Permanent, beneficial brain hormone effects were found when greater amounts of *Lactobacillus* florae were given to germ-free infant mice than found in average baby mice. By the same token, when studies introduced undesirable bacteria early on, lasting increases in stress behaviors were seen. If healthy flora was introduced only to older germ-free mice, after the age of weaning, benefits were not found. These findings suggest that youngsters have a sensitive period when flora can greatly impact brain development. Beyond this early period, flora may have less effect—good or bad—on the brain's stress and mood regulating receptors.

When studies introduced undesirable bacteria early on, lasting increases in stress behaviors were seen.

Although germ-free human babies don't exist, definite differences in human infant floral makeup are seen to be dependent upon their earliest environment. Diet and antibiotic usage are two early influences with great impact. Highly sterile environments are found to be less optimal. Measurable brain differences can be found between mice growing up germ free, those growing up with average flora, and those with high levels of the friendliest of flora. Definite brain differences are likely to be found in human children and adults—dependent upon many flora-affecting factors from their earliest weeks and months after birth.

Many other kinds of studies on animals and humans suggest this same kind of permanent influence on brain receptor formation based upon the earliest environments of infants. Besides stress hormones, researchers have measured direct beneficial effects from the flora on several other brain chemicals, including regulatory factors such as GABA and the "happy hormones," **serotonin** and dopamine.

The take-home message here is this: paying special attention to floral development and giving high priority to the health of your baby's gut can positively influence the permanent brain development and psychological health of your child. Psychologists know that frequent closeness and skin-to-skin contact with infants strongly encourages their emotional health. Can floral development be part of this process?

Establishment of Flora in the Newborn

The standard mantra has always been that babies are born entirely sterile, meaning they have no bacteria in their bodies before the moment of birth. In 2008, Spanish researchers discovered bacteria in the amniotic fluid of mice and in

the cord blood of healthy human infants. In order to confirm their contention, the researchers fed a labeled strain of bacteria to pregnant mice and later found the same labeled bacteria in the first stools of the baby mice, though delivered by C-section so as not to be exposed during birth. Although newborn intestines do not appear heavily colonized by bacteria, apparently babies are not born sterile. The chief bacteria found were common strains of *Enterococcus* and *Staphylococcus* that are already known to reside in newborns in the first days after birth. They did not find the healthy types of bacteria that dominate in breastfed intestines by a week after birth. There apparently hasn't been much interest in this topic as there appear to be no further studies to confirm or deny the presence of bacteria before birth. Most pediatric literature still refers to the newborn as sterile.

During birth, the passage of the child against mother's rectum generally causes some maternal stool to be passed. Babies are typically born facing mother's back side where their mouth becomes exposed to some of mother's intestinal flora as they head out. This occurrence is believed to be an important exposure for the infant and appears to have long-term impact on the eventual array of bacteria the child maintains. Even if born in a different position, babies will be exposed at least to vaginal flora. Their nose and skin likewise become seeded with what is, hopefully, healthy and protective flora provided by mom just before baby enters the outside world. The newborn's next exposures are from the air and people around her, mother's nipples, and mother's kisses. Somewhat different floral signatures can be found in infants based upon the environment they are born into (i.e., every environment has its own spectrum of bacteria and will provide a different array of flora to a newborn).

Infants born in large urban hospitals tend to harbor flora that is less favorable than that derived in smaller centers. A less desirable character to their flora is found to persist for a long time. Whereas hospitals tend to harbor a high portion of potentially infection-causing bacteria, a child home birthed to a healthy family tends to become inoculated with a healthier spectrum of flora. Imagine the huge change that must have occurred in the collective flora of entire populations within developed countries since birthing first moved from homes to hospitals during the 1930s through the 1950s.

In the months and years before delivery, mother's efforts to eat healthy and to otherwise maintain a healthy intestinal environment likely go a long way toward enhancing the health of her offspring.

During birth, through other contact with her infant, and through her breastmilk, mother has a large impact on the floral development of her newborn. With this realization, expecting mothers will want to do the most they can to bring their flora into an optimal state before birth. In the months and years before delivery, mother's efforts to eat healthy and to otherwise maintain a healthy intestinal environment likely go a long way toward enhancing the health of her offspring. Certainly, father's flora comes into the picture as well.

Establishment of Flora after Cesarean Section

Studies find infant flora in the first days after a cesarean birth to be much less diverse than that of vaginally delivered babies. Infants born via cesarean with no prior labor (elective C-section) have the least diverse flora, suggesting that mother passes some flora to baby during labor. Greater diversity of intestinal bacterial species is linked to greater health.

For allergic parents, a home-birthed child showed half the risk of future food allergy and asthma as one born vaginally in the hospital.

Additionally, the valuable bifidobacteria are conspicuously absent in the days after cesarean birth. Even though mother's milk is known to contain plenty bifidobacteria and lactobacilli, these are slow to appear in the guts of cesarean born babies.

Irregularities in the flora of infants born by cesarean are still measurable 6 months after birth. Particularly, an increased appearance of challenging clostridia bacteria is seen in the months after C-section. One study found that an increase in allergy symptoms correlated with higher clostridia levels and another found increased C. *difficile* at one month to coordinate with increased asthma symptoms at age 6 to 7 years.

A Netherlands study also found C. *difficile* more often in babies born vaginally in the hospital versus those born at home. For allergic parents in this study, a home-birthed child showed half the risk of future food allergy and asthma as one born vaginally in the hospital.

Children born by cesarean are known to suffer many more maladies than those born vaginally, and their less perfect floral establishment correlates with these findings in many studies. Scientific reviews have found children born by C-section to suffer:

- 20% more asthma
- 23% more diabetes
- 36% more of a certain skeletal disease (aseptic necrosis of the femoral head)
- more hospitalizations for intestinal infections
- more celiac disease

In addition, children of allergic mothers were more likely to develop allergies when born via C-section.

Continued Establishment of Flora in the Infant

Infants with siblings tend to have a slightly higher amount of friendly bifidobacteria than those without, confirming the great value of diverse, natural exposures in the early days. Formula-fed infants develop a more adult-like spectrum of challenging florae—including E. *coli*, *Staphylococcus*, and *Clostridium*—and will carry far fewer bifidobacteria. Exclusively breastfed infants will harbor many lactobacilli and yield around 90% bifidobacteria by a week after birth. Premature infants are found to have very limited flora, are low or lacking in health-promoting bifidobacteria and lactobacilli, and possess many kinds of unfriendly flora, including nasty **Clostridium difficile**. While living in the neonatal intensive care unit (**NICU**), limited exposure to mother and family, excess hygiene, antibiotic use, and formula supplements are all factors that hinder floral development in preemies.

Canadian professor, James Scott, compared the flora in stools of 3-month old infants to the bacteria in dust found in their homes and found great overlap. Skin flora was expected in the dust, as it lives in air, but fecal flora is designed to live in oxygen-free environments. Scott explained that the non-aerobic intestinal bacteria can release spores that can live outside the body. These can then bloom whenever they find a warm moist body to live in again. Families evidently share their flora a great deal, even beyond initial colonization of the infant. Clearly, the health of parents and siblings can impact the health of an infant through their flora and probably vice versa.

Scientists from San Francisco investigated the reason that babies who grow up with pets have fewer allergies. The scientists found a more varied gut flora when their study mice were living with dogs, especially when the dogs would go outside and come in again. An increased variety of such dog-introduced flora was linked not only to reduced asthma but also to reduced respiratory infections. They suspect this same kind of floral influence may occur with human babies. I suspect that decreased intestinal infections and possibly even decreased food allergies could be found as well. Of course, if a child is already allergic to the dog or other pet, the constant irritation from living with it would probably be worse than any floral benefits. There are other ways to gain good flora boosts from the out of doors.

Babies love to have fingers in their mouths—their own and those of others. This universal behavior is certainly a means of gradually obtaining more and more exposure to the microbes in their environment in order to increase the variety, and thus the strength, of their gut flora. I've heard of parents who are afraid of kissing their babies on their mouths, but this sharing of flora is also beneficial. Babies whose parents "clean" their pacifiers by sucking on them themselves have been found to experience two-thirds less asthma, eczema, and other allergic sensitization.

Flora of a Lifetime

Scientists are finding that the first moments, days, and weeks of life outside the womb play a large role in what will be a child's lifetime assortment of intestinal flora. At one time, researchers had difficulty understanding how this could be, with the common thinking that flora only lived inside the lumen, or the open space inside the intestines, thus being regularly pushed through. Scientists recently learned that colonies of bacteria actually live in little crypts, or caves, inside the walls of the intestines. Researchers have found it difficult to replace one intestinal colony with another strain, revealing the stable nature of these colonies. The finding of these crypts helped to create an increased understanding about the more permanent nature of bacterial strains.

Though floral makeup drifts from day to day and year to year, everyone has their own particular spectrum of flora, with genetics playing some role in the makeup. Early environmental factors of maternal influence, antibiotic use, mode of birth, and diet play considerable roles. A person's entire makeup of flora, including that on their skin, in their sinuses and other orifices, as well as intestinal flora, is referred to today as their **microbiome**, with the microbes involved being referred to as their **microbiota**. A child's array of flora, or microbiome, gradually shifts toward adult flora as her diet grows into chiefly solid foods, but her earliest infant microbiota still has significant impact.

Though health specialists have known for a very long time that flora affects a person's health, in-depth research is only beginning. Research about the environmental influences on infant flora, and the impact of infants' flora on their health, is truly in its infancy. Many studies suggest long-term or even permanent impacts of certain early influences on an individual's microbiome, but discovery of these influences is only the first step. Research on the use of supplemental probiotics and nutrition to improve intestinal health, and thus overall health, is also just leaving its infancy, especially when it comes to young children.

The Road to Health

Birth, infant feeding, and care seldom go exactly as we've planned. Although the road will likely be easier when optimal measures are followed in the first days and weeks of life, many years of childhood still remain and many options exist for reducing and healing any negative consequences resultant from any unavoidable straying from your plans. In this chapter I have covered key information on the establishment of and various effects from infant flora; in later chapters I will present ways in which good flora can go bad. I will also discuss some of the latest research findings on ways parents may be able to optimize their children's health through the gut via diet, probiotic supplements, and other measures.

Messing with the Microbiome

Throughout the last chapter, I've used terms such as *friendly flora* and *challenging flora*. Whereas certain flora, such as strains of *Bifidobacterium* or *Lactobacillus*, are pretty much always helpful, there is not exactly such a thing as "bad" bacteria among what is considered natural flora in healthy babies. Although some kinds of intestinal bacteria are only ever beneficial, nearly every child carries many bacteria that are generally quiet or even helpful but that can cause illness when the body's defenses are down. A child who is extremely immune-compromised can develop an infection from even the friendliest bacteria among normal flora, but generally some kind of interruption in intestinal or other bodily defenses is needed for what I call *challenging flora* to be allowed to flourish and cause illness. Outside of the challenging flora, some terrible deadly bacteria are never considered a normal part of natural flora, such as anthrax or the bacterium responsible for the bubonic plague. Ultimately though, a whole spectrum of bacteria, and some fungi, co-exists within humans and ranges between flora that could cause great illness and the friendliest of flora. This chapter discusses how important these challenging flora have been to humans and how efforts to wipe some of these bacteria out of our microbiome can—and have—backfired.

Good Efforts Gone Bad

A number of factors can lower your child's immune system and can create an environment for bacteria to take advantage of a situation, invade, and to flourish. A harsh cold virus and/or the use of antibiotics—possibly combined with other weakening factors such as a less-than-optimal diet, insufficient sleep, inadequate sun, or low levels of exercise—can awaken otherwise quiet bacteria in a child's respiratory system or gut. These bacteria are referred to as **opportunistic**; they can invade, overgrow, and cause, for example, a sinus infection or diarrhea when the opportunity arises.

On first thought, it seems that we should just wipe out any bacteria in our collective human microbiome that could possibly cause illness, but hard lessons are being learned today from that very effort. Our human microbiome seems to have settled over the millennia into a best possible situation in which certain opportunistic bacteria are maintained so that they keep out much more serious microbes by competing for attachment sites on the intestinal walls and for nutrients. It is these lesser bullies that challenge greater bullies and that are responsible for preventing frequent and dire illnesses in all of us.

Scientists have recognized for many decades now that the use of antibiotic drugs has a downside. Though these antibiotics have acted as miracle life savers, their overuse is causing more and more drug-resistant strains of opportunistic bacteria to develop and spread. Of great concern is the fact that some of these are showing up to be even more potent than the original strains.

> *Our human microbiome seems to have settled over the millennia into a best possible situation in which certain opportunistic bacteria are maintained so that they keep out much more serious microbes.*

Unsuspected villains have also caused serious consequences. A highly unexpected misfortune has grown out of the pneumococcal vaccination program. Pneumococcal vaccines fight against potentially dangerous pneumococcal pneumonia, meningitis, and infections of the heart. It's been discovered that a different kind of bacteria, called *Staphylococcus aureus* and known as **staph** for short, has replaced part of the niche in our microbiota created by the reduction of pneumococcal strains (also known as *Streptococcus pneumoniae*) via pneumococcal vaccines. It's becoming evident to researchers that pneumococci and *S. aureus* have been competitors within human microbiomes.

Pneumococcal bacteria were apparently keeping more serious staph infections at bay but now S. *aureus* has expanded greatly throughout populations globally. Once practically unheard of, suddenly S. *aureus* was causing *flesh-eating bacteria* to become a household term. This once-rare infection became more prevalent than anyone would wish to see.

The new invading flesh-eating bacteria have been coming from a newly prevalent strain of S. *aureus* that has since been monikered methicillin-resistant S. *aureus*, or **MRSA** (pronounced "mersa"). The name MRSA was given because these bacteria,

In the number of yearly U.S. MRSA deaths per citizen is more than triple the rate of polio deaths during the peak of the polio epidemic.

which can cause several types of very serious or even deadly infections including pneumonia, are resistant to common antibiotic drugs (methicillin). Over-use of antibiotic drugs (another tampering with human collective flora) is responsible for the drug resistance of this bacterium, whereas reduction of pneumococcal bacteria from the human microbiome, via vaccines, has allowed MRSA to flourish.

Since the year 2000, the same year that the pneumococcal vaccines began, infections that were rare and limited to hospital patients who had been treated with antibiotics began suddenly popping up in previously healthy children and adults throughout the community who had not been hospitalized and had not been taking antibiotics—and the trend has continued. In England, a study compared 2003 rates of various MRSA infections with those prior to the introduction of the pneumococcal vaccine. They found serious staph skin infections of impetigo and scalded skin syndrome increased by *5 to 8 times* for children under 4, and dangerous staph blood infections increased by 2 to 6 times.

UCLA researchers found a few hundred U.S. deaths per year are being saved by the pneumococcal vaccine introduction. At the same time, MRSA deaths have grown as described above to 7 in 100,000, or over 20,000 people per year in the U.S. The number of yearly U.S. MRSA deaths per citizen is more than triple the rate of U.S. polio deaths during the peak of the polio epidemic (polio deaths reached 3,000 in 1952, with half of today's population).

Swedish researchers have found S. *aureus* to be living in infant intestines at an increasing rate over recent decades and are now finding it in 73% of infant stools. Although no particular problem with intestinal staph illnesses has been recognized, from this home staph can provide a reservoir to seed infections in other body areas when immune defenses are down. Finnish scientists found these problematic bacteria could be reduced by many strains of *Lactobacillus* probiotic supplements. This finding not only reveals the impact of the floral makeup in fighting opportunistic bacteria but suggests that there is hope for healing damaged flora.

Antibiotics: Friend and Foe

I am absolutely *not* here to tell you to *not* use antibiotics. That question in the health of your baby is not for me to address. I feel it prudent and educational, however, to demonstrate the negative effects that antibiotic use may be having on the health of some of our children overall. Concerns about over-usage of antibiotics leading to the development of antibiotic-resistant strains have gone on for decades. New evidence suggests that the damage from antibiotics is much more far-reaching.

Allergies, autism, diabetes, obesity, and various bowel syndromes have grown by leaps and bounds over the last 5 or 6 decades, and millions of children are suffering. Sound answers as to why these are growing so incredibly are not yet available, but solid research suggests that children's microbiota play a role. Evidence also indicates that antibiotic drug use is responsible for a good portion of floral woes. Antibiotic usage wipes out large portions of good flora and allows undesirable flora to overgrow. Some antibiotics directly damage intestinal linings as well, adding to the suffering of the flora. Researchers are finding today that the floral results of an antibiotic onslaught are very large and very lasting, especially in infants.

Researchers are finding today that the floral results of an antibiotic onslaught are very large and very lasting, especially in infants.

As knowledge of extended effects from antibiotic usage trickles into the collective wisdom, clinicians and parents will have more information upon which they can base educated decisions about antibiotic usage. There is no question that antibiotics have saved countless lives, but clinical decisions about their use need to be far more cautious and alternatives need more attention. Limiting antibiotic prescriptions has long been called for by medical authorities, but actual practice barely changes.

In order to reduce antibiotic usage, improved diagnosis of the source of infection in a patient has been called for. Some medical experts have also suggested that when doctors provide parents with an antibiotic prescription, they should encourage the parents to wait 2 or 3 days before giving the drugs, to see if the child improves on her own. As this is an approved measure, it can be safe and useful in non-critical cases and in appropriate circumstances to hold off on drug prescription and wait for results of a culture of the infected area. While waiting to learn whether the infection source is even bacterial and, if so, the type of bacteria it is, the child may recover on her own.

If finally deciding to medicate, this measure allows for the prescription of antibiotics that are more specific to the offending microbe rather than using broad spectrum antibiotics. Sometimes an antibiotic sensitivity test can be ordered along with a culture. The sensitivity test reveals which antibiotics the particular bacteria are most susceptible to. Replacing broad spectrum antibiotic usage with appropriately targeted antibiotics can reduce intestinal damage, limit the kinds of normal flora damaged, and assure better recovery from infection.

Through decades of pharmaceutical industry promotions, parents have been trained to want to address every symptom in a child with a medicine. Some parents feel as though their doctor has not performed her job if sending them home without a prescription for their sick baby. The information in the table below has been provided to the public domain by the Centers for Disease Control and Prevention (CDC) to remind parents and clinicians that antibiotics are not always required.

Some conditions not needing antibiotic drugs

Illness	Antibiotic
Cold	No
Flu	No
Chest Cold (in otherwise healthy children and adults)	No
Sore Throat (except strep)	No
Bronchitis (in otherwise healthy children and adults)	No
Runny Nose (with green or yellow mucus)	No
Fluid in the Middle Ear (otitis media with effusion)	No

Source: Centers for Disease Control and Prevention as presented by the U.S. Food and Drug Administration, 2011.

Antibiotic Over-Usage

After the first many weeks beyond term birth age, a child's immune system should be able to handle simple infections well when its flora is balanced and health is otherwise good. Though professional monitoring is always important during illness, this is what immune systems are designed to do. In the case of ear and sinus infections, studies show that antibiotics may shorten the duration of an infection slightly but they also show that children tend to recover well regardless of treatment and that antibiotic use may lead to more frequent returns of ear infections overall. Diarrheal illness also occurs in response to such antibiotic treatments in upwards of 30% of children, depending upon the antibiotic prescribed. For starters, in so many of

Diarrheal illness also occurs in response to antibiotic treatments in upwards of 30% of children.

these cases, the cause of infection is viral or possibly fungal—not bacterial—though antibiotics are very often prescribed anyway. Antibacterials do nothing to reduce a viral or fungal infection and may worsen it.

A scientific review of many studies on antibiotic usage for respiratory infections found no difference in the clinical outcomes for those who received antibiotics and those who did not. Those not receiving antibiotics did show a little more fever and fatigue. That's just the immune system fighting the infection—likely gaining some useful immunity along the way.

Fevers are one mode of attack a child's body uses to effectively destroy invading microorganisms—one of the immune system's own "antibiotic" actions. Fever-reducing drugs not only add demand to the kidneys and liver in an already ill child but also diminish this body defense mechanism. They can prolong infection and illness and increase the eventual need for antibiotics. The fatigue and discomfort of an illness are the immune system's means of keeping a child resting during an infection so her body can concentrate on getting well.

Current studies are finding that one exposure to antibiotic drugs can leave flora imbalanced for up to 4 years and maybe longer. The drugs can also create a strong presence of dangerous, drug resistant strains of bacteria. Usage of anti-biotics for non-life-threatening illnesses can present risks for more severe and difficult to treat infections later on.

Antibiotics Given to Laboring Mothers

Obstetricians are aware that when a bacterium known as group B strep (GBS) is colonizing a mother's vagina during pregnancy, her baby is more likely to develop an early infection with this bacterium after birth. Around 20 to 30% of U.S. mothers are found to be colonized with GBS during late pregnancy screenings. Standard practice is to screen pregnant mothers for presence of this bacterium and provide antibiotics to colonized mothers during labor in attempt to prevent early GBS infections in their infants. A 2014 scientific review of available studies on such provision of antibiotics to mothers during labor finds reports of a reduction in infections in infants but states that this finding "may well be due to bias." In other words, they found a high risk of bias in study reports, making their conclusions weak.

I find it difficult to analyze the effects of preemptive antibiotics on GBS rates because some studies report rates of all colonized infants, some report the rates of seriously ill infants, and some studies report and compare the rates of infant deaths among those with early GBS infections, rather than the rate of infection. Infant death rates in those with early GBS infections dropped dramatically before preventive antibiotics were first studied: from 55% in 1970; to 22% in 1980, before clinical trials began; to 12% in 1990, just before standardized testing and treatment became recommended. From 1990 to today, there has been a continuation of the slow but steady decline to today's 5% death rate for those infants who become infected with GBS.

U.S. early infant GBS disease rates prior to the establishment of precautionary antibiotic provisions are reported at 10 to 17 per 10,000 births. The CDC reports the current rate at 3 in 10,000, with some sources reporting slightly higher rates. A significant jump in the number of U.S. mothers who initially breastfed their newborns—from 52% in the year prior to the beginning of GBS preventive antibiotics to 60% only 6 years later, and to 70% not long after that—surely accounts for some of the reduction reported in early infant infections. Although cesarean births pose many health problems to infants, early GBS infection risks are lower. A 50% increase in C-section births (from 22 to 33%)—from before the preemptive antibiotic measures to the present—has likely also accounted for some of the drop in early GBS infection rates. Other factors may be involved as well. Antibiotic provision does not always prevent early GBS illness; one study reported that 38% of infected babies were born to mothers who had taken antibiotics during labor. Also, many babies who *are* infected are born to mothers who tested negative and who were therefore not treated.

Even if early serious GBS infections are being reduced by antibiotic practices, there has been an emergence of other types of early infections from bacteria not affected by the kinds of antibiotics used—including a surge of drug-resistant *E. coli* infections affecting preemies. Most importantly, the scientific review found that the use of precautionary antibiotics did not reduce the number of infant deaths—neither from GBS infection nor from all causes—and the number of later, serious infections is increased by the use of antibiotics during labor. (Late-onset infections are defined as developing after one week of age.) Serious *Candida* (yeast) infections are among these, as a direct result of antibiotic exposure. Later bacterial infections are also increasingly occurring from antibiotic-resistant organisms.

> **The use of precautionary antibiotics did not reduce the number of infant deaths, and the number of later, serious infections is increased by the use of antibiotics during labor.**

These are making the illnesses even more challenging to treat. Today, half of late-onset infections are with MRSA. The conclusion of the above comprehensive review is that evidence is lacking to support preemptive antibiotic usage.

Another large review of available studies looked at the occurrence of premature births in relation to antibiotic usage. A predominance of undesirable vaginal bacteria is also associated with an increased rate of premature deliveries. This review found that antibiotic provision did decrease the appearance of vaginal bacterial over-colonization (vaginosis), but it did not reduce the rate of preterm births—the purpose of the antibiotic drug prescriptions.

Women in some other countries average far lower rates of GBS colonization than those in the leading industrialized nations. Rates are as low as 7% among nations measured, reflecting greater intestinal health in these nations.

A 2012 study provided either probiotic yogurt or antibiotics to over 300 GBS colonized pregnant mothers and found equal resolution of vaginal bacterial infection with either treatment. Another study gave garlic tablets or antibiotic drugs to 120 non-pregnant women with bacterial vaginosis. A statistically similar level of bacterial resolution was found between the two treatment groups, while more side effects occurred in those treated with antibiotic drugs. Other women use freshly cut garlic cloves vaginally and find long-term relief of GBS vaginosis whereas antibiotic treatment is medically recognized to provide only temporary relief and to result in great imbalance of vaginal and intestinal flora. Vaginal vitamin C tablets have also been shown to reduce bacterial vaginosis. Some mothers regularly apply probiotics or yogurt vaginally to help balance their florae. Of course, a wide spectrum of oral antimicrobial herbs and nutritional practices can help to improve mother's floral balance before birth. This can certainly provide other large benefits for mother and baby. More studies are needed on alternatives to antibiotic treatments for the prevention of infant GBS infections.

A pregnant mother can use oral and vaginal treatments with probiotics and other immune-supporting antimicrobials, such as garlic and vitamin C, during her pregnancy. She can then be tested—or re-tested—for GBS to find out whether these flora-protecting measures are providing the results that doctors would like to see.

Prematurely born infants are the most susceptible to serious infections of all kinds. Kangaroo care, in which a large amount of skin-to-skin contact is provided for an infant, along with frequent and near-exclusive breastfeeding, is shown to cut this risk in half. Studies also show significant reductions in newborn infection rates in term infants when exclusive human milk feeding is available. These measures help to optimize baby's flora and help to protect against all kinds of potential infections, not just GBS.

The infant health effects from exposure to maternal antibiotics during labor have avoided scrutiny because the drugs are given to the mother, not directly to the infant. Because of the potential ramifications of such a study, no one really wants to do it. In 2014, researchers did look into the effects on newborn floral development and found significant reductions in the numbers and variety of health-promoting bifidobacteria in babies from antibiotic-treated mothers. Moreover, they found deficiencies in the very species that actually help to fight against GBS.

Antibiotics create havoc in newborn intestines. They not only increase the risk of serious drug-resistant infections during baby's first few weeks after birth but also create serious impacts on floral balance that influence many other short-term and long-term health factors (as discussed below and in Chapter 14). In many cases, there are healthier options to antibiotic drugs that may bring few or no side effects and greater overall health to a child.

farming and Children's flora

Estimations are that 70 to 80% of antibiotics used in the United States are given to farm animals. These antibiotics are given for prevention of illnesses in the face of unnatural diets and poor living conditions, as well as being used for actual infections. The greatest amount is given to increase weight gain in the animals through the encouragement of unhealthy flora. Such use has not only caused a vast array of antibiotic-resistant bacterial strains among animals, but some of these bacteria are passing to humans with many being found in the gut flora of young children. Studies vary greatly as to whether today's use of growth-promoting antibiotics is even economically advantageous for farmers. The **World Health Organization (WHO)** has suggested essentially that farms—if run as well as those exemplified by the well managed farms in Denmark—should discontinue such use of antibiotics.

> *Antibiotic-resistant bacterial strains among animals are passing to humans with many being found in the gut flora of young children.*

A newer culprit may also be killing off friendly intestinal flora and promoting bad flora. Glyphosate-based herbicides such as Roundup, created by Monsanto, are designed to be used on their genetically modified (GMO) crops. Research has shown that this widespread usage is greatly interrupting the flora of cattle who eat the crops. Humans are being exposed to traces of this herbicide as well. Such studies on floral effects have not yet been performed on humans and may not even be possible because GMO products are seldom labeled, and some of the genes spread to other crops. A widely used Dow pesticide, which was found in the urine of 91% of people tested and in 70% of umbilical cord blood samples from pregnant women, has also been shown in laboratory studies to have great potential to disrupt the human microbiome.

Epidemic Results

As mentioned, one risk of widespread antibiotic usage is the development of antibiotic-resistant strains. On an individual level, your child can develop drug resistant strains while taking antibiotics, and this can lead to returns of the infection with microbes that are more difficult to treat and that require stronger drugs with possibly greater side effects. On a larger scale, antibiotic-resistant strains develop and spread frequently in hospitals, especially among the older adults and in pediatric units. This means that your child is at risk for acquiring some kind of drug-resistant infection during a hospitalization or even in the community. Such an infection could be very difficult to battle and could require exposure to more powerful antibiotic drugs and their related risks and damages.

Diarrhea is another common side effect of antibiotic usage. The hospitalized elderly adults have long been susceptible to the development of **Clostridium difficile** infection during or shortly after broad spectrum antibiotic use. Since the turn of the 21st century, the number of C. *difficile* diarrheal infections has greatly multiplied, and a growing number of infants and children are succumbing to **C. *diff*** inside and outside of the hospital. As antibiotic medications quickly wipe out friendly flora, any C. *diff* bacteria a child was harboring, or becomes exposed to in a hospital, easily take over. C. *diff* can cause severe diarrhea and colon-damaging inflammation and is presently killing 29,000 people per year in the U.S. Yes, you assumed right—not only has the presence of this bacterium billowed but also ever-increasing drug resistance has appeared in North America and Europe.

What has come as a shock is that a very severe strain of C. *diff* has become prominent and is affecting babies and children as well as older adults. Known as **NAP1**, this strain creates 10 or 20 times more damaging toxins as original strains of C. *diff*, causes more severe cases of diarrhea, and is much more deadly than older strains. This now prevalent strain is so infectious that not only is it infecting many children outside of the hospitals but it is also affecting children who have not even been taking antibiotics, though they likely have some kind of flora challenges. At some point in time, C. *diff* was pretty much confined to older people in hospitals and nursing homes, and it was generally not too tough to treat. Now, millions of antibiotic prescriptions later, C. *diff* has spread to the community and to our young children and has become far more dangerous and difficult to treat.

Now, millions of antibiotic prescriptions later, C. diff has spread to the community and to our young children and has become far more dangerous and difficult to treat.

Medical experts have declared the new C. *diff* strain to be on par with MRSA, while overall C. *diff* deaths have surpassed those from MRSA.

What's the medical treatment for C. *diff* infection? More and stronger antibiotics, and it's often a tough battle needing hospitalization, and risks of developing other bowel disease are a result of the treatment. It's a dangerous infection and anything more than a light case needs some kind of medical attention. Even after recovering from treatment, infections return 30 to 65% of the time.

Startling Treatment for a Serious Epidemic

A new treatment now exists for C. *diff* diarrheal infections that hasn't yet hit the mainstream—it's shocking but amazingly logical once you understand the incredible importance of gut flora. It's also remarkably effective. Several research trials have been performed that treat serious C. *diff* cases with **stool transplants**. Yes, they take some poop from a healthy individual and insert it into the colon of a diarrhea patient. All trials are reporting around 90% success in relieving the diarrhea *and* preventing its return, including cases of superbug NAP1. Compare this 10% failure rate to the normal failure rate that is upwards of 65%. In addition, these patients will not only be avoiding future consequences from repeat antibiotic treatments but also definitely reaping many benefits from the new flora they've acquired. To date, published studies have only been performed on adults, many of them with complicated prior illnesses. I'm eager to see positive results in young children. Unfortunately, financial profitability differences between the development and sales of increasingly stronger antibiotic medications and the use of human waste may have a strong impact on the future of this therapy.

Evil E. coli

Another serious diarrheal illness that has burst onto the scene, as a result of antibiotic over-usage, is that from some dangerous new strains of E. *coli* bacteria. Although E. *coli* have always been a part of normal human flora, certain antibiotic resistant E. *coli* superbugs—able to cause severe illness—have developed over recent decades, largely affecting children as well as older people. Antibiotics given to people for any kind of infection wipe out large portions of normal flora, including the usual tamer versions of E. *coli*, allowing tougher strains to develop, survive, and spread. These long-lasting diarrheal illnesses also carry a high rate of kidney damage and blood infection, along with a high death rate. Found in hospitals, in the community, and sometimes in the flora of a mother who has used antibiotics, E. *coli* blood infections are increasingly harming premature infants.

Early Flora, Allergies, and Asthma

Food allergies, hay fever, asthma, and other conditions of excessive immune reactions have grown by leaps and bounds over the last half century in the developed world, and they are growing in the rest of the world as areas westernize.

The answers as to why this is happening have not yet been found, but there are many suspicions. Likely, an array of new environmental factors is the cause, but it's pretty apparent that some change in the collective intestinal microbiota is involved to some degree. The previous chapter already discussed that the floral discrepancies found between cesarean, vaginal hospital, and vaginal home births can be correlated with later development of environmental allergy, food allergy, and asthma in children.

You've surely heard the **hygiene theory** of allergies: children raised in more sterile environments—meaning exposure to fewer and less variety of bacteria—may have a greater propensity for developing allergies. Ample research supports this contention, and some pieces are being put together now regarding some conflicting findings. A pair of New York microbiologists have now proposed an addendum to this theory. They propose that modern medicine, diet, hygiene, antibiotic use, and other modern factors have caused quite a drift in flora over the decades that increases our tendencies for autoimmune and allergic conditions. Our exposure to diverse bacteria has certainly diminished as antibiotic use and hygiene measures have altered the collective microbiota of industrialized nations. Studies show strong links between floral balance and diversity, and certain diseases.

New York microbiologists have now proposed that modern medicine, diet, hygiene, antibiotic use, and other modern factors have caused quite a drift in flora over the decades that increases our tendencies for autoimmune and allergic conditions.

Many studies find a correlation between exposure to antibiotics in early infancy and development of asthma and allergies later in life. Some researchers argue that this is not well proven, though other studies have accounted for each of the various arguments against this theory. It seems rather well confirmed that exposure to antibiotics in the first months after birth increases the likelihood of a child developing asthma or allergies later on. Studies that look at the earliest of antibiotic exposures tend to find stronger correlations.

A Swedish study found that early inflammatory signs of celiac disease, a type of food allergy, occurred nearly twice as often in infants who had antibiotic exposures as in those who did not. University of North Carolina researchers found antibiotic use in babies increases the risk of developing **eosinophilic esophagitis (EE)** by an amazing 6 times! EE is an allergic condition in which the throat swells, making it very difficult to swallow food. Babies with EE will cough, spit-up, and vomit often.

They also found that the risk of EE increases with cesarean section and formula feeding. **Eosinophilic gastroenteritis**, the same condition affecting the stomach or intestines, is likely encouraged by these same floral disrupting factors.

Through many animal studies and emerging human studies, one factor of floral imbalance is being confirmed. It seems that when plenty of less desirable microbes are hanging out in one's intestinal microbiome, they allow for impairments in the tightness and completeness of the cellular junctions along the walls of the intestines. This allows proteins and various other components to leak through the incomplete barrier and into the bloodstream. The presence of uninvited proteins in the bloodstream can cause allergic and immune reactions. Another way of wording this scenario is that poor floral health allows for a **"leaky gut"** and this encourages autoimmune reactions to occur.

Whether resultant from early antibiotics, early diet, mode of birth, or other factors, the connections between the character of early flora development and later allergic and autoimmune symptoms appear well established. In 2012, Swedish researchers looked at infants with **eczema**, a skin rash that tends to accompany allergies. They demonstrated that infants who eventually went on to develop eczema harbored much lower diversity in their gut flora at one month of age. Danish researchers recently showed low diversity of infant flora to be associated with allergies in childhood. An attempt at correlating specific bacteria to allergic developments was made by Dutch scientists. They found *E. coli* among a child's flora at one month correlated with a higher risk of eczema at 2 years, and early *C. diff* corresponded to more eczema, allergies, and asthma. Other researchers found early colonization with *L. casei*, *L. paracasei*, and *L. rhamnosus* to be associated with a lower risk of childhood allergies, even when the parents have allergic tendencies that could be inherited by the child.

Experiencing multiple infections in early childhood is linked, in many studies, to a lower risk of developing allergies—except when illnesses have been treated with antibiotics, which cause the opposite effect. Some early studies on the number of respiratory infections, measles, Hepatitis A infections, and such showed conflicting results in terms of allergy risks until the antibiotic factor was discovered.

Intestinal worm infections are also well known to reduce the chances of developing allergies and autoimmune diseases such as inflammatory bowel disease (Crohn's disease and ulcerative colitis). A South African study found that any report of childhood worm infection was associated with an 80% lower risk of this bowel disease. Worms and other parasites are quite common in undeveloped and developing parts of the world. A childhood brush or two with these may benefit the immune system, but chronic worm infection is draining to the immune system.

A very large study of people living in highly different hygienic and economic situations on either side of a border has really brought life to the hygiene theory. A group of Finnish researchers has studied, in great detail, the experiences and health parameters of border residents between wealthy, modern Finland and the underprivileged Karelian Republic of Russia. They found the Russian Karelia to have far more and varied microbes in their minimally but adequately processed drinking water and much more variety and density of microbes in the dust in their homes. Whereas Finnish home dust contained chiefly body and plant microbes, Russian homes also had a great amount of soil and animal flora.

E. coli among a child's flora at one month correlated with a higher risk of eczema at 2 years, and early C. diff corresponded to more eczema, allergies, and asthma.

The reason the study of environmental factors among these residents is so interesting is that Finland has the highest rate of childhood type 1 diabetes in the world whereas the Russian Karelia just across the border—who share the same genetic ancestry and same amount of diabetes genes—have one-sixth the rate. Both share the same number of gene markers for **celiac disease** (gluten sensitivity), yet Finnish children experience 5 times the rate of such intolerances to wheat and other grains. Finland has many times the number of other autoimmune diseases and allergies as well. In addition to the contrasts on either side of the border, those Russian Karelia with the highest number of microbes in their drinking water were found to have the lowest rates of allergies.

Early Flora, Obesity, and Diabetes

A recent research trend is the investigation of ways that intestinal flora makeup influences the development of obesity. At first, the suggestion of such a correlation seems quite peculiar; however, many studies now support and explain this assertion. Earlier, I mentioned that farmers give antibiotics to their animals to increase their weight. Apparently it works for people, too, with exposure during early infancy having the greatest effect, at least on childhood weight. Overweight is an important issue because it is so commonly associated with diabetes, heart disease, and many other disabling and life-shortening disorders.

Finnish researchers found that children who maintained normal weight as they grew tended to have high levels of bifidobacteria in early infancy, whereas later development of obesity was more often associated with high early levels of *Staph aureus.* Another study showed that antibiotic drug use in infancy reduces bifidobacteria and bacteroides and discussed ways in which these bacteria are thought to protect against obesity. Current research is further investigating the specific strains of bacteria that might be promoters or preventers of excess weight.

> **Antibiotic drug use in infancy reduces bifido-bacteria and bacteroides. These bacteria are thought to protect against obesity.**

A New York medical research team found that exposure to antibiotic drugs in the first 6 months after birth correlates with higher body mass development in the first 3 years. Another such study found that antibiotic use in the first 6 months leads to a greater risk of overweight among children of normal-weight mothers. Interestingly, the researchers also found that antibiotic use decreased a child's risk of excess weight among those born to mothers who were overweight before pregnancy. Apparently, obesity-related flora can be obtained from an overweight mother and then wiped out with early antibiotic use. Research evidence suggests that early flora of infancy may have an impact on weight gain not only throughout childhood but into adulthood as well.

Type 1 diabetes is an autoimmune disease in which one's body attacks its own insulin-producing cells of the pancreas, eventually leading to a need for insulin injections. Multiple animal studies implicate the health of the intestines in the development of type 1 diabetes. Human studies are now linking diabetes to increased gut barrier weakness, or leaky gut, as well as to diet and to infections. Studies of microbiota are finding similar disturbed floral patterns in those children who develop diabetes and those who develop obesity.

Notable differences have also been found between the flora of type 2 diabetic adults and those adults without diabetes. Once referred to as adult-onset diabetes, type 2 diabetic insulin resistance has also become quite prevalent in children over recent decades. Links between infant diets and development of type 2 diabetes later in children's lives are being established.

An interesting experiment transplanted stool flora of lean subjects to overweight diabetic individuals, which improved their insulin sensitivity. This was a study on adults, but—with ever-increasing incidence of diabetes in children at ever-younger ages—this finding adds to the importance of optimizing infant flora. The development of diabetes in childhood is known to be more common in formula-fed infants, which also suggests a link between early flora and the disease.

Flora and Autism

Many differences have been found between the flora of children on the autism spectrum and that of those who are not autistic. The new DNA sequencing techniques have allowed researchers to pin some of these differences down even further, in terms of bacterial numbers and strains, although they're still not sure what it all means. The floral distinctions are not simply those of immune-compromised children but do have characteristics in common with some other bowel diseases. Certain species of *Clostridium* are found to be much more numerous in—or nearly exclusive to—autistic children, and special attention is being paid to bacterial species of the seldom heard of *Desulfovibrio* and *Sutterella* genera.

Many differences have been found between the flora of children on the autism spectrum and that of those who are not autistic.

Intestinal flora is known to communicate with the brain and can affect mood, and it's a fact that intestinal disturbances are very common among autistic children. Some researchers suspect that early floral disturbances, including antibiotic exposure, may be involved in many cases. Other researchers suggest that antibiotic treatments be used in attempt to correct unwanted floral microbes in autistic children. Much more research is on the horizon, yet wise parents are finding many good answers together. The ways by which diet, medications, and flora influence autism are no simple picture at all, but many parents are finding improvements in their children by avoiding common allergens—chiefly dairy and gluten—and through other dietary measures. In Chapter 14, I will demonstrate how specific attention to the floral balance in babies and children is one key to preventing and treating autistic disorders.

Flora, Colic, and Reflux

Colic used to be the main diagnosis for heavily crying babies; however, **gastroesophageal reflux** has become the newly preferred diagnosis, though the primary physiology of the condition hasn't changed: a crying baby and digestive system clues. Like all of the disorders discussed in this section, the causes of colic are multifactorial, but an exploration of any floral associations may bring highly welcome relief to some sad babies and tired parents. Studies have not shown colic to have any strong connection to antibiotic usage or to whether an infant is breastfed or formula fed, so it does not appear to be largely related to floral imbalance. Flora-related diseases seem to take time to develop, though there are hints that smaller flora alterations may still be involved in some or many colic cases.

A small study looked at exclusively breastfed babies and found more gas-forming bacteria in colicky babies versus non-colicky babies. The researchers studied and compared babies who were exclusively breastfed so that the dietary factor could be removed from the equation (though mother's diet needs to be looked at, too). Other studies have demonstrated that certain probiotic supplementations may help colic. Probiotic supplements can help to improve food tolerance. Food intolerances to formulas and to foods in the breastfeeding mother's diet definitely play a large role in colic and reflux. These will be discussed more in later chapters.

Antibiotics and Inflammatory Bowel Disease

The greatest amount and most damaging effects from early antibiotic exposures have been suggested by a 2012 study of **inflammatory bowel disease (IBD)**. The term inflammatory bowel disease represents a group of painful, chronic intestinal irritations generally involving diarrhea and ulceration of intestinal tissues and leading to poor absorption of valuable nutrients (not to be confused with irritable bowel syndrome, IBS, which is covered elsewhere in this text). The main types of IBD are **Crohn's disease** and **ulcerative colitis**, and these are occurring today at younger and younger ages.

A United Kingdom (U.K.) study of over one million people found a strong association between antibiotic usage in childhood and the later development of IBD. The disease effect was most powerful for antibiotic exposure prior the age of one. Most studies discussed in this chapter have found something like 40 to 60% increased risks for the various disease correlations presented. In contrast, this U.K. study found a surprising five and a half times, or 550%, the number of IBD developments after antibiotic exposure before the age of one, versus no antibiotic exposure in childhood.

Although multiple antibiotic exposures increased the IBD risk slightly more, most of the effect came from the first exposure. As opposed to antibiotic usage in the first year, exposure before the age of five led to 2.6 times the risk of developing IBD, and use before the age of 15 led to one and a half times the risk. A 2012 Canadian study found a nearly identical risk; children who were exposed to antibiotics before the age of five were 2.8 times more likely to develop IBD.

Highly suggestive of a flora-hygiene connection, IBD is mainly an illness of industrialization and affluence. The numbers of new cases are growing every day. In the United States, some 20,000 children under the age of five are diagnosed with Crohn's disease today, and an even larger number have ulcerative colitis. In the 10-year span between 1996 and 2006 alone, the rate of IBD in children more than doubled in a Northern California Kaiser study. Amid the world's nations that were measured, the rates of Crohn's disease affliction are nearly 10 times

A U.K. study found a surprising five and a half times, or 550%, the number of later IBD developments after antibiotic exposure before the age of one.

higher in the most affected areas than in the least affected regions. Nations with the highest rates include Canada and Sweden, with the United States close behind. The least affected nations among those measured include Brazil, Argentina, and China. Such diseases were practically non-existent in undeveloped nations only decades ago. The research findings are here. Now it's time to get a handle on the explosion of autoimmune diseases.

Thoughts on Choosing Our Microbial Friendships

Hygiene can be a double-edged sword, but it can be used wisely. To avoid writing a book on this topic alone, I'll put some ideas in a nutshell. In environments such as preschools or large gatherings, people would do best to try to avoid exposure to the virus-of-the-month. When out in the world, or when a sick individual is in the home, hand washing is important before eating, touching one's face, or sucking on one's fingers. People need to be encouraged to drop the habit that was once thought of as good manners: sneezing and coughing all over their hands. It's better to cough or sneeze into a sleeve, into one's shirt, or into a tissue.

Your child will receive her share of common colds and mystery viruses and probably be better off for it. With good overall health and a solid set of flora, these viral illnesses should seldom allow opportunistic bacterial infections to ensue. If a secondary bacterial infection does occur, give the immune system some time to work it out on its own, with medical monitoring, as this can prevent worse infections in the future.

Highly sterile practices around childbirth, baby care, and childcare can reduce your children's immune development and future health potential. The more exposure children have to healthy people and varied environments, the better off their immune systems are. Soil and bodies of water are full of valuable microbial and submicrobial (bacteriophage) exposures that supplement, train, and strengthen immune systems. Children should play in ponds and dirt, organic produce may not need washing, and antibacterial soaps with their estrogenic and carcinogenic ingredient—triclosan—are seldom of positive value.

Some Final Thoughts

Clearly, the development and maintenance of your baby's flora play a highly important role in the healthy function of his immune system. Wiping out opportunistic flora is not as important as gaining a vast variety of bacterial troops to stand guard and to play immune roles. Optimal health depends upon a widely experienced and populous microbiota that has not been attacked by medications. Rather than trying to outrun common microbes and viruses—for there will always be other, probably tougher microbes

> *Wiping out opportunistic flora is not as important as gaining a vast variety of bacterial troops to stand guard and to play immune roles.*

and submicrobes to take their place—a healthy diet, sleep, sun, and play will go much farther in preventing detrimental infections and in preserving overall health throughout your child's school years and into adulthood.

The Poop on Breastmilk

Mammary Intestinal Integration

Born from an entirely protective environment where mother's body tends to baby's every immune and nutritional need, mother's breasts take over the role of the placenta and transition the newborn safely into childhood as his own immature immune and digestive systems continue to develop. Nursing provides physical protection and warmth alongside mother's body to the regulating tune of her familiar heartbeat in consort with biochemical imprinting, brain-developing interplay, and emotional wellbeing. Baby is designed to gain great comfort and positive neurological development from the act of suckling at the breast and from the pheromone scents from mother's nearby armpits. All the while, breastmilk delivers optimal nutritional and hormonal support along with a multitude of immune protective factors and actions. Additionally, through the **broncho-entero-mammary pathway**, mother's body can detect infective agents that her baby is exposed to and can supply specifically tailored antibodies through her milk. Through this same amazing pathway, mother provides useful flora to baby. Mother's breasts, which even have the ability to modify many milk factors according to her infant's age, function intricately with her child's intestines to powerfully provide for his health and wellbeing.

Although human milk's nutrition has been passably replicated artificially and a bottle-fed baby can be affectionately nursed in arms, nothing comes close to providing the wellness that breastmilk alone affords. Newborns have very little immune functioning of their own. For the most part, breastmilk *is* their immune system. Even an older infant, without mother's milk, would be missing very important factions of his intended immune system. The result is more frequent and harsh illnesses.

Microbes—good or bad—will generally enter a child's system through the mouth, pass through the throat, and enter the intestines; thus, the digestive system is a baby's greatest vulnerability, by far, in terms of infections. Auspiciously, breastmilk travels this same course and has tremendous influence on the development, wellbeing, and protective capacities of the digestive tract and its flora—and thus the child. Even microbes that enter through a child's nose will meet with breastmilk-nurtured floral defenses in the throat. The floral balance and, thus, the infection risks for the sinuses and ear canals depend upon the mouth and throat flora, which are influenced by the gut flora and by the same factors that affect gut flora, mainly breastmilk. Even lung flora and function are strongly influenced by gut flora. Via its passage through the baby, breastmilk protects against dental, sinus, ear, throat, lung, stomach, and intestinal infections. And, we have already seen how optimal gut flora protects against the development of asthma, diabetes, and other diseases. Through its floral benefits and via many other modes, breastmilk feeding provides your infant with long-term protection far beyond weaning.

In the Beginning

Baby's tummy is teeny tiny at birth, holding little more than a teaspoon at most. Good colonies of florae that are important to digestion are not yet established, and her own digestive juices are not yet revved up. The newborn digestive system is not ready at birth to handle much in the way of food, and the breasts know this. Immediate and near continual skin-to-skin contact between mother and baby with frequent suckling efforts day and night—and in a calm, supportive, and rather romantic environment—can allow mother's breasts to begin to fulfill their destiny. Immune protection is the first order of business. In intentional coordination, the intestines are preparing for digestion over the first few days as the breasts ramp up for significant milk making, which typically kicks in around 3 to 5 days after birth.

The importance of healthy flora to a child has been established. When uninhibited by antibiotics, formula supplements, or delayed feedings, breastmilk can essentially seal the deal. It's been shown that the health of the floral environment into which an infant is born can have positive or negative impact on the creation of his long-term microbiome. If only a magical concoction existed with which a newborn's digestive membranes could be quickly coated immediately after birth and then, if repeatedly applied, it could possibly head off some less desirable environmental influences. Of course, there is one. A few drops of **colostrum** from mother's breast is all it takes.

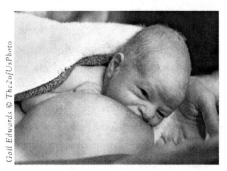

Even the mother who faces challenges with the establishment of sufficient milk supply can generally yield a few initial drops of this invaluable potion. Even when circumstances create an inability to latch, hand expression or an electric pump may do the trick. Interestingly, when birth occurs through a planned C-section—meaning no labor has occurred—mother's milk is found to contain less healthy flora to pass to her newborn. Apparently, labor is not only a signal for mother's placenta to pump antibodies into the soon-to-be-born child (and probably part of the physical process) but also a signal for the conveyance of important flora to mother's breasts to enhance her colostrum for added newborn protection. Mother's colostrum provides valuable flora to homestead in the newborn gut, some 700 different species in fact, along with special fiber-like sugars to perfectly feed the flora. A dense package of antibodies and anti-inflammatory agents are also provided by mother's colostrum to assure the infant's immature immune system is not overwhelmed by the initial introduction of hundreds of different kinds of bacteria in the first days outside the womb.

Either good flora provided in colostrum or bad flora from a hospital environment have an exceptionally high opportunity to establish themselves in the first many hours after birth.

The newborn's stomach acidity at birth is quite neutral because it contains amniotic fluid. Acidity does not become high for about a day, so either good flora provided in colostrum or bad flora from a hospital environment have an exceptionally high opportunity to establish themselves in the first many hours after birth.

Successful initiation of breastfeeding and establishment of a responsive milk supply are important to the best success of the newborn gut and the child's long-term health. In addition to generations of misinformation—stresses from birth interventions, insensitive hospital attendees, drugs, bright lights, disturbing noises, an uncomfortable and foreign atmosphere, frequent separations, and/or poor lactation facilitation can all impede the process for both mother and baby.

Cells lining the newborn's intestinal walls have loosely knit junctions with spaces between them that allow valuable colostrum factors to pass into the bloodstream. Epidermal growth factor and other components of colostrum help to slightly close these junctures and to mature the intestinal walls so that good digestion can begin within a few days. Feeding of infant formula to the newborn can lead to the passage of large foreign proteins into the bloodstream, which is a factor in the development of allergies to soy or cow milk proteins—or even to corn, as traces of corn proteins are found in almost all infant formulas. This vulnerability is especially true in the first several days after birth, although ultimate tightening of cell junctions, known as **closure**, doesn't occur until around 6 months of age, at which time it's safer to introduce some formula or other foods.

Newborn intestines are full of meconium that needs to be cleared before much more can go on in there. Having spent her life until birth floating in liquid, the baby's body can afford to lose a little excess fluid and does not need significant quantities of milk. Very frequent feedings of little bits of colostrum are what's important. Colostrum's laxative effect helps to move the meconium through, and this helps to limit the buildup of bilirubin in order to prevent excessive jaundice.

Every additional day that human milk can be provided exclusively, with no added formula or fortifiers, is another step toward optimal, short-term, and long-lasting immune protection for the child.

When mother's milk is unavailable, donor milk is the safest option. The immune protection offered from mature milk is not as powerful as colostrum, and the pasteurization of donor milk, necessary in medical settings, damages some of the immune factors. Regardless, donor milk is still plenty potent and will prevent the risky, undesirable floral development that occurs with formula supplements. Every additional day that human milk can be provided exclusively, with no added formula or fortifiers, is another step toward optimal, short-term, and long-lasting immune protection for the child. Sugar-water supplements, sometimes given, though seldom warranted, interrupt the establishment of mother's milk supply but do not appear to interrupt breastmilk's immune provisions.

Regulation

Your baby's digestive system knows just when it's time for more nutrition, and it sends signals to baby's brain for him to communicate with the bearer of the breasts. A very young baby will usually start out with some squirming and rooting. If that doesn't work, they'll let out a whimper and, soon, a cry. When not rehearsed away because of formula feeding, increased blood flow is then sent to mother's breasts, and her brain responds to the cry by leading her to caress the baby and position him so he can nurse. Eventually, baby and mother learn to understand and recognize each other's signals and develop their own cues so that crying for feeding is seldom needed.

Based upon his current growth needs and his genetic destiny, baby's body also knows just how much food he needs in a day, at least when his own signals and cravings are not regularly overwhelmed or ignored. Mother's breasts help baby to manage his caloric needs by gradually increasing the fat content of the milk during a nursing session in order that the milk will feel more and more filling, thereby signaling baby to take a break. **Leptin** is a hormone in breastmilk that helps baby to gradually feel full and to limit his milk intake to just the right amount. Wisely, leptin levels are reduced in mother's milk when she gives birth prematurely and increased when mother gives birth to an extra-large baby.

When baby's inborn knowledge of when and how often to feed is spoiled by scheduled feedings, possible consequences are failure-to-thrive, obesity, or other unhealthy food issues. At the same time, the frustration affects the portions of baby's brain that manage stress, and receptors may permanently reorganize toward excess stress reactions. Stress responses in mother to excess infant crying from delayed feedings can also damage mother's milk production and cause inflammatory reactions as a result of excess stress hormone releases.

Releases of soothing nursing hormones can occasionally impede newborn feedings. Some newborns become so overwhelmed by the comforting hormone releases from suckling that they will fall asleep before taking in significant nutrition or will sleep for excess periods of time. The concept of scheduled feedings then should be one of increased regularity, not delaying. Excess sleepiness usually lasts for only a week or two and the child should be examined if it lasts longer.

Nursing is also nurturing, and babies thrive on nurturing. The act of suckling and the hormonal releases from nursing at the breast, particularly **oxytocin**, provide a strong sense of comfort, calm, and wellbeing to the infant. These hormones also provide beneficial regulation of the development of baby's stress-handling brain receptors to establish lifelong balance in baby's stress reactions. For these reasons, babies benefit highly from non-nutritive suckling as well, and some babies need it more than others. Powerful hormonal releases occur in mother while breastfeeding, too, which also provide calm and sense of wellbeing. Both mother and baby enjoy biochemical reinforcements of their bond every time they nurse. These feelings serve to regulate optimal feeding for the baby by keeping the source of nutrition and protection close by. When mother and baby's regular pattern of nursing is interrupted, they suffer negative physical and mental sensations of withdrawal.

Bottle feeding of breastmilk can also override some of baby's natural controls for regulating the volume of her nourishment, with excess feeding being the risk. Thinner foremilk and fattier hindmilk are now mixed, and mother may have a strong temptation to encourage finishing whatever amount of milk is in the bottle. Though it may be best to match the infant's intake cues, rewarming restrictions may provide practical constraints. Once desired nutritional intake is met, further important nurturing can be provided to the exclusively bottle-fed baby by holding the baby in a nursing fashion while providing a finger or pacifier to suck on.

The breasts also know what nutritional and immunological needs the baby has at every age. Prematurely born babies receive a minimal amount of antibodies from mother's placenta and have even more immature immune systems than term newborns. The breasts coordinate with this status and provide a greater amount of antibodies to a premature infant, as well as extra **lysozyme,** an antibacterial protein. All breastmilk gradually transitions from dense, but less fatty, colostrum at birth to mature milk over the first couple of weeks. The immune provisions and nutritional balances of breastmilk continue to change slightly as a child ages. Breastmilk even follows a daily rhythm with certain sleep-inducing nucleotides present in higher quantities at night and other nucleotides higher in the day.

Many varied proteins in human milk provide immune protective functions and/or aid in absorption of important nutrients. Certain basic proteins are broken down in digestion to provide amino acids necessary to the child's nutrition, whereas many proteins with specific functions are protected from digestion until they can perform other duties. In fact, human milk has over 1600 different proteins, monkey milk just over 500, and cow milk far fewer. The following are examples of a few of these human proteins: haptocorrin, antitrypsin, transforming growth factor, bile-salt-stimulated lipase, kappa-casein, and folate-binding protein.

Antibodies from Mother

Babies are all born with very incomplete, weak immune systems. Along with weakness of many other immune pathways, newborns are barely able to develop any microbe-fighting antibodies for themselves. Part of an infant's intended immune protection is provided by mother's infection-fighting **IgG antibodies** passed through her placenta and into her baby's bloodstream while in the womb. These antibodies provide baby with partial protection against a wide array of microbes that mother has been exposed to in her lifetime.

For instance, if mother was exposed to measles virus in her childhood, she would pass measles-fighting IgG antibodies through her placenta to reduce the impact of any measles exposure her young infant may encounter. To continue the example, if mother were vaccinated for measles during her childhood rather than attaining natural immunity, her antibodies would have likely waned, and she would pass on fewer or no measles antibodies to her vulnerable newborn.

The immune provisions and nutritional balances of breastmilk continue to change slightly as a child ages.

Not being an ideal consequence, the hope is that the vaccination program will simply reduce the chances that newborns will be exposed at all, and this plan seems to have worked well for measles and several other vaccinated-for diseases.

This same dilemma is true for antibodies that are provided in mother's milk. Luckily, breastmilk provides many other kinds of infection protection, besides antibodies.

The defensive antibodies obtained through the placenta before birth dwindle in the baby's body over three to nine months after birth whereas breastmilk can continue to provide defensive antibodies for much longer.

A good portion of the intended IgG antibodies are passed during labor, so a baby delivered by a scheduled cesarean section—without going through any labor—receives significantly fewer of these antibodies. Born too early, premature babies miss out on a majority of placental IgG antibodies as well.

Another important kind of antibodies to protect against illnesses are **IgA antibodies**. These antibodies are highly valuable for protecting vulnerable linings of the throat and intestinal tract, which are an infant's chief sources of exposure to potential infections. The newborn has no IgA antibodies of his own and won't make significant amounts for himself for months. Fortunately, mother's milk delivers plenty of IgA antibodies, along with some IgG antibodies and others. Mature immune systems continually develop antibodies to whatever environmental microbes they are exposed and carry antibodies or memory cells of past exposures. Mother's body intentionally directs plenty of these IgA antibodies and antibody-making cells into her breastmilk to protect her infant against a wide array of microbes in mother's own flora, from her past exposures, and in mother's recent environment, which should be the baby's environment as well.

The antibodies provided in mother's milk will not be specifically directed toward many microbes in the hospital unless she's been there for a few days.

The antibodies provided in mother's milk will not be specifically directed toward many microbes in the hospital unless she's been there for a few days, thereby having developed antibodies in response to her exposures there. Remember that some hospital germs are much tougher than community germs and quite antibiotic resistant. The antibodies in mother's milk will protect baby more completely at home and at mom's other regular haunts.

Just as with placental antibodies, in terms of most diseases for which there are vaccines, if mother was vaccinated as a child, she'd pass on minimal milk antibodies for such diseases, as vaccine-acquired immunity generally wanes over time. Her infant is at greater risk if exposed to any of these before he is old enough to be vaccinated himself. Still, plenty of other infections exist besides those for which there are vaccinations. Human milk provides antibodies to many of these, and other

Through continued close contact with her infant, mother becomes exposed to any microbes that are challenging her baby.

immune pathways in mother's milk will prevent or reduce severity of most. An infant born prematurely or without labor, and for whom human milk is unavailable, will be at greatest risk of illness and needs greater isolation measures.

It was once thought that antibodies in mother's milk would be digested in her infant's stomach and unavailable to help the child. It's been well shown, though, that breastmilk antibodies indeed survive, and they coat the linings of baby's throat and intestines. Breastmilk's antibodies are packaged in a special way that helps them survive their trip through the infant's tummy. The acidity of a young baby's stomach is less than that of older children or adults. This feature allows for the survival of many factors in mother's milk. Although nearly all breastmilk antibodies remain along the digestive tract, it is thought that in premature infants some IgA and IgG antibodies may pass through the intestinal wall and into the bloodstream where they can home to more sites and effect even greater protection.

Broncho-Entero-Mammary Pathway

Through continued close contact with her infant, mother becomes exposed to any microbes that are challenging her baby. Skin-to-skin contact, kisses, sharing breath, and the act of diapering provide much of this valuable sampling. Baby's sneezes provide definite exposure to mom. Microbes from all such exposures are presented to lymphatic immune centers in mother's body—chiefly, to those in her respiratory tissues and to Peyer's patches in her intestinal linings. There these viruses, bacteria, and fungi incite immune system signals for the creation of custom antibodies for each particular microbe. IgA antibody-making cells home to the breasts to fortify mother's milk with relevant immune provisions specific to the infant's exposures. The level of IgA antibodies in mother's milk is much denser than that found in her blood. In addition to this signaling process, saliva from baby's mouth enters directly into pores in mother's nipple, signaling the vast antibody-producing immune cells in her breasts to provide specific antibodies.

These viruses, bacteria, and fungi incite immune system signals for the creation of custom antibodies for each particular microbe.

If a baby is obtaining all of her breastmilk from bottles, with no breastfeeding attempts, some mothers like to regularly apply saliva from baby to their nipples in hopes of increasing their opportunities to alert their own immune system to provide specific antibodies. When premature infants in the hospital NICU rely upon pumped milk because they are too weak to extract all of their milk from mother's breasts, suckling attempts should still be encouraged. Along with plenty of close contact in the fashion of kangaroo care, these practices can help mother's breasts provide custom-made antibodies for her weak preemie and help to regulate the infant.

I take this opportunity to also mention that mothers certainly may continue breastfeeding when they themselves are ill. Importantly, the breastfeeding mother will create specific antibodies against the microbe that she is infected with, and these will be passed on to help protect her nursling from becoming ill, or as ill, from exposure to the same microbe.

In addition to antibody-producing cells making their way from lymph centers in the intestines and respiratory tissues to the breasts, healthy flora also travel from these areas to mother's milk, to boost baby's flora. These immune system cells and healthy bacteria are found to travel (transported by dendritic cells) chiefly through the lymphatic system as well as through the bloodstream. These roadways—by which the body provides such valuable factors to mother's milk— are referred to as the broncho-entero-mammary pathway.

More Health Protection from Human Milk

In addition to antibodies and healthy flora, a slew of other protective factors in human milk are worth mentioning. Some factors energize the infant's own immune responses, and several agents simply help mother's immune elements survive the trip through the stomach:

- Cells called phagocytes directly gobble up undesirable microbes.
- Special fats impair viruses from reproducing.
- Various fatty acids penetrate tough outer coats of certain kinds of viruses.
- Interferon is a powerful anti-viral.
- Fibronectins and mucins tag viruses and bacteria for other immune cells to destroy.
- A full spectrum of cytokines regulates immune reactions.
- B12 binding factor starves microbes of vitamin B12.
- Bifidus factor promotes the growth of healthy flora.
- Lysozyme destroys unwanted bacteria.
- T cells kill infected cells.

And though a few are found in cow milk, human milk is abundant with over 100 different kinds of **oligosaccharides**. Besides feeding and maintaining a preponderance of friendly flora in the breastmilk-fed gut, these fiber-like factors serve to prevent unwanted bacteria, viruses, and even parasites from gaining hold on the intestinal walls. Some of the oligosaccharides appear quite specialized toward just one kind of infective agent.

This is only a taste of all that goes on between mother's milk and baby's system. Mother's breasts become an arsenal of protective health and wellness agents designed especially for her baby.

Imagine that the world had created a new "dream product" to feed and immunize everyone born on earth. Imagine also that it was available everywhere, required no storage or delivery, and helped mothers plan their families and reduce the risk of cancer. Then imagine that the world refused to use it.
—Frank Oski, editor of leading medical pediatrics textbooks

Lactoferrin, Iron, and Infant Protection

Lactoferrin is a breastmilk protein that binds with iron. Nutritional iron is provided by mother's milk in this bound manner. Lactoferrin will also bind any free iron found in the breastfed intestine, such as tiny amounts released by expiring bacteria or any rogue red blood cells. The more challenging bacteria—found in the stool of formula or solid-food-fed infants—require free iron to survive and proliferate. Lactoferrin, which is 50 times higher in breastmilk than in cow milk, holds on to the iron in the breastfed intestine, makes the iron unavailable to feed unwanted bacteria, and provides safe haven for desirable lactobacilli and bifidobacteria to proliferate. Although lacto-

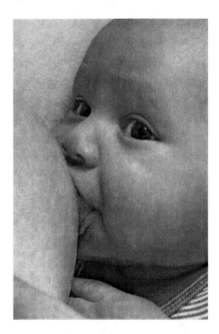

ferrin has other antimicrobial and antiviral activities, this iron-restricting ability appears very effective at preventing serious diarrheal illnesses and at keeping down challenging florae that could otherwise seed other areas of the body, such as the lungs and sinuses.

If free iron is added to a breastfed child's diet, it will saturate and overwhelm the lactoferrin, feed challenging bacteria, and allow them to flourish. Free iron exists in all formulas (even low-iron formulas) and pretty much in any solid food besides pure fats or refined sugars. It doesn't take very much formula, juice, or baby food to overtake the protective lactobacilli and bifidobacteria florae provided by exclusive breastmilk feeding and to allow for the growth of the more challenging types of bacteria, including enterococci, enterobacter, clostridia, streptococci, and *E. coli*. In fact, baby's flora has been shown to change within 24 hours after just one bottle of formula. Once your infant's stools begin to develop unpleasant odor and darken in color, you can tell that the floral transition from protective breastfed flora to more adult-like bacteria is taking place.

Formula Supplementing and Floral Health

The picture, of course, isn't quite as simple as this. Efforts to fortify formulas with ample lactoferrin unfortunately provide no apparent benefits. Most likely, several other factors in breastmilk facilitate the actions of lactoferrin, and factors other than iron also interrupt the virgin flora of a previously exclusively breastfed gut. Lactose is a special sugar found only in baby milks and certainly must play a helpful role. Studies on premature infants show greater infections occurring when mother's milk is fortified with proteins derived from cow milk, which suggests the negative influence of these proteins on the flora. Free fatty acids in formulas have also been discovered to cause injury to intestinal cells whereas breastmilk fatty acids are packaged in such a way as to protect the infant's intestines from the development of damaging forms of fatty acids during digestion.

Studies suggest that if any formula is given to a breastfeeding newborn within the first 7 days after birth, there is little chance of ever developing the highly acidic, strongly protective floral environment found in an exclusively breastfed baby. Of course, there are still many, many benefits to continuing breastmilk, but some of the immune protection potential may be damaged for good. If only a small amount of formula or juice are given somewhere beyond the first 7 days, the infant's flora could still possibly recover after a few weeks of return to exclusive breastfeeding.

In fact, baby's flora has been shown to change within 24 hours after just one bottle of formula.

A couple of very old journal reports suggest that a baby's stools can return to resemble exclusively breastfed stools in around 4 weeks if mother returns to exclusively feeding breastmilk after some formula or other feeding have been given. There don't appear to be any newer or more detailed studies on this topic. Odor and color should give good clues.

Formula supplements impair the immune provisions of breastmilk in many ways. If formula is used too early or more than a few times, the protectiveness of baby's flora is permanently decreased. Early formula supplements can increase a child's risk of developing allergy to cow milk proteins; the allergy may be caused by such proteins leaking through intestinal cell junctions that remain quite open in the first weeks after birth. Formula supplementation also reduces baby's demands at the breast, which impedes mother's milk supply. Although a final loss of breastmilk's protective flora is inevitable with the eventual introduction of solid foods, the longer this event can be put off, the longer the child's status of lower risk for infections can be maintained. Six or more months before introducing other foods is the recommended goal. Still, after this flora alteration occurs, breastfeeding continues to provide many nutritional, hormonal, neurological, and immune protective advantages.

More about Iron

When a breastfed infant is provided with iron supplements, the iron fills up all available lactoferrin binding sites, and the excess free iron feeds the more challenging kinds of florae, which ends the highly protective gut environment provided by breastfeeding exclusively. Excess iron is also quite oxidizing, leading to toxic reactions in the intestines. When supplemental iron is actually needed by the child's body, then the iron is absorbed more quickly, and little oxidation occurs. Although the addition of iron to a breastfed child's diet can cause a considerable drop in her intended immune protection before the time she is beginning solid foods (which also marks the end of this protective stage), if an infant is truly anemic, it is important that he receive iron supplements or high-iron foods of some kind.

Although a final loss of breastmilk's protective flora is inevitable with the eventual introduction of solid foods, the longer this event can be put off, the longer the child's status of lower risk for infections can be maintained.

Children who are exclusively breastfed for long periods sometimes demonstrate little or no extra iron *storage* on blood testing (**ferritin**), allowing some to label them as iron deficient even though they are robust and do not display **iron deficiency anemia** (low **hemoglobin**). Those feeding exclusively on mother's milk, according to studies going up to 9 months of age, typically do not demonstrate anemia.

Nonetheless, pediatricians commonly recommend iron supplements for these infants because of low stores. Giving iron supplements to a breastfed infant who may have low stores, but is not truly anemic, is not a beneficial measure. Studies reveal that iron supplementation can only reduce the health of a baby who is being exclusively breastfed when actual anemia is not present. Higher amounts of free iron allow the growth of challenging bacterial flora, allowing for more infections. Too much iron leads to damaging oxidation and can cause intellectual decline.

On the other hand, too little iron in baby's red blood cells (anemia) reduces the cells' ability to carry adequate oxygen, increases baby's risk of infections, and can also cause intellectual decline.

Too much iron leads to damaging oxidation and can also cause intellectual decline.

Unless hemoglobin levels are quite low, just one low blood iron measurement still should not necessarily precipitate supplementation, as it is a natural immune system mechanism to lower available blood iron if a child is fighting off some kind of infection, sending iron to ferritin stores. The immune system knows what it is doing, and iron levels will return once the immune system action is over.

Infants who receive formula in addition to mother's milk are found to possibly be at higher risk of anemia than those fed exclusively on either. Adding formula to a breastfed infant's diet is suspected to interfere with the absorption of iron from mother's milk. At the same time, formula iron is poorly available. The high calcium and dairy proteins from formula bind quickly with any available iron, and most formula iron (96%) is passed unused into the diaper. This is one reason that formulas are supplemented with such high levels of iron. Soy protein and phytates from soy formulas also inhibit iron absorption. Whereas formula or solid foods reduce the absorption of mother's iron provisions, the iron from formula is poorly absorbed by baby's intestines. Formula feeding also may introduce microscopic intestinal bleeding, which reduces iron stores.

Similarly, the first months of introducing solid foods to an exclusively breastfed baby pose a vulnerable period for developing some anemia, especially in a child with other risk factors. The free iron in the foods reduces lactoferrin's ability to supply iron to the infant and allows adult-type flora to grow. As the new flora flourishes, it quickly consumes much of the available iron from small portions of baby foods and leaves little iron for baby to absorb. Those at greatest risk are babies who were born prematurely, who had experienced bleeding due to intolerance of foods in their mother's diet, who received a high amount of reflux medications, who have had some kind of surgery, who have mothers who smoked during pregnancy, and those babies who have had much diarrhea during their little lives. Immediate clamping of the cord after birth robs newborns of a good amount of their intended blood supply and also increases their risk for developing iron deficiency anemia. Once parent and child decide to be committed to solid foods, beyond tests and tastes, researchers suggest that plenty of high-iron foods may be beneficial in the first few months. An infant or toddler fed much cow milk, rather than formula or breastmilk, has a high risk of developing anemia.

As mentioned, anemia can lead to an increase in infections, and severe anemia can lead to neurological impairments; on the other hand, high blood iron levels can also lead to neurological impairments, along with other concerns. For this reason, a simple blood test is recommended if you have concern about anemia. An iron supplement is not advisable in an exclusively breastfed baby, or any baby, without demonstrated need.

Unless a child was born near term, benefited from delayed cord cutting, exhibited no blood in her stools, experienced minimal diarrhea, and received only breastmilk for the first several months, one or two measurements of the child's iron levels as he approaches 9 months (when he is not ill) may be of benefit to look for anemia, which is rare—but occasional—occurring in about 3% of exclusively breastfed babies. These rare occurrences are likely due to other factors mentioned, rather than breastmilk itself.

Although mother can increase the amounts of many nutrients passed through her milk by increasing her own intake, increasing her iron intake does not increase the level in her milk, unless she was very anemic, as the milk is *determined* to maintain only enough iron to keep baby healthy without feeding unwanted bacteria. Breastmilk is designed to get it just right.

About Formula and Other Breastmilk Substitutes

There are times when breastfed babies are simply not getting enough milk. Donor human milk is highly recommended at least for the youngest of such babies, and especially for preemies, in attempt to keep their diet entirely human sourced until they become a little older and stronger. Milk banks are institutional sources for donor milk. There are two additional worldwide options: EatsOnFeets.org and HM4HB.net (Human Milk 4 Human Babies). These three alternatives each have differing sets of guidelines. Parents will want to learn some basics about them and select the one that is right for their family. When supplementing mother's own milk is recommended by a lactation consultant and when donor milk is unavailable or not desired, infant formulas are available to provide needed extra calories to infants.

Because the absence of human milk poses so many health risks to infants, people sometimes point their fingers at infant formulas as the cause of these problems and seek out whole goat milk or raw cow milk to feed their infants. Cow milk, or any whole animal milk, is incredibly different from human milk nutritionally and highly inappropriate to feed a young infant in any significant quantity. Around the year 1920, well after pasteurization of cow milk was common practice and boiling of bottles and nipples was also commonplace—and after it was well known that sugar needs to be added to whole cow milk in attempt to give a child a fighting chance—the death rate of newborn infants who were fed whole animal milk was 10 times that of infants who were breastfed.

Milk banks are institutional sources for donor milk. There are two additional worldwide options: EatsOnFeets.org and HM4HB.net (Human Milk 4 Human Babies).

For this reason, highly amended infant formulas have been developed and continually improved over a century of research and experience. Every several years, in fact, formula is determined to be deficient in another ingredient, which is then added. To attempt to mimic this kind of experience on your own, through homemade formula, is not highly recommended. It's less of a concern if you are only using a homemade formula to supplement a mostly breastmilk diet and in an older baby.

The baby sugar, lactose, in animal milks is the same as that in human milk and is good stuff, providing slight immune properties; however, in cow or goat milk, the amount of this sugar is too low for the proper brain development of a human child. The most essential modification to animal milks for human infants is the addition of extra lactose, or other sugar, in prescribed amounts.

In addition to having proteins that are difficult for a baby to digest, the protein content of goat and cow milks is much too high for a human infant and puts the child at risk of kidney damage. For this reason, dilution of animal milk is also important if much is to be fed to an infant.

Dairy's extremely high calcium content causes relative deficiencies in magnesium and other bone-building minerals. This calcium also binds with the small amount of iron available in milk, making the iron unavailable and rapidly causing anemia, and the calcium binds with certain fatty acids, forming complexes that are lost in the stools. Additionally, the excessive phosphorous in animal milks reduces the availability of calcium for absorption. The dilution of animal milks helps to dilute the calcium and phosphorous as well.

Cow and goat milks also contain inadequate amounts of vitamins A and D (usually added to commercial milks and probably high in milk from range-fed cattle raised in the sun), boron, copper, magnesium, manganese, zinc, selenium, vitamins C and K, and omega-3 fatty acids, and more so after dilution. They also contain no prebiotics to feed flora (neither do most formulas). You will find most of these ingredients added to infant formulas. Fresh goat milk is also exceptionally low in folic acid and vitamin B12, although folic acid is added to powdered goat milk along with vitamin D.

Pasteurization, performed on commercial milks for bacterial safety purposes and necessary for large mainstream cattle farms, damages whatever active immune factors that may be available in raw milk. Homogenization, for consistency and convenience purposes, poses some unnatural, possibly unhealthy, qualities to the good natural fats. All milk fats are typically removed in the making of commercial formulas. One advantage to this removal is that most drug residues, toxins, and hormones are stored in fats. A disadvantage is that vitamins A, E, and K are stored in fats and, for a cow raised in the sun, vitamin D as well. The fats added back in to formulas are not the most ideal kinds and, although each of these vitamins naturally occurs in multiple forms, only one synthetic form of each is added back in.

Cow and goat milks also contain inadequate amounts of vitamins A and D, boron, copper, magnesium, manganese, zinc, selenium, vitamins C and K, and omega-3 fatty acids.

Of course, no whole animal milk or soy or milk formula comes close to providing the extensive immune support found in human milk alone. Raw animal milks do carry a few antibodies and possibly low levels of a few other active immune factors, although antibodies would be chiefly directed toward common diseases of cows, not of humans. Antibodies to **rotavirus**, a common diarrheal disease in human infants, have been found in a portion of raw cow milks. Bacterial floral counts are high in raw cow milk, and assumedly goat milk, and may pose some positive experience for a child's immune system and flora.

The Weston A. Price Foundation has homemade formula recipes on their website that are the only recipes I've seen that appear to be appropriately diluted and fortified. They use wholesome ingredients and seem, with my rough calculations, to cover all of the vitamin, mineral, and fatty acid needs, along with suitable ratios of proteins to carbohydrates to fats. I have heard of parents wanting to reduce the fat or sugar content of formula recipes, thinking they are making them healthier. This would be a mistake. Nearly half the calories in human milk come from fat, and over 40% come from sugars.

Formulas and Preemies

Human milk is a definite lifeline for infants born too small. Ample evidence suggests that formula is damaging to already delicate premature infants and that donor human milk should be the default standard of care in the NICU when mother's own milk is unavailable. In Chapter 6, "Preemie Poops," I'll show that even when a baby has ample access to human milk, supplements are commonly used and are seldom beneficial. These supplements are called "human milk fortifiers," but they are actually products derived from cow milk. These may speed growth of a prematurely born infant, but they also increase the number of risky infections, slightly impede brain development, and reduce survival. A life-threatening intestinal condition, known as **necrotizing enterocolitis**, is almost entirely linked to formula feeding in premature infants. Although formula companies will boast about increased growth results for preemies, the known health effects from faster growth are increased risks of diabetes, obesity, and heart disease, and possibly cancer.

Although formula companies will boast about increased growth results for preemies, the known health effects from faster growth are increased risks of diabetes, obesity, and heart disease, and possibly cancer.

Highly motivated by financial profits, formula companies are in a powerful position to persuade pediatricians to use their products. Vulnerable parents must assert their rights to be informed and must demand the best evidence-based care for their tiny vulnerable infants.

Measurable Impact

We've seen that breastmilk and infant intestines are intricately intertwined to act against most infectious threats and many other potential ills. What does all of this intestinal immune protection really come down to? If you're interested, take a look at some numbers with me about diarrhea and some other illnesses. Because a protective gut microbiome also provides for friendlier flora throughout the respiratory tract, we'll look at some of these numbers, too. Illnesses not only occur more often in the absence of breastmilk but also studies consistently show that infections are more severe when formula is fed before 6 months. Whereas any number of days or weeks of exclusively feeding breastmilk clearly shows a good margin of benefit, a large body of evidence shows that major benefits occur when breastfeeding remains exclusive for at least 4 to 6 months, with continued benefits from breastmilk well beyond the introduction of solid foods or formula.

Even when a mother desires to and is fully able to breastfeed, forces from every angle tend to encourage her to add in a little formula here or a little rice cereal there. The knowledge is not yet mainstream enough as to what a large difference such a seemingly small act can have. It is important for mothers to have reliable infant-feeding information available so they can make decisions that fit best into their own family's abilities, needs, and priorities.

A multitude of studies have demonstrated how highly valuable it can be to exclusively feed breastmilk for at least the first 6 months, with nothing else being fed other than maybe occasional bits of water (not recommended but not damaging immunity). The respiratory and gastrointestinal illness rates for breastfed babies who receive formula along with breastmilk are much closer to the rates for those fully formula fed, although other physical benefits of breastmilk continue to be measurable. The bonding, emotional, and neurological benefits of any breastfeeding always remain. Once it is time to introduce solid foods, the differences between breastfed and formula-fed infants are not as  great, yet physical health benefits from breastmilk are still measurable for a couple of years of breastfeeding, and they likely go beyond. The emotional benefits of breastfeeding certainly extend beyond this point for both mother and baby.

Breastmilk, Diarrhea, and Gastroenteritis

Breastmilk is a powerful preventer of rotavirus and all other kinds of infectious diarrheal illnesses. Although the differences between diarrheal illnesses and deaths in breast and formula-fed infants are far greater in the developing world, the differences are still significant in industrialized nations.

Study findings have revealed from 6 to 15 times the rate of diarrhea deaths in formula-fed infants versus exclusively breastfed infants in various developing nations. A large, recent analysis of a great number of studies reported the average risk to be ten and a half times. Besides the lack of breastmilk protections, two factors that are involved in these statistics are unsafe water and the dilution of formula due to its high cost. Sanitation challenges in developing regions provide a much larger spectrum of ills that a child, who is unprotected by breastmilk, can succumb to. Some are quick to suggest that sanitation challenges are the only reasons for increased illnesses in formula-fed infants, but the differences in illness rates are significant even in the industrialized world. As illustration of its strength, exclusive breastfeeding was found to cut diarrhea in moderately developed Brazil by 90%, whereas rotavirus vaccination was shown to cut infant diarrheal deaths in the similarly developed nation of Mexico by only 40%. The industrialized nation statistics to follow reveal the true protective powers of breastmilk.

In terms of study findings in industrialized nations, critics point to various factors known to complicate the picture, such as the mother's smoking, educational level, and socioeconomic status. For decades now, researchers have been compensating for these factors before reporting their numbers. The most current studies account for all known significant confounders but find that most of these elements actually have little impact on the final results. We'll take a look at what a majority of studies find in the developed world.

Although diarrhea is a major cause of infant deaths among less developed nations, it accounts for 1.3% of U.S. infant deaths, or about 350 infants per year. U.S. infants suffer an average of 2.2 diarrheal illnesses per year with some three to seven in 1,000 infants requiring hospitalization.

Among industrialized nations, a 2008 Canadian study found that, during their first 6 months, infants who were exclusively breastfed suffered fewer than half as many cases of **infectious diarrhea** as those who were fed any amount of formula. A 2011 U.K. study also found fewer than half as many diarrhea cases in babies fed breastmilk. Many other studies in industrialized countries have found one half to just one third as many cases of diarrhea in exclusively breastfed babies as those fed formula. Many studies also report that when breastfed infants do suffer diarrheal illnesses, they tend to get less ill and to get well faster.

Other Intestinal Health

A scientific review of a large number of studies found breastfeeding to reduce the later development of serious **inflammatory bowel diseases** (IBD; i.e., **Crohn's disease** and **ulcerative colitis**) in childhood by one third. A more recent study found that breastfeeding for over 6 months reduced the chances of developing Crohn's disease by two thirds. A recent Danish study found that being breastfed for over 6 months as a child reduces the risk of IBD in adulthood by half. A recent New Zealand study had the same finding for those who had been breastfed for at least 3 months. This study looked at breastfeeding for up to 12 months and found that the risk of IBD continued to lower the longer the child was breastfed.

It has been found that the risk of a child developing sensitivity to wheat gluten, known as **celiac disease,** is half if the child is receiving breastmilk and no formula or animal milk at the time that wheat is introduced into the diet. In this and other manners, it is seen that breastmilk aids the digestive system in gaining tolerance to foods.

Statistical effects of formula feeding on gastrointestinal health in industrialized nations

Study	Risk	Effect	Feeding
Fisk 2011 U.K.	2.3 times	diarrheal illness	full formula
Duijts 2010 Netherlands	2.5 times	diarrheal illness	full formula
Monterrosa 2008 Canadian	2.5 times	diarrheal illness	any formula
Ip 2007 combined studies	2.8 times	diarrheal illness	full formula
Hlavaty 2013 Slovak	2.7 times	IBD (Crohn's)	< 6 months breastmilk
Hlavaty 2013 Slovak	1.7 times	IBD (ulcerative colitis)	< 6 months breastmilk
Hansen 2011 Denmark	2 times	IBD	formula fed
Gearry 2010 New Zealand	1.8 times	IBD (Crohn's)	formula fed
Gearry 2010 New Zealand	1.4 times	IBD (ulcerative colitis)	formula fed
Barclay 2009 combined studies	1.4 times	IBD	formula fed
Sullivan 2010 U.S.	10 times	surgical NEC	any formula in premature infants
Akobeng 2006 U.K.	2 times	celiac disease	full formula when gluten introduced

Palmer, L. F. Baby Poop. 2015.

Note: IBD = inflammatory bowel disease; NEC = necrotizing enterocolitis, dangerous inflammatory condition of intestine.

Breastfeeding helps to keep stools soft and results in far less **constipation** than formula feeding. Hard stools have been measured to occur more than 8 times as often in infants given both formula and breastmilk as those exclusively breastfed, whereas exclusively breastfed infants showed triple the number of healthy stools per day.

A more unusual finding is that, compared to those breastfed, infants who receive only cow milk formula developed 2.3 times the number of cases of **intussusception**, an odd folding of a piece of intestine inside itself that leads to dangerous intestinal blockage. The mechanism for this is unknown. Similarly peculiar, formula-fed babies have been found to suffer 4.6 times as many cases of **pyloric stenosis**. Exhibited by extreme vomiting, pyloric stenosis is a thickening of the sphincter that controls emptying of the stomach into the small intestine. Surgery is typically required for both of these conditions.

More Breastfeeding Impact

A professional analysis of a large number of studies on **respiratory infections** and breastfeeding in developed countries found that formula-fed babies suffer three and a half times as many severe respiratory tract infections versus exclusively breastfed babies. Another very large study found more than 4 times as many cases of **pneumonia** and double the *ear infections* for infants who were fully breastfed and who began formula or other foods between 4 and 6 months versus those who received nothing but breastmilk until after 6 months. Again, the power of a longer duration of exclusive breastfeeding is emphasized in these reports, as is the fact that the length and severity of such illnesses tend to be less among breastfed babies. These numbers are significant in that respiratory infections account for some 6% of U.S. infant deaths.

Studies on early feeding and diabetes have generally found, on average, that more than double the cases of type 2 and nearly double the cases of type 1 **diabetes** develop in children who received any formula.

The most recent analysis of studies on **sudden infant death syndrome** found 4 times as many cases of **SIDS** among formula-fed infants as among exclusively breastfed babies. SIDS accounts for 9% of all U.S. infant deaths.

I've often been confused by motives when I hear of a pediatrician recommending early vaccines by saying "no disease risk is too small," and then, in the same visit, suggesting early formula supplements that can easily double a child's risk for infections—contagious infections—and raise other risks for the child as well.

Breastfeeding Success

In a natural human condition, as in many less industrialized parts of our world, girls grow up seeing and learning about breastfeeding all their lives. If we—as mothers—could grow up this way, we would learn about the challenges and the solutions, and we would not be hindered by negative social mindsets. We would have the support of members of the family circle who are older and experienced in the practice of nurturing children. Like so many other ills of the industrialized world, breastfeeding success is found to be much more difficult to achieve in highly westernized nations, though mothers' malnutrition may be a downfall to optimal breastfeeding in parts of the developing world.

Our hormones and instincts, along with cues from the newborn, should also be strongly aligned to make breastfeeding happen quite naturally. But in addition to our loss of collective maternal wisdom, many lifetime environmental exposures, which are so common in the industrialized world, may impair our ability to breastfeed. These chiefly involve estrogen mimics found in pesticides, plasticizers, petroleum products from cosmetics and other personal care items, mercury, solvents from many household cleaning products and dry-cleaning products, fire retardants, synthetic scents, and many other unnatural chemicals in our environment. Antibiotics and growth hormones used in animal farming may also pose hormonal balance problems. Stress, too, can certainly interfere with optimal hormonal functioning, as can trans fats and many other messed up modern dietary trends.

With such added challenges, we need assistance even more. One might think that pediatricians would be a source of information on the natural feeding of babies, but you will find optimal breastfeeding help from only a very special few. Pediatricians are highly educated by formula companies on the use of their products and tend to receive any breastfeeding education from this same, biased source. Beyond this, their educations

Like so many other ills of the industrialized world, breastfeeding success is found to be much more difficult to achieve in highly westernized nations.

are importantly geared more toward discovering and treating infant disorders and illnesses, so let them be heroes; you can find your own special breastfeeding support network among lactation consultants, at La Leche League International, and through connections with local moms.

If you haven't already guessed, one very important key to breastfeeding success is to actively insist that the newborn nursery not provide any formula supplements to your newborn. Better yet, insist on keeping your baby in your room with you.

Some Final Thoughts

Many mothers have an ideal image of the way they want their baby's beginnings to be. Often, things don't go as planned. All is not lost. The best way to prepare is to be informed. You can broaden your options and optimize outcomes for your entire family by being informed about available evidence-based choices in pregnancy, birthing, parenting, feeding, and treating illness and by striving for the best physical and emotional health for you and your baby.

First Poops

What's Normal and What's Not

If new parents are not well exposed to other new families, the first stuff found in their baby's diaper can be quite surprising; so can the next stuff. Just like lochia experienced by the new mother, it's just not often talked about. Like other stool issues, it's important to define what is normal for these early poops and understand what symptoms may be cause for concern.

Meconium

In the womb, your baby begins rehearsing her digestive system by swallowing bits of the amniotic fluid with which she's surrounded. Bile and mucus from her digestive system join this fluid. Babies develop a dark hairy covering in utero that is replaced around the eighth month by lighter newborn fuzz. In babies born after it has shed, this hair invariably contributes to meconium. Dead cells that slough off from the intestinal linings mix in with all these other components, and the resultant muck will become your baby's first bowel movements—hopefully, in the first few days after birth. This first poop is called **meconium**. It presents as blobs of dark green-black sticky stuff with no unpleasant odor. Meconium is a great parental initiation. If you can clean this, you can change any diaper.

Meconium Timing

You may feel that it's poor taste to place such attention on what kind of stuff comes out of a newborn's bottom, but it's truly very important. Passing of meconium is the first test that your baby's body works right—that the intestines are open and ready to push food through.

If your baby's tummy is bloating, he's vomiting, or he refuses to feed, these should greatly add to your level of concern.

If a newborn is not passing meconium, it could mean one of several possible problems that need to be addressed early, so doctors need some kind of standard in order to determine which babies may need attention. In the case of meconium, the question of which baby to be attentive to is easier than other stooling questions as there's not a lot of leeway.

When should meconium pass? Classic medical advice is based on a large 1977 U.S. study, which found that only 1.5% of term babies had not passed any meconium within 24 hours after birth. Though a larger 1991 study of Chinese babies found that 2% of term births had not passed anything in the first day, the standard mantra is that 99% of babies should pass something within the first 24 hours.

More recently published research studies differ quite a bit from the early 99% standard that's still used today. A study of Nigerian mothers found that 24% of healthy newborns had not passed meconium within 24 hours and another Nigerian report found that 12% of babies delayed beyond 24 hours. In a study from the Netherlands, 21% of term newborns had not produced meconium within 24 hours. Preterm infants will more often pass beyond the 24-hour mark. Very preterm infants can definitely take more time but, typically, will already be under medical observation.

Okay, I know, that's way too much math for one simple matter, but I'm personally quite curious as to why recent study findings differ so much from the older and why this has never been addressed. I think that questions like this are always important to ask, but I have no solutions to venture here. The current high rate of cesarean sections can't be the reason because the rate is not high in Nigeria. Medications would not be the cause, as their use in the Nigeria and the Netherlands studies would have been lower than in the earlier U.S. study.

The basic take-home message is that if your baby has not passed any meconium after maybe 36 hours, you certainly want to contact your doctor, and you may want to do so sooner. If your baby's tummy is bloating, he's vomiting, or he refuses to feed, these should greatly add to your level of concern. When it comes to delayed meconium, several kinds of obstruction could be the cause, and these are certainly for your doctor to diagnose and care for. Just to name a couple of the most common possibilities, cystic fibrosis or Hirschsprung's disease may be on the mind of a physician who is attempting to diagnose such a baby.

When should the passing of this dark sticky stool end? Your newborn's poop will likely transition a bit gradually from tarry meconium to light brown or mustard-colored loose infant stools. Generally, this transition should begin by Day 4, and there should be no more meconium appearance by about Day 6. Meconium lasting longer than this is suggestive that a baby may not be taking in enough nutrition to push their pre-birth accumulation out.

Meconium and Baby's Microbiome

As mentioned in Chapter 2, babies were once thought to be born sterile, with no bacteria in their bodies. It's recently been determined that, at least humans and mice are born with established bacterial colonies in their meconium prior to any exposure to the outside world. These were found to come from mother, as one study tagged certain bacteria in mother mice and found these tagged bacteria inside the meconium of the mothers' pups, born via cesarean. Apparently, these fetal gut bacteria pass selectively through the placenta.

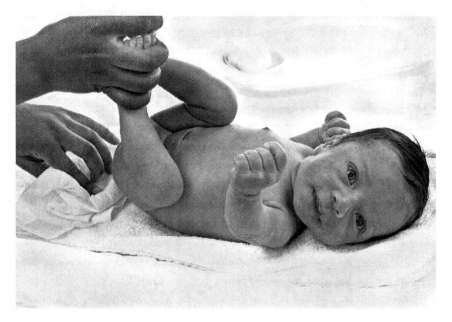

Researchers found that these bacterial colonies tended to be one of two kinds: either friendly *Lactobacillus* with other health-promoting, lactic-acid-producing bacteria, or strains of challenging *E. coli*. This time, it's not baby's birth or diet making this determination; it's mother's health and diet practices. Scientists found that factors such as college education and making organic food choices were linked to *Lactobacillus*-dominated meconium, whereas smoking and other less healthy habits in mothers were linked to predominantly *E. coli*-inhabited meconium in their newborns.

This early initiation of friendly or challenging bacteria is likely to be at least partly responsible for the reason that, among formula-fed infants, some will have a good number of *Lactobacillus* and *Bifidus* colonies, along with their challenging bacteria, and others will not. These differences can influence their overall immune system capabilities. Researchers' studies with mice suggest that a creature's very earliest microbiome can affect their mental health as well. This level of affect was not alterable after 7 days of age in mice studied. Can a human mother's health habits during pregnancy influence her child's psychological and immune development? Plenty of research clues point in that direction.

Meconium Concerns

As said, if meconium is not passing at all, it is a definite concern requiring prompt attention. Another worry arises when meconium has passed into the amniotic fluid before baby is born. Referred to as **meconium staining**, this finding can signal that the infant may have been under some kind of stress, but it is rather common, being seen in some 12 to 17% of births. The existence of meconium in the amniotic fluid can pose a risk to the fetus if it becomes breathed into the lungs with baby's first gasps. Meconium aspiration into the lungs can irritate or lead to infection and can be life threatening. Light or medium amounts of

Can a human mother's health habits during pregnancy influence her child's psychological and immune development?

meconium staining have been found statistically to be of little concern. Wise midwives know that it's safest to suction the baby's nose and mouth before cutting the cord because the umbilical cord will continue to provide oxygen while the baby's nose and mouth are suctioned. Deeper suctioning down the baby's throat is an option used medically when baby is judged to have potential for meconium aspiration. Studies pose controversy over the wisdom of suctioning practices, especially in babies who appear "vigorous," with the most recent study suggesting that wiping is as good as suctioning.

Medical interventions during the birth process can lead to meconium staining, especially labor induction. Use of dinoprostone or misoprostol creates a greater risk of meconium staining than does oxytocin for induction, as they stimulate the fetus's bowels, along with mother's uterus and bowels. Artificially breaking the amniotic sac may increase risk. Having little oxygen access in the womb and being well past the due date are two other common links. If the baby has been living in meconium-stained amniotic fluid for some time, he can actually be born with a green tint to his skin and nails.

First Feedings

Newborn tummies are very tiny and have been found to have little ability to stretch in the first few days. If fed an ounce or two of milk with a bottle, most of it will likely come right back up. Milk volume is better thought of in milliliters or teaspoons at this stage. A day or two old newborn may want somewhere around one half a teaspoon (2 to 3 mL) per feeding, totaling possibly one half an ounce (15 mL) to a full ounce in an entire day. Formula-fed babies may take 3 to 5 ounces by the second day.

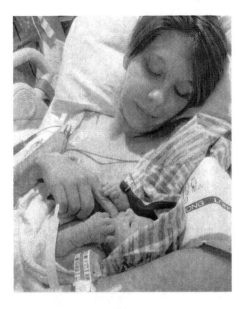

Breastfeedings should be quite frequent to keep things moving and to encourage milk development. Milk passage does not need to be measured. A breastfeeding mother can look to see that her baby appears to be doing some drawing of milk (pausing with chin down) and some swallowing. It may take baby a day or two to get this whole suck and swallow thing coordinated. Remember that baby's system is designed to require only very small amounts of nourishment in the first days and that formula supplements given to a baby who is intended for breastfeeding can interrupt a large part of the benefits of breastfeeding.

The newborn baby's minimal milk requirements coordinate with mother's breasts, which produce only small amounts of colostrum for the first 3 to 5 days. Whether human or formula milk fed, newborn digestive systems require time to ramp up for milk intake and digestion. This time is needed, in part, for meconium to clear out, for some intestinal maturation to occur, and for digestive flora to become established.

A baby should begin to urinate within a day, and then pee several times per day; in very small amounts, the first days. Most pee passed the first day is likely still from in utero fluids. Salmon-colored pee a few days after birth can be surprising but is not a concern as long as it doesn't last for long.

Initial Weight Loss

Most babies lose weight in the first several days after birth. Living in a fluid-filled environment, babies are born a bit plumped up. Meconium passage accounts for some weight loss. Babies are not designed to take in much nourishment in the first few days, leading to a bit more loss. It's all part of the plan and is not cause for concern. Of course, at some point, loss needs to turn around to gain, and loss that is much greater than average can rouse worry that the newborn is not receiving milk from her mother's breasts. You should not expect any weight gain from breastmilk feeding until 3 to 5 days after birth. The question of milk delivery to formula-fed babies is generally not a mystery, as long as you observe that the baby is not spitting up as much milk as she takes in. In the breastfed newborn, separation from mother, minimal skin-to-skin contact, spacing feedings out to every 3 or 4 hours, and limiting

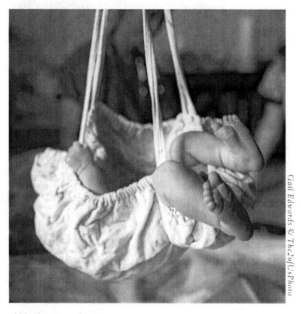

Gail Edwards © The2ofUsPhoto

Weighing newborn

time per feed are often causes of insufficient milk intake and production. Passage of the baby through the birth canal helps to stimulate milk-producing hormones. Cesarean births tend to delay milk production a bit.

Five percent of birth weight is the expected amount of weight loss for formula-fed newborns. In breastfed babies, 10% weight loss during the first 3 or 4 days is a common guideline beyond which investigation is warranted. The American Academy of Pediatrics states that 7% is the acceptable limit, yet that number is also the *average* loss in several studies, and 20 to 65% of breastfed babies reportedly lose beyond that mark. Use of 7% weight loss as a guideline by pediatricians can lead to excess parental worry as well as excessive and inappropriate formula recommendations by doctors. A healthcare or lactation consultant visit can't hurt beginning at 8% loss, is a good idea at 10%, and most will agree that 12.5% or greater loss calls for very serious medical and lactation attention. If things aren't turning around in a day or two, donor milk or formula supplementation will be recommended. If the child is deemed quite dehydrated, supplementing is more critical and some intravenous fluids may be of benefit.

> *Use of 7% weight loss as a guideline by pediatricians can lead to excess parental worry as well as excessive and inappropriate formula recommendations by doctors.*

It is important that weight-loss guidelines be used to suggest examination, consultation, and observation rather than immediate formula supplementation. For one, supplementation does not help the breastfeeding mother to get things going right; rather, it can jeopardize her supply. Supplementing causes a baby to be fuller and to demand less at the breast, which leads to lesser production by the breast. As mentioned earlier, formula given to a breastfed baby in the first week may prevent his flora from ever reaching its full protective potential. There is no evidence of damage to health or development by such weight losses in the first week, as long as a child is not dehydrated.

Another reason to look at the whole picture, and not focus tightly on the percentage of weight loss, is that newborn weighings are often not highly accurate, and they often measure baby in different states. For instance, a baby born with a full bladder who does not empty it until after weighing will have more apparent weight loss than a well-peed newborn. Variability between scales is another common complicating factor.

Two separate studies found that the most consistent factor linked to greater weight losses was not lesser milk availability; rather, it was greater amounts of intravenous fluids pushed into the mothers in their last hours of labor. A highly hydrated mother will be sending highly hydrated blood through her placenta and into her soon-to-be-born. This well-hydrated baby will weigh extra at birth and will then appear to have lost several ounces on his next weighing, having peed out all this excess fluid.

Babies born via cesarean without labor also tend to show more weight loss. We know that fluids are whooshed out of the lungs during labor and vaginal delivery. For babies who make larger stools or pee less often, I believe that bladder and stool status should be considered at early follow-up weighings. Lastly, bigger babies at birth tend to lose a tad more than those smaller to begin with, whereas those born a bit early tend to lose more than term babies.

How can you tell a baby who has lost extra weight because his mom received a high level of intravenous fluids from a baby who's receiving limited colostrum or milk? The former will pee a lot in the first 24 hours or so, then will experience a drop in urine quantity, which will gradually build up again over the next few days. The latter will not be peeing much in any day.

Use of a space heater in the home has been found to be occasionally linked with weight loss that is actual dehydration. This study finding leads to suspicion that the warmers in hospitals can be dehydrating as well. A newborn can be kept warm more safely against a warm chest.

Next Poops

Now the meconium is gone, and the transition stools are over. Mom's milk has come in or baby is taking more formula. The next stools to be seen by about Day 7 are called milk stools. Breastfed stools will likely be yellow mustard color, rather runny, and often referred to as "seedy." They may have a bit of orange or bright green to them and may be a bit bubbly. We'll call these within normal range, for now. They tend to have a bit of a sweet scent and no negative odor. Formula-fed stools may be rather mustard colored or may be more on the bright green or tan side, and they will be thicker, maybe like toothpaste. They will develop a more adult stool-like odor. Many babies on high iron formula will have a deep green hue to their stools. Parents will be able to discern it from meconium as it's less "tarry" and more odiferous. Generally, 3 or 4 or more soiled diapers are

Breastfed babies may dirty a diaper for every feeding, and the stool may look quite runny. This is not diarrhea; it's normal.

expected daily at this stage. Breastfed babies may dirty a diaper for every feeding, and the stool may look quite runny. This is not diarrhea; it's normal. Formula-fed babies tend to have fewer stools, with a little more matter each time. It's not uncommon to see watery stools in babies fed hydrolyzed Nutrimigen formula.

By one week after birth, babies should be urine soaking somewhere around 6 diapers a day. Pee from an amply fed baby will mostly be very light in color and pretty much odorless. A breastfed newborn who does not seem to be soaking diapers at one week and is not producing at least one or two bowel movements a day, with substantial matter, should probably be seen by a lactation consultant, to be sure things are going okay.

By the end of this first week, parents will know if their formula-fed baby is having feeding problems or not. Their baby will typically be drinking somewhere around 12 to 24 ounces (350 to 700 mL) per day by now.

After about a month, stool frequency may slow down a little—and in breast-fed babies, possibly a lot. Other changes may be seen over the months before solid foods are introduced, a time when big changes in stools occur.

Jaundice and First Poops

Over half of all newborns gradually develop a little yellow coloration to their skin and to the whites of their eyes, often lasting for 2 or 3 weeks. This appearance, known as **jaundice**, develops from a rapid breakdown of red blood cells that occurs after birth. In utero, babies maintain more red blood cells to carry oxygen from the placenta than they need for breathing air after birth. Rapid breakdown of excess red blood cells after birth leads to a buildup of a yellow pigment called

Jaundice is an appearance, not a disease. Now known as physiologic jaundice, it should be considered normal.

bilirubin. While waiting to be broken down and excreted in the poop, bilirubin is deposited into the skin and eyes. Once processed by the liver, products of bilirubin breakdown leave through the stools. The newborn liver may need some time to process this excess amount of bilirubin for elimination, and elimination in stools does not occur until meconium is cleared and good stooling begins.

Mild to moderate jaundice is highly common in newborns and is harmless, and possibly beneficial. Jaundice is an appearance, not a disease. Now known as **physiologic jaundice**, it should be considered normal. Various liver disorders and several other rare problems can lead to greater jaundice with threateningly high levels of bilirubin. Most of these will lead to a tell-tale pale color of the stools. These are entirely different from physiologic jaundice of newborns. Such pathologic jaundice needs definite attention, and newborns who develop higher levels of normal jaundice are monitored to be sure it is only normal newborn jaundice. Whereas physiologic jaundice develops gradually over days, an infant born with—or very quickly developing—jaundice alerts pediatricians to check for certain disorders.

Boston University School of Medicine performed a review of medical textbooks and found breastfeeding information to be both greatly lacking and largely inaccurate.

Strangely, the yellow coloring of jaundice begins in the head and face, with greater amounts of bilirubin causing coloration in the upper arms and trunk, and then spreading lower. Still greater levels, which warrant serious attention, will bring yellowing to the palms and below the knees. Pale-colored stools, dark-colored urine, and reduced alertness are other signs that warrant a prompt call to the doctor. With examination and a simple skin test, and possibly a few blood tests, your pediatrician can discern simple physiologic jaundice from rare health problems that require medical attention. A little cautious observation can prevent very rare brain damage that can occur when bilirubin levels climb well above simple newborn jaundice levels.

In general, over-reaction to newborn jaundice has been common for decades, with treatments that are not healthy and that can complicate the situation. In our book, *What Your Pediatrician Doesn't Know Can Hurt Your Child*, pediatrician Susan Markel explained that pediatric textbooks have long fed an excessive jaundice anxiety in doctors through treatment recommendations that are intended for babies who are much sicker. Boston University School of Medicine performed a review of medical textbooks and found breastfeeding information to be both greatly lacking and largely inaccurate. Parents need to be informed and proactive when medical recommendations threaten to interrupt exclusive breastfeeding without very good cause.

Not only is physiologic jaundice not found to be harmful, it may actually serve a purpose. We know that inflammation and a weak immune system are normal challenges to be overcome by all newborns. It turns out that bilirubin beneficially acts as a powerful antioxidant and, in newborn infants, it helpfully regulates inflammation created by certain immune cells (neutrophils) and increases their antioxidant production, when needed.

Sometimes newborn jaundice is deemed to be increasing because baby is not receiving enough breastmilk. Called **breastfeeding jaundice**, it would be better to change this term to "not-quite-enough-breastfeeding jaundice." Bilirubin products are not being removed well when baby is not pooping quite enough. Less pooping comes from breastmilk delivery being less than optimal. Although formula supplements are typically recommended, these can endanger the establishment of a good milk supply, which is the opposite of what is needed to both clear the jaundice and sustain healthy breastfeeding. Lactation assistance and more intensive breastfeeding are the beneficial responses. To keep things moving, excessively sleepy newborns need to be wakened to eat, day and night, with 10 to 12 or more feedings per day. In cases of greater concern, a little intravenous fluid can reduce bilirubin concentration quickly and prevent dehydration while milk supply is being improved.

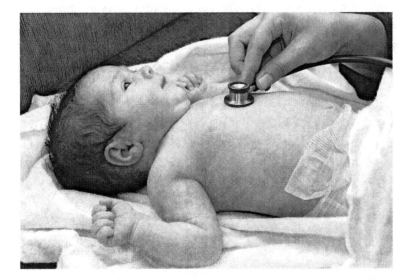

Another newborn jaundice seen in some one third of breastfed babies tends to develop a bit later, grow a little greater, and last longer. Often hereditary in manner, this occurrence is referred to as **breastmilk jaundice**. Curious, but harmless, it used to alert strong medical responses because formula feeding and mixed feeding were once so common that those babies were used as the benchmark of normal. It was once believed, and the idea continues to be promoted, that some mysterious factor in breastmilk detrimentally causes greater jaundice; in fact, at least 10 different components of breastmilk have been accused. Okay, a link to breastmilk does exist, but as breastfeeding is the human norm and no actual damage from the jaundice occurs, I find it a funny way to look at it—thinking that humans somehow made it through all these millennia with breastmilk being somehow harmful to so many newborns. Sometimes doctors ask for breastfeeding to be stopped for a couple of days to see whether the jaundice lessens (formula feeding can reduce the bilirubin levels) and, if not, they assume that they should look for some other problem in the infant. This is certainly not an optimal means of handling the situation. There are other, more informative ways of diagnosing problems that are so rare, and interruption of breastfeeding can lead to problems itself. How rare? A review of infant jaundice suggests that, up to the year 2007, there were *no* reports of brain damaging

It turns out that bilirubin beneficially acts as a powerful antioxidant and, in newborn infants, it helpfully regulates inflammation.

excess bilirubin in babies specifically with breastmilk jaundice. Still, there is no reason not to *monitor* the situation, when levels are in higher ranges, as there is no distinct cut-off level of bilirubin at which damage does or does not occur.

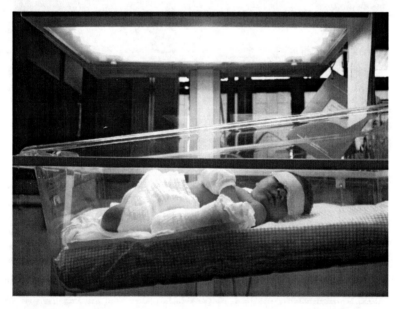

As a matter of fact, a significant portion of newborns showing prolonged jaundice, and possibly fast onset, actually have a hereditary condition known as **Gilbert's syndrome**. It's been found that people with this condition, which brings on mild bouts of jaundice and itchiness throughout life, have much longer lifespans than the rest of us. The assumption is that the longer lifespan is a result of the powerful antioxidant benefits of bilirubin. This finding demonstrates that common bilirubin buildup just can't be all that bad for breastfed babies.

Providing bottles of sugar water to a breastfed baby is another common recommendation in presentations of newborn jaundice. Although sugar water may not cause much interruption in the immune provisions of the flora in an exclusively breastfed baby, it can still impair breastmilk intake. Thirty years ago, and several times since, reports stated that this practice has yet to be proven at all beneficial.

Rather than complicating matters through formula feeding of a breast-fed baby, or reducing nutrition by giving sugar water, there's a very natural treatment to speed up the reduction of bilirubin levels, when desired. Simple sunlight can penetrate baby's bare skin and react with bilirubin to break it down so it can exit with the stools. Often, people imagine that it is UV light from the sun that is needed, the kind found to be greatest in the middle of the day, in the summer, and not through a window. Although UV light is great for vitamin D production, it's not what's needed here. It is the blue and green light portions of visible white light that are useful for encouraging bilirubin breakdown. Any time you can see light that's provided by the sun, the blue light and all colors of light are in it, whereas indoor lighting tends to have very little blue in it. Even in the middle of winter, and even early in the morning or later in the afternoon, mom can sit next to a sunny window with baby, exposing the jaundiced skin areas. Ten to thirty minutes of such sunlight, twice a day, is typically recommended, though more is certainly not harmful, and longer would be needed if it's dark and cloudy. Outdoor exposure under a shady tree will work, too, when it's not cold.

Just as it seems to happen so often with even the seemingly simplest interventions in natural processes, medical blue light therapy is found to cause unwanted side effects. Oxidation and damage to red blood cells result.

Medically, blue light phototherapy is recommended; however, placing a baby in a basinet in the hospital for phototherapy can complicate matters by impeding frequent breastfeeding. A blue light therapy blanket can be provided to be used in the home, but truly, more blue light is to be gained from sunlight. Just as it seems to happen so often with even the seemingly simplest interventions in natural processes, medical blue light therapy is found to cause unwanted side effects. Oxidation and damage to red blood cells result, and now some studies are calling for green light instead. Likely, the natural full spectrum of light colors from the sun would be the more optimal treatment.

Some Final Thoughts

In many cases, medical customs tend to sound the alarm too soon or too heavily, only worrying new parents needlessly, and sometimes exposing babies to undesirable treatments. Still, awareness of where dangers can lie helps parents know what to watch for. Health-damaging circumstances are very rare in terms of newborn weight loss and jaundice, but a little caution can head off such occurrences.

Preemie Poops

Optimizing the Health of a Baby Born Too Small

In case of a preterm birth, I believe it is highly important for expectant parents to learn a little bit about factors over which they may have some influence. A premature birth can come quickly, as a complete surprise, and there's no time to go searching for information during delivery or in the first many days after birth. Premature infants can face many critical health challenges, and their survival chances are much lower than for term babies. Most challenges have to do with feeding and with the digestive system. The tiniest of preemies face the greatest challenges, yet even babies born just weeks early can share some of the same potential risks. Even though premature infants are cared for in the hospital, with experienced medical staff playing heroic roles, generally parents can take measures to increase their baby's chances for optimal outcome.

Supporting Optimal Care

One important move you as parents can make, with greatly proven benefits, is to practice **kangaroo care** with your preemie as much as possible. You can learn the "why to" science about this in *Baby Matters*, and *www.KangarooCareUSA.org* should provide all of the "how to" that you will need. A large 2014 review of 16 studies on kangaroo care found an overall 40% lower death rate for preemies who spent most of their time in kangaroo fashion, snuggled on a warm bare human chest, rather than flailing alone in a plastic bassinet. Once oral feedings begin, parents can have great potential impact on their preemie's outcome by advocating for pure human milk feedings, including donor milk if needed,

and excluding any cow milk-derived fortifiers. Practices that do not support the interests of big industries, such as formula companies, tend not to dominate medical realms, but parents who strongly advocate for their tiny infants may find that such practices are more possible and more beneficial than hospital staff may lead them to believe.

UNICEF and the WHO released recommendations in 1991 designed to improve infant survival through practices that especially encourage human milk feeding for newborns. Hospitals following this **Baby Friendly Hospital Initiative** are shown to have greatly superior infant outcomes. When babies are born prematurely, their mother's milk production is sometimes slow to grow. This initiative is designed to provide appropriate support for mothers to help them enhance their milk production. It's also important for hospitals to maintain access to donor milk when needed and to not provide unwanted formula supplements that jeopardize preemie breastfeeding and health. With over 3200 hospitals and birth centers providing maternity care in the United States, including over 1500 NICUs among them, only 158 have achieved Baby Friendly status as of 2013—*5% of maternity wards, 22 years later*. Most all other countries have better rates than the United States, and a large portion of countries have notably higher percentages of Baby Friendly status designations, with a global average of 28% of hospitals. You may wonder why it would take so long for hospitals in a wealthy industrialized nation to take this rather simple and highly effective step. So do I. Money should not be a roadblock. Although there are added expenses with providing support to mothers and with banking of donor milk, the benefits of reduced demand for disease care are proven, through solid studies, to balance the economic scale.

It's All about the Intestines

Generally, the greatest challenge that premature infants face is the ability to obtain enough nutrition without significant negative reactions to feeding attempts. The hurdles are all about the intestines: digestion, absorption, inflammation, and infection. Intestinal health, in turn, is all about what goes in. Preterm newborns often receive intravenous fluids with various nutrients, and these valuable intravenous fluids do not impair intestinal health. Often preemies receive a full nutrition solution through a major blood vessel. This is known as **"TPN,"** for **total parenteral nutrition**. TPN also does not impair intestinal health, but it is quite rough on the immature

With over 3200 hospitals and birth centers providing maternity care in the United States, only 158 have achieved Baby Friendly status.

liver and poses infectious and other risks; thus, efforts are made to limit the amount of time TPN is used in preemies. Although TPN does not impair the intestines, avoiding early introductions of oral feeding can. Even when other feeding modes are required to provide adequate nutrition, early oral feedings in tiny but increasing doses are shown to generally provide great benefit, as long as these come exclusively from human milk: mother's milk or donor milk, not supplemented with cow-derived products.

Necrotizing Enterocolitis

Sadly, a common intestinal condition of preemies presents a predominant reason for seeking exclusive human milk feedings for preemies. **Necrotizing enterocolitis (NEC)** is a devastating condition seen mostly within 6 weeks after birth in prematurely born infants, in small-for-gestational-age (SGA) infants and in otherwise unwell babies who are being cared for in a neonatal intensive care unit (NICU). In this condition, which affects 7 to 12% of very tiny premature infants and a smaller percent of larger preemies, part of the intestinal lining becomes inflamed and dies off as acids build and secondary infection sets in. Intensive medical management is needed and surgery is often required to repair or remove damaged portions of the intestine. If the bowel must be considerably shortened surgically, some infants end up with lifelong challenges in obtaining adequate nutrition. There are many other possible complications from NEC; for instance, neurological deficits often occur, including blindness. NEC has a 22 to 50% death rate.

This terrible disease is a powerful demonstration of the way human milk is an integral part of a young infant's gut and literally keeps the intestines alive. The large majority of NEC cases are in babies who are fed some amount of infant formula or cow milk-derived fortifier in the NICU.

A review of studies, in which preterm infants were fed either donor human milk or formula, found 80% fewer cases of NEC occurred in babies who received no formula. A broader review the same year found 60% fewer cases of NEC. NEC occurs even less often in infants fed their mother's own milk than in those fed donor milk, as the pasteurization of donor milk damages some nutrients and immune components. Additionally, preemies suffer less than half as many other infections when receiving mother's milk versus donor milk or formula.

NEC cases are not only more frequent in those receiving formula or cow milk-derived fortifiers, they are also more severe. One study found that 90% of NEC cases needing surgery or leading to death occurred in those preemies who received cow milk products in addition to mother's milk versus those who were fed mother's milk and supplemented with only human-derived products. If comparing premature infants who were fed exclusively with mother's milk to those who were exclusively formula fed, the disparity would certainly be even greater—approaching 100%.

Providing a good milk supply is difficult for many mothers when their infants are born very early. Their breasts and hormones are not yet fully prepared. Mainstream hospital routines and a lack of appropriate support add greatly to the problem. Luckily, donor milk performs quite well. Babies do better with *any* human milk versus none. Donor milk from mothers of premature babies brings slightly better results than that from mothers of term babies. Any amount of mother's own milk added to donor milk improves the results of donor milk use. The actual responses are all dose dependent. The World Association of Perinatal Medicine declared in 2010 that donor milk is the preferred supplement when there is not enough mother's milk, thereby reducing infections and NEC and improving long-term outcomes.

At the end of this book, please find more detailed information in the descriptive notes that have been added to many of the references cited for this section and following sections.

Fortify Human Milk?

Often pediatricians are determined to provide animal milk-derived fortifications to human milk feedings, even when mother's and donor milks are ample. These are called **human milk fortifiers**, although they are *derived from cow milk*. Many recent studies that discuss use of human milk in preemies use language such as "though nutritional fortification is necessary," without ever demonstrating exactly why it is necessary. Formula suppliers boast of faster weight gains when their fortifiers are used, and this *is* a consistent finding, but it is well shown that feeding of cow products is also consistently associated with greatly increased chances of NEC, respiratory infections, other infections (sepsis), and other health risks including reduced survival. Re-hospitalizations are also more frequent in preterm infants who had been receiving formulas.

All the while, there is no evidence that faster weight gain is advantageous in human milk-fed infants. There *is* at least one study showing that faster early growth in preemies is neurodevelopmentally beneficial, but this study pays no attention to infant diet. One can assume no mainly or fully human milk-fed infants were in the study as it takes special attention to encourage this feeding or to seek these mothers out. So, it's possible that growth may be positively linked to neurodevelopment in babies receiving only formula, absorption of many of formula's nutrients is a great challenge; therefore, more formula, or a different balance of formula nutrients, may be required to provide adequate nourishment for the nervous system. Another feeding choice, however, shows even better neurodevelopment than slow or fast growing formula-fed preemies. The studies that *have* taken diet into account show greater developmental and intellectual benefits to fully human milk-fed preemies, as well as overall survival benefits, even though their weight gain is slower. Regardless, this one study on predominantly formula-fed preemies is the one that is widely promoted and used to sell human milk fortifiers, unfoundedly praising faster growth. As each new fortifier is brought to market, their safety is tested and reported only as compared to other fortifiers, not compared to human-only feeding.

Neurologically, those preemies who do not receive any cow-derived products are found in many studies to have slightly higher IQs and other good neurodevelopmental indicators. The deficits are not necessarily *caused* by the cow milk products; rather, it appears to be the interruption of human milk influences, as studies reveal that breastfed infants also show slightly higher intellectual skills over those who receive soy formula. Though study reports about the intellectual advantages of breastfeeding are sometimes contested, researchers take these complaints into account; every new study is designed to address each additional factor accused of confounding research findings, such as mother's education level

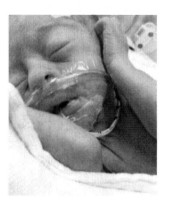

or the family's income. Among the large number of available studies measuring developmental achievements in relation to diet, no suggestions are ever made of any intellectual or other neurological detriments associated with absence of formula supplements or human milk fortifiers, even when there is slower premature infant growth. It's known that later catch-up growth occurs in breastfed preemies, so slower growth is not a concern in terms of final size. Although current thinking is strongly in favor of fortifying human milk with additions of cow milk products, I am unable to find one study that shows human milk fortifiers provide survival benefits; reduced disability, such as blindness or cerebral palsy; or other neurological or health benefits. I find only studies showing increases in early growth along with increases in illnesses, with formula additions to breastmilk.

With the evidence weighing so heavily against *formula* supplements to human milk and in favor of donor milk supplements when mother's milk is not available, human milk *fortifiers* have been brought in as the new "necessity." There are fewer studies on fortifiers available, but these are still just cow milk proteins and other components; they're still cow milk formulas, just with altered balances of nutrients. The name "human milk fortifiers" was certainly given in attempt to set them apart from the negative study findings associated with preterm formulas.

Suggestions are that these fortifiers are needed chiefly to increase the amount of protein that a human milk-fed preemie receives. Studies use definitions of preemie protein requirements derived through different energy use measures. The studies do not base protein recommendations on overall survival and on developmental outcomes from use of their fortifiers. In fact, they do not even take into account the fact that human infants more easily assimilate human milk proteins than cow milk proteins.

A large analysis reviewed all pertinent studies of protein levels in preterm formulas through 2006. This review reported that, though higher protein levels led to faster growth, the (supposed) benefit "could not be weighed against the adverse consequences" of excess protein residues in the blood and neurodevelopmental abnormalities. Researchers haven't even proven greater

protein to bring more benefits than detri- | *As each new fortifier is brought to market, their safety is tested and reported only as compared to other fortifiers, not compared to human-only feeding.*
ments among formula-fed preemies.

With speed of growth not shown to provide any health, development, or survival benefits in preemies, I believe ultimate survival, neurological development, and lack of other disabilities are the parameters of greater importance. These are found to be improved with purely human milk-derived diets for prematurely born and SGA infants.

I'm sure you've tired now of my growth versus outcome arguments, but there is another consideration I need to mention. Researchers have reported that the slower growth of preemies associated with human milk feedings directly leads to reduced risks of future, potentially life-shortening diseases such as obesity, diabetes, heart disease, and possibly cancer.

And one final issue is that of bone density. Complaints are that several bone nutrients are lower in breastmilk than the estimated needs of preterm babies, which presents another opportunity for the promotion of fortifiers. Sometimes bone growth indicators *are* lower in human milk-fed preemies than in those fed formulas. Researchers find, however, that preemies eventually catch up to their term-born counterparts. Formula supplements or fortifications of breastmilk may increase bone indicators for a few months, but they do not provide any long-term bone advantages. In fact, the more unfortified human milk a set of study subjects received as premature infants, the greater whole body bone size and density they exhibited at 20 years of age.

Studying Fortifiers

Through the influences of formula companies, human milk fortifiers have been made the standard of care without good studies to compare their use to that of unfortified human milk. A New Zealand analysis seeking research evidence of safety and advantages of fortifiers concluded that insufficient data exists to comment on neurodevelopmental effects or to be sure there were no other adverse effects, though a possible increase in deaths is associated with fortifiers. This 2004 review by Drs. Kuschel and Harding surmised, "Despite the absence of evidence of long-term benefit and insufficient evidence to be reassured that there are no deleterious effects, it is unlikely that further studies evaluating fortification of human milk versus no supplementation will be performed." I can't explain why.

An example of a study that supports cow-derived fortifiers for human milk is one that was performed in the pediatric medicine department of the University of Iowa in 2012. This report summarized earlier research reports of slower growth along with lower rates of NEC and sepsis, better survival, and better neurodevelopmental outcomes when only mother's milk is fed to tiny preemies, as opposed to formula supplements or full formula feedings. It then goes on to support current routine fortification of human milk, using the inappropriate formula-fed study finding that I mentioned before, that slower growth in formula-fed infants was associated with poorer neurological development. To quote this University of Iowa report, it read, "Although neurodevelopmental advantages were associated with human milk intake . . . slower in-hospital growth associated with a maternal milk diet in [pre-term] infants remains a concern, because poor in-hospital growth . . . is associated with poor neurodevelopmental outcomes." I find it difficult to believe that policies today are based upon this broken argument that simply does not make sense.

The more unfortified human milk a set of study subjects received as premature infants, the greater whole body bone size and density they exhibited at 20 years of age.

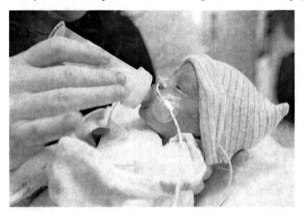

To make fortification policy matters even more puzzling, a huge French study, also from 2012, directly compares the neurodevelopment of 2- and 5-year-old children who were preemies being either breastfed or formula fed at the time of their release from the hospital. This study found a significant neurodevelopmental advantage for those who had been breastfed. Breastfed children also had larger heads, an indicator of brain growth.

In 2012, a large multi-hospital Utah study reported that a preponderance of deadly NEC cases among human milk-fed preemies was associated with an increased concentration of cow-derived human milk fortifier being fed within the 48 hours previous to diagnosis. This finding begs for similar analyses in other hospitals but does not bode well for fortifiers.

The arguments for the supposed necessity of human milk fortifiers are to promote increased early growth, to address a supposed need for greater protein, and to lower a risk of neurodevelopmental deficits. Yet no benefits are shown from increased early growth; no overall benefit has been proven from increased protein provision; and neurodevelopment is much better without formula or fortifier supplements. The very large increase in potentially devastating NEC, when any formula is used, should tip the scale strongly against the use of human milk fortifiers. In 2012, a Harvard-based medical team reviewed the "best available evidence" in terms of feeding infants at risk for NEC, which means those born quite early or small. They stated, "We suggest the exclusive use of mother's milk rather than [cow]-based products or formula in infants at risk for NEC." Still, human milk fortifiers are the absolute standard of care.

Fortifiers Made from Human Milk

Human milk fortifiers developed entirely from human milk sources have become available over recent years and do not cause such health and survival risks as do cow-derived products. These should be the first choice if a doctor is determined that a specific child requires certain concentrated nutrients. Actually, as fortification of human milk for preemies has basically become a standard of care—whether truly beneficial or not, then so should human-derived fortifiers, as cow-derived fortifiers are clearly detrimental. Because pasteurized donor milk provides slightly lower benefits than exclusive mother's milk, I believe that a benefit from human-derived fortifiers, a form of donor milk, still needs to be proven over only mother's milk when exclusive mother's milk is available. In personal communication with a researcher of human-derived fortifiers, it was explained to me that some mothers of very prematurely born infants have lower levels of protein and/or fat in their early milk than others do, and this concerns many doctors. When mother's milk availability is insufficient, and donor milk is used, this donor milk may come chiefly from mothers of term infants and may be lower in protein than typical milks from mothers of premature infants. With bedside devices available to easily measure breastmilk's fat, protein, and lactose levels, the makers of human-derived products believe that there could be benefits to boosting protein and/or fat by using human products, when milk levels are found to be lower. I'm eager to see further studies with human-derived fortifiers. Safety and superiority to cow-derived fortifiers are already well established.

Probiotics for Preemies

By now it should be clear how powerful a healthy and diverse infant flora is for disease protection and nutrient absorption—and these health issues are especially significant to the good survival of premature infants. Human milk and kangaroo care both support optimal floral development. A comprehensive review of 24 studies on the provision of **probiotic supplements** ("good" bacteria, such as that in yogurt) to preemies found a 55% reduction in severe forms of NEC and an overall 35% reduction in all-cause infant deaths. A recent, small Israeli study gave probiotic supplements to breastfeeding mothers of tiny preemies, which resulted in a 78% reduction in NEC. A simple provision of optimal flora to both mother and baby, along with measures to protect baby's flora and intestines, may bring even greater results than any of these measures alone.

Some Final Thoughts

Parents of prematurely born or SGA infants can provide additional research study information to their medical team, who are constantly bombarded by formula company messages and regularly provided with carefully selected studies, chiefly those that the formula companies themselves have sponsored. Many of these teams are stuck in tradition, as seen by the glacial pace of U.S. hospitals that gain Baby Friendly status. Parents can convince doctors that they are eager to agree upon the best evidence-based care for their baby, despite standard protocols, as they are seeking optimal long-term outcome for their child.

Parents enjoying kangaroo care with their preemies will help to demonstrate their commitment to optimal care. They can encourage medical staff that the use of donor milk and human milk-derived fortifiers has been shown to save hospitals money due to decreased costs from NEC, sepsis, and other infections, and from fewer re-admissions. Parents can help to find sources for these if they are not readily available in their hospital. Parents can show studies to the hospital about the benefits of probiotics for preemies as well. All of these actions may not only improve the chances for their own infant but could also encourage positive changes in that hospital for future preterm babies.

The Character of Poop

There's a huge spectrum of possible findings in babies' diapers. Before we can begin to talk about abnormal poop, we need to know what normal poop is. Infant stools are surprisingly different in appearance and frequency from what adults are used to, and most every parent of a new baby wants to know whether their child's stools are normal. A large portion of infant maladies present themselves in the diaper. As a child grows and the diet changes, baby poops then change just as distinctly. Depending upon the age and diet of the baby, normal healthy infant stools can appear every couple of hours to once every several days, can be green to brown to yellow, partly formed or entirely runny, can be seedy, have mucus or lumps, and can be barely scented to rather smelly. Given these wide variations of "normal," it's a challenge to know when to be concerned.

How Often?

Frequency can vary greatly from one healthy baby to the next. Once the first days of dark green meconium movements have transitioned out, we'll hope to see at least one or two stools per day, with very frequent stools being nothing out of the ordinary in the first weeks, especially among breastfed babies. Some young infants may skip a day here and there. Babies who start off with frequent stooling tend to drop off in frequency over the first few months. Around 3 months of age, most infants are producing zero to 5 stools per day. Over the next year or two, frequency tends to drop slightly more, reaching less than once to 3 times per day.

Different formulas are found to have different effects on baby poops. According to the company's research, infants on Nutrimigen tend to have stools as frequently and as loose as breastfed infants. ProSobee and several other formulas tend to create less frequent, firmer stools.

Whereas adults generally use frequency as a guideline to discern diarrhea or constipation for themselves, for an infant, the consistency of stools, changes in stool frequency, and changes in the child's behavior should all be considered to determine whether a baby has diarrhea or constipation that needs attention.

A healthy child can have soft bowel movements many days apart. After the newborn stage, we are mostly only concerned about infrequent poops when they are hard or hard to pass. After the first several weeks, some breastfed babies actually go 7 or even 11 days without pooping. In terms of adequate milk consumption, this is not considered to be a concern. But are there other reasons for concern? Some advisors are determined that a baby is not healthy without multiple stools every day, but skipping days is so very common that it's difficult to imagine all of these children are experiencing harm. A Turkish study reports that at 2 months, 39% of babies pass stools less than once per day. They also found less frequent stooling in infants with colic at this age. This finding does give some clue that maybe something is not optimal in children with infrequent stools. We'll investigate all of this in Chapter 11, "Hard Poop: Causes of Constipation and Withholding."

A Turkish study reports that at 2 months, 39% of babies pass stools less than once per day.

What Color is Poop, Really?

It's difficult to believe, but all stool—whether it results from a diet completely of white breastmilk or formula, or from a diet of all colors of solid foods, mixed with the billions of various bacteria being eliminated, plus the cells sloughing off from the pink intestinal linings—would be *white* if it weren't for the color imparted to it from **bile**. Yup, poop would be white without this digestive juice and in the absence of things that actually color the stools, such as blood, supplemented iron, beets, or artificial food colors. Colorful antioxidants and nutrients in foods are broken down and absorbed from the intestines. It's natural to think that at least the bacteria in poop are brown, but think about probiotic supplements with all the various bacteria in them. The powder is white. Bacterial infections of most kinds create white build up. Even a test tube full of E. coli is white.

Okay, but no healthy person has stools without bile in them. Bile is bright yellow-green. When it has time to be broken down normally in the digestive tract, it turns first to yellow or yellow-orange. If staying for longer—which it may with foods that take longer to digest, such as formula—it becomes light brown. When solid foods are part of the diet, stool remains long enough to turn bile fully brown.

> *Once much formula is introduced to a breastfed baby's diet, her poop will become tan to brown, and with the feeding of any solid foods, it will become brown. Poop browns as mature flora become established.*

The fats in breastmilk are more easily digested than other dietary fats, and breastmilk contains a special fat-digesting enzyme (bile-salt-stimulated lipase) that babies make very little of themselves. As a result, less bile is released in the intestines of breastfed babies. Bile breakdown is then handled a little differently when digested by the chiefly lactic acid-forming bacteria that grow in breastmilk-fed intestines. The result is yellow, rather than brown, like the yellow coloration that bile breakdown products impart to urine.

If stool has gone through very quickly, the bile is still bright to dark green. Green and white stools are discussed in Chapter 8, "The Color of Poop," along with other colorful presentations that may pose cause for investigation.

Normal Infant Poop Color and Consistency

Typical stools of exclusively breastfed babies are a mustardy yellow—that's somewhere between the duller *Grey Poupon* and the bright yellow of *French's* mustard. They're often seedy or they may contain little lumps or some mucus and, generally, they're rather runny or even slightly watery. If the poops are browner during exclusive breastfeeding, look at the section on brown stools for ideas. Once much formula is introduced to a breastfed baby's diet, her poop will become tan to brown, and with the feeding of any solid foods, it will become brown. Poop browns as mature flora become established, feeding on the free iron found in any formula and nearly any food.

Typical formula or mixed-feed stools are a slight orange-ish brown, light brown, tan, yellow brown, or just plain brown, with a consistency that's a lot like peanut butter. Some babies fed a mixture of formula and breastmilk maintain more of the yellow breastfed coloration, and I've even heard this coloring reported in exclusively formula-fed infants. This may mean that their flora has somehow, favorably, not converted as much to the more adult-like flora of most

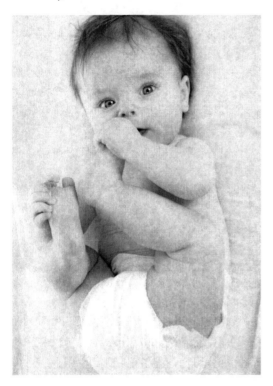

formula-fed children or possibly that their stool goes through a tad quicker than most, not giving the bile as much opportunity to be broken down into brown. Green stools are also so common in formula-fed babies that it's widely considered to be normal for this diet, though a little investigation might be a good idea if these are seen regularly.

As babies begin to eat any bits of solid foods, their poops will become browner, but portions of what comes out may closely resemble what's gone in. This clearly demonstrates that the baby's system is not mature enough to digest the foods found partly intact in the diaper. This food-like appearance in stools is considered normal enough, and harmless, and it may turn around in just a few days. If this finding is a regular occurrence, it may be best to back up on solid foods and retry them some weeks later.

One of the most common little surprises in baby poop is the sudden appearance of tiny little black threads. These are alarming, as they look like little worms, but usually they represent a first feeding of banana. These are a normal finding, although again, it may be best to wait a little while before re-introducing this fruit. Are you finding little white threads? These could actually be worms, especially if they wiggle.

Baby poops can be found in many more colors, with red, black, and white being the colors of greatest concern.

Some consistency surprises that may be found in a baby's diaper are foamy, frothy stools, mucusy stools, or greasy stools. If found more than rarely, these characteristics require further investigation. These are all covered later in this book. One more consistency indicator is that poop should sink in the toilet, not float. Poop floats when it has too much fat in it. If this finding is frequent, it means that baby is not absorbing fats properly. If noticed along with diarrhea, then the intestines have likely not had enough time to absorb the fats. If noticed with greasy and smelly stools, tell the doctor.

The Shape of Poop

Generally, babies poop in diapers, and so the shape is pretty simple; it's usually flatly spread out. If you happen to have a diaper-free baby, or you've just enjoyed a between-diapers surprise, you'll see that normal breastfed poop has little shape at all, except for the occasional lump or curdiness. Formula-fed poop will pile up, come out in odd soft pieces, or even take on some soft sausage shape. A very firm sausage, a sausage with sections to it, or hard balls, do not fit in with the definition of "normal," and are covered in Chapter 11. Any poop that manages to keep some shape inside a diaper is probably too hard, though formed stools are expected to be seen in the training potty with a solid food diet. Very watery stools—and floaters in the toilet when you dump the diaper contents in—are appearances that require some scrutiny.

How Much Poop?

We've already looked at newborns—the time when the first real poops signify that the baby's intestines are formed normally and their mother is making milk. After the first weeks, the real question associated with poop volume is whether a baby is taking in enough nourishment, though efforts to actually measure the total amount of stool are seldom made. If you are really interested, it's going to be around 3 to 5 ounces per day, depending on the amount of moisture it contains and the size of the baby. Another ounce or more of water could be lost with the stools if they are watery. Urine volume should go down when more liquid is lost in the stools. Daily baby poop volume will be roughly about one quarter of what an adult makes. Obviously, if a baby has several poops per day, each movement will have much less stool than if he doesn't poop for two or three days. Wetter poop will create a larger overall volume than dryer poop.

It used to be that formula-fed babies produced more stool than their breastfed counterparts, but the difference is not as great as it used to be, as newer formulas are more digestible than those of decades past—especially the fats.

Parents tend to be hugely concerned over whether their infants are getting enough food. I believe it's partly instinctual and partly a remnant attitude passed down from a century ago when weigh stations were developed by the early formula industry to tell breastfeeding mothers that their babies were underweight and needed their new scientific formulas. Pediatric doctors become overly concerned due to regular encouragement from formula companies to watch for any lower-weight babies. Weight charting is a standard part of every pediatric visit. This is not a bad thing, but so many other factors need to go into a determination of whether a baby is achieving adequate nutrition, absorption, growth, and development.

When charting baby weights, you must realize that a baby who only poops every few days, or maybe even just once per week, will have fluctuations in weight as her stool builds up over days, and then is lost all at once. This can make a 3 to 5 ounce per day difference, depending especially on the amount of moisture in the stool, and should be taken into account when there is an apparent drop along the weight curve. I recommend that parents pay attention to this, as doctors have little way of knowing where a baby stands in terms of stooling.

Those Growth Charts

When charting weights on growth charts, the first matter of importance is that your doctor use the new WHO growth charts released in 2006. They can be found here: www.cdc.gov/growthcharts/who_charts.htm. The American Academy of Pediatrics endorsed the use of the WHO charts in 2012, but many pediatricians are still using old U.S. government charts—supplied to them by formula reps. The old charts were created using chiefly formula-fed babies. The WHO charts were developed based upon the average weights of babies who were breastfed for at least 3 months, thus these charts better represent normal infant growth patterns.

Breastfed babies, on average, tend to gain weight a little faster during their first 3 months and then gain more slowly than formula-fed babies between 3 months and a year. Their head circumferences and lengths are the same, however. The use of charts derived from formula-fed infants can lead doctors to determine that a healthy breastfeeding baby is dropping off the curve when, in fact, they are following normal breastfed patterns. The WHO also recommends that the 2 percentiles and 98 percentiles be used as indicators of a child's deviation from normal, rather than the previous 5 and 95 percentile recommendations, prompting concern much less often.

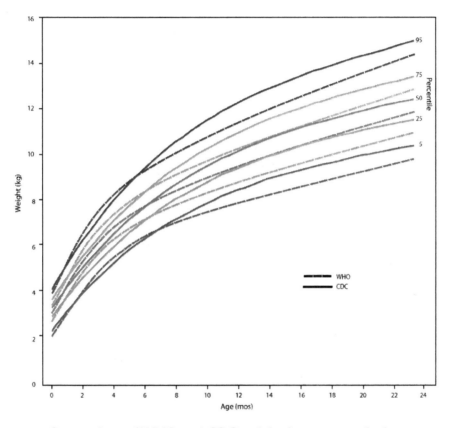

Comparison of WHO and CDC weight-for-age growth charts

Growth charts indicate to doctors and parents when a child is growing more slowly or more quickly than most infants her age. This finding should help alert those concerned to be sure that nothing is hampering a child's healthy growth. In some instances, for example, a child may be suffering from some kind of malabsorption or the mother needs more assistance in breastfeeding. For such reasons, dropping on growth curves are a time to evaluate feeding habits and to evaluate whether the child is experiencing frequent vomiting, diarrhea, rashes, or other signs of a problem that needs attention. It's also a time to look at other factors, such as the size of the child's relatives and whether a child is reaching developmental milestones.

Prematurely born babies certainly need to be charted by their gestational age. Preemies often develop even a little more slowly than term infants of their same actual age from conception. There seems to be this concept that a prematurely born child should eventually "catch up" to others their same birth age, in terms of size and development. This idea should be dropped. There is no reason to expect that a child's development should jump weeks or months ahead of their actual gestational age.

Periods without weight gain are always expected. Flat portions are obviously not seen on standardized growth charts because the curves are averages of hundreds of babies.

Most of the time, a child who appears to be low on the growth charts is actually steadily gaining weight at his own destined rate. Periods without weight gain are always expected. Flat portions are obviously not seen on standardized growth charts because the curves are averages of hundreds of babies. If a child is happy and alert and is approximately achieving suggested milestones for his gestational age, it's likely that the child is healthy and needs no feeding intervention or worry.

More often though, practitioners use the percentiles from weight charts as if they were grades of sorts, as if above 50% were akin to an "A," 15% a "C," and poorer grades below that. When a baby's weight lands in low percentiles on the charts, doctors—without paying attention to other characteristics of the child—may worry the parents by insinuating that their baby is starving. Typically, this kind of interpretation leads to recommendations for supplementing breastfed babies with unnecessary formula or solid foods, even though such measures are not shown in studies to increase growth rates, and there are no studies suggesting that an increased rate of growth is beneficial. Studies do show that early introductions of formula or solids are associated with increased gastrointestinal infections.

Basically, children will instinctually eat how much they are genetically destined to eat, unless their natural weight control mechanisms are greatly interrupted. Interruptions can be caused by frequent force-feeding, which commonly happens by strongly encouraging babies to finish what's in their bottles and by feeding them unnaturally sugary and fatty treats. When the weaning from breastmilk and the introduction of formula or solid foods begins, babies are often challenged with mild illnesses or food intolerances, resulting in drops on their growth curves. Although usually nothing to be alarmed about, such a drop may not be the result that was desired if asked to supplement because of slow weight gain.

Although there seems to be a large preoccupation with attempts to fatten lean babies, possibly we should give more attention to the fact that one third of all U.S. children are overweight or obese. Obesity increases the risks for many health issues. Slenderness does not.

Dropping Off the Growth Curves

For several reasons, babies' birth weights do not tend to strongly reflect their destined sizes. Rather, newborn weights are very dependent on gestational age and many other dynamics besides genetic factors. This means that a baby may be bigger at birth and then drop off their growth curve if they are destined to be thinner or shorter. Possible causes of a baby being born large for his destiny are a mother gaining a considerable amount of weight during pregnancy or suffering gestational diabetic tendencies, or a baby simply staying past term. Second and third born babies tend to be born larger than a first.

There are so many reasons why babies do not cling to standardized growth curves. Babies often gain in spurts. I've especially noticed that some babies will seem to gain only in length for a while, or possibly head circumference, and then gain only in weight for a time. Some say that babies tend to grow fastest in the summer and more slowly in the fall.

I'm amazed at how many times I've been contacted by parents who were frightened by their pediatrician's comments that their baby was in a very low percentile on the weight charts or was simply dropping from their previous percentile. Then I came to learn that not only was their child happy and meeting milestones, but both mother and father were small people. A smaller child is to be expected in this case. The use of a weight-for-length chart rather than the weight-for-age graph may give a clearer picture in many situations.

It's also common for babies to stop gaining weight for many weeks, or even lose a little weight briefly, when they begin crawling, scaling furniture, or walking, due to the extra energy expenditure. Again, this is no cause for concern or intervention. Babies also commonly experience a flattening or even a drop in their growth curve when switching from breastmilk to formula or when starting solid foods.

All of these instances I've described are examples of normal reasons for infants to land along low percentiles in the charts or to show flattening or drops in their own growth curves. Some babies may even fall from near the 50th percentile to the 15th percentile to the 3rd and be perfectly healthy. Let's consider

Being small, in itself, is not a disorder and does not impair health nor intellectual development. If a baby appears healthy and happy and is meeting most milestones, there is no reason to try to fatten him just for the sake of gaining some mark on a curve.

a baby at the one percentile. One in every hundred other babies are at that same point or below it, and these babies are certainly not all sick, underfed, or disordered.

Charting against standardized curves should be used as a tool to alert health practitioners when it may be prudent to examine a child to see whether there's a condition that needs to be addressed. They should not be used as indicators to attempt to fatten babies up. Being small, in itself, is not a disorder and does not impair health nor intellectual development. If a baby appears healthy and happy and is meeting most milestones, there is no reason to try to fatten him just for the sake of gaining some mark on a curve.

Other babies will certainly increase among the percentiles, as certainly many did among those used to gather these averages to begin with. I don't hear from these parents, though, as they are not frightened by their doctors. Yet, although no evidence of harm is associated with slower growth, much faster growth is linked to later tendencies for diabetes, heart disease, and obesity. Still, a baby growing faster due to his own genetic fruition should not be a concern. Just be sure that encouragement to finish bottles is not a factor.

Normal Sound and Smell

Breastfed poop can arrive stealthily, without sound or smell. Because it tends to be so liquidy, breastmilk stools can also expel quite explosively, with great sound effects announcing their arrival. As long as baby isn't more than momentarily upset by this auditory event, there's nothing to be concerned about. When not associated with some kind of upset, such as an illness or during or after the use of antibiotics, breastmilk stools or such gassy explosions shouldn't have much odor.

Poop from a child who is fed formula or solid foods will normally smell pretty much the way adult stools smell. Because they're generally thicker, they tend to bring less melodic accompaniment upon arrival.

Gas odor is different from stool odor, and it certainly can come at times other than during stooling. It's normal for all babies to expel gas several times a day, but it shouldn't have much odor, especially in exclusively breastfed babies. Smelly gas is often attendant with a fussy baby. When this happens often, you may wish to search for clues as to the cause. This is covered in Chapter 9, "Loose Poop: What is the Reason?"

More on Normal Gas

Gas *is* normal and is not a concern as long as baby is not too uncomfortable. One common cause of increased gas in some breastfed babies is mother's consumption of cruciferous vegetables. These include broccoli, cauliflower, cabbage, Brussels sprouts, kale, arugula, bok choy, rutabagas, and turnips. Onions and garlic sometimes cause gas as well. These are all healthy foods, of course, and do not cause excess gas in all breastfed babies, but if baby appears uncomfortable from gassiness associated with mother's consumption of these, mom will want to cut back for a while. Most of the time, these are not food allergies, per se, but simple, common, "normal" results of certain elements in these foods passing through very young digestive systems. In spite of these common breastfeeding dietary encounters, formula-fed babies are found to generally be a little gassier overall.

> *One common cause of increased gas in a breastfed baby is mother's consumption of cruciferous vegetables.*

Other causes of gas, that I'll call normal because they are not associated with inflammation or illness, are things that cause excess air swallowing. This can occur with bottle feeding, no matter what's in the bottle. It can occur with excessive crying, and it can occur when a breastfeeding mother has a powerful milk letdown that overwhelms the baby, who gulps in an effort to take it all in. These are cases in which a good "burping" for baby can come in handy. A lactation consultant can offer some good advice on letdown. For those receiving bottles, some babies do better with one kind than with another.

A baby who does not pass stool for days in a row may be more likely to have gas that announces itself well, as it may build up in areas between stool segments and then finally finds passage out.

Sometimes gas goes along with other symptoms to help paint a diagnostic picture, such as seen (heard) with food sensitivities or illness. In these, the effects go beyond simple and brief discomfort. Gassy illnesses, and methods of dealing with baby's undesirable reactions to formulas or to foods in breastfeeding mother's diet, are dealt with in later chapters of this text.

Is My Baby Normal?

You may notice that I generally try to avoid giving any kind of strong proclamations when it comes to the behavior of babies' poops. Normal healthy babies vary in so many ways. The diets of babies, of breastfeeding mothers, and even the diets of all the cows used for milk formulas all vary widely. Formula ingredients also vary widely. Parents do want to observe what *their* infant's normal is so they can monitor for important changes in usual patterns and can compare their baby's stool characteristics to those described for the many maladies presented throughout the rest of this text.

Standardized weight charts should not be used to proclaim that certain babies require efforts to fatten them up when they fall in lower percentiles and even below the one percentile. Rather, charts should be used as one instrument among a kit of tools and indicators to signal that a baby may need evaluation for the presence of feeding or absorption-inhibiting conditions. If a slower-growing baby is generally happy, meeting most milestones, and showing no other signs that present concern, lower weight can simply mean "smaller genes." Efforts to override natural weight controls may only introduce a propensity for diabetes, obesity, and heart disease later on. This by no means is to suggest that a rapidly growing infant should be put on a diet. When fast weight gain is not a result of overriding her natural appetite regulation, this baby is also fulfilling her genetic destiny.

The Color of Poop

Orange, lime, black, purple, red, white: the possibilities are surprising. Baby poop color changes can be alarming to parents, yet they can be important signals of what's going on inside their child's body. As a parent, you will wish to determine the cause of a new color in your baby's diaper, so you can know whether any kind of response is indicated. Some color changes only require parents to recollect baby's recent diet, whereas others can signify a need for urgent medical attention. Most color changes lie between these two extremes and pose opportunities for parents to act to improve their baby's intestinal health which, of course, impacts their child's entire wellbeing.

We've covered the first green-black stools of newborns and the yellow to light brown hues of normal infant stools. Once solid foods begin, the brown will become darker, like adult stool (and smellier too). Now we'll look at the causes of other possible colors. Sometimes an entire stool is a changed color and sometimes there are only streaks, blobs, or stains of a color. Either way, we want to know why.

Moderate amounts of blood can show up in infant poop as red or black. Outside of that, many pediatricians are not interested in stool color changes. Generally, they'll assume that parental reports of color alterations are related to a change in diet or a little stomach bug and, more often than not, this is the

> *A baby cannot describe her own sensations, and pain signals can be difficult to decipher, so the things coming out of the two ends of a baby are essentially all we have to go by in terms of determining the presence or absence of some disorder.*

case. This profession tends to hear about poop a lot, more than most would care to, and they may occasionally become desensitized to the degree of severity that certain presentations can potentially pose. A baby cannot describe her own sensations, and pain signals can be difficult to decipher, so the things coming out of the two ends of a baby are essentially all we have to go by in terms of determining the presence or absence of some disorder. If a parent's observations and instincts say that something may be awry, some medical testing or reassurance can't hurt. If there is fever, vomiting, bloating, or the appearance of pain, along with a stool color change, there is more reason to investigate.

Colorful Bile

Stool color alterations often result from the speed that food is passed through the digestive tract. As (solid) food moves through normally, stool becomes green from the addition of **bile** just after leaving the stomach, and then progresses to orange-yellow, and finally to brown as bile is broken down by the flora and as certain components of bile breakdown are re-absorbed. Let's look at this more closely, to better understand where some poop colors come from and what they may represent.

Let's review how the breakdown of **heme**, from iron-carrying hemoglobin in red blood cells, leads to the formation of **bilirubin**. Excess red blood cell breakdown in newborns leads to a buildup of bilirubin, creating skin-yellowing jaundice in newborns. As a part of the natural daily breakdown of old red blood cells, iron is released from black heme and the remaining portion is converted to green *biliverdin*, which then turns to orange-yellow and yellow bilirubin. If you have light skin, you've probably seen this happen many times. When you suffer a bruise, it starts out deeply purple. This is the black of released heme showing through skin that is pinked from red blood cells in capillaries. In a day or two, the bruise turns green, and eventually yellow, before it disappears.

Stool color changes may represent changes with bilirubin production and bile handling. Yellow and slightly orange forms of bilirubin, and its green associate, biliverdin, are deposited into the digestive juice bile and provide most of its color. This bile is released into the small intestine right after food leaves the stomach. Digestive enzymes from the pancreas are released along with bile. Digestive factors in saliva and the stomach have already acted on the food, but added color comes from bile.

The bile factors are broken down in the intestines by flora. This occurs chiefly in the large intestine after passing through the small intestine. In this discussion, the two important breakdown factors are colorless *urobilinogen* and brown *stercoblin*. Don't worry about all these names. They just help us to keep the colors straight. Urobilinogen is reabsorbed through the intestinal wall, into the bloodstream, and is captured in the kidneys, where it finally provides the yellow color of urine (as *urobilin*). Stercoblin stays in the intestine and provides the final brown coloration of normal, mature poop.

Exclusively breastfed babies release less bile, and they have a special spectrum of flora that processes bile less. Rather than tan or brown poop, these babies end up with yellow poop.

Many metabolites from drugs, supplements, and foods, including trace minerals and other colorful components, are deposited into bile for disposal through the stools. Large changes in any of these metabolite deposits can alter the shades of bile, hence, the color of the stools. It is likely that changes in floral balance can bring slightly different bile handling and create different balances of bile salts. These shifts in floral balance can also bring on slight changes in the shades of poop.

Technicolor Poop

Whenever any unusual color appears in baby's poop, the first question is whether baby—or possibly breastfeeding mom—has consumed a quantity of artificial food coloring. The coloring in gelatin desserts and artificial juice drinks (including Pedialyte), in colorful candies, and in decorative icings can certainly taint portions or all of a child's stool. Urine may be tainted as well. As certain elements of the coloring may break down more than others, sometimes the end color result of a food coloring is not the same as it was when it went in. Regardless, the look is typically artificial, and a judgment call can generally be made rather easily.

The coloring in gelatin desserts and artificial juice drinks (including Pedialyte), in colorful candies, and in decorative icings can certainly taint portions or all of a child's stool.

Next, after artificial food colorings, are natural food colorings. Food pigments may sometimes be less broken down by infant intestines than by adult digestive systems, although adults can also pass some fun colors at times. Beets may be the most intense stool and urine coloring food. Orange pigments can remain in poop from high doses of carrots, and dark berries can provide some nice blue or black hues. Curcumin (turmeric) supplements or large amounts of curry spice can bring beautiful shades of yellow orange to urine and stools.

The measurement of time between ingestion of corn and appearance in the poop is a great test for transit time.

If pumping or expressing, breastfeeding mom may see coloration in her milk, though by the time the color appears in baby's diaper, that dose of milk is probably gone from mom's breasts. You don't need to be concerned about feeding colored breastmilk to baby, if noticed. If it's a pigment from a natural food, such as beets, the pigments are typically wonderful antioxidants and aren't to be avoided. If much of the food pigment or coloring has remained colorful in mom's milk, this means it has gone through her system intact, rather than being fully digested, and will most likely go right out of baby's system the same way.

Other colorful, and often chunky, appearances occur in baby's poop when solid foods are simply coming out much the same way they went in. Pieces of tomato can mimic blood and could be probed a bit to distinguish between the two. Partial and whole corn kernels are quite common after a meal with this grain, even in adults. Actually, the measurement of time between ingestion of corn and appearance in the poop is a great test for transit time, if you're interested. It will likely be between 12 hours and two days. Such occasional appearances of undigested food are of no concern in the established solid food eater. For babies in the first days of starting solid foods, however, if food comes out looking the way it went in, it's a good sign that baby's digestive system is just not ready. Although it's likely not particularly harmful, it seems more appropriate to just wait some weeks before trying again. Food that doesn't digest can cause some tissue irritation and floral disturbance, and it's clearly not providing any nutrition.

Stool color and consistency variations can occur with many kinds of medications, which can affect bile or directly affect stool. A few common drug effects will be discussed here, but there are too many less-common medications and effects to cover each possibility. Basically, if things start changing soon after a new drug is being used, you can probably make an accurate connection. If you feel concern, read the drug package insert as it may give clues, and call the doctor to help confirm the connection.

One more occasional colorful event in baby poop that needs mention is the appearance of little pieces of brilliantly colored stuff. This comes from eating crayons left around by big sister. Luckily, today, most crayons are non-toxic.

Green Poop

Green is the most common color alteration seen in baby stools and should not cause great alarm. If a newborn leaves the green-black poops of the first few days of meconium, only to return to bright or dark green stools days later, this can be caused by a loss of excess bilirubin into the stools associated with jaundice. If this is the case, it's good that the bilirubin is being cleared, and it's most likely this child is already being monitored for bilirubin levels. If this child has yellowing of much of her skin and the whites of her eyes, and is not being monitored for bilirubin levels, it's possible she should be. Jaundice is covered in Chapter 5, "First Poops: What's Normal and What's Not."

Beyond the newborn stage, the first matter of order when seeing green is to determine whether baby has eaten some especially green food, including kiwi, spirulina, or green veggies. It's said that grape-flavored Pedialyte hydration drink can turn baby poop a bright green. If a child is being given iron supplements, these can turn his stools a dark evergreen.

Pea or Bright Green Poop

If it's not from jaundice recovery, it's not the dark green of iron, and if it's not a food pigment, then a basic swamp green to a strikingly lime green color is the digestive juice bile; the same stuff that, when properly digested, imparts the normal yellow to brown colorations of poop. When bile comes out green, it's because the stool has been rushed through baby's digestive system for some reason and has not hung around long enough for the bile to be broken down. The question to ask then is why.

Antibiotic use will commonly cause stool to rush through and have green showing for possibly the full duration of the antibiotic exposure and, likely, a few days beyond. Probiotics are shown to balance some of the negative effects of antibiotic intake, both during and after the drug use.

When bile comes out green, it's because the stool has been rushed through baby's digestive system and has not hung around long enough for the bile to be broken down.

Many parents report a greening and loosening of the stools associated with periods of teething. It's thought to result from the excess saliva being swallowed. The large amount of saliva can irritate the system, causing it to rush food through. If it seems as though this may be the cause, it should go away in a few days and is of no concern. Some parents notice a greening of the stools when

baby has a cold, maybe with some frothiness. This is likely from excess swallowing of mucus. Some attribute the occasional green stool to stress or anxiety in the baby.

Temporary bouts of green stools are not of concern. If the green appearance is only occasional and does not go along with any other symptoms, just jot down any new foods from the last 36 hours or so, and then don't worry about it.

Anything that causes diarrhea can certainly bring green stool coloration along with it. If green is generally only seen along with runny stools, then the course of action is to investigate the reason for the loose stools. If such appearance is only very rare and accompanies a fussy or listless baby, possibly with a fever or vomiting, it can be an intestinal infection, or what some call the stomach flu. Infected stools are often foul smelling as well. If you know that infection is the cause of the green, there's no need to worry about the bile appearance itself. Most intestinal infections are viral and mild and are little cause for concern. Good monitoring, pushing fluids, appropriate professional consultations, and good home care are called for. Causes, clues about when to call the doctor, and info on home care for infections are covered well later in this text.

If loose green stools are more frequent, the source may be reactions to diet, including formula, foods in the breastfeeding mother's diet, and any additional foods and supplements. When attended by other symptoms of allergy or intolerance, the call is more likely. Eczema and other rashes, often on the face or diaper area, a bright red ring around baby's anus, congestion, colic, chronic reflux, constipation (can be seen intermittently with diarrhea), blood in the stools, and excess gas can all suggest food reactions as do waking with screams, arching of back in apparent discomfort, and frequent spitting up or vomiting.

Chronically loose green stools with ongoing weight gain challenges, occasional bleeding, and frequent discomfort are characteristic symptoms of the child who is eventually diagnosed with an inflammatory bowel disease (IBD) at an older age, either ulcerative colitis or Crohn's disease. Both of these disorders, though rare in babies, are typically exacerbated by food intolerances. On the other hand, chronic inflammation resulting from food intolerance reactions is possibly the initiating factor for these disorders in some cases, when linked with a genetic propensity. Discovery and strict avoidance of all offending foods found through food elimination diets can limit inflammation and thus progression of these diseases (see Chapter 15, "Understanding, Detecting, and Treating Food Sensitivities").

Green Poop in a Formula Fed Baby

Frequent or constant green stools are common in formula-fed infants, so common that it's usually referred to as normal. If it's quite dark and black-green, the color is coming from the iron in their formula. This is of little concern, unless attended by a problematic level of constipation. My own interpretation of a regular appearance of dark green iron in poop is that a good portion of the iron is not being absorbed—likely, because it is not needed. It makes sense to try a lower-iron formula in this case to see if it reduces any problems with constipation. Excess iron is very oxidizing. It's generally antioxidants that are wanted for health. Too much oxidizing produces free radicals and can increase some health risks over time.

My own interpretation of a regular appearance of dark green iron in poop is that a good portion of the iron is not being absorbed—likely, because it is not needed.

Although it's been shown that some 50% of formula-fed babies are having regular green stools by 3 months of age, no distinction is mentioned in such studies between iron stools and bile stools. Likely, many stools are green from both. If stools in formula-fed infants are generally a brighter color than the dark green of iron, this is still called normal because it's so common. Of course, common does not mean optimal. These green stools likely *do* mean that baby is having some level of intolerance or digestive difficulty with the formula. This green may not be associated with loose stools, as formula is typically constipating, so the end result may produce more normal stools in terms of consistency. Infant intolerance of non-human milk proteins is quite typical. To ensure that a child is absorbing the most nutrients he can from his diet, it's worth trying different formulas to see if the green will reduce. Organic, soy, hydrolyzed milk protein, and basic amino acid formulas are options to try. Even just a switch of brands may help. Many formulas have disparate ratios of whey to casein and assorted sources of fatty acids. Babies typically produce different stools with different formulas.

When Martek's DHA/ARA was first being added to infant formulas, there were formulas available on the market both with and without this product. During this transition period, lactation specialists found that many babies were fussy and had some green stools, and possibly diarrhea, when using formula with this added ingredient but not when consuming formula without it. They suspected the reactions had to do with residual traces of the chemical *hexane* used in the production of this fatty acid supplement. Although an organic brand may be available without the ingredient, today most formulas contain this ingredient.

If it turns out that baby continues to have green stools with any formula option, then as long as the child is happy, energetic, and gaining weight, it is time to decide that this baby is just going to have lovely green poops and be fine. It may be advisable to begin solid foods around the earlier 4-months gestation mark with this child, if tolerated, to provide some relief from the formula.

Green Poop in a Breastfed Baby

A common theory explaining frequent green and often frothy poops in breastfed babies is that of an imbalance of **foremilk** versus **hindmilk**. Many moms have successfully reduced the green appearance of their baby's stools by making certain efforts to balance the milk delivered to their baby. Intolerance of certain foods in breastfeeding mother's diet is the most common link to green poops in breastfed babies. Mothers can try to use other symptoms to help determine whether efforts to discover food intolerances or efforts to balance foremilk and hindmilk would be a better first endeavor. Unfortunately, many reported symptoms from these two potential causes are the same; thus, the symptoms may offer little to no definitive conclusion. Moms will need to use their own instincts, observations, and trials to determine the culprit, with added guidance from a lactation consultant.

Most likely, the degree of discomfort a baby appears to have and the adequacy of his weight gain will help mother decide how determined she might want to be in finding green poop causes and solutions.

The symptoms that many attribute to **foremilk-hindmilk imbalance** include green frothy stools, explosive stools, frequent stools, mucus, colic, gassiness, and slow weight gain. Higher acidity of the stools may lead to a diaper rash with a burned skin appearance. All of these symptoms are also found to be associated with food sensitivities. Either milk imbalance or food intolerances may lead to blood in the stools as well. Eczema or other rashes outside of the diaper area are more suggestive of food sensitivities.

A common theory explaining frequent green and often frothy poops in breastfed babies is that of an imbalance of foremilk versus hindmilk.

Constipation can be seen with food sensitivities, either as a determined symptom or interchanged with diarrhea. Foremilk-hindmilk imbalance should not cause constipation.

After the early colostrum phase of mother's milk, foremilk comes out of the breast first during a nursing session. It is watery, sweet, and full of the milk sugar, lactose. This sugar is important for brain development, and this more watery

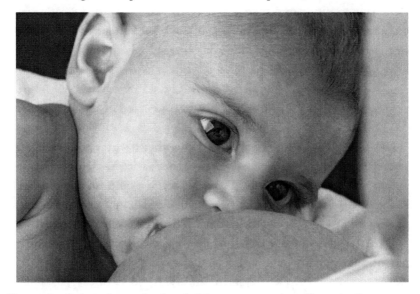

milk satisfies baby's thirst. As the child nurses, mom's milk gradually transitions and becomes fattier and less sweet. The fattier milk created later in a nursing session is referred to as hindmilk. Hindmilk is more nutrient dense, designed to fill baby up. If a baby switches breasts frequently, or takes only frequent, small snacks at the breasts, he can consume much more sugar and less fat. This practice can become self-perpetuating, with baby continuing to be hungry because he's not consuming much fat. This eating style may overwhelm baby's digestive system with more lactose than there is available lactase enzyme ready to digest it. And, with less hindmilk intake, there is less fat for secreted bile and enzymes to work on. Sometimes moms are super milk makers, and this oversupply can lead to a preponderance of foremilk being consumed.

In an effort to solve foremilk-hindmilk issues, mothers are often advised to try some form of **block feeding.** Discouraging frequent snacks at the breasts and having baby nurse for a longer block of time on one breast can moderate such imbalances. Some will use just one breast per nursing session, or maybe per two- or three-hour period, no matter how many times the child nurses in that time block. Some mothers have found more success by pumping off a little milk before putting baby to breast. Be aware that young babies are meant to nurse some 12 times per day, and there is no reason to try altering a baby's nursing preferences if potentially related symptoms such as green stools and attendant discomfort are not present.

Many lactation consultants report that green stools can sometimes be associated with a **tongue-tie** issue, or a tongue that is over-anchored to the bottom of the mouth, interfering with adequate milking of the breast. If tongue-tie is preventing a baby from milking the breast well, she may obtain only the milk that lets down easily at first, which will be the foremilk. She may then nap, exhausted from

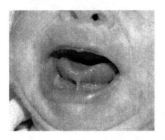

milking efforts, and wait for more milk to let down easily. This can be another cause of foremilk-hindmilk imbalance. Sore nipples in mother can be an added clue that it's time to investigate the effectiveness of baby's suck—helping baby to establish a better latch while ruling in or out tongue-tie or lip-tie. Tongue-tie could also cause problems with bottle feeding. Tongue-tie is often treated with a tiny

Tongue tie in infant

little clip to the piece of tissue attaching the tongue underneath, providing baby's tongue with more ability to move up and out.

When poops are frequently green, efforts to reduce the appearance may improve baby's absorption of nutrients. If colic, reflux, or other signs of discomfort are attendant with the green stools, determining the dietary source or other cause can result in a more comfortable baby. If moderate efforts fail, yet baby is gaining weight, is bright, and generally happy, you may just accept that this is how it's going to be for a while. Babies typically develop quite normally, in spite of frequent green stooling.

If a breastfed baby's green stools will not resolve, this is certainly no reason to stop breastfeeding, as it's still providing the best nutrition plus powerful immune advantages. Remember that green stools are more common in formula-fed babies, so a switch to formula is not the answer.

Are You Seeing Green?		
Possible causes of green coloring in your baby's stools		
colored icing, candy, or gelatin dessert	spirulina, spinach, or kiwi	grape Pedialyte
excess bilirubin associated with jaundice	foremilk/hindmilk imbalance	tongue-tie
artificial DHA/ARA ingredient in formula	reaction to formula	iron supplements
bile from food intolerance reaction	iron from formula	a common cold
inflammatory bowel disease	bile from intestinal virus	teething

Clear Poop (Mucus and Fat)

A curious surprise in the diaper can be little bitty, round, clear sticky grains. These are not poop at all. In fact, they didn't come out of the baby; they come out of the diaper! They are absorbent material that has broken out of the inside of baby's disposable diaper.

The most common clear poop is *mucus* in the stools. Mucus may be tainted in color by the surrounding poop, but it will have a distinct (excuse me) thick snot appearance to it. Mucus can be in clumps or in long strings, or it can surround the stools in a liquidy soup. A child may rarely pass only mucus, once or twice.

If baby has quite a cold, the mucus in the diaper could have been swallowed from her sinuses, but most mucus in the poop comes from the intestines. Mucus is made in cells inside the intestinal walls to lubricate passing stool. Typically, not enough is produced to be seen, but if there is irritation in the intestines, extra mucus may be made. Hence, the appearance of excess mucus is generally considered a sign that something is causing intestinal irritation. Mucus is most often seen along with green stools and loose stools. It can be used as a diagnostic clue that something is aggravating baby's system, be it a food allergy or sensitivity, some kind of blockage, or an infection. Multiple instances of moderate or large amounts of mucus should be mentioned to the doctor. When mucus is present with more than tinges of red blood, in an unhappy baby, urgent medical attention should be sought.

There is the slight possibility that a long mucusy-looking string is a big intestinal worm, but it's not likely. If you truly suspect that it is, save the stuff, and take it in to the pediatrician for testing. Typical worms are tiny white threads. If they're wiggly, that seals the diagnosis.

When mucus is present with more than tinges of red blood, in an unhappy baby, urgent medical attention should be sought.

Other clear stuff found in stool may be fat. If poop looks greasy, the child is probably not absorbing fats properly and needs a medical workup to determine the cause of such malabsorption. One common cause of malabsorption is gluten intolerance. A specific presentation of gluten intolerance is known as celiac disease, for which there are simple medical tests. At times, however, gluten intolerance does not show up in medical celiac tests. If a child continues to have grease in his stools without good medical explanation, a trial of strict gluten avoidance is best. Additional elimination of cow milk proteins or possibly a more complete food elimination diet may be needed before recovery is achieved.

Rarely, oily stools can mean **cystic fibrosis**. CF is a hereditary disease that affects one in 3700 U.S. babies and presents itself in infancy. Though routinely screened for in newborns, occasionally CF is missed by the tests. CF causes mucus to be extremely thick, which clogs the lungs, liver, pancreas, and intestines, and causes breathing and digestive problems. Although it's most known for lung problems, occasionally, an appearance of oily stools, often orange in color, is the symptom that finally attracts a diagnosis. When oil appears in stools of a baby that coughs a lot and possibly has suffered constipation or slow growth, cystic fibrosis needs to be looked for. A simple clue to CF presence is that the baby will taste salty when you kiss him.

Unexpected Yellow Poop

Before solids or formula are introduced, exclusively breastfed babies are expected to have yellow stools, and this is healthy. Occasionally, a tan or brownstooled baby will suddenly show yellow. If this yellowing is short-lived and infrequent, there's nothing to be concerned about. If it appears to be a distinct change and is sticking around, it's prudent to look for the cause.

If baby is receiving a multi-vitamin with high levels of B vitamins, this can certainly turn stools more yellow and urine a deeper yellow. If you want to be sure this is the cause, simply withdraw the vitamins for a couple of days and then try them again.

If newly yellow poop attends a very sick baby, who displays fever and vomiting, the protozoan, *Giardia*, could be the unfortunate cause. This bug, much larger than a bacterium or virus, comes from contaminated food or water. This baby would benefit from medical guidance. Some other causes of yellow poop can also bring fever and vomiting, so a confident diagnosis should be reached without long delay so that proper treatment can be initiated.

Yellow stool can represent a malabsorption disorder, such as celiac disease. In such case, unabsorbed fats may be seen in the stool, adding a light yellow coloration. Speeding of food through the digestive tract, as a result of irritation from a malabsorption disorder, can bring yellow as well. Any visible fats accompanying stool should be mentioned to the healthcare provider.

Other disorders that affect the speed of food passage, the amount of bile, or the handling of bile can present themselves with yellowing of the stools, including gastroesophageal reflux, gallbladder disorders, liver disorders, and inflammation of the pancreas. Although intestinal infections often bring green poop, they can sometimes bring yellow.

One possible diagnosis can alleviate—rather than cause—concern. **Gilbert's syndrome** is a little known genetic quirk that actually affects 3 to 7% of Americans. People with Gilbert's syndrome have reduced functioning of an enzyme that helps clear bilirubin from the bloodstream. These people may develop occasional bouts of non-harmful jaundice. This syndrome poses no health risks, though it can lead to some fatigue at times.

Babies with these genes tend to have prolonged periods of harmless newborn jaundice. They also tend to have periods of yellow-colored stools throughout their lives. Dark urine may attend the yellow stools. Because this is such a mild syndrome, parents will often not know that their child has it until, one day, they have blood testing for some other reason. If parents do learn their child carries these

A large study showed that those with Gilbert's syndrome tend to have markedly extended life expectancies. It's thought to be from the powerful antioxidant effects of bilirubin.

genes and has bouts of elevated bilirubin, they need not fret. A large study showed that those with Gilbert's syndrome tend to have markedly extended life expectancies. It's thought to be from the powerful antioxidant effects of bilirubin.

If the cause of new and lasting yellow stools isn't apparent, it's best to have a healthcare consultation, whether or not baby has other symptoms.

Pale Yellow Poop

Pale yellow stools can represent pancreatic problems. Unabsorbed fats may contribute to the yellow coloration. Mostly pale yellow stools represent the same concerns as for gray to white poop, as discussed below.

Orange Poop

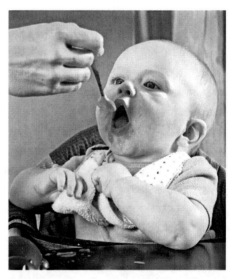

Salmon- or brick-colored dusty stuff toward the front of the diaper isn't orange poo; rather, it's pee that's high in uric acid crystals. This is a common finding in newborns in the first week. If found more than once or twice, you will want to make sure your new baby is receiving ample milk. If this is found in an older baby, it may be a sign of dehydration from diarrhea or of some other problem.

A large dose of carrots, sweet potatoes, or paprika can orange up baby poop, and enough daily carrots can even orange up baby's skin. Antacids containing aluminum hydroxide can lighten the color of stool, giving an orange appearance. Mylanta and Maalox are two examples of antacids that are sometimes prescribed to babies and children for reflux. *Rifampicin* is a strong antibiotic sometimes prescribed to young children. It can impart a red-orange color to the urine and stool.

Orange poop may represent the presence of less bile, which leads to stool that is less brown. If this finding persists, it should be investigated. The oil in the greasy poop of malabsorption often looks orange. Other times, stool appears more waxy orange. These poops are reason for concern and should lead to testing for the cause of malabsorption.

Today, a large portion of white tuna sold is fake—it's actually escolar. Escolar fish irritates the intestines and causes an unusual, waxy diarrhea.

There is one more possible cause of orange oily or waxy poop. This is consumption of *escolar* fish. Although escolar is not a commonly chosen meal for young children, tuna is. Today, a large portion of white tuna sold is fake—it's actually escolar. Escolar fish irritates the intestines and causes an unusual, waxy diarrhea that represents the release of an indigestible fat from the fish. *Oilfish* is another species that can cause this; sometimes labeled as cod.

Blue Poop

The cause of blue poop must be food coloring or blueberries.

Brown Poop in a Breastfed Baby

If your yellow-pooping exclusively breastfed baby begins developing tan or brown stools, the most likely explanation is that someone is sneaking him some formula, prune juice, or other solid foods. Any of these will have free iron that feeds adult-type bacteria, which changes the balance of flora and slightly reduces the immune protection from exclusively breastfed intestines. Breastmilk protects iron from becoming lunch for the less protective bacteria. Low dose iron supplements or a multi-vitamin with iron would also cause the stools to turn brown, as the iron feeds the adult-type bacteria, and thus bile is processed differently by them. Some other nutritional or herbal supplements may do the same. Larger amounts of iron supplementing will turn stool green-black. In this case, the color comes directly from the iron. Antibiotic use may also alter the flora, which allows more challenging bacteria to take hold and turn the poop brown. Once breastfed poops have gone brown from any of these causes, they may never go yellow again.

If your breastfed baby begins developing tan or brown stools, the likely explanation is that someone is sneaking him food.

Some exclusively breastfed babies just make browner poop from the beginning. They may have been cesarean born, may have had formula bottles in the hospital, or may have been prevented from breastfeeding for some hours after birth by being given sugar water. All of these interventions can allow more adult-type flora to become established.

Light Tan Poop

If a child who makes normal brown poops begins having much lighter colored stools, this should be questioned. The reasons would be the same as for gray to white poop—see below.

White Threads in Poop

Little white threads in baby's poop are likely worms, especially if they're wiggling. Medical worm medications work swiftly, with occasional mild side effects. Today there are worm medications available over the counter, but if this is your first encounter, you may prefer your doctor's diagnosis and advice.

Some parents try to rid their baby of worms using ginger and garlic. Both are shown through many research studies to have powerful anti-parasitic effects in the intestines. It's a bold move, best made with advice from someone who's done it successfully. These can prevent candida—a frequent result of worm drugs.

The biggest challenge of having a child with worms is keeping the whole family from catching them and keeping them from returning once your child is rid of them. The eggs can fall from baby's diaper or baby's bottom. If hands go in there to scratch—and they will—then eggs are pulled out onto pajamas and sheets, and eggs are now under baby's fingernails. Hands then go into the mouth, re-infecting the child. It's useful to check all family members for worms once they're found in baby, and keep plenty of salsa on your menu. It's also useful to find some advice online about ridding your home of worm eggs and preventing their spread.

Gray to White Poop

Little pieces of solid white things inside the poop come from baby chewing on the store tags from new clothing or plush toys.

Little plops of white pus-like material alongside the stool could truly be pus, which is a buildup of dead white blood cells and bacteria from an infection inside the wall of baby's large intestine. It's probably just mucus, but if it's rather white or slightly yellow, as opposed to rather clear, and if you think it may be pus, you'll want to contact the doctor. This would not need to be an emergency call unless it's attended by a fever, which would signify a larger infection.

Many anecdotal reports tell about white poop occurring when a child is drinking lots of cow milk. I can't find any reports of this from medical sources or research studies. At first, it makes no sense, as babies drinking human milk or cow milk formula are consuming nothing but these milks all day, and their stools are not white. Could it be that cow milk discourages bile release? Or is just not digested? I don't think so. Calcium supplements are reported to lead to a whitening of baby stools. Compared to human milk or infant formula, straight cow milk contains a huge amount of calcium. A lot of calcium is removed from milk to make infant formula appropriate for human babies. I'm banking on it being high calcium content that is the cause of whitish stools coming from heavy cow or goat milk diets. White skin, from anemia, is a likely sequel.

Whitening stools likely signify that something is blocking the bile duct and preventing bile from entering the small intestine.

Several antacids are high in calcium and can whiten infant poops. Other antacids containing aluminum hydroxide can also lighten the stools. If your child has had a barium enema study, she will poop out the white barium for a while.

A serious illness in the developing world creates what is referred to as rice water stools. This is *cholera* infection, causing highly watery poops that contain little bits of white matter. Overall, the poop appearance is watery gray or white. Haiti has recently suffered a high rate of cholera that has lasted for several years, and it affects many other parts of the developing world with occasional cases arising in Florida and nearby states. Profuse diarrhea in a child requires quick medical attention due to the risk of dehydration.

A rare but serious disruption in liver function leading to pale stools and jaundice can result from use of acetaminophen (paracetamol, Tylenol).

Beyond these possibilities, stool that is truly approaching white—sometimes referred to as clay colored or chalky—may denote another serious condition. Unless a child with white stool is vomiting seriously or otherwise appears to be in great distress, it's not considered to be an emergency room or a "wake-the-doctor" situation, but it does warrant a call during office hours. Be sure to explain any other symptoms that develop.

Whitening stools likely signify that something is blocking the bile duct and preventing bile from entering the small intestine. It is bile that brings most color to poop, and without it, poop is white. As bilirubin builds up in the system, being unable to exit through the stools, the occurrence of white poops may be accompanied by itchy skin or dark urine. Bile obstruction can come from an inflammation of the bile duct, the liver, or the pancreas. Sometimes, a simple virus can cause such inflammation, and the blockage will clear up soon. Other times, there is a problem that needs more serious medical attention. A rare but serious disruption in liver function leading to pale stools and jaundice can result from use of acetaminophen (paracetamol, Tylenol). Pale stools after use of this medication should be treated as an emergency situation.

Silver Poop

One more kind of light stool appearance is referred to as silver or aluminum in color. This occurs when a bile obstruction is coupled with the presence of digested blood. Typically, digested blood turns brown stools into black, but it turns white stools into silver. Silver stools can also occur in a child being treated for diarrhea with sulfonamide antibiotics. If not a result of medication, silver stools need quick medical attention.

Black Poop

Below I list several possible explanations for poop that has traces of black in it or is, overall, remarkably dark or black. Once the simpler possibilities are ruled out, black may mean digested blood, and blood is serious. Even slight traces of unexplained black in baby's stools should be discussed with your healthcare provider. Any greater amounts of unexplained darkening or blackening of the stool should prompt a call right away, and be sure to save the diaper or a stool sample. Refrigerate it until you can bring it in. There are many possibilities as to the cause of bleeding, and this is for a professional to determine.

Be sure to save the diaper or a stool sample. Refrigerate it until you can bring it in.

Little short black threads in baby's poop may look like worms but actually come from a fresh banana that has been fed to an immature digestive system.

Red Pedialyte can turn stools dark. Oreo cookies, blueberries, blackberries, grape juice, prunes and prune juice, black jelly beans, black licorice, or deglycerized licorice (DGL) can all cause blackening of stools, as can consumption of pencil leads (which are harmless carbon, not lead), cigarette ashes, fireplace ashes, or charcoal. Chronic lead exposure from baby eating paint dust or peeled chips of paint that had been applied before 1960 unfortunately does not announce itself in the stool coloring, although it's unhealthy. Larger doses of lead, from baby eating lead shot, lead fishing sinkers, or lead solder will taint baby's stool black. Lead is sweet, so it's eagerly consumed by little ones, when discovered. If there's any reason to believe this is the cause of baby's dark stool coloring, medical attention is necessary. The baby colic remedy, "Colic Calm," contains charcoal and will harmlessly introduce little black specks or black tinting to baby's poop. Black stools can result from use of Pepto-Bismol, Kaopectate, or other **bismuth** containing products. These can also cause a black tongue. It's not blood, and it's harmless.

It's said that highly concentrated bile can make stools look almost black or a very dark green-black. Iron supplements, a switch to a higher iron formula, or enough iron-fortified cereal can also bring green-black to the stools. Gummy kid supplements with iron are yummy. If found, a few extra may be munched and the excess iron can turn the stools quite green-black.

Digested blood would have no green to it at all. If unsure about a dark color, you can smear some of the dark matter onto a piece of white paper to see if there's any green to it. If you find just black, blood is of concern. Of course, a baby could have excess bile or iron along with blood. Use your intuition and err on the side of caution.

Black stools can come from baby consuming blood. Nutritious blood pudding or similar sausages made with high amounts of blood are quite out of style in the United States but are still consumed in other countries; however there's a small raw meat movement in the United States. Tiny bits of black blood can appear in baby's poop when mother is experiencing bleeding nipples. If this happens, there is no reason for mother to avoid feeding her milk to baby. It's entirely harmless for baby, but mother may need a lactation consultation.

A little black stool could come from swallowing the blood from a bloody nose. Occasionally, a baby can experience little tears in her throat from forceful vomiting. Swallowing this blood would bring some darkening of baby's stool. Likely, in this case, the doctor has already addressed the blood in the vomit. If you know your baby to have severe reflux, the finding of black in her poop can mean that the acid has burned her esophagus to the point of bleeding. This certainly needs attention.

If other causes can be ruled out, especially dark, faint black, or very black stools are likely coming from bleeding in the stomach or upper intestines. When bleeding occurs lower down, in the large intestine, it will appear in the stools as red. When blood comes from far up enough to be subjected to digestive enzymes in the stomach and small intestine, the blood becomes digested and comes out black. Sometimes, when in greater amounts, this appearance is described as *tarry* stools, whereas another presentation can look more like coffee grounds.

Though usually associated with red blood, food intolerances can occasionally cause traces of black blood in the poop when affecting higher portions of the digestive tract.

The use of non-steroidal anti-inflammatory drugs, or **NSAIDs**, typically used for pain, fever, and inflammation, can cause damage to the stomach lining and cause bleeding. These include aspirin and ibuprofen (Motrin). Acetaminophen is a pain reliever thought to have less potential for damaging the stomach, but it can as well. Steroid medications also pose risk of such ulceration, which causes bleeding from the stomach. Fluoride supplements or swallowing toothpaste can rarely cause some bleeding.

Although old school thinking taught that there should be no bacteria in the stomach, it's now been proven that many species inhabit the stomach.

Rarely, a young child is diagnosed with bleeding ulcers or gastritis. This finding is often connected to *Helicobacter pylori* bacterial infection in the stomach. Besides treating this symptom, parents will want to ask why baby became vulnerable to stomach infection in the first place. *H. pylori* is also found in very healthy stomachs, so balance is key. Probiotics are found to be partly helpful here. Although old school thinking taught that there should be no bacteria in the stomach, it's now been proven that many species inhabit the stomach. It is hoped that helpful species predominate.

Red Currant Jelly Poop

Poop that looks raspberry colored, like red currant jelly, with gel-like blood and mucus, represents a kind of intestinal blockage known as **intussusception**. This needs urgent medical attention. *Don't wait for a doctor to call you back.*

Red in Poop

If it's not tomato pieces, tomato sauce, red Jell-O, or Fire Cheetos, and it's not pinkish, as from beets or raspberries, red can mean blood. It can show up in spots and/or streaks; it can be blended in, coating the stool, or mixed with diarrhea. Blood shows up red in the poop when it's not coming from high up the digestive tract, where it's digested into black. Though it's seldom serious, the appearance of blood should be reported to the healthcare provider. Anything beyond spots and little streaks should be reported quickly. There are many possible causes of bleeding, and only a few are mentioned below.

Some antibiotics, such as *cefdinir*, sometimes produce a red color in the stools, but antibiotics can also lead to true intestinal bleeding. You may be able to differentiate the two causes by the shade of red.

Traces of intestinal bleeding are seen occasionally in babies due to reactions to their formula. The cause is often found to be due to sensitivity reactions to milk, soy, or corn in their formula. It's possible that a change from cow milk formula to soy formula, or from either of these to a hydrolyzed or amino acid formula would be appropriate. This is especially true if baby also experiences colic or reflux. Bleeding is even more common with the feeding of straight cow milk to babies under the age of one year. This is not advised.

Bleeding is even more common with the feeding of straight cow milk to babies under the age of one year.

The decision about trying a change in formula may be based on the kind and extent of other symptoms and whether allergies or intestinal challenges run in the family. Often doctors express no concern over the appearance of blood. Yet, with iron absorption from formula being difficult, if regular bleeding goes on, baby can become anemic. Regular small traces of blood in a formula-fed baby's poops should be discussed with the pediatrician, and a blood test for anemia may be a good idea. If traces of bleeding in a formula-fed baby cannot be stopped, the child may benefit from introduction of iron-fortified cereal or other solid foods as early as 4 months. Especially meats or vegetables, as tolerated, can provide good iron and other good nutrition while giving baby some break from any possibly irritating formula proteins.

Occasionally, traces of blood are found in an exclusively breastfed baby's diaper as well. A common cause can be baby reacting to cow milk proteins passed on from mother's diet. Other food proteins may offend as well, especially wheat or soy. If bleeding is a concern or parents have other reasons to suspect it is a reaction to diet, mother can perform dietary trials in order to find and eliminate any offending foods from her diet. This provides baby with comfortable, nutritious, and immune-providing meals. Foremilk-hindmilk imbalance can occasionally be the source of a little bleeding in breastfed babies due to irritation caused by lactose buildup.

An Ohio study found that one third of chronic infant intestinal bleeding cases resolved without diet changes.

Likely, the food sensitive or allergic baby will have rashes or other symptoms that will increase the likelihood of such a diagnosis. If parents are unsure whether dietary changes are helping enough, the infant's stools can be tested for unseen blood. It's not uncommon for microscopic bleeding to go on that can be measured but not seen. If wishing then to confirm dietary suspicions, parents can try re-introduction of the suspected offenders and see what happens, possibly testing the stool again.

An Ohio study found that one third of chronic infant intestinal bleeding cases resolved *without* diet changes. The cause of bleeding may not be a food reaction at all. Many cases of bleeding, in an otherwise well appearing baby, can

be a virus that may not be making baby outwardly sick but is still irritating intestinal tissues. Studies find unknown virus particles to be involved in a portion of cases of bleeding. Baby will gradually recover from bleeding if this is the case.

Bloody diarrhea can result from a bacterial or, more often, a viral digestive bug. Likely there will be other symptoms of illness. Bloody diarrhea needs medical observation. Be sure to save a sample for the doctor.

A common source of fresh bloody *streaks* along the stool or in the diaper is tiny tears along and just inside the anus, from the large size, the roughness, or the excess pushing of hard stools. If you are sure this is the source of blood, it doesn't need urgent attention, but if constipation is a problem, you will want to investigate options for relieving it.

Rarely, a baby girl will have a tiny bit of menstrual flow for a few days, generally occurring within a week after birth, though there are many reports of it occurring later. It may take a little visual or delicate Q-tip investigation to determine whether the blood is coming from the stool or vagina.

Maroon Poop

This color—between blood red and perfect black—occurs when bleeding comes from somewhere in the middle of the intestines, such that the blood is only partly digested. Treat seriously, as with any blood in the stool.

Port Wine Purple Poop

A set of very rare disorders involves missing enzymes in the formation of heme, a part of blood hemoglobin. Intermediates to the heme formation process, known as porphyrins, build up and are excreted in the urine and stools. The disorders are known as *porphyrias*. A child suffering from a porphyria will have occasional or frequent wine purple stools as well as urine. The color comes out more intensely after being exposed to light for some time, with the shade of red to purple depending upon the wavelength of the light, and looks quite different in room light than in sunlight. These children will be sensitive to sunlight themselves and will need to stay out of the sun.

Violet Purple Poop

Some anecdotal reports tell of purplish poo when a baby starts eating bananas. I have no idea why, but then I haven't figured out the more common little black threads from bananas either. Of course, concord grapes, grape juice, purple potatoes, or artificial colorings can cause purple poop. Some mothers use gentian violet on their nipples or inside baby's mouth to treat thrush. This incredibly deep violet dye is reported to not come out purple in the stool, yet I personally witnessed some quite violet poop in a young child treated for worms with this dye. Likely the higher dose did the trick.

Pinky Red Poop

An attractive pinky red can come from beets and other foods or from an old package of laxatives, such as Ex-Lax. Newer versions do not contain the pink ingredient *phenolphthalein*.

Stool Color Presentations Suggesting Need for Urgent Medical Attention	
bloody diarrhea	more than slight amounts of unexplained black stool
red blood with mucus and distress	white stool with vomiting or great distress
white pus with fever	red currant jelly appearance is emergency
silver stools	moderate or greater amounts of red blood
any time parent feels urgent concern	

Some Final Thoughts

If you pay attention, your baby's diaper or potty chair can provide you with a frequent indication of her health status. You may be able to quickly determine the source of your baby's sudden fussiness, lack of energy, or change in feeding behavior, and find a solution that may have otherwise evaded you. Or you may discover a mild but chronic issue for which remedy can bring more daily comfort to your baby and probably bring better future health. Some parents may notice certain rare health problems early, thereby heading off greater illness. Keeping one eye on your baby's stools and the other eye on his behavior can help you to detect smaller problems before they become bigger ones.

Loose Poop

What is the Reason?

Runny or frequent poops in a baby can be caused by various bacteria, viruses, inflammatory conditions, food sensitivities, teething, various kinds of sugar intolerance, gluten intolerance, antibiotic treatments, and a lot more.

Diarrhea is the body's mechanism for rushing unwanted materials out of the body. In the case of food or chemical poisoning, this is particularly advantageous. Our primary goal is not to stop the diarrhea; rather, our goal is to determine the cause and decide how best to prevent or treat it. In the meantime, a moderate or significant amount of diarrhea can cause dehydration that can quickly become dangerous for a baby. Diarrhea reduces or prevents the digestion and absorption of nutrients, and this too can become problematic over time. In the next chapter, we'll deal with the home care of children with diarrhea of various causes.

Is It Diarrhea?

Whether yellow, green, brown, or other, a sudden poop change to looser or watery is generally a signal that your baby is off track in some manner. An occasional light presence of looser stool should be of little concern. When diarrhea is more frequent, lasting, or more severe, or is attended by a very unhappy baby or by other concerning symptoms, you will want to determine the cause so that you know what kind of attention to provide.

Medical definitions for diarrhea generally refer to three or more episodes of loose stools in one day. Supposedly then, one or two episodes of significantly more watery stools in a day are of no concern. I'll assure you, though, that even

Grandfather at DrMomma.org

one episode of much looser or watery stool *does* certainly mean that *something* is different. Although it may not be serious, it also may not be a sign of baby's best health.

In terms of frequency, one baby's usual stooling pattern may be a healthy 6 times per day while another may be once per week. Should a baby's stools speed up in frequency, but with little change in the consistency of the poop or in the demeanor of the child, there is little concern. In a baby, the number of stools per day is not highly indicative of anything, unless stools get to be much too rare an event. By the same token, one baby suffering from loose stools might release several squirts per hour while another might just unleash one giant mess and have little left to give. Either way, it's a sudden change of consistency in stools with which we are concerned. Of course, one baby can have, at different times, different kinds of diarrhea for different reasons. The truth is, if it's something very different coming out of your baby, there's likely a reason behind it.

You might get corrected in the pediatrician's office if your suddenly fussy child had two and not three watery stools that day. The doctor's answer to your diarrhea complaint may be "that's not diarrhea," even if you feel there's cause for concern. It may be best not to use the diagnostic term, diarrhea, but to just describe the reasons for your concern.

One medical definition for diarrhea is the passing of more than 10 ml/kg/d— that's ten milliliters of stool per kilogram of the child's weight, per day. Oh my, if I find you measuring that out and doing the math then we'll know you are poop-crazier than I. The absolute best indicator of a worrisome loose stool is the caretaker's observations and instincts.

The truth is, if it's something very different coming out of your baby, there's likely a reason behind it.

There are those who will say that having random or even regular bouts of mild to moderate diarrhea is normal and not worth worrying about, as long as the child is gaining weight. Well, what they really mean is that it's *common*. Common is not the same as healthy, in my book. By now you know that I'm interested in helping you to provide optimal health for your child, as I know you'll both be happier, and your baby's whole life will be healthier.

Of course, babies go through natural transitions in their normal stooling patterns. Most commonly, we see a newborn's stools gradually reduce from frequent to something like one per day. A baby who normally was producing infrequent stools several days apart may begin to increase his frequency. It is a marked increase in the looseness or wateriness of the stool that is of concern. The appearance of blood or mucus adds concern, and other symptoms that may accompany a change in baby's poop are important to help determine the cause and the seriousness of the condition.

Is It from an Infection?

When loose poop comes on rather suddenly, is distinctly runnier than a baby's normal stools, and the child shows other signs of illness, such as fever, vomiting, or acting sick, it's quite likely that they have developed a viral, bacterial, or protozoal intestinal infection. Viral gastrointestinal infections are quite common in young children and generally pose no cause for alarm. Sometimes respiratory or other kinds of infections will cause diarrhea as well.

Fever much over 100 degrees Fahrenheit (38°C) is likely a sign of infection, although fever is not necessary to suspect infection, and other things can cause fever.

Mild diarrhea may occur within a week after a rotavirus vaccine and is not considered cause for alarm.

Should You Call the Doctor?

Call your doctor soon if your baby has loose poop and exhibits any of the following:

- passing of a worrisome amount of liquid,
- passing of blood,
- passing of much mucus,
- a very high fever,
- much vomiting,
- very poor eating,
- signs of dehydration,
- signs of a stiff or painful neck,
- a hardening and reddening abdomen, or
- signs of reduced alertness.

Babies cry often and can't tell you their reason for crying. Of course, babies cry and fuss more when they're sick and not feeling well. Parents can generally tell this discomfort cry from their child's usual cries. Then there's another cry that tells there's something very wrong. Often, long inconsolable crying will be written off as colic, but a mother can tell when her child is in great pain. If this is what you think, tell the doctor.

Pediatricians strongly recommend that a rectal fever of 100.4 degrees Fahrenheit (38°C) or higher in a baby less than 2 months of age warrants a call and probably a prompt examination, depending upon the information you provide. Babies this young have immature immune systems, and a fever could possibly signal a dangerous infection. Although it is rare for this to truly be an emergency, the delicacy of such a young child makes it important to be sure they are doing alright.

Doctors also recommend that they should be called if a 3- to 6-month-old child's temperature reaches 101 degrees Fahrenheit (38.3°C) and if a baby over 6 months of age develops a temperature of 103 degrees Fahrenheit (39.4°C). If you've been recently traveling abroad, the source of illness may be of more concern. Your doctor may have different guidelines, and the other symptoms your baby is displaying are important in determining how quickly or whether the child needs to be examined at all.

Fever or no fever, moderate or slight diarrhea, how is your baby behaving? Does he act sick? Is she alert? Does she engage your eyes the way she normally would? Is she terribly fussy and unable to be consoled? Does her crying come in waves? Is your baby unusually pale or flushed red? Is he eating? Does he draw his knees up to his chest or arch his back? Your observations and instincts are the most important indications when it comes to the question of how serious your baby's symptoms are.

Sometimes a child's diarrhea does not seem worrisome enough for a call to the doctor initially, but over time the symptoms do not go away or the child is getting worse. When symptoms are prolonged, if baby gets worse after the first couple of days, or if baby is continuing to lose weight after some expected lost ounces, these too can be reasons to make that call.

Signs of dehydration include the following:

- dryness or stickiness inside the baby's mouth,
- a near lack of tears (in a baby old enough to develop tears),
- sunken eyes,
- a sunken appearance to the soft spot above the baby's forehead,
- an increased pulse rate,
- a darkening of baby's urine, or
- no wetting of diapers for 3 or 4 hours.

Dehydration may have become *severe* if, in addition to some of these signs, baby:

- seems unusually drowsy or confused,
- becomes extremely fussy,
- looks pale
- has a mottled skin appearance,
- develops cold hands or feet,
- has no sweating,
- has a weak pulse, or
- is breathing rapidly.

If pinching baby's skin, it may stay momentarily pinched before bouncing back. Signs of severe dehydration require immediate medical attention.

A baby is more likely to become dehydrated when diarrhea is of considerable amount and is quite watery, when it's accompanied by much vomiting and an inability to keep liquids down, and when baby just does not want to nurse or drink for some time.

Different mothers have different sensitivity and confidence levels when it comes to symptoms in their child, and that's totally okay. One mother may have more experience with or information about such events, and another may become quickly anxious over symptoms in her infant. Do what feels right to you, while watching for major warning signs. No matter what guidelines you learn about, if something just does not seem right, call your healthcare provider. If you don't think your baby is getting the attention he needs, be persistent, or find another source for care.

Continual Diarrhea from Birth

Continual diarrhea from birth could rarely signify *short bowel syndrome*. If a newborn's stools are quite runny and frequent, as soon as the meconium has cleared, it's possible that she was born with intestines that are shorter than usual. Normal breastfed stools can be rather runny. If you're unsure, you may want to show some diapers to your lactation consultant, midwife, or pediatrician to see whether they think they are normal.

Medications That May Cause Diarrhea

Antacids such as Maalox or Mylanta, commonly given for reflux, contain magnesium that can cause loosening of the stools. These are typically given to children as one component of reflux treatment and should not be used in babies without medical advisement. Propulsid, Reglan, and Maxalon are other reflux meds that can also cause diarrhea. These prescription medications are designed to speed up stomach emptying. Some women take higher than usual doses of magnesium for certain disorders. This has been known to speed up stooling in breastfed babies.

You must remember that food sensitivities that could cause reflux may also be a cause of diarrhea. Certain foods or baby's medication could be the cause of diarrhea, and this could be determined by correlating symptoms with days of medication usage and with days of intake of suspected foods. Of course, it could be both.

If your child is or has recently been receiving antibiotic medications, this could account for her diarrhea. Antibiotics greatly disrupt the floral balance in the intestines. Mild or moderate diarrhea for some days during or after antibiotic treatment can be expected. Children can generally recover on their own, though their flora will not be as healthy as it was before. Probiotics can be given to your child during antibiotic treatment to help reduce negative effects and should be continued after treatment in attempt to re-establish healthier flora.

If baby's antibiotic-associated diarrhea begins to worsen, if blood appears in her poop, or if your baby seems sicker, you will want to contact her doctor, as she has likely developed a new kind of infection. **C. difficile** is a tough bacterial intestinal infection that can take hold after antibiotic use. **Salmonella** is another bacterial infection that has recently increased in incidence after antibiotic use. These bacteria could have been recently obtained when visiting the doctor or hospital, or they could have been quiet established parts of baby's flora that were kept in check by other bacteria.

Teething and Diarrhea

Is your baby teething? Many babies experience looser stools when they are teething. Many doctors say there's no clear physiological connection between teething and stools and assume that looser stools during this time are just coinciding with an age when fruit juices are usually started. Some explain that loose stools at this age represent a time when maternal antibodies from the womb are wearing off, allowing mild infections. Other doctors, who observe their patients well and who listen to moms carefully, understand that the association between teething and looser stools is quite common and distinct. They assume it to be caused by the excess saliva production during teething. Looser stools could even be a mild stress reaction to the discomfort of teething.

Far too many bright and observant caretakers have compared notes, ruled out other causes, and associated teething with loose stools, a runny nose, and sometimes maybe a little fever or some diaper rash.

A dental researcher found strong associations between teething and various symptoms. Slight temperature, irritability, increased drooling, runny nose, and loss of appetite all showed strong correlations with tooth eruption. Other studies demonstrate such correlations as well.

Experienced moms know. Far too many bright and observant caretakers have compared notes, ruled out other causes, and associated teething with loose stools, a runny nose, and sometimes maybe a little fever or some diaper rash. Fever may be a result of gum inflammation. Some babies also develop some rash around their mouth from the excess drool.

As teeth are coming in, you can feel them under the gums. Your child may begin biting on your fingers and chewing on all kinds of things, biting during nursing, and being occasionally fussy at the breast if his gums are sore. Before blaming mild diarrhea on teething, be sure baby has no other signs that could be cause for concern.

Change in Routine

Has your baby had a significant change in routine? Travel can sometimes present more opportunities for infectious illnesses, but a child can also just react to travel by presenting some simple diarrhea. Other alterations in baby's daily life, such as a change in caregivers, attempts at sleep training, or noisy construction next door can bring a little stress-related diarrhea. Some such changes also bring about dietary alterations that might mildly disturb the digestive tract. Some babies seem to react to a change from boiled water to tap, or from one area's tap water to another.

Soiling or bedwetting exhibited by a potty-trained child is occasionally a reactionary behavior to changes such as a new baby being brought home or a move to a new house. You may wish to focus on some calming and reassuring activities, especially familiar ones, and you may be able to use a return of stool normalcy as a measure of emotional recovery.

Dietary Changes and Diarrhea

A young child's digestive system learns what foods to expect and maintains enzyme levels and flora designed to meet the calling. New kinds or large amounts of fruits and vegetables, a large amount of sugar, or a larger than usual amount of fat may catch the digestive system off guard. The gas-forming foods—such as cabbage, beans, onions, garlic, broccoli, or cauliflower—may cause some diarrhea when a child is not accustomed to them. You can cut back some on such new foods to see if your child's poop levels off, then make diet changes more gradually. You child's poop may find a new normal frequency and consistency as his diet grows, but as long as he seems happy and comfortable, things should be fine.

If things don't settle down after a gradual change in diet, and your child is becoming uncomfortable or developing rashes, sleeplessness, or other symptoms, you will want to consider allergy or intolerance of one or more of the new foods. You can remove the new foods from the diet until baby's stools normalize and then re-introduce the foods one at a time while you watch for symptoms.

A Change in Formula

Did you just change your baby's formula? Many formulas are made with the milk proteins partially hydrolyzed, meaning partially pre-digested in order to be gentler on the tummy. A move from one of these to a formula with complete milk proteins may be a little more than a young system can handle. If your child was successful with the previous formula, a return to it is a good idea.

Is your formula-fed baby reacting to the DHA and ARA additives? The percentage of babies who react to these unnaturally derived versions of what should be healthy fatty acids is unknown at this time. A high number of reports of diarrhea and vomiting seem to be associated with DHA- and ARA-supplemented formulas. Breastfeeding consultants often work with formula feeding as well, when needed, and are in agreement that these added ingredients are more than occasionally associated with diarrhea, vomiting, and dehydration, and—rarely—are associated with seizures.

A high number of reports of diarrhea and vomiting seem to be associated with DHA- and ARA-supplemented formulas.

It's believed that one reason why formula-fed babies don't quite keep up with breastfed babies in some areas of development is the lack of certain fatty acids in formula that are found in breastmilk. Formula manufacturers have found it difficult to add these to formula in a stable manner. To remedy the difficulty, they've settled on artificial forms of these fatty acids by using the neurotoxic chemical hexane to extract them from algae and fungi. The U.S. Food and Drug Administration (FDA) has never approved these unnatural fatty acids. Besides possible effects from traces of hexane likely left behind, these artificial fats could have unknown risks, just as artificial trans fats produced from hydrogenated vegetable oils, once considered safe, are now known to cause heart disease and other disorders.

To find out whether these ingredients are the cause of your baby's diarrhea, try a switch to a formula that does not have DHA and ARA added. Organic infant formulas are beginning to drop these non-organic ingredients while the USDA tries to determine its position on allowing these in products labeled as organic. Some organic formulas may have found healthier versions of these fatty acids to add.

Formula companies have acknowledged that these added ingredients are, unfortunately, not providing the developmental advantages desired, so your baby won't be missing out on a valuable additive if you choose a formula without them. You may wish to add 1/4 to 1/2 teaspoon per day of a good quality children's cod liver oil or a recommended dose of a children's DHA supplement to your formula-fed baby's diet for a natural source of DHA.

Diarrhea, Reduced Appetite, and Facial Rash

Babies can be a little vulnerable to mild zinc deficiency, depending upon circumstances. Soy blocks zinc absorption, and a baby fed fully on soy formula can become a little low in zinc over time. If, after months on this formula, baby begins a solid food diet of only vegetarian foods, a mild deficiency risk becomes greater, albeit low. Diarrhea, reduced appetite, rashes on the face and bottom, and slowing of growth are common symptoms of zinc deficiency. A facial rash tends to remain in a rather symmetrical butterfly-shaped area around the mouth and is sometimes misdiagnosed as eczema. The symmetry may help to distinguish from a food-allergy rash. In a child who is already borderline, zinc deficiency can also result *from* serious diarrhea of another cause and can confuse the picture when trying to resolve the original illness. Zinc deficiency can increase a child's susceptibility to illnesses. Major zinc deficiency is uncommon in industrialized nations. Mild deficiency can be difficult to detect with blood tests.

Premature infants are born with lesser stores of zinc, iron, and other nutrients, making them more vulnerable to eventual deficiencies. Infants with sickle cell anemia may also be vulnerable to zinc deficiency.

Iron competes with zinc for absorption. This is one reason why it is difficult to provide enough of either of these in formulas. Iron supplementation can thus reduce zinc stores. Most iron-fortified baby cereals today are also zinc fortified.

Juice Diarrhea

Has your child been on a sudden juice kick? Has she been to a party or relative's home where unrestricted juice was served? Excess juice intake can loosen the poop. Various fruits in the rose family, such as apple, pear, cherry, apricot, and especially prune, are high in a sugar known as **sorbitol**. This particular fruit sugar is not digested well by children or adults, and is only partly absorbed. Sitting in higher quantities inside little bodies, sorbitol can cause water to be drawn into the intestine, leading to watery poop. You've probably heard about "sugar-free" lollipops that can cause diarrhea. They're made with sorbitol or something similar. Berries are high in another barely digested sugar, xylitol. Berry juices may also cause diarrhea.

Sorbitol, xylitol, and the like are actually antimicrobial—fighting certain bacteria and viruses, including those that cause cavities—and they feed the healthy flora in the intestines.

When these sugars are naturally found in fiber-filled whole fruits, diarrhea is seldom a problem. Less sugar is generally taken in when eating whole fruits rather than extracted juices, and fiber tends to normalize stools, preventing both diarrhea and constipation.

These weakly digested sugars, often called indigestible sugars and also known as **sugar alcohols**, are healthy. Sorbitol, xylitol, and the like are actually antimicrobial—fighting certain bacteria and viruses, including those that cause cavities—and they feed the healthy flora in the intestines.

Such sugar alcohols are often added to sugar-free and diet foods. Again, in higher quantities and outside of their natural environments (the fruits and veggies they come from), these sugars can attract water to be drawn into the intestines of young children, making runny poop. If you suspect these may be the cause of your child's diarrhea, look for the ingredients sorbitol, xylitol, mannitol, maltitol, lactitol, erythritol, or isomalt in foods you've recently fed to your child, such as sugar-free cookies or low-calorie fruit spreads.

Aspartame and some other artificial sweeteners found in diet sodas and such are not health foods, but they are also not linked to diarrhea.

Again, you want to rule out other possible causes. A juice-related diarrhea isn't going to be associated with other symptoms, except that a little excess gas may go along with it and may cause the child a little discomfort. Juice diarrhea isn't particularly unhealthy or harmful. It's good to know when juice is the cause of your child's diarrhea so you don't need to be concerned that he's ill. Either way, it's better to cut back on the juice or to water it down. Whole fruits have wonderful fiber and are so much healthier.

Fructose Diarrhea

A baby may experience diarrhea with both fruits and juices, even when taking in good amounts of fiber. Some children and adults have a lower ability to absorb fructose than others do. This is called fructose malabsorption or **fructose intolerance**. Some with fructose intolerance may also have problems with *fructans*, found in high quantities in onions, garlic, cabbage, and wheat. Of course, high fructose corn syrup is a problem for such children.

Combining high fructose or high fructan foods with any of the sugar alcohols mentioned earlier can make a child's symptoms even worse. Gas is likely an uncomfortable and smelly component of this situation.

One or two rare genetic defects involve the lack of an enzyme needed for the absorption of fructose, affecting somewhere between one in 10,000 and one in 20,000 people. If a baby had one of these genetic defects, he would have diarrhea whenever consuming any fructose. However, it has recently been recognized that, on a dosage basis, most people will eventually exhibit inadequate absorption of fructose. Some people will just handle a much higher dose than others before they reach that point. Young children tend to be more susceptible.

If your baby with frequent loose stools is a big fruit eater, try limiting the amount of fruits, fruit juices, and other sweeteners to see if she improves. Then, if you wish to prove this theory in your child, go for a day with plenty of fructose sources and see what happens. Eventually, you will be able to determine your child's fructose tolerance level.

Some of the highest fructose-containing fruits include watermelons, raisins, figs, papayas, mangos, apples, pears, and cherries. Also high in fructose are honey, agave nectar, and sugar snap peas. Maple syrup, brown sugar, and white sugar are low-fructose sweetener choices.

Unlike other fruits, apples and pears also contain a much higher portion of fructose compared to the amount of glucose they hold. Fructose requires glucose in order to absorb well. When in excess of glucose, fructose has more reason to be poorly absorbed, again causing diarrhea in small children.

Studies are finding that some children diagnosed with irritable bowel syndrome or functional bowel disorder may be only suffering from fructose intolerance. There is disagreement about this point today, but it's easy enough to find out in your own child with simple dietary experiments. Fructose intolerance will generally improve as a child grows.

Is It Lactose Intolerance?

Many are mistaken about lactose intolerance when it comes to babies. Lactose is baby sugar and babies are designed to digest it well. It's available only in the milks of mammals to provide for their offspring. This includes, of course, human milk, cow milk, and goat milk. Lactose is great for babies as it aids calcium absorption, ensures sugar is released at the proper rate, nourishes healthy flora, and supplies carbohydrates that are important for a baby's brain development.

Many older children and adults eventually develop lactose intolerance because they are not intended to be nursing; that is, they are not intended to be drinking the baby mammal food, milk.

A baby born with the extremely rare defect causing total inability to digest lactose quickly suffers brain damage and would not be expected to survive to pass on her genes—at least not prior to the relatively recent development of lactose-free infant feeds. Thus, a true genetic inability to digest lactose is almost never found in very young children. It is, however, common for an infant reacting to cow milk proteins or recovering from some other intestinal irritation to suffer a *temporary* reduction in **lactase enzyme**, used for lactose digestion. Whereas most digestive enzymes are created inside the mouth, stomach, or pancreas, lactase is produced by cells along a delicate brush border that lines the small intestine walls. When a child has diarrhea or intestinal irritation for any reason, these cells can be damaged and sloughed off, lessening the number of cells producing lactase, until they are able to re-populate.

> *It is common for an infant reacting to cow milk proteins or recovering from some other intestinal irritation to suffer a temporary reduction in lactase enzyme, used for lactose digestion.*

This temporary reduction in lactase enzyme production may cause some babies to test positively for lactose intolerance, via laboratory or breath tests, and to be diagnosed as lactose intolerant. This condition will reverse quickly, however, as soon as a child recovers from illness or, if it's caused by food sensitivity, is given a feed without cow milk proteins or other problematic proteins in it.

Though a breastfed baby may temporarily have less lactase enzyme after an intestinal infection and may test positive for lactose intolerance should a doctor decide to test, mother's milk is the one thing that will help him recover the quickest from his illness and help the intestines heal and recoup lactase enzyme production. If becoming gassy during an intestinal illness, then shorter, more frequent feeds are all that's needed. This helps to provide frequent hydration and anti-inflammatory action, as well as comforting. This feeding pattern will likely continue to be helpful for a time after the illness has cleared.

If a breastfed baby regularly develops diarrhea and fussiness after mom's consumption of cow milk products, this is not lactose intolerance. The child is reacting to cow milk proteins being passed on from mom's milk. Mom's milk is full of healthy lactose and her consumption or avoidance of lactose would not matter at all to her nursling, except that lactose added as an ingredient to foods is generally contaminated with traces of milk proteins. Removal of any milk-containing foods from mom's diet will afford relief to her milk protein intolerant baby. Her breastmilk will then help baby's intestines recover.

A formula-fed baby suffering from or recovering from a diarrheal illness may be more comfortable on a lactose-free formula for a couple of weeks as the intestines heal and lactase enzyme returns. This is because frequent small feeds are more difficult to provide when formula feeding, and healing may be slower without the growth factors in breastmilk. On occasion, a significant diarrheal illness can lead to a baby developing intolerance to the cow milk proteins in her formula, as poorly digested proteins leak through the irritated intestinal walls during the illness. If a baby does not seem to ever do as well with formula as prior to an illness, a switch to a hydrolyzed formula, in which milk proteins are broken up into smaller pieces, may be the solution. The most sensitive formula-fed infants do best with an amino acid formula.

Breastmilk Oversupply and Diarrhea

Do you have a high breastmilk supply? Forceful letdown? Some moms are super milk makers and their babies may get a little overwhelmed with the speed of the milk delivery. Their babies might cough or gag at the breast, not want to feed, or take quick but frequent feeds. In attempt to slow the milk flow, some babies may clamp down hard on mom's nipple, leaving it a little pinched and causing mom some pain. Spitting-up may be excessive. If nursing lying down, baby may leave a little pool of milk. This baby's poops may be watery, frothy, mucusy, smelly, and possibly green. They may also show a little blood. Some poops may be explosive, being pushed out by gas.

The fat content in the milk increases the longer a child nurses, and the lactose level drops.

Weight measurements for a baby dealing with **milk oversupply** will show baby to be gaining quickly even though she is spitting up and has diarrhea. This baby will often be diagnosed with food sensitivity because the symptoms are so similar. The presence of coughing or gagging at the breast may help discern between these two potential causes of diarrhea. Children with food sensitivities also tend to gain a little more slowly.

In response to a forceful milk delivery, babies tend to stop nursing before emptying a breast. They may come back frequently for short feeds, and they won't be found comfort nursing. The first milk to come out of the breast is waterier and higher in the milk sugar lactose. The fat content in the milk increases the longer a child nurses, and the lactose level drops. If a baby frequently empties only the first milk, known as the foremilk, she will take in a high amount of lactose. This is known as **foremilk–hindmilk imbalance**.

Although babies are not born to be lactose intolerant, they may have difficulty with higher amounts of lactose at one time. Lactose may come in faster than baby's available amounts of lactose digesting enzyme, lactase, can respond. In this case, some of the lactose can sit undigested in the bowel, causing water to rush in to dilute this sugar, leading to loose stools, and allowing bacteria to ferment it, which causes smelly gas. Over time, this situation can keep the intestines irritated and cause a little bleeding. Such chronic irritation can also cause a drop in lactase enzyme production. This can create a vicious cycle.

A doctor may measure excess acid in the baby's stool, or hydrogen gas in baby's breath, and diagnose the child as lactase enzyme deficient (i.e., lactose intolerant). Sadly, a switch from mother's milk to lactose-free formula is sometimes recommended, but this poor irritated intestine does not need to lose its healing, anti-inflammatory breastmilk; it just needs a little change in the feeding plan.

If this sounds like you and your baby, you may want to seek the help of a lactation consultant right away, or try first resolving the situation on your own.

By allowing the baby to feed only on one breast during every two-hour period, you can help him to gain more of the fattier hindmilk. Over time, with this **block feeding**, the breasts should adjust to the altered milk demand and the supply should level off. If your baby tends to want to sip quite often, you may want to gently delay him with distraction techniques. If this only leads to lots of tears, the hormonal response to crying can cause your breasts to respond by making more milk. We don't want that. You may have to make this transition gradually if your breasts are feeling too engorged. Some moms express some milk before putting baby to breast. In the long run, expressing or pumping off more milk than the baby can drink will only serve to increase rather than decrease the milk supply, but it may just be the answer that works for some. A little sage tea also helps some moms decrease their excess supply.

If you wish, you can put a dose of lactase enzyme drops from the drugstore into your expressed milk and refrigerate or freeze it for a later feeding. It takes time for the drops to work, so if you want to freeze the milk, it has to sit with the enzymes in the refrigerator for a few hours first. Some moms try giving the drops directly to baby. There's no reason not to give this a try, but many moms have reported it to be not as helpful as desired. Remember, if things are not going well, contact a lactation consultant.

> *A child can have reactions to wheat or all glutens without having positive celiac tests, though, so dietary challenges are still important.*

Food Allergy and Intolerance

Diarrhea that repeatedly comes and goes, or is present most of the time, and doesn't fit into any of the above possibilities, is most likely some kind of food protein allergy or intolerance, although there are still more possibilities. Does your baby also suffer from colic, reflux, rashes, or sleeplessness? Reactions to dietary proteins are likely involved when colic or reflux are associated with bouts of diarrhea, possibly interrupted by constipation, and with other possible symptoms such as fussiness, resistance to eating, frequent spitting up, green poop, mucus or blood in the poop, rashes, gassiness, a red ring around baby's anus, sleeplessness, or waking with screams. Such symptoms usually improve with discovery and removal of offending foods from breastfeeding mother's diet or the child's formula or other diet. Cow milk proteins are the most common cause, with soy and gluten intolerances running close behind.

Gluten Intolerance

Gluten is one of many proteins found in wheat, rye, and barley. Commonly known as celiac disease, gluten intolerance is a common kind of food intolerance with some quite distinct findings on blood tests that make it sometimes easy to diagnose, once it's suspected. A child *can* have reactions to wheat or all glutens without having positive celiac tests, though, so dietary challenges are still important to the final decision about grains. There is a large hereditary component to celiac disease.

Both diarrhea and constipation can occur with celiac. When gluten is regularly consumed, the irritation to the intestinal linings causes poor absorption of nutrients and this malabsorption can lead to slow weight gain, anemia, and other problems for the infant. Early symptoms will be similar to other food intolerance symptoms, but with rashes sometimes appearing on elbows and knees. If symptoms begin not long after baby's first exposures to wheat, rye, or barley products, or if a parent has known difficulty with grains, one can suspect gluten intolerance. Although breastfeeding is shown to often delay and reduce the effects of celiac disease, some babies may react to gluten in their nursing mother's diet. Because of its hereditary nature, many mothers who begin eliminating gluten from their diet to provide healing gluten-free milk for their intolerant babies find that they themselves are feeling better health than ever before.

IBS, IBD, or Eosinophilic Gastroenteritis

Although most anyone diagnosed with one of these diarrheal conditions likely had symptoms in infancy, these diagnoses are typically not made in babies. They are generally made based on distinct diagnostic findings in older children, adolescents, and young adults, after years of symptoms. Inflammatory bowel diseases (IBD) include Crohn's disease and ulcerative colitis and involve diarrhea with inflammatory damages going on inside the intestines. Eosinophilic gastroenteritis symptoms result from a stomach or intestinal membrane concentration of eosinophils, which are typically allergy-responding blood cells. **Irritable bowel syndrome (IBS)** may present with frequent diarrhea or may involve both diarrhea and constipation. It is a more

Irritable bowel syndrome (IBS) is a more vague diagnosis that is often made when no other causes for intestinal symptoms can be found.

All of these conditions have hereditary components, but dietary and lifestyle factors can strongly impact whether or not these conditions will develop and how serious they may become.

vague diagnosis that is often made when no other causes for intestinal symptoms can be found. Sometimes blame is laid on excessive sensitivity of intestinal nerves. All of these conditions mentioned have hereditary components, but dietary and lifestyle factors can strongly impact whether or not these conditions will develop and how serious they may become. Almost always, elimination dieting— when strict and consistent— can bring great relief. To reduce or eliminate the need for drugs, many other things can be done to reduce symptoms when one of these diseases is diagnosed.

Other Dietary Causes of Diarrhea

Alcohol—found in certain herbal remedies, cough syrup, or in mom's milk from her own alcohol consumption—can cause some loose stools. Caffeine can cause diarrhea in some little ones. It may come from a chocolate treat, from tea, or from soda. Mother can also pass caffeine in her milk. Have you had a bit of a coffee splurge?

Diarrhea after a Cold, Pulling on Ear

Ear infections are rather common in toddlers and may be attended by some diarrhea and possibly vomiting. The child may lose her appetite from the pain. A toddler holding or tugging on her ear is a pretty good sign that her diarrhea is related to an ear infection. Sometimes the baby with colic, reflux, or food reactions grows into the toddler with frequent ear infections. Antibiotic treatments for ear infections are not shown to be of great benefit and can cause more serious diarrhea from intestinal infection with antibiotic-resistant bacteria. Antibiotic treatments also tend to cause many more returns of ear infections with bacteria that are more drug resistant. Often antibiotics are prescribed when the infection is only viral, but the infection can then become bacterial as well, from the elimination of the competitive floral balance, allowing a take-over by resistant bacteria. Bacterial flora in the ear canals is slightly different from, but dependent upon, intestinal flora. Probiotics can help to better balance ear flora too.

Diarrhea with Night Restlessness

Has your baby developed diarrhea and, at the same time, become suddenly quite restless at night? I'm not talking the fussiness of pain or illness—just plain restless. Or is your child itching his bottom at night? Take a good look at his poop. You might see thin white little worms. Also try looking at his anus with a flashlight after he's fallen asleep at night, to look for wiggly heads greeting you.

Even if you don't see worms with these efforts, there's a way you can help your doctor to diagnose them quickly. On the evening before baby's appointment, do this **tape test**. Take a piece of Scotch Tape and tape it to itself to make a ring with the sticky side out. Place this sticky ring of tape in close to your baby's anus, just before bed time, and leave it there for the night. The tape should pick up eggs from the worms as they come out to lay their eggs during the night. You may even catch a worm. Remove the tape in the morning to bring to the doctor. In the morning, you can take another piece of tape and press it firmly over the anus and pull it right off, in another attempt to pick up any possible eggs. They'll be too small to see with your unaided eye, but your doctor or a laboratory technician can see them easily with a microscope.

Hyperthyroidism

An overactive thyroid gland is a rare but possible cause of chronic diarrhea in a baby. If mother has had Graves' disease or some other hyperthyroidism, it's more likely to occur in baby. Symptoms include diarrhea, poor sleep, restlessness, and a fussy baby with poor weight gain. Some babies' eyes won't close completely when sleeping, or they have an unusual stare during the day. Simple blood tests help diagnose thyroid conditions, and there are effective medical treatments. Autoantibodies stemming from gluten intolerance or other food sensitivities may initiate or worsen some kinds of hyperthyroidism; dealing with these may improve the condition.

Autism

Recent reports reveal that gastrointestinal (GI) symptoms are common in a considerable proportion of children who are diagnosed with an autism spectrum disorder. Those children with stronger autism diagnoses account for the larger percentages of GI symptom reports, and any children on the spectrum who experience GI problems tend to display greater behavioral symptoms. Diarrhea is the most common GI finding. Although reactions to foods or chemicals in a child's diet may not be the *cause* of most or many autism cases, a large number of parents who explore such options find that focusing on gut health, including dietary reactions, can reduce problems with diarrhea, abdominal pain, and constipation, and can often improve other autism symptoms as well.

Constipation Followed by Loose Poop Soiling

Frequent leaking of watery poops may be seen in the diapers of a child who has shown constipation or who has undetected constipation. Accidental soiling of underpants can occur in a previously potty-trained child. These can occur when poop from higher up the colon is squirting past a collection of **impacted stool**. This occurrence of watery poop is actually a bad case of constipation.

Diarrhea with Hardening of Abdomen

Signaled by a hard and painful abdomen, necrotizing enterocolitis (NEC), covered in Chapter 5, is initially not an infection. Rather, it's a serious inflammatory condition that is more often seen in hospitalized preemies but may rarely occur in the first few weeks after your premature or term baby arrives home. The symptoms include poor feeding, abdominal bloating turning to a red shiny hard abdomen that is clearly painful for the infant when you press on it, green vomit, diarrhea or lack of stools, and bloody stools. Most cases occur in infants who have received at least some formula or fortifier since birth, although NEC is seen in fully breastfed babies as well. Your baby's physician should be contacted right away if you see such an abdominal appearance or a significant amount of any of these other symptoms.

Greasy, Smelly Diarrhea

Greasy, smelly diarrhea may result from the malabsorption often seen with advanced celiac disease. Add in the symptoms of coughing and salty tasting skin, and this may be a more serious problem. Along with slow growth, diarrhea and/or constipation, and frequent respiratory infections, these are the signs of **cystic fibrosis**, a disorder that can occasionally be missed by newborn screening.

Red Currant Jelly Diarrhea

Severe pain that comes and goes, along with a red currant jelly stool appearance can represent a rare bowel obstruction found mostly in babies 5 months of age or older. Known as **intussusception**, abdominal pain will come on suddenly and cause loud, inconsolable crying. The baby may draw his knees up toward his chest. Bloody diarrhea may occur, being thick and dark,

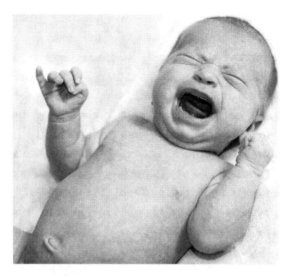

thus referred to as currant jelly stool. Vomiting may occur and may be green.

The pain from intussusception can go away and the child may return to his normal state, or seem a little disturbed, only to begin distressful crying again in 15 to 20 minutes. The abdomen may become hard and swollen, and you may actually be able to feel a hard, long, and narrow portion, which feels rather like a sausage inside the abdomen. Of course a child with some of these symptoms requires quick medical attention.

An interesting and fortunate feature of medical attention for intussusception is that the same procedure used to diagnose the condition most often also resolves the condition. Typically a barium enema is given to the child to help the intestines to be seen on X-ray or another imaging study. In possibly 80% of cases, this thick enema also serves to relieve the intussusception.

Those who receive a rotavirus vaccine may be at slightly increased risk of intussusception, but the risk is smaller than from the original 1998 vaccine that gave rotavirus immunization a bad name. The current risk is estimated to be one case of intussusception for every 20,000 infants fully vaccinated with a newer rotavirus vaccine. This is about a quarter of the number associated with the original discontinued RotaShield vaccine. The math suggests that the new vaccines could produce under 200 intussusception cases per year in the United States, with a hypothetical loss of under two infant lives per year. See below for more info on rotavirus.

Food Poisoning and Tummy Flu

The most typical intestinal infection comes from what is called food poisoning. The virus or bacteria lives and grows in improperly handled food and then reproduces further inside the intestines of the unfortunate child who consumes this food, thereby causing illness. Sometimes these microbes release toxins into the food or inside the intestines, and these toxins cause illness. Such infections can generally be spread other ways besides directly from spoiled foods, and these modes of transmission are more common in babies. Many infections can be spread from person to person, especially from baby to baby in childcare, once they are mobile. Babies do not eat restaurant foods, fancy homemade dishes, or old leftovers as often as adults do, but they spit up frequently, their diapers leak, their noses are down near where these things land, their hands touch everything, and their hands frequently go into their mouths. This sampling of the environment is not fully a bad thing, except when a nasty bug is going around.

> *When an intestinal illness has not been connected to a food consumed, then such a tummy bug is commonly called a stomach flu, though these have nothing to do with "the flu," which is influenza, a respiratory infection.*

Though mostly caused by the same bacteria and viruses, when an intestinal illness has not been connected to a food consumed, then such a tummy bug is commonly called a stomach flu, though these have nothing to do with "the flu," which is influenza, a respiratory infection. Any such intestinal diarrheal illness, from food poisoning or not, is referred to medically as **gastroenteritis**.

Norovirus and Rotavirus Infections

The two most common gastrointestinal infections in babies are known as **norovirus** and **rotavirus**. Infections from these intestinal viruses can be spread by food or other means and can cause anything from minimal discomfort to very serious illness with severe diarrhea. More often than not, you will not find out what virus is troubling your baby, but some familiarity with these newsworthy viruses can be beneficial. Symptoms of both of these, and many other gastrointestinal infections, include vomiting, fever, watery diarrhea, and a basically unhappy baby. Dehydration resulting from the vomiting and diarrhea is generally the chief threat to infants.

There has reportedly been a significant 33% overall reduction in U.S. children's hospital visits for all causes of gastroenteritis since the beginning of rotavirus vaccination in 2006, with most of the drops noticed during rotavirus seasons. No reduction in U.S. rotavirus deaths have yet been reported by the CDC or published studies, though the U.S. rotavirus death rate has always been low, at 20 to 60 deaths per year. An emergence of alternative strains not covered by the vaccines is just beginning to be found in the United States and could eventually lead to a renewed increase in rotavirus cases, though the vaccine industry will likely respond by expanding their vaccine strains.

One minor precaution should be taken when your child is vaccinated for rotavirus. RotaTeq is a live virus vaccine, and it is known to shed live viruses in babies' stools. Typically, this action helps to increase "herd immunity," by initiating immune development in some unvaccinated children who are exposed to newly vaccinated children. The concern expressed by researchers is that serious illness could result in individuals with weak immune systems if exposed to these shedding live viruses. It may be a prudent measure to keep some distance between a newly vaccinated child and an unvaccinated newborn or a frail house member. The RotaTeq manufacturer cautions against vaccinating an infant who has contact with any immune-deficient individual. Shedding has been shown to last for up to 15 days.

In industrialized nations, studies find 64% fewer serious diarrhea cases in exclusively breastfed infants. Compare this to the 33% reduction from the rotavirus vaccine measured in the United States.

In developing nations where the numbers of mortalities from diarrhea are more significant, measures of the results from interventions are also more significant. A 2010 study on the introduction of rotavirus vaccination in Mexico found a significant 40% cut in diarrheal deaths there. In terms of other efforts available to reduce diarrheal deaths, a review of a large number of studies in developing countries found that exclusive breastfeeding cut all diarrhea cases by over 90% versus a diet of formula and/or other foods. In industrialized nations, studies find 64% fewer serious diarrhea cases in exclusively breastfed infants. Compare this to the 33% reduction from the rotavirus vaccine measured in the United States. Rotavirus vaccine may be an especially valuable option for a baby who is receiving infant formula.

Norovirus is well known for causing epidemic illnesses on cruise ships, but you don't need to take a cruise for baby to catch it. Once norovirus gets started somewhere, it's highly contagious. More serious than rotavirus, norovirus is responsible for one million healthcare visits in U.S. children and 570 to 800 total U.S. deaths per year, chiefly among young children and elder adults.

It turns out that these viruses are also spread by particles in the air; that is, viruses simply fill the air around an infected person and are especially found floating around the toilet and diaper changing areas, and wherever vomiting has recently occurred.

References are commonly made to such gastrointestinal bugs as being spread by the *fecal-to-oral* route. This suggests that poor bathroom or diapering hygiene leads to fecal material contamination of food and objects that others then touch and get into their mouths, or directly eat or suck on. I rather like to think that common bathroom hygiene is not so poor that it could be responsible for the hundreds of people who will become infected in a short amount of time during a cruise ship norovirus outbreak, for instance. It may start with one bad kitchen incidence, but it continues to spread. It turns out that these viruses are also spread by particles in the air; that is, viruses simply fill the air around an infected person and are especially found floating around the toilet and diaper changing areas, and wherever vomiting has recently occurred.

These two particular viruses tend to survive outside the body for longer than many common viruses. Rotavirus may live for 4 hours on hands and for a few days on some surfaces. It's thought that norovirus can live on hard surfaces for up to 12 hours and on softer surfaces for up to 12 days.

E. coli

E. coli bacterial infections are responsible for only a few percent of children's diarrheal illnesses, but I bring them up because the name has gained much notoriety, and this bug's activities can be very confusing. All different kinds of *E. coli* make up a normal part of everyone's intestinal flora. Some strains behave in tougher manners and can cause infection when allowed to get out of line. These are more common in formula-fed babies than young breastfed babies, but all children eventually acquire these bacteria with the consumption of solid foods. We're mostly glad to have them, after breastmilk, as they can keep down even meaner bacteria. Then, there are a few kinds of extremely dangerous *E. coli* out there that I hope never make it into your home. These are the ones coming from bacteria in the stools of poorly cared-for cattle or chickens, and these strains are often strengthened by overuse of antibiotics in animals. Occasionally, these powerful *E. coli* are allowed to become established on poorly packaged meat or to get into produce fields from animal waste. These bacteria die easily with appropriate cooking but are very occasionally passed to humans on undercooked meat or fresh vegetables.

Diarrhea from such *E. coli* is more often bloody. Again, it's unlikely you will be told that your sick baby is specifically suffering from an *E. coli* infection, except in rare instances in which there is a community outbreak, and widespread testing is being performed.

Poisoning from Household Chemicals

Sudden vomiting and diarrhea, possibly with sweating and trembling, can certainly signal an infection of some kind, but if there is any cause for suspicion, do what it takes to find out if your child may have ingested some form of household chemical. Poisonings can even cause fever, sometimes quite high, so the presence of fever does not rule out poisoning. If you have any concern, call 911 (in the United States). Bring the suspect chemical along with you when you go to the hospital. If your child has vomited, or you've been instructed to induce vomiting, collect some of the vomit and bring it along as well.

Collecting and bringing some of the diarrhea can be helpful, too, if you don't have something else to bring.

If you suspect or know of some kind of ingestion but do not feel your child is in immediate danger, you can also call Poison Control. They will give you the advice you need. Throughout the United States, the phone number is 1-800-222-1222. Some things to keep handy in the house in the event of poison ingestion are syrup of ipecac and activated charcoal, to use if instructed to.

Poisoning from Eating Common Plants

If eaten, many plants can cause diarrhea and vomiting. This response is the body's efficient means of ridding itself from undesirable toxins. Some common plants that can cause diarrhea are azalea, daffodils, foxglove, hyacinths, narcissus, oleander, rhododendron, wild mushrooms, and wisteria. You can talk to your doctor, poison control, or dial emergency, depending upon the severity of your baby's symptoms.

Some Final Thoughts

We've covered many potential causes of diarrhea, and hopefully you are able to narrow down the possibilities now. In the following chapter, we'll look at many ways you can help to protect the health of, and to comfort, your sick baby.

Caring for Loose Poop

Helping Your Sick Baby

Though the numbers are far higher in the developing world, diarrheal illness accounts for over 1.5 million outpatient visits for U.S. children, with some 200,000 hospitalizations and around 300 child deaths per year. Medications for such illnesses are seldom of much help and can be harmful. Maintaining adequate hydration is the most important key to baby's safe recovery.

Beyond a visit to the doctor, it's on parents to provide care for their ailing child. Good observation of the child's symptoms is always important and significant changes in condition can be reported. Over and above observation and loving comfort, the most important role for a caregiver of a child with diarrhea, and possibly vomiting, is to prevent dehydration. Your baby will also be very grateful to you if you apply lots and lots of your favorite diaper rash cream to his bottom after every loose poop—enough to keep most of the acidic diarrhea from touching baby's tender skin.

Outside of these measures, you can trust that your child will be active if her body doesn't need the rest and will rest if she needs to, as long as her symptoms are not covered up by medications. If she has little appetite, it's okay—this seldom lasts much beyond a day. As long as she's drinking, she'll be fine.

During any diarrheal illness, report any signs of dehydration, any red or black blood in baby's stool, or any observations that baby may be in great pain. Also let the doctor know if you don't believe your baby is keeping fluids down or if he's losing a large amount of water in his stools. Any time you think your baby just does not seem right, trust your instincts and seek advice.

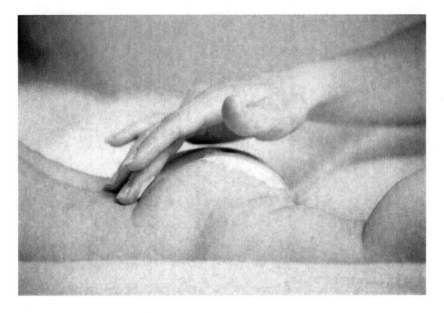

Signs of Dehydration

I'm going to repeat myself here: Signs of dehydration include dryness or stickiness inside the baby's mouth, a near lack of tears (in a baby old enough to develop tears), sunken eyes, a sunken appearance to the soft spot above the baby's forehead, an increased pulse rate, a darkening of baby's urine, or no wetting of diapers for 3 or 4 hours. Dehydration may have become *severe* if, in addition to some of these, baby seems unusually drowsy or confused, or becomes extremely fussy, looks pale, has a mottled skin appearance, develops cold hands or feet, has no sweating, has a weak pulse, or is breathing rapidly. If you pinch baby's skin when she is quite dehydrated, it may stay momentarily pinched before bouncing back.

In addition to these signs, standard guidelines denote a 5% loss of weight as mild dehydration, and 10% loss as severe. If you have access to weighing your baby, it's great to do so when first recognizing diarrhea, so the progression can be followed. If you cannot, it's not of concern. Baby's behavior and appearance are the greatest signs of the intensity of his condition, and his caregivers' observations are of great value.

A child showing signs of severe dehydration requires immediate medical attention.

Oral Rehydration

When baby is losing too much fluid to diarrhea and vomiting, he needs to have it replaced. It's been found that adding sugar and salt to fluids helps restore baby's electrolyte balance so his body holds on to the right amount of fluids. This can be done in the hospital with intravenous (IV) fluid, but studies and medical recommendations point out that appropriate electrolyte fluids given by mouth, known as **oral rehydration**, can be just as good in most cases of mild to moderate dehydration. Only when rehydration is deemed urgent or when baby cannot keep liquids down is IV hydration especially necessary. Oral rehydration is so important during diarrhea, no matter the cause, that John Hopkins researchers estimate that its proper use can prevent 93% of all diarrhea deaths.

Oral rehydration solutions can be used to prevent dehydration when the need is suspected or to replenish fluids after dehydration is observed. The WHO recommends a recipe that they have tried and perfected over many years and across many nations. This recipe, provided later in this chapter, contains water, of course, and additionally, it contains salt and sugar. Salt is lost from baby's body through diarrhea and must be replaced to bring baby back to healthy balance. Salt must be in the right concentration. If the solution is too salty, this can cause new problems for baby. Sugar is also necessary as it transports salt across the intestinal membranes. The sugar needs to be the right concentration as well. When sugar in rehydration liquid is too high, it actually pulls more water out of the body and into the intestines.

Oral rehydration is so important during diarrhea, no matter the cause, that John Hopkins researchers estimate that its proper use can prevent 93% of all diarrhea deaths.

Zinc has been shown to be quite helpful in the developing world for reducing the severity and for shortening the course of diarrheal illnesses. Today, some researchers believe that zinc isn't just for emergent nations any more, although others disagree. It's been shown that even when there is no zinc deficiency, zinc supplementation during a diarrheal illness can help babies to better absorb electrolytes, boost their immune system, and help their intestines to heal. There is no evidence of harm from short-term zinc supplementation in children, and it may help. The occasional child becomes nauseous or vomits from zinc supplements, just as some do from B vitamin supplements. This doesn't mean it's bad for everyone, some systems are just sensitive to concentrations of some nutrients. Pedialyte recently began adding zinc to their rehydration solutions.

Potassium is the next nutrient that is easily depleted from diarrhea and vomiting. Potassium is easily found in most fruits and vegetables. If your child is eating, or consuming ample breastmilk or formula, and keeping some of his food down, he's getting potassium, but if he's losing a considerable amount of fluids, potassium replenishment can be valuable. Again, it's available in Pedialyte as well as in generic solutions and instant electrolyte salt packs.

Fluids and the Exclusively Breastfeeding Baby

It is rare for a breastfeeding baby with gastroenteritis to stop nursing. When baby has diarrhea, with or without vomiting, offer breastmilk more frequently. Frequent nursing will keep hydration more consistent and can reduce the amount of milk taken each time. In the case that intestinal irritation is reducing lactase enzyme production, smaller, more frequent doses of breastmilk intake will help baby better digest milk's lactose. This may also be a nice time to allow baby to comfort nurse, taking in little or no milk as he suckles. Comfort nursing can provide great relief to the sick child. By the way, staying close to your infant and receiving exposure to her saliva through your nipples should lead your body to create antibodies to whatever illness your baby is suffering. You can then pass these on in your milk to speed baby's recovery.

When nursing unusually frequently, you may want to keep baby coming back to nurse on one side for 2 or 3 hours before switching breasts, if baby tends toward gassiness or is not accustomed to frequent snacking. This will assure more hindmilk delivery. Most babies don't need this kind of extra effort.

Generally, baby's body will adjust appropriately to a moderate fluid loss for a day or so without any other measures. A baby whose diet has been nothing but breastmilk—who has not started solid foods and receives no formula—typically does not need anything more than breastmilk when ill.

If dehydration signs are lasting or if baby is showing some signs of progressive dehydration, he will need some electrolyte fluids in addition to breastmilk. You'll likely want advice from your baby's healthcare provider at this point.

Typical electrolyte solutions contain no iron and no proteins, thus they do not interrupt the protective flora of an exclusively breastfed baby. In terms of intestinal floral balance, immune protection, and other benefits, your baby is still, essentially, exclusively breastfed if given these solutions. Coconut water or soup broth may be wonderful natural electrolyte fluid sources, but they contain a little protein and a little iron. It's likely that these nutrients would feed challenging florae and reduce the immune provisions of the exclusively breastfed intestine the same way that introducing formula, juice, or any solid foods would. During an illness would not be a good time to begin to wean from breastmilk as that would further weaken the immune system.

It's perfectly fine to make a homemade rehydration solution, but for an exclusively breastfed baby, it should be made from basic ingredients of water, table sugar, and table salt, as opposed to whole food sources.

Give fluids to compensate for observed dehydration and fluid losses. Standard recommendations are that if your breastfed baby is vomiting repeatedly, you may want to stop nursing for a short time (up to 4 hours) and give 1 to 2 teaspoon (5 to 10 mL) of oral rehydration solution, probably by spoon or dropper, about every 5 minutes. A toddler or older child will need larger amounts. If baby does not vomit for 4 hours, then gradually return to breastfeeding. You may want to pump or express some milk during the 4-hour break if your breasts are not accustomed to waiting this long. If your breastfed baby continues to vomit and you feel her dehydration may be worsening, or if baby is becoming more dehydrated from excessively watery diarrhea, even without vomiting, her doctor may recommend intravenous fluids. IV fluids will not interrupt baby's good flora, and you can stay close to her and nurse her during treatment.

Fluids and the Formula-Fed Baby

Gastroenteritis can decrease the amount of lactase enzyme that baby makes. A formula-fed baby may do better with a lactose-free formula until a few days after he's well again. Even lactose-free formula can be hard on some irritated intestines. A hydrolyzed formula may provide nutrition more comfortably. Try to feed small amounts, more frequently, when baby has diarrhea and is not feeling well.

If your formula-fed baby vomits more than once, standard recommendations are to feed a teaspoon or two (5 to 10 mL) of oral rehydration solution in place of formula, about every 5 minutes, for 4 hours. After this, try resuming formula feeding if vomiting has stopped. Toddlers and older children will need larger amounts of solution.

If it seems more appropriate, after vomiting slows down, you can mix oral rehydration solution with formula. It is *important* that you dilute powdered formula with plain water in the usual manner, and then add this normally mixed formula to a properly made or ready-made rehydration solution.

A pacifier can help bring some relief to an ailing baby between bottles. Be sure to nurse your sick baby affectionately with his bottles. You can do this with the pacifier, too.

If a baby typically receives a mix of breastmilk and formula, it can be highly advantageous, if possible, to increase the portion of breastmilk over formula during an illness.

Oral Rehydration Solutions

All sugar-containing soft drinks—and just about any juice or artificial juice drink—have too much sugar to be given full strength to the dehydrated baby or one at risk of dehydration. As mentioned, high sugar content will pull water into the intestines, which means out of baby's blood and organs, thereby dehydrating her body. Also, as we've learned, the high fructose in fruit juices or drinks can especially increase diarrhea, as fructose digestion can be impaired. Additionally, these drinks don't provide needed salt. Gatorade, the popular sports drink, has an unfortunate reputation for being appropriate for true dehydration. It's not. Their G2 product has similar sugar but less than half the salt as the WHO's recommendation. It may be okay when serious rehydration isn't needed and if you are not concerned about the added artificial sweeteners, artificial flavors, and colors. Their other products have more sugar.

All sugar-containing soft drinks—and just about any juice or artificial juice drink—have too much sugar to be given full strength to the dehydrated baby or one at risk of dehydration.

Pedialyte is the gold standard and reflects what is currently believed to be a perfectly balanced rehydration solution when serious rehydration is needed. Along with generic versions and various powdered electrolyte products, it's most appropriate for babies who are too young to be given solid foods or juice. One drawback of Pedialyte is that it cannot be given to a child with a corn allergy because the dextrose and citric acid are derived from corn. A rice-based product, Infalyte, used to be the allergy alternative, but it's no longer available. The unflavored version of Pedialyte may not always be available when you want it. Some parents may not care for the artificial sugars, flavors, and colors added to the flavored varieties or most alternative products carried on drugstore shelves; I must say, though, the flavored products do go down much more easily in a fussy child who is not feeling well.

For a baby who has already started eating solid foods, the options are much wider. If they are eating well, then they only need extra water or herbal tea in addition to their formula or breastmilk. Just make sure that something in their diet is salty.

Rehydration Solution Options

If baby has moderate signs of dehydration or a doctor has ordered rehydration therapy, it may be best to start out with one of the professional products. You may then use a homemade formulation for continued maintenance, once baby has improved. You can also use homemade formulations for light dehydration or for prevention from dehydration. Still, even when it's time for serious rehydration, there are many reasons a family may want to go for a homemade electrolyte solution. Some parents just prefer to use home-selected ingredients. Another reason for making something at home is that stores may be closed when parents are told or decide to provide a rehydration solution, or baby is so sick that it's not convenient to go out.

Pedialyte has added potassium and zinc. These things are not easy to add on your own. Again, potassium is not necessarily needed if baby is holding down her baby milk or some fruits or vegetables. Zinc is more of an optional ingredient, though a good one. It's interesting to note that Pedialyte once contained many more kinds of electrolytes, including calcium, magnesium, phosphorous, and bicarbonate. These have been dropped and apparently are no longer considered essential to rehydration.

Homemade Rehydration Solutions

If you happen to have an old family recipe for a rehydration solution, you should know that current experts believe they should be weaker than what was once recommended. An old recipe will also likely contain baking soda. This is fine, but no longer endorsed.

Below is the basic rehydration solution recipe recommended by the WHO:

World Health Organization Recommended Rehydration Recipe
30 mL sugar : 2.5 mL salt : 1 L water or
2 tbsp sugar : 0.5 tsp salt : 1 qt water

In a child over 12 months, honey is a healthy, gut-healing sweetener to use.

If your baby has a corn allergy and you are making your own solution, remember that iodized salt contains corn-derived dextrose. You can buy non-iodized salt in most grocery stores.

Some people prefer to use sea salt. Sea salt contains free iron that one would not want to give to an exclusively breastfed baby. Its use would contribute 0.12 mg of iron per liter of rehydration solution—enough to jump start a few bad bugs in a baby who is already ailing.

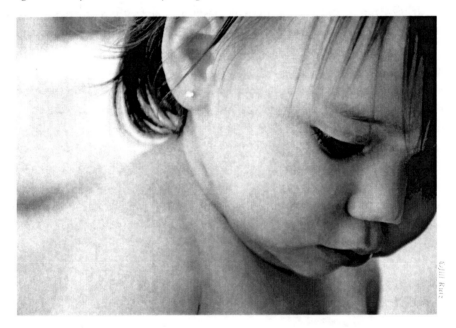

If you want to add zinc to this or to another solution, standard recommendations for short-term zinc supplementation during diarrhea are 10 mg per day for babies under 6 months and 20 mg for older children. These guidelines are created with poorly nourished children in mind, so I would consider them upper limits. Pedialyte provides 8 mg per liter of solution, and a child is assumed to consume around a liter, and up to two liters, per day. A wide variety of zinc lozenges are available in grocery and health food markets that could be dissolved into a solution. You may want to try a little zinc supplementation if developing a homemade rehydration beverage.

Adding potassium is more difficult, as supplements sold contain quite low amounts compared to what would provide a worthy fortification for a child who's lost a lot of fluid. For comparison, Pedialyte provides 800 mg of potassium (20 meq) per liter, yet potassium supplements are generally 100 mg or less in rather large-sized tablets.

Rehydration for Baby after Solid Foods

For babies already on solid foods but who don't want to eat while they're ill, a lightly salted and lightly sweetened, diluted homemade bone broth should be a healthy rehydration solution full of electrolytes and many other nutrients. Use the WHO recipe to estimate the amount of salt and preferred sweetener to use. Some may wish to use 4 tablespoons (60 mL) of apple juice concentrate per quart or liter, but only if your child doesn't tend to get gassy from higher doses of fructose. She'll have even less tolerance for it now. You can also simmer in various veggies and then strain them out. These will impart potassium to the broth. When broth is made from simmering of a whole organic chicken for 6 hours or more (ideally 24 hours), the gelatin-forming cartilage will provide intestinal healing properties, the meat provides zinc, and the marrow provides excellent nutrients along with immunoglobulins that may have immune providing qualities.

Instant or canned chicken or vegetable broths are nothing but salt, water, and various forms of MSG. (You can look up the many names used for free glutamates. Be *especially* wary when it says "No MSG" because that usually means other forms of glutamates *are* added.) These broths have no nutrition, and they're far too salty for rehydration. If you think you're buying real chicken broth—something beyond having had a chicken swim through it briefly—it should be jelly-like and deep in color, and it should list at least several grams of protein per serving. I've never seen one available.

Coconut water has recently been discovered by health food proponents as nature's perfect rehydration solution. Make sure you get coconut *water*, not coconut *juice*, *drink*, or *milk*. Coconut water amazingly contains the same amount of sugar and salt as the WHO recipe, and has 3 times the potassium as Pedialyte. This high amount of potassium is not a concern; it's great. A tricky thing about potassium is that, although fruits containing it may taste great, straight potassium supplementation does not. Coconut water is tolerable tasting. In addition to these electro-lytes, it contains many other nutrients and has just under 1 mg of zinc per quart or liter.

Coconut water has recently been discovered by health food propo-nents as nature's perfect rehydration solution.

Also for a baby who has already started solids foods, many parents prefer using diluted juices. When given along with something salty, such as cheese or olives, this option is good enough when serious rehydra-tion is not needed and when the child tolerates fructose well. A liter (just over a quart) of juice contains around 100 g of sugar (of course you would never give that much juice), whereas the WHO recipe calls for 30 g of sugar per liter. Hence, juice can be diluted by two parts of water to one part of juice. This would supply only a portion of the amount of potassium desired for serious stool and vomit liquid loss, and no zinc.

Among the higher dietary sources of potassium, one whole medium banana (a half cup) provides 400 mg of potassium. A half of a medium-sized baked potato provides 460 mg and a half cup of avocado, 550 mg. Orange juice has a reputation for being a good source of potassium. A half cup of juice or one medium-sized orange provides 250 mg, although its high acid could be irritating to an already aggravated tummy.

Again, coconut water, soup broth, or juice should not be given to an exclusively breastfed infant. The first two of these should be fine for most infants who already receive any formula, over maybe 4 months of age, or as suggested by the health-care practitioner. It may be best to wait until after 6 months to give diluted juice.

Cow milk has a nice amount of potassium but cannot be counted as liquid for rehydration because it's quite protein and phosphorous dense and high in lactose. For a milk-drinking dehydrated child, dilute, or match the milk 50:50 with water and it will be fine.

Fevers and Sick Children

"Fever does not cause brain damage. Fever is a good thing," says pediatrician Scott W. Cohen, MD, author of *Eat, Sleep, Poop*. Pediatrician Jo Ann Rohyans, MD, writes for BabyCenter.com: "Most children can tolerate a temperature of slightly higher than 107°F without long-term effects from the fever itself." She explains that this is unless the child is overdressed or trapped in a hot space. The U.S. National Institutes of Health (NIH) post about children on their Medline Plus website: "Brain damage from a fever generally will not occur unless the fever is over 107.6°F (42°C). Untreated fevers caused by infection will seldom go over 105°F (40.5°C) unless the child is overdressed or trapped in a hot place." Pediatrician Barton Schmitt, MD, states in his American Academy of Pediatrics book, My Child is Sick, "Fevers with infections don't cause brain damage. Only fevers above 108°F (42.3°C) can cause brain damage." Need I go on?

A child stuck in a hot car can become heated to higher than 108 degrees Fahrenheit and suffer injury or death. Certain severe chemical poisonings can cause excessive, damaging temperatures. These are not infection-related fevers, rather they are unnatural overheatings. The body will not destroy itself through its own immune system process of warming up to kill infections.

Pediatrician Susan Markel, MD, in our book What Your Pediatrician Doesn't Know Can Hurt Your Child, states,

> Despite the common fear that fever can cause brain damage, this has never been confirmed by any scientific tests or investigations. Only in the rare cases of meningitis or encephalitis, conditions which themselves can cause brain damage, can the brain's ability to control the body's temperature be disrupted. In neurologically normal children, the brain has an internal regulatory mechanism that does not allow fever to rise out of control. Fevers produced by viral or bacterial infections will not cause brain damage or permanent physical harm, despite the myths about children being severely compromised by having a high fever.

Fever is not to be feared. Fever is useful. It's the body's means of getting itself better. We want baby to get well as soon as possible. Fever is one of the body's immune system processes for killing infections. We want infections killed. There is no reason to block the body's efforts to recover. The goal of caring for a sick child should be to keep her protected while her body tackles the infection and repairs itself. A child is not truly healthy and well just because she behaves better when her symptoms are covered up by some chemical medication—while the drug hinders her immune system—for the sake of short-term relief.

Some children experience febrile seizures. These are frightening to see, but according to the American Academy of Pediatrics, and other authorities, febrile seizures do not cause brain damage or other long-term harm. As well as having seizures, a child can experience hallucinations or suffer a "swimmy head" feeling when her fever is in higher ranges. These all come from the head being hot, when the benefits of fever are mostly needed for the rest of the body. A child's head can be cooled by using cool cloths, bringing comfort without stopping the benefits of fever to the rest of the body.

We all get sick. It's *okay* for a baby or child to feel uncomfortable sometimes. You don't have to *fix* it. The best medicine for your child's ill feelings is your warm affectionate attention and tender embraces. Your child will not only gain great comfort, but this is a special opportunity for your child to learn empathy and caring through your compassion, and have opportunity to really feel how much you care. Besides the emotional feel-good, your touch and especially skin-to-skin contact lead to oxytocin releases that invigorate the immune system. Baby's neurological feedback systems are also designed to gain great relief and physiological normalizing through sucking. Whether on a finger, breast, bottle, or pacifier, help your sick baby or toddler achieve as much as desired.

Fevers and Pain Medications

Pain and fever medications do not cure, reduce, or shorten illnesses. If anything, they may lengthen them. They stress baby's liver and kidneys when he is

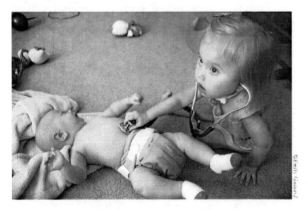

already ill, and they put baby at slight potential risk for damage when we actually want him to be getting stronger. By causing a child to feel much better through the use of pain and fever reducers, his body will be prevented from telling him when to slow down and when to lie down. Unimpeded, the immune system tells the body when it needs rest in order to focus on efforts toward recovery. Masking of symptoms with drugs can also cover up important signs of worsening, which could possibly delay the pursuit of important medical attention.

Accidental medication overdoses are risky, of course, but each kind of fever and pain medication has its own health risks even at recommended doses, which is what I discuss here. **NSAID** is common lingo for a **non-steroidal anti-inflammatory drug**, which includes aspirin, ibuprofen (Motrin), and naproxen. Acetaminophen is another common, non-prescription pain medicine. Also known as paracetamol, or Tylenol, this medication is not classified as an NSAID. All of these pain-reducing medications are also fever reducers. There are other drugs in these same categories with similar actions and side effects, but I will focus on these.

Aspirin is known to cause non-permanent liver damage in half of all who use it regularly. In a small number of children, more severe complications can occur. All of the above meds are known to pose slight and—on rare occasion—severe liver risks, even at recommended dosages. Ibuprofen and aspirin are known to occasionally cause gastrointestinal (GI) discomfort or bleeding in children. Acetaminophen can do the same but less often. Acetaminophen is labeled as safer overall than ibuprofen in some studies, although other studies claim it has worse side effects. NSAIDs and acetaminophen are also implicated in occasionally causing an autoimmune blood disease, thrombocytopenia, from which recovery is generally good.

Exposure to acetaminophen before the age of 15 months is associated with a more than tripled risk of later developing allergies and a doubled risk of developing asthma.

Acetaminophen and other medications rarely can cause severe skin reactions such as Stevens-Johnson syndrome or toxic epidermal necrolysis. These can be fatal. If a medication ever causes a skin reaction, it should be stopped and never used again. In addition to these threatening skin reactions, there is also a risk of severe or fatal skin staph or strep infections when NSAIDs are used with chicken pox or shingles infections. A risk in using these medications for a child with diarrhea and vomiting of unknown origin is that they could be exhibiting early symptoms of chicken pox or shingles, though the chance of a child actually having chicken pox or shingles is low today in vaccinated young children. Shingles rates are higher in children over 10 years of age than before the era of chicken pox vaccination.

Further safety studies for these meds are sorely needed. Studies have been performed in animals with influenza and with pneumonia, finding increased death rates when fever reducers are used. In animal studies, fever reducers were found to lengthen the time of illness in diarrheal infections from *Shigella*. Small studies of humans with influenza have found prolonged illness with the use of fever reducers. Only three different microbes were included in this study so this finding doesn't exclude such an effect with other infections.

Parents continue to be warned about the risk of Reye syndrome when giving aspirin to young children with chicken pox or other viruses. There are many dangers from giving medications to sick children, but this actually is not one of them. It'll likely take another decade for this information to trickle its way into mainstream medical education. The whole aspirin and Reye syndrome connection has been fully debunked in the medical research literature since the year 2000 and, even a decade before that, it was strongly suspected that anti-vomiting drugs have been responsible for most of the serious effects in children who showed symptoms that were associated with Reye syndrome. Still, aspirin, like all of these medications, may rarely be linked to serious skin, organ, or neurological disorders, especially when combined with bacterial or viral infections.

Some parents may understandably have concern about seizures after witnessing one in their child, but a large review of studies found that fever reducers actually do not prevent the return of febrile seizures. These results also imply that they do not prevent a first febrile seizure. An even larger review looked at the use of all kinds of anti-seizure medications as well as fever reducers and found that no drugs reduced the return of febrile seizures or provided any benefits, yet a full 30% of children suffered adverse effects from such drugs. Although a very small percentage of children who experience febrile seizures go on to be diagnosed with epilepsy, there is no evidence that this occurrence can be prevented with drugs.

Cooling of the whole feverish body through cool bathing has also not been proven beneficial; if anything, it slightly increases complications.

Other Medications

Like fever and pain reducers, anti-diarrheal and anti-vomit medications do not cure intestinal illnesses either. They may prolong illness, and they carry risks for side effects. Vomiting and diarrhea are the body's means of ridding itself of viruses, bacteria, parasites, toxins, or food allergens. Some of the common drugs traditionally used for these symptoms have some rather scary side effects, but medical researchers believe a couple of newer medications have good safety profiles: ondansetron for vomiting and racecadotril for diarrhea. I am not recommending these at all, and they are absolutely not appropriate for most cases of diarrhea and vomiting, but medical opinions find these prescription drugs to have occasional benefits in preventing or shortening hospitalization in certain cases when excessive fluid losses are preventing good nutrition and hydration from being achieved.

Most diarrheal infections in developed countries are viral, and antibiotics do not treat, shorten, or cure viral infections, and can make them worse. Excessive use of antibiotics, even for bacterial infections, has created many dangerous, antibiotic resistant bacteria today. Most bacterial infections will resolve on their own—that's what the immune system is for. Treating infections with antibiotics and other medications often provides no improvement and can potentially make things worse.

> *Most bacterial infections will resolve on their own—that's what the immune system is for.*

Medical reviews commonly recommend that physicians prescribe antibiotics chiefly only for *Shigella* and cholera diarrheal infections, for certain parasites, or—in some other cases—when any bacterial gastroenteritis is causing severe illness.

Bismuth salicylate, found in Pepto-Bismol and Kaopectate, has some nice antimicrobial actions, may reduce diarrhea somewhat, and can absorb *E. coli* toxins, but there are concerns over its use in children because of the aspirin (salicylate) it contains. Aspirin is hard on stomach tissues anyway. Pepto-Bismol-type products are not recommended for use under the age of 12. It's unfortunate that there does not appear to be a bismuth product available without the aspirin, as it's the bismuth that has bacteria-fighting and toxin-absorbing properties. Additionally, no side effects are reported in studies on bismuth. Bismuth salts were used in the 1700s.

Caring for Antibiotic-Caused Diarrhea

Between 15 and 25% of all children treated with antibiotics for any reason end up with antibiotic-caused diarrhea, which is a result of friendly and guardian-type flora being wiped out and opportunistic bacteria being allowed to flourish. Some 16 to 20% of antibiotic-caused cases are *Clostridium difficile* infections. Other *Clostridium* species, staphylococci, and *Salmonella* are some other sources of infection that can arise from antibiotic use.

It's likely in the child's best interest to make efforts to avoid the need for another, stronger, potentially more adverse antibiotic. Careful parental and professional observation of the child's progress—while giving her immune system time to handle the infection itself—may allow for avoidance of further drugs.

Because an imbalanced flora is the reason for this kind of diarrhea, providing ample probiotic supplementation (as discussed below) makes good sense.

When this diarrhea is known to be caused by C. *difficile*, there's a great alternative treatment for the infection when it is severe. The insertion of healthy stool from a healthy subject into the intestine of a person desperately ill from C. *diff* has been shown many times to be at least 90% curative. It doesn't yet appear to help with other kinds of infection. Insertion is accomplished through a tube that goes through the nose and down into the tummy or a tube that goes up the colon. Currently, a pill is being studied, which will make this treatment much easier. An early pill trial reported a 100% cure rate. Further trials, including children as young as 7 years, began in July of 2013. Hopefully this treatment will be available to young children soon. In the meantime, unfortunately, powerful antibiotics are used to treat serious antibiotic-caused C. *diff* intestinal infections in children today, with risks of failure of treatment, return of more serious infection, and unwanted side effects.

Tummy Tamers

Once your baby is old enough and is consuming solid foods, many options are available for trying to tame an upset tummy. Breastmilk contains a vast array of anti-inflammatory agents and other natural tummy-tamers, and there's no need to desire herbal or nutritional tummy soothers when breastmilk consumption is ample.

Ginger—real ginger from the ginger plant, not artificial ginger flavoring and not the tiny drop of natural ginger flavor found in various grocery store ginger ales—is well known to reduce nausea and some other tummy miseries. Unlike anti-vomit drugs that dampen neurologic pathways with possible unwanted consequences, ginger's soothing action is through its ability to protect digestive tissues. Ginger also serves to reduce oxidation and to directly fight microbes, including bacteria, viruses, and parasites—even worms. Its action is generally not as strong as that from drugs, but there is nothing undesirable known about its use in a child who is old enough for things besides her baby milk. Ginger is a highly researched herb and its actions are well documented.

Chamomile has been shown in several rat studies to have protective effects on digestive tissues, and it's well known to have calming, soothing effects. **Peppermint**, as from tea or essential oil, is shown to have relaxation effects on intestinal tissues and to have strong antioxidant and antimicrobial actions.

Raw honey has been found to be both healing to intestinal tissues and promoting of healthy intestinal flora. Unfortunately, it's not advised to give honey to a child under one year because of a tiny risk of botulism. After that age, you can use it as a healing sweetener and even use a direct half teaspoon here and there as a medicine. For extra microbe-fighting power in a child struggling to battle infection, you may choose to spend the big bucks for a jar of *high UMF manuka honey.*

You can combine some of these ingredients to concoct your own healing tea, or you may find a nice formulation in the health food store. In a sensitive child, or a baby who is rather new to solid foods, you may want to try ingredients one at a time in order to see how your child responds to them.

For the caretaker looking for further natural antimicrobial action, **garlic** has been shown to fight against *E. coli* and many other intestinal infectious bacteria, including antibiotic-resistant bacteria, as well as fighting yeasts, viruses, and parasites.

Probiotics

Probiotic supplements are shown to have moderate benefits for children suffering from diarrheal illnesses. They can be given to even the youngest breastfed or formula-fed infant. One needs to be sure they're milk free if the child is allergic.

A large review of European studies found the probiotic **Lactobacillus rhamnosus GG** significantly shortened the length of diarrheal illnesses. Though most probiotics are bacteria, a fungal probiotic known as **Saccharomyces boulardii** has also been found promising for treating diarrhea in children. These two probiotic strains are reported to be among the most successful of those studied for treating and preventing diarrhea in children. Other studies have shown specific success using these products against rotavirus, *Salmonella*, and *Candida* infections, often shortening child illnesses in industrialized countries by a couple of days. Treatment with both of these microbes together may be ideal. Another review finds *L. reuteri* to also be effective in children. If the products you find have other additional strains, that's fine and probably beneficial.

Breastfeeding mother can take probiotics herself and pass a stronger balance of probiotics to baby through her milk. Some moms provide pediatric probiotics directly to an exclusively breastfed baby. This should not interfere with the immune bubble provided by exclusive breastfeeding.

The occasional baby gets a little fussy from probiotics fed directly to him, for unknown reasons. Some health professionals suggest that this is related to a die-off of unwanted bacteria. Starting with a small dosage and gradually increasing the dose should help when this occurs.

Industry additions of probiotics to infant formulas have not yet proven effective. Adding your own fresh probiotic supplements to your baby's formula at home (not before warming) may be effective, especially when accompanied by a prebiotic. Prebiotics and probiotics are discussed in more detail in Chapter 16, "Healing Baby's Gut for Lifelong Health."

Preventing Spread of Infectious Diarrhea

In general, in a healthy family, I consider excessive hygienic practices to only interfere with maintaining a varied, experienced, and protective flora, but when there's an easily sickening bug lurking, it's a different story. It certainly can be miserable when much of the family is sick at the same time. Keeping sick children away from well children is likely quite a task, but efforts to do so are recommended. When there's a bug in the house, a worthwhile effort would likely be to provide healthy meals and favorite nutritional or herbal supplements

such as vitamins C and D, *Echinacea*, and the grape seed extract, resveratrol, for the whole family (with breastfed baby's through mom's milk).

Probiotic usage can moderately reduce the risk of acquiring antibiotic-caused diarrhea when taking antibiotics. It would take too large a study to determine the risk reduction provided for the general population with various exposures to contagious infections, and I see no studies on protecting household members, yet we know that those with healthy flora generally become infected less often. I think it couldn't hurt to give probiotic supplements or fermented products to all household members daily when an infectious diarrhea is in the house.

As mentioned before, viral or bacterial particles are found suspended in the air around infected individuals. Certain diarrheal infections, including certain food poisonings, can be spread in this manner. The greatest density is around an area where vomiting recently occurred or where diarrhea was released. Some bacteria are also released into the air during cleaning of surfaces. Good ventilation and good hygiene around diapers, toilets, and vomit areas are important. It's also important to be sure that baby's diapers are well covered to prevent even the most minute amount of leaking (though a bare bottom outdoors in warm weather can sometimes be a convenient way to deal with baby's diarrhea). Soap or standard cleaning agents are sufficient in cleaning contaminated surfaces.

Don't use antibacterial products. Antibacterial soaps have not been shown to be any more effective in removing microbes than standard soaps. **Triclosan**, the ingredient used in most antibacterial products including soaps, wipes, and hand sanitizers, absorbs into the system and is strongly suspected to be a hormone disruptor—affecting thyroid hormone as well as estrogen—and to be a mild carcinogen. Scientists also fear that triclosan use may lead to the development of resistant bacteria. This unwanted chemical is already bio-accumulating in our waterways and affecting fish. Chloroxylenol, another antibacterial sanitizer product, is toxic when inhaled or ingested. Fragrances added to these products represent a wide range of chemicals, but a large portion contain phthalates or other toxic ingredients and, as a whole, they're placed high on toxicity scales.

Though the mechanical action of hand washing or wiping surfaces clean provides the greatest portion of microbe removal, standard non-antibacterial soaps are found to work better than water alone and are quite adequate for removing infective bacteria from hands and surfaces. Ethanol or alcohol found in many products do absorb into the skin and may not be desirable for use by children, though they are not highly toxic. Brief use of these with good rinsing may be fine and use by adults is of little concern. They are shown to be effective in lowering bacteria and viruses on hands and surfaces and are sometimes found superior to soap and water alone, though two studies measuring C. *diff* contamination specifically found soap and water to work better than alcohol-based products. Oregano oil, thyme oil, and similar ingredients found in natural sanitizing products are shown to be both effective and safe.

Feeding the Sick Child on Solid Foods

Of course, if diarrhea is determined or suspected to be the result of an intolerance to certain foods, total elimination of any traces of any suspected foods is wise. Recovery should then be rather quick. After giving the intestines some time to heal, days beyond the point of return to normal stooling, you can begin experimenting with suspect foods if desired. Re-introduction of foods one at a time can allow for discovery of which may be the actual offenders.

If baby is vomiting regularly, it's often advised to stop giving foods for some hours while giving only oral rehydration solutions, as described earlier. Once vomiting is reduced, you can return to giving foods to a baby who typically receives solid foods. Food should always be in sight but not strongly encouraged. On the other hand, fluid, formula, or breastmilk intake is always important, and moderate encouragement should continue when appropriate.

There is a time-honored tradition for feeding children with diarrhea, known as the **BRAT diet**. BRAT stands for bananas, rice, applesauce, and plain toast. These are in addition, of course, to the child's baby milk and any rehydration fluids and are only for the child who has already started solid foods. These foods are known to be gentle on the tummy and add a little binding fiber. Whereas much apple juice could possibly increase diarrhea, apple sauce has a special fiber known as pectin that can help to reduce the liquid content of stools a tad. Truly, the BRAT diet should serve only as a suggestion for foods that may fare well in a sick child. There is no reason to avoid many other foods if the child may have an appetite for them.

Yogurt can add some good flora, and the lactose in milk yogurt is largely digested by the bacteria in it. There are coconut, almond, and soy varieties for the cow-milk intolerant child. Chicken soup is, of course, another time-honored tradition that can provide good gentle nutrition, especially when the broth is homemade from boiling bones and joints for a long time. Acidic fruits, such as citrus or pineapple, may be mildly irritating to baby's upset tummy. Fatty foods may increase diarrhea in some unhealthy adult guts but doesn't have this effect so much in children. Fats may be absorbed more easily than complex carbohydrates during a diarrhea bout, thereby providing useful calories. Foods known to typically bring a little gas, such as broccoli, cabbage, and beans, are healthy foods but may not be the best choices right now. Raw vegetables and any whole corn kernels often don't digest well and so may not be beneficial to the sick child.

These are only guidelines that many parents find effective. If a sick child has a poor appetite but does crave certain foods, those may be just what they need.

Some Final Thoughts

Your affection, attention, close observation, avoidance of unnecessary drugs, and provision of good hydration and nourishment will see baby through her diarrheal illness with healthy success.

Hard Poop

Causes of Constipation and Withholding

A simple case of constipation in a child can quickly turn into a big one, and then it can become a chronic problem, causing frequent pain and unwanted use of medications. On occasion, chronic constipation can lead to threatening consequences, such as a condition called megacolon. Constipation in young children can be quite challenging and uncomfortable, often carrying great emotional overtones. It can be equally frustrating for parents, who share their child's obvious discomfort and who want to resolve the issue without causing emotional discords or dependence on laxatives.

Very rarely, a baby is born with a little abnormality that interrupts proper stooling. Typically, this is discovered and addressed early on. Also rarely, something can cause an obstruction later on. An enlarged hard abdomen and a baby crying in desperation are warning signs that need to be addressed quickly.

The cause of constipation is seldom a physical disorder; rather, constipation is more often a consequence of diet, reactions to diet, and resultant behaviors.

One researcher reports that constipation is as common in children as asthma or ADHD and is as costly to our health system, yet constipation receives far less attention in public health campaigns. More public awareness of child constipation could certainly help caretakers prevent the distressing cycle.

Especially in toddlers, **withholding** of stool is a common challenge that requires delicate attention. During or after potty training, rectal leaking and soiling of underwear is sometimes interpreted as behavioral insecurity or defiance rather than recognized for what it is: a direct result of constipation.

Is It Constipation?

Constipation has multiple medical definitions, depending on age, timings, and various symptoms. Different sets of criteria lead to different cases being labeled as constipation and to a difference in the attention each child receives. We aren't going to discuss these diagnostic criteria. If a child is uncomfortable, we want to try to help him. If the problem persists, we want to investigate the cause and try to remedy it. Painful, time-consuming, toilet-clogging, or skin-tearing poop is not healthy poop, and it needs attention. Generally, if baby spends much time straining in unsuccessful efforts to poop, he has a problem. If stool is firm to hard and is accompanied by cries, it's a concern. Although medical criteria require constipation symptoms to last for at least 2 weeks before warranting attention, the truth is that, in little ones, one small brush with clogged intestines can quickly turn into a big predicament. My usage of the term *constipation* may not fit into proper definitions, but I'll use the term for hard, slow moving, or painful cases of poop that we don't prefer our children to experience.

Painful, time-consuming, toilet-clogging, or skin-tearing poop is not healthy poop, and it needs attention.

In order to become disagreeably hard, stool usually has to hang around in the colon and rectum for a few days while the colon continues to absorb water from it. Some babies have hard, uncomfortable poops almost every day though. Constipated poops may consist of a lot of firm dry pellets or they may be larger segmented chunks. Some parents report stools being passed that are nearly as thick as a coke can and that clog the toilet. Hard poop may cause a painful little tear along the rectal wall, inside the anus, or a tear in the anus itself, that is revealed by a red streak of blood along the stool or by blood on tissue paper. None of these poops are easy to pass and none are a sign of health.

Beyond some straining and maybe grunting, a constipated baby may be quite colicky and may cry as the stool is passing. Some babies vomit with constipation. An older child may frequently report abdominal pain that comes and goes.

If your child's colic or abdominal pain complaints go away after passing a good amount of stool, you can probably blame her pain on constipation.

If you think your baby has missed pooping for a few days and you are wondering whether he's constipated, you can feel his abdomen. If it's generally hard and tight, or if you are able to feel some hard portions when pressing around with deep gentle pressure, baby is likely constipated. A finding of hard stool just inside the rectum confirms constipation, for the parent who feels comfortable exploring here with a finger. Stool blockage can be up higher, so absence of stool in the rectum does not eliminate the possibility of constipation. The benefits of a little rectal exam are that you can insert petroleum jelly, or another good lubricant, that will ease the eventual passage, and the stimulus may cause the stool to pass.

If a child has had diarrhea, it could take 2 or 3 days to build up enough poop for the next normal passage. Some parents are surprised by this occurrence and worry about constipation, but the stool will typically come out soft, if fluid loss has been adequately replaced. On occasion, a bout of diarrhea can lead to a bout of constipation.

A few weeks or months after birth, babies typically reduce the frequency of their poops. Sometimes the transition happens rather suddenly, causing concern in parents who are used to changing dirty diapers several times a day. Eventually, babies may poop only once per day or even just twice per week, which isn't uncommon. As long as things go smoothly, there should be no major concern. Many exclusively breastfed babies will go 7 or 10 or even several days more between stools. When stool is finally passed, there will be a lot of it, but usually it is neither hard nor painful. This infrequent stooling is quite common, is not believed to be harmful, and is not constipation. You might consider doing a little investigating though, as most of us can agree that it doesn't seem to represent a system that is functioning optimally. Some babies fuss, strain, get red-faced, and maybe even grunt when passing very normal, peanut-buttery poops. This also is not constipation.

Soiling: Your Child Has Accidents in His Pants

Squirts of runny poop, in the absence of a good amount of bowel movement, actually signify a bad case of constipation. These squirts are different from a watery diarrhea explosion, which more often comes out green. Rather, the colon becomes blocked and backed up with accumulated hard stool, leaving new poop coming in from higher up to squeeze and squirt its way around the blockage before excess moisture is absorbed from it. Such occurrence can lead to uncontrollable soiling of underwear in a previously potty-trained child.

Five percent of children who cannot successfully keep underclothing free of stool have some kind of damage to, or irregularity of, their anal sphincter. In the other 95%, soiling is from constipation. Don't chastise a child for leaks in his underpants. It's not laziness, carelessness, unwillingness, or defiance; it may be a problem with his sphincter control, and most likely it's a sign he needs help with constipation. Such staining squirts in diapers or pants can fool caretakers of a constipated child. It's possible to lose track and be unaware of the actual deficiency in stool production, especially when multiple people are in charge of diapering or bottom-wiping at the potty.

When a child is this impacted, they must have their rectum and any higher blockages fully cleared out with some method. This disimpaction is only the beginning of the process toward turning this tendency around for good.

Functional Constipation

Only 5% of the time is constipation in a child caused by a distinct physical abnormality, such as a malformation, a twisting of or growth in the intestine, or a neuromuscular, hormonal, or digestive abnormality. Most constipation is caused by diet, reaction to diet, or behavior. This is referred to as having a **functional** cause, as opposed to an organic cause, which is discussed a bit later. Sometimes, the term functional is thrown out in such a way as to sound dismissive, but don't take it that way. When the doctor uses this term, it's really a matter of relief to her, as she's been able to eliminate more serious causes that will require more serious remedies, and that's her most important purpose. Most commonly, some sort of laxative is prescribed at this point, but caregivers can do a lot more to remedy the situation and to reduce future bouts.

Changes in a child's daily routine can cause stool irregularities. A busy home holiday or vacation travel can present unfamiliar people, heightened activities, altered diet and eating schedules, and different levels and kinds of attention. A disruption, such as a move to a new home or beginning a preschool program, can also alter a child's stooling pattern. Some children just don't want to stop playing to go and use the potty. They keep ignoring signals, and eventually stool gets harder. When some such occurrence leads to one difficult poop and then things return to normal, that's just something to take note of. Keep in mind, however, that more serious and chronic cases of constipation most commonly begin with one uncomfortable brush with hard poop.

Once a child experiences painful pooping, or exhaustive pooping, they commonly desire to avoid experiencing that pain or work again, and hence they consciously avoid pooping when the urge comes.

Use of a space heater near a baby can reportedly cause some dehydration and, consequently, constipation.

An occasional functional cause of constipation in babies is an inability to control the anal sphincter well—unable to relax it properly to allow stool to pass. This improves with age.

Once a child experiences painful pooping, or exhaustive pooping, they commonly desire to avoid experiencing that pain or work again, and hence they consciously avoid pooping when the urge comes. Even if a nice soft stool is on its way, it will become drier and firmer the longer it sits in the rectum. Now this harder stool, when finally released, causes discomfort and only goes to confirm the child's fears and to encourage further withholding. As stool backs up and enlarges, intestinal walls stretch and muscle tone reduces, allowing stools to grow wider and reducing the ability of the intestinal walls to push them out. Frequent overriding of the body's signal that it's time to poop also teaches the mind and body to ignore such urges, further reducing adequate stooling. Eventual passage of this harder, bigger stool can cause tears along the rectal wall or in the anus, bringing even greater pain. Clearly, constipation can become a terrible, self-perpetuating cycle.

This cycle is the most common cause of persistent child constipation problems, especially in toddlers and preschoolers. Often a child will release a little bit of stool but not empty himself completely. This can cause progressive and problematic backup. It's important for parents to not only monitor how often their child is moving her bowels but to keep track of the quantity of stools. The commonness of such constipation developments is the main reason caretakers will also want to pay some attention to every little case of difficult poop.

Dietary Causes

The most common initial cause of functional constipation is reactions to diet. This may be a sensitivity reaction to the milk or soy proteins in baby's formula, corn syrup or corn solids in formula, or a reaction to some other formula ingredient. This can also be sensitivity to something in breastfeeding mom's diet.

At least four different recent studies on diet and recurring constipation in children found cow milk allergy to be involved in approximately 80% of chronic constipation cases.

Sometimes food-sensitive babies will alternate between constipation and bouts of diarrhea.

Different from a sensitivity reaction, the high iron in infant formulas directly causes firming of stools and affects some babies this way more strongly than others.

At least four different recent studies on diet and recurring constipation in children found cow milk allergy to be involved in approximately 80% of chronic constipation cases. This is huge and an important factor for you to investigate. Many parents also find this link with infrequently pooping breastfeeders. Although laboratory confirmation of milk allergy was performed in the majority of children in these studies, a few intolerance cases were determined simply by dietary elimination and re-introduction.

A child who consumes large amounts of milk products (besides infant formula), and few vegetables, may simply be magnesium deficient. If such a child does not have other symptoms of food intolerance, such as rashes, a red ring around anus, or reflux, then magnesium deficiency is a possible cause of constipation. Magnesium supplements will cause stool softening in anyone, regardless of magnesium status. For this reason, it's important to distinguish whether magnesium supplementation is correcting a deficiency or simply masking a symptom of inflammatory intestinal intolerance reactions to milk. Magnesium blood tests are not reliable indicators of magnesium stores. If you monitor your child's response to ongoing magnesium supplementation, the true issue will be revealed because, if the child was deficient, symptoms should resolve after some weeks of supplementation. Other symptoms will be ongoing with food intolerance, and stools will gradually harden again, even with ongoing supplementation.

Constipation can result from reactions to other foods in addition to, or instead of, milk. IgE food allergy blood tests are not considered effective in children under 2 years. Beyond that age, these tests are often not positive in food-reacting children, even when they have very definite reactions to foods.

Patch tests catch some cases that IgE tests miss but not all. Skin prick tests are less effective. Your removal of 100% of suspected food allergens, and then re-introducing these one at a time, is the best means of determining whether and what foods are involved in your baby's uncomfortable constipation.

Such food reactions can certainly begin at any age. As baby grows older, the number of possible causes for constipation grows, too. At the same time, children can also outgrow food allergies—often during the toddler years.

As a child begins solid foods, constipation may be caused by the initial effects on digestion. Constipation after first food introductions doesn't always mean food sensitivities. An increase in grain or fat consumption can incite some constipation. Though fiber is good stuff where healthy pooping is concerned, if a baby starting solid foods receives plenty of fiber foods without added liquids for the fiber to absorb, this can plug baby up. At the same time, a low fiber diet can make things quite dry, especially if the only liquids are formula or cow milk. Low fiber foods include refined grains, such as white rice cereal or white flour crack-ers, eggs, meats, dairy, and juices. A switch from breastmilk to formula, a switch in formulas, or a move to cow milk commonly hardens things up. Consuming large amounts of dairy products in general is known to encourage constipation. When it's suspected that a switch or certain alteration in diet is the cause of constipation, it's best to return to the softer stool producing diet.

Organic Constipation

In contrast to functional constipation, **organic** constipation is when hard stools are caused by some organ malfunction or a response to a medication. The term organic refers to processes that are more medically observable and measurable than in functional causes. Hormonal disorders, neuro-logical disorders, and anatomical abnormali-ties fall under organic causes.

> *Reflux medications and simple antacids can cause constipation in infants.*

Reflux medications and simple antacids can cause constipation in infants. ADHD medications, some epilepsy drugs, cough suppressants, and many other drugs can also plug up a child. Iron supple-ments often cause constipation.

Celiac disease, which is one kind of gluten intolerance, receives more medical recognition than other food sensitivities, outside of immediately life-threatening food allergies. This is because it creates distinct characteristics that are more easily measured in the lab for medical interpretation, compared to many other non-immediate food reactions. Hence, celiac disease tends to earn the label of an organic disorder whereas other food intolerances are called functional.

Hypothyroidism, a disorder that occurs when not enough thyroid hormone is available, is another potential cause of constipation in a baby. Thyroid hormone controls the rate of body processes. Babies are often born with enough hormone from mother's blood, but hypothyroid symptoms can turn up in a baby during the first weeks or months after birth. Symptoms could also appear years later. Some signs that should incite suspicion that hypothyroidism may be the cause of regular constipation in an infant are being born large or late, experiencing prolonged jaundice after birth, not feeding well, or possibly having cold limbs or a hoarse cry.

Cystic fibrosis is a cause of constipation as thick mucus clogs the digestive as well as the respiratory system.

Megacolon and Hirschsprung's Disease

The term **megacolon** refers to an enlarged section of colon. Megacolon can be acquired when a child continually withholds stool, and a portion of the intestine becomes progressively stretched. The muscles in that section weaken, and the section of colon may even become paralyzed. Periods of total blockage may result and serious infection can occur above the obstruction. Both situations require critical medical attention. The possibility of dangerous megacolon is one main reason that constipation in children requires earnest attention from caregivers. Prolonged training of proper bowel habits, and persistent constipation treatment, can usually heal a child's megacolon.

An abnormality known as **Hirschsprung's disease** is an occasional organic cause for child constipation. When the nerves that control the muscle contractions responsible for moving stool through the colon are not completely formed as a fetus develops, the condition is called Hirschsprung's. It's a congenital form of megacolon. Serious buildup of hardening stool is the result. This disorder is sometimes hereditary and, other times, it may just be an alteration in fetal development. It may affect one small section of the colon or larger parts of the intestine.

Hirschsprung's is typically caught in the first few days after birth, when no pooping appears, but milder cases may not be recognized for some time. Occasionally, the early signs are diarrhea, which can lead the diagnosis off track. Generally, surgical removal of the non-functioning section of intestine is performed, which results in a well-functioning system.

Botulism

Botulism is a fear-striking term. Although it's actually a rare disease, parents tend to hear warnings about botulism in terms of feeding honey or corn syrup to an infant.

Honey often contains spores of the bacterium, *Clostridium botulinum*. A baby exposed to uncooked honey could rarely become infected with this bacterium. As these bacteria multiply, they release a potent toxin—have you heard of Botox? This toxin can cause gradual paralysis over many days and, untreated, possibly death. One of the first signs of botulism tends to be constipation. Most botulism cases occur in babies under 6 months of age, but the rule of thumb is to not give honey to a baby under a year old. Older children and adults have mature digestive systems that easily handle these tiny spores and are not at risk of botulism from eating honey.

Not only in honey, the spores of *botulinum* are quite commonly found in soil as well as in the dust in vacuum cleaner bags. The greatest risk factor for infant botulism is not from honey but from living on or near a farm. Of course, it is extremely rare for babies to develop botulism, even living in a world full of dirt and dust.

Curiously, though fear over corn syrup and botulism continues to be passed around, corn syrup, such as Karo syrup, is often prescribed to treat constipation in babies. Supposedly, an actual case of botulism has never been caused by corn syrup.

If a baby develops constipation along with some weakness, such as a reduced ability to hold his head up or to suck, or his eyes stray unusually, these symptoms should be brought to the attention of a doctor.

Infrequent Poop in an Exclusively Breastfed Baby

Hard poop constipation is quite rare in a baby fed nothing but mother's milk. It's so uncommon that a medical consult is probably in order if it arises. Infrequent or hard poop in the first weeks after birth especially call for attention, as a possible anatomical or neurological shortfall could need attention. Once formula, iron supplements, or solid foods enter a breastfed baby's diet, hard stools are more of a possibility. If your breastfed baby has been temporarily exposed to a few bottles of formula and is now suffering from firmer stools, probiotic treatment for both mother and baby may help return baby's stools to more typical, looser breastfed stools. If your breastfed baby regularly receives formula supplements, you will want to use the guidelines in the next chapter for treating formula-fed babies.

Of course, the first matter of importance when stooling is infrequent, whether hard or not, is to be sure baby is eating adequately. As long as baby is

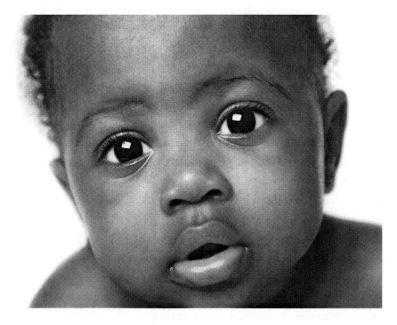

soaking several diapers daily with urine and has been gaining weight (after the first several days), you should be assured she is feeding well. If baby started out with regular poops in the first weeks after birth, you can be more assured that adequate feeding is not an issue; however, a reduction in feeding frequency to follow a timed feeding schedule can reduce baby's intake, and hence mother's milk production. Remember that if stool is building up inside, baby will gain of a few ounces per day and then lose it when much stool is released. Keep this in mind when going by weight to determine adequate feeding. Urine soaked diapers are a sure sign of milk intake and, if the color of urine is light, that's also a good sign.

As mentioned, some exclusively breastfed babies will go 7 to 10 days, and dare I say even 17 days between poops, without having any hard or painful stools. This is common enough that most doctors call it normal. In my experience, any such baby I've worked with has had some other issues going on and has benefited from working through the issues. You may wish to think of it like constipation, in terms of searching for causes, especially when it regularly goes beyond 3 days. However, laxative treatments should only be considered if the stools are hard.

If you've gone through some unsuccessful sleuthing and your infrequently pooping nursling seems otherwise quite happy and healthy, I wish to comfort you by telling you that it happens a lot, medical doctors are largely unconcerned, and babies generally come through it without big problems.

The most likely cause of infrequent stooling in a breastfed baby is sensitivity to foods in mom's diet. Sometimes, a long period of no stool is ended by a diarrheal explosion. I'm certain that, in this child, something is going on. If your infrequent pooper has this or other symptoms—such as colic, rashes, reflux, waking with screams, excess and uncomfortable gas, or frequent ear infections—there is even more reason to suspect intolerance to cow milk, gluten, and/or other foods in your diet. It's certainly worth some dietary elimination trials to see whether baby can be made to be more comfortable and likely more healthy. I find it quite common for food sensitive babies to come from moms with intestinal issues. Often when a breastfeeding mom goes on an elimination diet for her baby, she ends up feeling better herself.

Hard Poop in Formula-Fed Infants

Constipation is more common in a baby receiving mixed breastmilk and formula feeds, or only formula. Again, if pooping is not going well in the first few weeks, it's best to have baby examined. After this age, it's likely the baby's individual response to the formula itself that is causing constipation.

Constipation and Iron-Fortified Formulas

Two studies reporting no link between high iron infant formulas and constipation in babies are referred to often in old and new discussions of the issue. There appears to be only one more published research study covering this topic since these 1980 and 1988 formula company-tied papers. The 1995 Mead Johnson study compares four of their own formulas and demonstrates double the constipation in their higher iron (8% hard stools) versus lower iron (4% hard stools) Enfamil. Oddly, these iron level links to stool hardness are not mentioned in their study summary, nor elsewhere. They found less stool hardness with their hydrolyzed Nutrimigen, also containing high iron, and reported much more constipation with their high iron soy-based ProSobee. Clearly, iron is only one variable that can affect stool hardness, with allergy being another chief variable, and allergy being lower with hydrolyzed formulas.

Formula companies claim that high iron formulas do not increase poop hardness. Although I have no outright reason to discount this claim, I also do not doubt the observations of a multitude of mothers who report improvements in their babies' constipation when switching to lower iron formulas. Don't take it from me though. If you happen to switch to a lower iron formula and believe it is helping, you can try going back to the higher iron formula again, if you want to be certain. On the other hand, you could leave well enough alone. You can always return to higher iron 2 or 3 months later, if you wish to, when it's likely to pose less of a poop problem. Most babies will have enough iron stores at birth to get them through their first few months, at least.

Prolonged higher iron exposure, when unneeded, is also linked to reduced mental abilities.

High iron fortifications of infant formulas are made because iron absorption from formulas is low and because iron deficiency anemia was once common among formula-fed infants. Once it was learned that anemia was linked mostly to homemade formulas and straight cow milk feeding, anemia significantly reduced, yet the high iron in U.S. formulas stayed. It's been shown that no good evidence supports the United States' use of higher iron levels. Additionally, high iron competes with other valuable minerals for absorption. This could potentially lead to mild deficiencies in minerals such as zinc or selenium. European countries typically carry lower iron formulas.

What's better? There are definitely unwanted health repercussions from iron deficiency anemia, including an increased rate of infections and slightly reduced intelligence. Babies who were born prematurely or who've often had blood in their stools are at higher risk for such anemia. Less commonly addressed, however, is the fact that prolonged higher iron exposure, when unneeded, is also linked to reduced mental abilities. What to do? Personally, I think that as blood tests for iron levels are simple and inexpensive, there's no reason not to rely on facts, rather than guessing. If a parent is worried or warned about use of a lower iron formula, a simple blood test can suggest the best course.

Some Final Thoughts

Finding the cause of your child's constipation can lead you toward preventing, rather than just treating, symptoms. For the most part, we'll find that what goes in has a lot to do with what comes out, and how it comes out.

Caring for Constipation and Withholding

Studies show that 20 to 30% of those who have difficult constipation problems as young children continue to have significant constipation challenges on into adulthood. It has also been demonstrated that the sooner a child's constipation problem is addressed, the less likely he is to suffer during adulthood. By sleuthing the cause of your child's constipation rather than only treating symptoms—and by working to train and educate your child well in terms of his intestinal health—you may reduce or prevent a great amount of suffering throughout his life.

When a bad case of constipation exists, the recommended response generally includes three steps: clearing out the poop, correcting the factors that are to blame, and re-training the digestive system. A wide range of options are available for getting stubborn stool moved out of children. Some will be a better fit for you and your child than others. Infant and toddler systems are delicate and easily disturbed. All laxative options, natural or drug, have the potential to disrupt tiny systems. It's quite useful to be aware of the wide range of options available, and their pros and cons. At the same time, it's important for your child's health provider to be involved in the process.

Responding to Infrequent Poop in Exclusively Breastfed Babies

When an exclusively breastfed baby is pooping less than once every couple of days and the stools are not hard, it is mostly the cause of the infrequent stooling that needs attention. The delayed poop itself does not need fixing unless parents feel their baby is suffering direct discomfort from the buildup of stool. Discomfort can be suggested when baby is much happier for the first couple of days after pooping than she is in the last days before a long awaited poop. If so, there are many ways to speed things up without giving foreign foods to a young nursling. Different parents and healthcare providers have different comfort zones when it comes to long periods without poop, and I can't blame them. Some can't stand to see 3 days go by without a movement. Others give up patience at 10 days.

Although some doctors will recommend giving juice to exclusively breastfed infants—even to newborns—please don't do it. Whether a cause for slow stooling is apparent or not, if you or your doctor decides that you should encourage some bowel movement, this certainly is not the time to wean baby from exclusive breastmilk by giving juice or formula in effort to make baby poop. Either of these would only cause an undesirable change in baby's flora and damage the highly protective state provided to exclusively breastfed babies. This would not be a step toward healing baby's slow-acting intestines. Eventually, formula would more likely thicken stools than speed them up, although irritation from the initial introduction of formula can lead to diarrhea.

> *Although some doctors will recommend giving juice to exclusively breastfed infants—even to newborns—please don't do it.*

As a rule of thumb, it's not advised to give water to breastfeeding infants before they are eating solid foods. They should receive plenty of water from their milk, and added water could reduce their desire to nurse. Although many professionals recommend giving water for slow stooling, studies suggest that extra water does not help constipation when the baby is not dehydrated.

Most of the physical methods mentioned below are ideal to try for breastfeeding infants. If these don't bring the results you desire, insertion of a half pediatric glycerin suppository is considered not harmful when not used too frequently, and it will at least make the parents more comfortable.

In the absence of hard stools, any kind of stool softener or agent that attracts water into the intestines will likely give your baby diarrhea and put him at risk for electrolyte imbalance. Most pediatricians also would not prescribe a stimulant to get stools moving when there are no signs of impaction. You really want to be sure there's a good reason before trying any of these if stools are not hard. Lactulose may be a good option if more help is really needed and if you wish to reduce the use of glycerin suppositories. Lactulose would neither replace breastmilk calories nor disturb breastfed flora. Because PEG kills some good florae, it would not be a choice I would make. These are all discussed further on.

Responding to Constipation in Formula-Fed Infants

If hard stools are a problem for your baby who receives infant formula, a switch of formula—possibly to a more hydrolyzed version—may be helpful, or baby may respond better to a lower iron or a soy formula. A really constipated formula-fed infant may do best with an amino acid formula such as Neocate, EleCare, or Nutrimigen AA. Use of one of these would eliminate most formula allergens, except for corn and any chemical residues to which some babies may react.

Newborns are not ready to be digesting juice, which only replaces their better nutrition formula. Try other means to clear backed-up poop out of a young infant. Some physical methods may help. Formula-fed babies may be ready by 4 months to receive a little pear or prune juice, or some other dietary efforts, to help soften their stools. These are often prescribed sooner, and a little may be fine. One of the sugar treatment options, discussed later in this chapter, or a half-glycerin suppository, may be your next best option before using medications.

Physical Measures First

Although it's common for medications to be prescribed right away for a constipated child, gentler techniques can be tried first in attempt to move that poop out. These methods are especially useful in babies who are too young for juice. It's best to attempt physical techniques right after a feeding, as the intestines are naturally stimulated by each intake of food or liquid.

The simplest technique to try when wanting to encourage baby to poop is gently inserting a **lubricated Q-tip** or rectal thermometer no more than an inch into baby's rectum and wiggling it around a bit. Hold baby's knees up to her chest while doing this. Results may be immediate, so be ready. If it doesn't work immediately, the lubrication in baby's anus will help to smooth and comfort a movement when it does occur.

Some moms use *castor oil packs* with their babies. One study with elderly people found that castor oil packs helped, not to speed up stooling, but to soften stools. There's no reason it shouldn't work for children or babies as well. It's an age old remedy without toxicity concerns. Soak a cloth in castor oil. Place it on baby's tummy, and cover with a hot water bottle or a carefully monitored heating pad. In case you have access to live castor bean plants, don't use them. They contain a poison, ricin. Only commercially processed castor oil is safe.

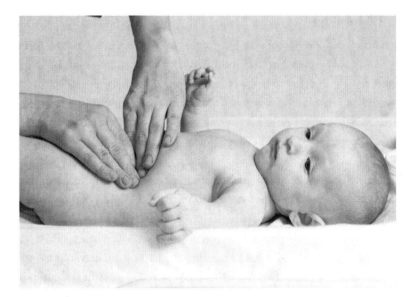

Abdominal massage may do the trick. Press gently, but deeply, on baby's lower right (to your left) abdomen, and work your way up to the bottom of the rib cage. Move more lightly across to the left side, and then press more deeply again, moving down baby's left side. This follows the path of baby's large intestine (colon). Repeat this several times. Move as if trying to move the poop along inside the colon. You just may be. This abdominal massage may also stimulate some natural squeezing movements that the intestines use to move poop along. You may be able to feel where stool is blocked, and you may even find yourself physically pushing poop out. Some moms use a little *peppermint oil* in this massage and find it helpful.

Some *leg exercising* can be added to the abdominal massage. Hold baby's shins and move his legs as if peddling a bicycle but pressing into the abdomen a little with each rotation. If you can encourage your baby to actively kick his legs, this can be beneficial, too, as can some speed-crawling if your baby is a crawler. Encouraging plenty of running may be helpful in a toddler or older child. A bouncy dance in dad's arms or some time in a *vibrating chair* may encourage gas bubbles to move along, thereby stimulating some other movements in the bowels.

Another physical technique favored by some parents is to press baby's back against your abdomen, holding her feet in your hands. Push her thighs into *her* abdomen. Baby may push her feet against your hands, causing her to bear down a bit, which would be helpful. Walk around like this, bouncing, gently pumping her legs against her abdomen. Don't do it over pricey carpeting.

Magnesium is an important mineral to health. Supplemental magnesium is known to be an effective natural laxative. **Epsom bath salts** consist of magnesium and sulfate. Both magnesium and sulfate safely absorb across the skin when taking a warm Epsom salt bath, soothing intestinal and other muscles. A warm soak may be just the thing to get baby's bowels moving. Levels of magnesium absorbed from a bath are lower than prescribed oral treatments, and it would be highly unlikely that an overdose of magnesium could be absorbed through the skin when using normal doses in occasional baths. Typically, we can all benefit from a little more magnesium.

Diet for a Constipated Child

Once a child has started solid foods, there are more reasons for constipation—and also more options for reducing and preventing it. Be certain your child drinks ample liquids, but there's no need to push high amounts of fluids. Studies do not support pushing of fluids.

> *Be certain your child drinks ample liquids, but studies do not support pushing of fluids.*

Fruits and vegetables are your fiber-filled, flora-feeding target foods for improving constipation and overall intestinal health. If your child is not much of a vegetable eater, fruits are amply helpful and nutritious when no sugars are added. Whole grains (when not intolerant), bran, and flax-added cereals can improve poops, as can tolerated nuts.

Probiotic foods contain beneficial bacteria and can be quite valuable. Today, yogurts made from almond milk, rice, soy, and coconut, as well as cow milk, give plenty of choices for the food allergic child. Other probiotic food options include miso soup, sauerkraut, Spanish olives, pickles, tempeh, and poi, as well as kefir and a spectrum of other probiotic drinks. Use of probiotic foods alone will probably not clear out a constipated child, but they are shown to be a valuable part of a complete gut health program.

Choosing a Laxative

Many products can help to soften your child's stools and move them through. The first considerations are your child's age and whether she's started solid foods yet. Initially, you'll probably just know that some choices are more your style or more appropriate for your baby. Mostly, you may want to start out with simpler measures and then add on or switch to other efforts until you find the right combination of methods for your child. Even starting from medically prescribed dosages, you will eventually grow to find the right dose for your child that softens and speeds up pooping and that overrides any withholding behaviors, with a minimal amount of wateriness to the stools.

Whether a medically prescribed drug or plums fresh from your tree, anything that's going to get a stopped up colon moving again is apt to produce some uncomfortable sensations.

Suppositories and enemas can work quickly—within minutes. Many medications will work within hours. Prunes, juices, or fiber supplements may take closer to 24 hours to work.

If your child is seriously impacted, probably exhibited by leaking runny stool that has had to squeeze past the blockage, he may do best with medical means for initially clearing him out. With first cases of constipation, medical consultation is definitely valuable, even if you choose to try some more natural efforts first. With serious constipation, depending on the cause, your child will probably require your close supervision for some time, as his dietary and behavior challenges are being resolved. Nutritious, or at least non-chemical, options could be healthier long-term choices versus medical laxatives.

Medical laxatives are prescribed if your child is going in for a *colonoscopy*, where a little viewing scope is inserted into her bottom to look up through much of the colon to see if something is wrong. A wide variety of colon clearing plans are prescribed to prepare for this procedure. These generally include one or two of the laxatives discussed here. The colon needs to be perfectly cleaned out and the timing needs to be right. You will need to follow your doctor's plan well, so the view through the colonoscope is not impaired by leftover stool and so the colon is not still actively clearing at the time of the study. If you are interested in some alternative method, you can discuss it with the gastroenterologist ahead of time. He may not be able to approve it if he's not had personal experience with the option.

Whether a medically prescribed drug or plums fresh from your tree, anything that's going to get a stopped up colon moving again is apt to produce some uncomfortable sensations. Fiber and sugar laxatives can cause extra gas formation. Gas can build up behind the clogs, which causes discomfort until it finds its way through and helps to push stool through. Lots of jiggling of baby, or chasing your child around the playground, can get that gas moving through better and can relieve some of the discomfort. The drawing of water into the intestines or the stimulation of intestinal movements by laxatives can cause nausea and even some vomiting. Any laxatives can cause cramping or colicky pain. If any such symptoms are occurring, you then know the effort is working, at least partly. If you think your child is in severe pain, longer than it should take to move a big gas bubble, you'll want to make a call for advice.

With most any laxative given by mouth or by bottom, diarrhea can result if the laxative dosage given works too well. Fiber supplements are generally an exception to this rule. It's best to start out any laxative use gradually, even with prescribed doses, if there's time to wait. Be sure to replace lost liquids if diarrhea does occur. If laxative use frequently causes watery stools, baby's electrolyte balance can be disturbed. Good rehydration liquids can be given, as described in Chapter 10, "Caring for Loose Poop."

Natural Oral Laxatives

Prune juice, *pear juice*, or watery baby food *prunes* or *pears* are wonderful natural gentle laxatives for babies over 4 months of age who are not exclusively fed breastmilk. Two chief components of these fruits contribute to their stool softening and bulking effects. Baby food prunes, pears, plums, and prune juice are all high in both soluble and insoluble fibers (listed from highest to lowest) that help to bring water into the stool and add bulk to help push things through. Prunes and pears are also high in the natural sugar, **sorbitol**, which acts to draw water into the intestines. Prunes are dried from a high fiber variety of plum and contain significantly more fiber and sorbitol than pears, though some babies prefer and respond well to pears or pear juice, as well as apricot. My health preference would be to opt for the higher fiber, lower sugar, stewed or baby food prunes, rather than juices.

Simple **supplemental fiber** is known to be beneficial for constipation. Fiber attracts and retains water, and adds bulk to help push stool through. A great thing about fiber use is that, as well as lessening constipation, it also reduces diarrhea. Fiber normalizes stools and feeds healthy bacteria. Some gas discomfort may occur with initial use of fiber for constipation, as gas builds up behind stool blockages before they are moved out and as the child's flora adjust to the new healthy diet. Over time, the child should experience greater comfort than before the addition of fiber.

> *A great thing about fiber use is that, as well as lessening constipation, it also reduces diarrhea. Fiber normalizes stools and feeds healthy bacteria.*

Many sources state that fiber supplements are not recommended for children under 15 months or under 2 years of age—generally because it's just not well studied. Many individual doctors will recommend fiber for constipation at younger ages. A study by Ross Laboratories, in which 9 g of daily fiber was added to an infant formula and fed to babies 6 to 20 weeks old, found no nutritional or other difficulties. Although studying this high dose of fiber was useful, you'd want to give less. A teaspoon of a fiber supplement contains 3.5 g of fiber and may be a good starting dose for a toddler—starting with even less for an infant. You may wish to increase to a total of two teaspoons per day for a child over 2 years, if needed, and increase a little more as the child gets older.

Swallowing safety is the key concern when giving fiber to little ones. A spoonful of pure fiber is a sure choking hazard. Adding fiber to baby's bottle will thicken the liquid over time, so it's best to add only to the portion you expect baby to drink in the next 5 minutes or so. Divide the desired amount of fiber over a few bottles during the day. Little pinches of fiber can also be sprinkled onto watery spoonfuls of baby food.

Psyllium husks are a popular form of supplemental fiber. Psyllium goes quite nicely in gelatin. You can make your own Jell-O-like recipe with either plain gelatin or vegetarian pectin. Either are good helpful fiber themselves, then the added psyllium provides more oomph, and you can sweeten the mixture by using pear juice as your liquid, for a tasty stool softening treat. Psyllium powder can also be stirred into any food or added to a smoothie. Whatever concoction you create will need to be consumed rather quickly, before the stuff becomes too gummy. Give ample liquid to drink any time you feed psyllium or other fiber or bran to your child. Without added liquids, there is no water for the fiber to retain for stool softening. It can become thick and bulky in the digestive tract and can actually contribute to blockage, rather than clear it.

Among all the various kinds of laxatives available, psyllium seems to have the most potential for allergic reaction, though psyllium allergy is not common. Of course, a child can be allergic to any food, and rare allergic reactions are reported with all the chemical laxatives as well. If your child tends toward food allergies, you'll want to scan your choices of fiber supplements, pick the one that seems least likely to cause a reaction in your child, and then start out slowly.

Acacia from the acacia tree is another common fiber option. **Inulin** is a specific kind of fiber found in many vegetables, and many varieties of inulin supplements can be found. Barley malt extract acts similarly—sold as **Maltsupex**. If you already know that your child tolerates rice, oats, or wheat, you can find each of these sold in bran or fiber powder forms. Besides bulk powder fiber options, you can find shakers of fiber powders that can be easily sprinkled onto foods. Fiber gummies, fiber cereals, products labeled as *pre*-biotic supplements, and high fiber muffins are all available options. **Metamucil** sells a cookie wafer with psyllium and oat fiber.

One study looked at a mixture of acacia fiber, psyllium fiber, and fructose sugar, and compared the concoction to the commonly prescribed medication, PEG. The mixture and medication were found to be about equally beneficial in treating constipated children. I doubt there's anything magical about this exact mixture, but the research verifies that the use of fiber and laxative sugars is evidence based. Another study found psyllium superior to docusate, an often prescribed stool softener. Other research publications support the use of fiber supplements in constipated children as well. I bring these studies up because some medical reports describe simple, safe, natural food treatments as unproven alternative practices, yet almost no studies actually compare prescription drugs to natural methods. Several studies report that most prescription laxative products are also not well studied for safety or effectiveness in children.

You can make your own Jell-O-like recipe with either plain gelatin or vegetarian pectin. Added psyllium provides more oomph, and you can sweeten the mixture by using pear juice as your liquid, for a tasty stool softening treat.

Many commonly prescribed laxative products, including PEG, are not actually FDA approved for use in children. This doesn't mean they can't legally be prescribed for children or that they are necessarily harmful. Options for children and babies are very much needed. It just means these drugs haven't been well studied in children—or possibly in any population.

Magnesium supplementation is a mild and natural means of softening stools. *Natural Calm* and Kids Natural Calm Multi are magnesium products that are highly trusted by natural health-oriented moms. I've also heard of mothers using a magnesium lotion. *Milk of Magnesia* is a popular drugstore oral magnesium

product that's often prescribed by pediatricians. Appropriate dosing of magnesium for your baby or young child should be left up to your healthcare provider. Long-term, high dosage use could potentially cause magnesium overdose, chiefly when kidneys are weak. For constipation, you don't want a magnesium supplement that contains much calcium, as calcium stops things up. Studies are mixed on whether breastfeeding mothers can pass higher amounts of magnesium through their milk by taking supplements, but many mothers report positive results.

Aloe vera juice from the aloe plant has been used effectively to treat constipation for centuries, but Medline Plus recommends against children drinking aloe, and the FDA had aloe removed from over-the-counter laxative products in 2002. Concerns stemmed from a small number of reports worldwide of negative effects with prolonged use of high doses and from lack of safety studies, and some of these concerns were related to the natural intestine-stimulating **latex** portion of the plant that is used when making aloe juice. Although aloe gel is still wonderful to use on sunburned skin, drinking much latex-containing aloe juice may cause some kidney or other problems in children.

Senna is a time-trusted natural herb that stimulates movement in the intestines, encouraging bowel movements. Its usefulness is medically accepted, and it's sold in drug stores as *Senokot*. It's reportedly best used along with something that softens the stool, such as PEG, prune juice, or lactulose. The Senokot-S version comes with a stool softener included. Purchase of senna in bulk herbal form or even in capsules poses a dosing challenge unless you work with an experienced herbalist or naturopath. You can buy senna in pre-measured teabags and try a portion of one teabag's worth with your child. Increase the dose slowly, according to response. For the most part, although it's sold over the counter, medical advice on the usage and dosage in young children is best. On the package, Senokot provides a dosage recommendation for children over two. Some pediatricians do not recommend the use of senna under this age. As a stimulant-type laxative, prolonged use of senna can potentially lead to your child's intestines becoming dependent upon it for movement.

Mineral oil, sometimes called liquid paraffin, is a pure oil distilled from petroleum. It's often prescribed as a stool softener to be given to constipated children by mouth or sometimes as an enema. Because several vitamins dissolve in oil, there is a little worry that frequent use of mineral oil by mouth could reduce some vitamin absorption. One study found mineral oil to be more effective than senna. There once was concern over some toxins that could be found in poorly refined petroleum products, but any reputable brand today (labelled USP) is entirely free of such toxins. Although there are no toxic concerns over mineral oil, other oils are available that are actually healthy and nutritious. Why not use one of these instead?

Although there are no toxic concerns over mineral oil, other oils are available that are actually healthy and nutritious. Why not use one of these instead?

Health benefits of *coconut oil* and *palm oil* have been reported in science journals since the 1990s. Their valuable forms of fatty acids are found to be anti-inflammatory, and they're high in antioxidant vitamins A and E, as well as vitamin K. Your grandmother was raised on spoonfuls of *cod liver oil*, known for its vitamins A and D, and omega-3 fatty acids (like the DHA found in breastmilk and added to many formulas).

Flax seed oil is high in DHA precursors, is anti-inflammatory, and promotes the absorption of vitamins. Omega-3 fatty acids can help baby to recover from food allergies. A common dose of oil for laxative effects is a teaspoon per day for babies and 2 teaspoons for toddlers. Freshly ground flax seed meal—added to food, smoothie, or juice—can be an even better laxative than just the oil, as it has fiber too. Recommended doses are the same, one to two teaspoons in divided doses over the day.

Straight oils can be a swallowing challenge for infants. Many parents supplement infants over a few months old with a daily quarter teaspoon or so of cod liver oil, for the vitamin and omega-3 fatty acid benefits. Oils do not contain iron and would not interfere with exclusively breastfed flora, but dosages large enough to soften or speed up stooling could be too overwhelming for children under about 12 to 18 months. There are concerns about babies aspirating oil into their lungs if spitting up the oil. You can mix the oil with breastmilk or formula in a bottle, using a portion of the dose per bottle. Yes, shaking breastmilk breaks up some of its protective factors, but this is not being done to all of the child's breastmilk—just a portion.

Sugars are often suggested for treating constipated babies. Excess sugar draws water into the intestines, thereby softening stools. Some parents use simple white or brown sugar. **Karo syrup** is a brand of corn syrup that's often prescribed by doctors for constipated babies. Many ask whether they should give light or dark Karo syrup. It seems the two variations once had differences that they no longer have. Either one is fine, and Karo no longer has any botulism risk, if there ever was one.

Corn syrup and other simple sugar treatments may feed some undesirable flora in breastfed babies. The baby sugar, lactose, is known to promote beneficial bacteria. If a formula-fed infant is receiving formula with only lactose for sugar, she too may do better without adding simple sugars before solid foods are introduced. Flora may be able to recover from some sugar exposure, but if a baby is having stooling problems, likely the flora needs to be improved, not hampered.

Sugars may be more easily handled than juices are by very young babies. If not used often, sugars may feel safer than chemicals. Over 40% of calories in both breastmilk and formula come from sugars, and sugar is important for infant brain development. Used regularly, high doses can, of course, displace too much of the other important nutrition that baby milks must provide. **Molasses** contains a little iron, so it would not be appropriate for an exclusively breastfed child, but otherwise, molasses will contribute some vitamin and mineral nutrition along with its sugar. You can add one teaspoon of molasses, corn syrup, or sugar to a few ounces of water and feed this solution gradually to baby throughout the day.

> *Breastfeeding mother can take probiotic supplements and pass a greater amount of probiotic benefits on to baby through her milk.*

If you don't like the idea of giving simple sugar to your baby, your doctor may prescribe sorbitol or lactulose. I like these better because they feed healthy flora, whereas sugar is less selective in the bacteria it feeds. Sorbitol and lactulose are covered in the next section.

Probiotics, or beneficial flora supplements, can be given to help with constipation. They aren't likely to cause any kind of movement within a day or two, but they are shown to be a useful part of a bowel maintenance program. They can gradually promote softer stools by improving baby's flora over time, whereas laxatives are used for more immediate needs. Probiotics are also known to provide some help toward baby's system eventually developing tolerance of allergenic foods. Breastfeeding mother can take probiotic supplements and pass a greater balance of probiotic benefits on to baby through her milk.

Medical Laxatives

Whereas most laxative products are available over the counter, and all laxative plans for babies require at least some initial professional consultation, I've grouped the more frequently medically prescribed, less natural treatments here. An advantage of some common laxative medicines over dietary measures is that they do not replace healthy baby milk calories with sugar calories and they don't interfere with exclusive breastfeeding.

Some newer drugs are being prescribed for (hopefully only) severe cases of constipation in children. Currently these are not studied for safety in children and do have slight potentials for harm. I will not be covering these. I'm certain that caretakers will try several avenues before resorting to such measures and will do their homework when such choices are to be made.

The most popularly prescribed laxative for children is *polyethylene glycol*, or **PEG**. It's sold over the counter as **MiraLAX**, but it's best not to use in young children without medical advice. PEG prevents water from being absorbed out of the colon. By keeping it inside the intestine, it loosens the stools and encourages movement. In addition to the usual kind of possible laxative side effects of gas and cramping, studies report headache to be an additional, occasional side effect of PEG.

PEG may be more effective than some natural approaches, but there are slight concerns about its long-term use. Many children are using this chemical for months or years. Simpler methods may or may not be enough, but personally, I feel safer with non-chemical solutions if they'll work. When urgent clearing is not required, I think it makes sense to try a couple of physical methods first, natural foods or nutritional extracts next, and then go for the chemicals, if all else fails.

Actually, PEG isn't the end of the treatment options. Some more serious drugs are offered, which are not actually approved for use in constipated children, and then there's surgery. Let's nip this thing in the bud, so we don't have to go there.

There has been a long standing medical perception that PEG is quite safe because it's thought to minimally absorb from the intestines into the bloodstream. It appears, however, that in some children, some PEG is definitely being absorbed. There is growing concern about serious effects from PEG that are being reported to the FDA. Between late 2000 and early 2013, *2,257 adverse events* involving PEG were reported to the U.S. FDA's Adverse Event Reporting System, largely among children. These complaints involve kidney problems and a great number of psychiatric effects.

Apparently, very little research has been performed on PEG absorption in children, who differ from adults and from the healthy, grown animals originally used in safety studies. Often, irritated little intestinal systems lose some of the strength of their intestinal barriers, allowing things to travel into the bloodstream that should not be passing through. This may be why so many symptoms are being reported in children given PEG. Reports of adverse events are not proof of actual effects, but when one medication has a far greater number of reports of specific kinds of reactions than other medications do, it's time to take notice.

The FDA has recognized these serious reports and posted them on its website as "potential signals of serious risks" but, as of date, they have decided not to do anything more about it. In 2012, a large group of citizens petitioned the FDA to perform safety studies on PEG in children. As of 2014, such studies have not begun.

The U.S. FDA website reads,

> *The Drug Safety Oversight Board discussed reports of metabolic acidosis… and neuropsychiatric adverse events in children using polyethylene glycol (PEG) products. Metabolic acidosis is a disturbance in the body's acid-base balance and causes too much acid in the blood. In some situations, metabolic acidosis can be a mild, chronic condition; however, it may lead to shock or death in severe cases. Neuropsychiatric adverse events may include seizures, tremors, tics, headache, anxiety, lethargy, sedation, aggression, rages, obsessive-compulsive behaviors including repetitive chewing and sucking, paranoia and mood swings.*

Outside of such concerns, PEG is not my favorite choice because it damages healthy flora. To me, upsetting the balance of a child's protective intestinal flora is not an ideal way to treat a distressed intestine.

In comparison to the large number of adverse events reported with PEG use, the largest and most recent review of adverse event reporting on natural products was performed in Italy, covering not one product but a wide spectrum of herbal and nutritional factors used as laxatives. A total of 26 adverse events associated with all natural laxative products were reported over an 8-year period. None were in children.

2,257 adverse events with PEG were reported to the U.S. FDA's Adverse Event Reporting System, largely among children.

Although other laxatives are known to soften the stools, *docusate* (**Colace**), usually prescribed for oral use, is specifically categorized as a stool softener. It does not have good evidence to support its effectiveness. One study found docusate to be no better than placebo. Many laxatives are found to be more effective, including psyllium fiber, and probably other fiber supplements. Ducosate is generally found to have very low toxicity by itself, but if taken when mineral oil is also being used, it can cause toxic effects.

Mineral oil, to be taken by mouth, is often prescribed. It's found to be safe, but I have described possibly healthier options. **Oral castor oil** is another common prescription. It's known, however, to cause a bit more of a wild ride than many other laxatives in terms of cramping, nausea, vomiting, and explosive stooling.

Lactulose is an artificial sugar made from chemically altering lactose. In the United States, it's only available by prescription, though the reasons for this have since been disproven. It has a very good safety record. Lactulose is not broken down in the small intestine and so is not absorbed and does not contribute sugar to the child's bloodstream. Instead, it persists, like fiber, and causes water to remain in the intestines.

Unlike PEG, which destroys much of baby's flora, lactulose feeds and supports good flora, just as natural fiber would.

Unlike PEG, which destroys much of baby's flora, lactulose feeds and supports good flora, just as natural fiber would. Like using psyllium, lactulose can aid in the child's gradual healing. Bacteria feeding on fiber or complex sugars, known as fermentation, causes gas. Ample gas caused by lactulose fermentation helps to push stool out. Acids formed by bacterial interaction with lactulose also stimulate intestinal waves—another manner by which lactulose works. On top of its high effectiveness, it tastes yummy, so cooperation is easy. Review studies find lactulose to be either just as effective or somewhat less effective than PEG. It has also been found to be about equal to natural fiber and to senna treatments.

Sorbitol is one more sugar sometimes prescribed for baby constipation. You've likely seen the warnings on "sugar-free" candies made with sorbitol, saying that sorbitol may cause some diarrhea. It may. That's why it's great for constipation. It's a slowly absorbed sugar, so it hangs around longer than simple sugars—but not as long as lactulose—to hold water in the intestines. Absorbing slowly, it does not cause the unhealthy insulin surges that come from eating moderate to high doses of sugar all at once. Like lactulose, sorbitol feeds healthy flora. Lactulose may be thought superior to sorbitol because it does not add sugar to the baby's bloodstream. Others may prefer sorbitol because it is a natural sugar, whereas lactulose is artificially created.

Treating from the Bottom

Suppositories do not interfere with infant feedings and do not involve the whole digestive system, making these possibly ideal solutions for younger babies

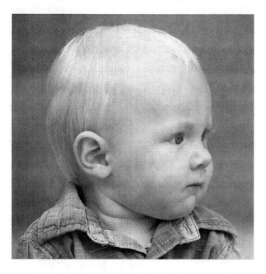

when physical efforts haven't worked. Both suppositories and enemas can be effective go-to's when oral efforts are disliked or are not working in older children.

Pediatric *glycerin suppositories* are commonly prescribed by physicians and are available over the counter for parents who've gotten the okay. These are one of very few choices that are useful for babies before they are receiving solid foods. Usually half, or less, of a suppository is used at a time, cut lengthwise for ease of insertion. If you've been planning to use a suppository and notice your constipated child straining to poop, this might be a great time to help him out by inserting the suppository right away.

Any time an enema is used, the child should be first provided with extra water to drink so the enema will not dehydrate him. Enemas are not generally recommended for children under the age of two. Store-bought enemas give dosing information for children over two. The most common type found and prescribed is **Fleet Enema**. This is known as a *saline enema*, but it is not made from table salt; it's a phosphate salt. I'm a little surprised that these are sold over the counter with doses recommended for young children, as a child can easily absorb too much phosphate into her system from these. This can especially occur when the enema fluid is kept inside the rectum for a long time. Phosphate enemas should be used only with detailed medical advisement.

Suppositories do not interfere with infant feedings and do not involve the whole digestive system, making these possibly ideal solutions for younger babies when physical efforts haven't worked.

Because of the known slight risk with phosphate enemas, a homemade enema of water and table salt is considered safer. Some parents simply use a little bit of warm tap water given with a nasal bulb. Large amounts of tap water held for long periods of time can cause water dilution of baby's bloodstream. By simply adding a tad of table salt, to make the water salty like baby's blood, there is no concern over too much water or too much salt flowing into or out of baby's bloodstream.

A simple *homemade saline enema* recipe is widely distributed and medically accepted. It consists of 1/2 teaspoon (2.5 mL) table salt added to a cup (1/4 L) of warm distilled water. The standard recommended amount to use would be about 2 tablespoons (30 mL, 1 ounce) of the saltwater solution that you made for a 20-pound baby, 2 ounces (60 mL) in a 2-year old, and not more than 4 ounces (120 mL) in an older child. Repeated use of enemas is not advised.

Another enema that some hospitals recommend is a **milk and molasses enema**. It sounds natural and nice, but it's used for serious impaction because it's actually quite powerful. The sugar in the rectum causes a large amount of gas formation, which can result in some serious cramping discomfort. Of course, it's not for a child with milk allergy. Otherwise, recent studies report this age-old enema to be safe and quite effective. Varying recipes and doses are used.

A simple homemade saline enema recipe consists of 1/2 teaspoon (2.5 mL) table salt added to a cup (1/4 L) of warm distilled water.

The rare mom will go gently into baby's rectum with a finger and gently coax out some hard pellets that are blocking baby's rectum. More stool will likely follow. Occasionally, medical personnel will perform such **manual disimpaction** as well, but this occurs less and less frequently as oral treatments become medically preferred over any treatments at this end.

Summary of Constipation Treatment Options

Agent	Action	Advantages	Disadvantages
Switch of formula or mother's diet	• Prevents constipation by eliminating allergens	• Prevention, not just treating symptoms	• Takes time and some sleuthing to find the right diet
Lower-iron formula for formula-fed	• Reduces constipation from iron	• If it works, elimination of cause	• Concerns over anemia but not well-founded
Physical measures	• Help move stool through	• No chemical or sugar ingestion	• None, generally harmless
Glycerin suppositories	• Attract water into rectum • Ease passage of stool	• Quick results • Appropriate for young infants	• Concerns over dependency with frequent use
Saline (phosphate) enema (Fleet)	• Adds and attracts water into colon • Stimulates movement	• Quick results	• Risk of phosphate overdose • Muscles can weaken with long-term enema use
Homemade salt enema	• Adds and attracts water into colon • Stimulates colon by expansion	• Quick results • Considered safe when properly used	• Muscles can weaken with long-term enema use
Milk and molasses enema	• Attracts water • Causes gas formation to push stool out	• Quick results • Highly effective • Natural ingredients	• Can be quite uncomfortable
Senna (Senokot) enema	• Stimulates intestinal movements	• Quick results	• Generally not recommended under age 2
Senna products oral	• Stimulates intestinal movements	• Natural herb	• Often need attendant softener
Bisacodyl (Dulcolax) oral, suppository, or enema	• Stimulates intestinal movements	• Commonly prescribed	• May cause nutritional or fluid imbalances with long-term use
Docusate (Colace) oral	• Softens stool	• Commonly prescribed	• Effectiveness not well-established
Prunes, pears	• Add fiber and special water-attracting sugars	• Natural • Regular usage is fine	• Not before solid food age
Prune or pear juice	• Adds fluid and special water-attracting sugars	• Easy acceptance	• Not before solid food age • Insulin surges • Tooth decay

Agent	Action	Advantages	Disadvantages
High fruit and vegetable consumption	• Adds fiber and special normalizing sugars (both also found in breastmilk)	• Promotion of gut and general health • Natural prevention	• Only toddlers and older can eat enough • Not strong enough for urgent impaction
Probiotic foods and supplements	• Provide healthy flora	• Flora support • Promotion of gut and general health	• Mild and slow effect • Require additional mode of treatment
Magnesium products (Natural Calm, Milk of Magnesia) oral	• Attract water into intestines	• Gentle • Simple • Valuable nutrient	• Slight risk of overdose
Mineral oil oral or enema	• Lubricates	• Time-proven remedy	• Reduce some vitamin absorption
Castor oil oral	• Lubricates • Stimulates movement	• Time-proven remedy	• Can cause strong sensations
Palm, cod liver, or flax seed oil oral	• Lubricates • Is anti-inflammatory	• Nutritious • Small doses okay under 6 months	• Difficult administration
Simple sugars, corn syrup	• Draw water into intestines	• Easily accepted • Okay under 6 months	• Empty calories • Insulin surges • Tooth decay
Lactulose sugar	• Holds water in intestines • Causes gas formation to push stool	• Not absorbed as sugar • Not cause insulin surges • Feed healthy flora • Easily accepted	• Prescription only, despite excellent safety record
Sorbitol sugar	• Holds water in intestines • Causes gas formation to push stool	• Not cause insulin surges • Feed healthy flora • Fight tooth decay • Easily accepted	• Adds sugar calories
Polyethylene glycol (PEG) oral	• Maintains water in the stool	• Frequently chosen by pediatricians	• Damages flora • Serious concerns over safety

Palmer, L. F. *Baby Poop*. 2015

The Evolution of a Withholder

Even if the original cause of constipation was a food allergy that's been remedied, many children develop ongoing constipation and impaction problems because they wish to avoid the pain they experienced in passing big hard stools. It's an instinctual human behavior to avoid something that hurts. Of course, in this case, this behavior is not beneficial, and it can take quite a bit of your sweetness, creativity, and psychology, and maybe even a bit of bribery, to counteract your child's natural instincts and confirmed fears. If withholding should occur in a young toddler, some parents end up relying on some kind of laxatives until baby is old enough to understand requests to make pooping efforts.

It can take quite a bit of your sweetness, creativity, and psychology, and maybe even a bit of bribery, to counteract your child's natural instincts and confirmed fears.

Some withholding babies will extend their legs straight out, possibly while crying. This posture helps them to hold their stool in. Without knowing this, many parents believe this behavior is their baby trying to push stool out. Walkers may stand with legs straight and back arched backward for the same reason. Some children become quiet and are visibly concentrating when overriding urges to poop. Others will run and hide to do their thing until the urge passes.

Withholding behaviors generally occur sometime after toilet training has begun. In fact, experts find that earlier toilet training, such as during the twos, is linked to more withholding behavior than children toilet trained closer to or after the age of three. Of course, withholding doesn't occur in every—or even most—early toileters, but this correlation tends to be found in children who are affected. This is chiefly because young children, who discover the control they have over their own bodies, may naturally choose to reduce the amount of time and effort spent making bowel movements, once supervision is diminished. Then their gradual progression

Experts find that earlier toilet training, such as during the twos, is linked to more withholding behavior than children toilet trained closer to or after the age of three.

toward constipation may naturally go unnoticed, until the problem is a big one.

There are those young ones who just have too much fun in their days and don't wish to interrupt their great day to sit and poop, gradually developing painful bowel movements and then avoidance behaviors. Some children ignore too many bowel movement signals because they don't like using school or public restrooms. This too can easily start a constipation cycle.

Other pooping peculiarities are not all that rare in children. Some seem to have simply developed an embarrassment over pooping. There are those who have memories of better stooling luck in diapers. Though they use the toilet to pee, they may refuse to poop until a diaper is put on them. Though the reasons may not be easy to understand, we need to respect that many children are deeply affected by this function of their body, the physical sensations, emotional impressions, and outside influences.

EC is not expected to carry the same possible risk of creating a stool withholder as early toilet training is.

Some parents use a method called **Elimination Communication**, primarily known as **EC**, to begin a progression toward appropriate toilet use from early infancy. EC is not expected to carry the same possible risk of creating a stool withholder as early toilet training is. EC is about both mother and child becoming highly aware of pee and poo signals and choosing less dependency on diapers. The higher attention to signals should hopefully maintain good toileting behaviors throughout the preschool years.

If your withholding child develops a bladder infection, you will then know that your youngster is trying to withhold pee as well. Bladder walls can become irritated and damaged from frequent overloading. Generally, this habit will go away as stool withholding is dealt with.

Bowel Training

Normally, intestinal movements are stimulated by food and liquid coming in. Things get moving inside the digestive system, though the intestines don't necessarily try to move stool all the way out every time we take something in. Our intestines are also more active when we first arise from bed. Bodies like to stick to a bit of a schedule for stooling, negotiating with daily activities and responding to various signals sent from hormones and nerve pathways. If "ready to move out" signals are regularly answered, they will continue to be sent, and the body will continue to prepare for the movements.

Following this bodily tendency, caregivers can help their constipated, toileting-aged children retrain their intestinal movements, re-invite signals to come, and re-initiate a daily stooling schedule. The key is to encourage your child to sit

©FOTCR

on her potty for several minutes when she first arises and after each meal. Young boys challenged with constipation can be taught to sit to pee, which increases the opportunities to feel an urge for passing stool. Over time, the body should recognize that its natural opportunities are returning and redevelop a regular pattern of intestinal movements. Teach your child to recognize, report, and get excited about such poopy signals, and then rush her to a potty or encourage her to fill her diaper.

There are a lot of options for things to do with your child as she sits. Let her know that you aren't necessarily expecting her to perform a bowel movement. It is good for her to either be very relaxed or to be thinking about moving her bowels with imagery of ease and success.

You can read calming books and tell comforting stories to relax your child, or you can read books about poop and pooping. You can educate and encourage your child by telling him, "You eat every day, so your body makes poop every day. That poop really wants to come out." Explain how, if the poop stays inside, it gets dried up and becomes really hard, like old dinosaur poop. If your child dislikes his leakage problems, explain how and why that will stop if he can make a real poop every day. Talk about how mom and dad poop, and pet Sparky, and cows, and even caterpillars poop, and how birds will poop on your head because they don't know any better. For the more creative family, a pooping contest may even be in order. Find the key to your child's intestinal motivations.

Caregivers can help their constipated, toileting-aged children retrain their intestinal movements, re-invite signals to come, and re-initiate a daily stooling schedule.

Any time that a real poop is made, not just leaking around a blockage, then it's time for excitement, praise, and hugs—maybe even a victory dance.

If your constipated preschool child is one who does not even want to sit at the toilet, you of course have a bigger challenge. Medical researchers have shown that, among constipated children who are toilet refusers, nearly all were constipated first, and the refusal behaviors followed. This indicates that it was likely pain and discomfort that led to the refusals.

> *Any time that a real poop is made, not just leaking around a blockage, then it's time for excitement, praise, and hugs—maybe even a victory dance.*

Now it's time not only for some natural stool-softening techniques but also probably for a quiet return to diapers and an avoidance of pressuring. When eventually parents are desiring a revisit to toilet training, it may be a time for listening to your child's fears, connecting with your child, and for creating incentives.

If your child wants a diaper to poop in, put it on him when he says he's ready to go. Diapers are better than constipation and, believe it or not, this phase won't last forever. You may be able to work toward his sitting on the toilet in the diaper. Maybe, eventually, you can cut a hole in the diaper …

A colorful calendar can be helpful for children to be rewarded with gold stars placed on their successful days.

Some Final Thoughts

Once constipated, the intestines lose part of their integrity and the flora become imbalanced. Allowing this condition to persist for a long period of time can set up a persistently problematic bowel that could possibly cause distress throughout the child's life. By trying to find and address the causes of constipation, you can reduce or prevent dependency on laxatives. The long-term goal is to have your child dependent upon a healthy and allergen-free diet rather than on laxatives. In the meantime, natural stool softening approaches may be milder than drugs and may be enough.

A child who does not respond well to all of your good love and efforts can be referred to a specialized clinic for professional help in resolving the problem so that is does not follow him into adulthood.

The Poop on Colic and Reflux

Chronic colicky symptoms of prolonged crying and excessive fussiness occur in a significant portion of babies, and the diagnosis of reflux is widespread today. Such symptoms often go along with those of diarrhea, infrequent stooling, constipation, green stools, rashes, excess gas, or waking with screams. Although other causes occur, all of these presentations in infants are frequently linked to food sensitivities.

Crying Babies

All babies cry, and for many reasons. Typical crying seems to be one important means for babies to find their way into our hearts as well as to teach us how to parent them. Babies can be frightened, lonely, hyper-stimulated, hungry, wet, tired—the list goes on. A certain kind of cry, though, lets connected mothers know that their baby is in great discomfort. If some kind of consistent problem is occurring and if parents can do something to relieve this discomfort, all involved will undoubtedly be grateful to have solutions found.

Whereas colic was once the simplistic verdict for babies with excessive crying and fussing—a diagnosis that merely means they cry and fuss a lot—today, reflux is the diagnosis of fashion, with weak and inconsistent diagnostic criteria and poorly substantiated treatment prescriptions. If you are a parent of a baby who was diagnosed with reflux, likely in part due to his frequent distress, you will want to take note that from this point on, when I use the term colic, I am also including reflux diagnoses.

What is Colic?

If a baby's cries are relieved by picking her up, providing attention, or giving something to suck on, this is not colic. Babies have inborn needs for consistent affection and responsive attention, and some babies appear to need more than others. By design, infants' hormones and neurons respond positively to such attachment behaviors, which leads to the developmental creation of permanent receptor pathways in their brains that add to good lifelong psychological and physical health (as detailed in my book, *Baby Matters*). If a crying baby regularly cannot be consoled, outside of heroic jiggling or Oscar-worthy distraction techniques, then there's a reason why.

The basic term—colic—refers to intestinal pain that comes in waves, known as "colicky pain," representative of the wave action of the intestinal muscles. Because parents generally perceive a highly fussy and desperately crying baby as having episodes of abdominal discomfort, colic has become the traditional descriptive term for such infants.

Infant colic is technically diagnosed as 3 or more hours of crying and fussing for 3 or more days per week, for at least 3 weeks. It's useful to have this definition for consistent research studies and also for a yardstick to be able to assure some mothers that their baby's hour a day of crying is entirely common and seldom linked to treatable disorders. Yet, with regards to any one family's challenges, I personally don't think it matters much as to whether a baby cries for 2 and 1/2 hours a day or for 3 and 1/2 hours. I also believe that the intensity of the cry, and attendant symptoms, may distinguish between a baby who is easily irritated or hyper-stimulated and a baby who is in physical pain. Both of these may be referred to as colicky infants, but one baby may just be going through a natural development stage, and the other may need some serious sleuthing.

> *If a baby's cries are relieved by picking her up, providing attention, or giving something to suck on, this is not colic.*

Reflux: The New Colic

When it comes to diagnosing heavily crying babies, reflux is the new colic. Ever since new (expensive) medications for reflux were released in the United States in the 1990s, more and more fussy babies are being diagnosed with reflux rather than the traditional diagnosis of colic. Just as earlier literature described colic to be found in 15 to 25% of babies, about this same percentage of babies are given a diagnosis of reflux today—based upon the same symptoms—with many infants exhibiting rashes, gas, poor sleep, and green stools.

Gastroesophageal reflux, or **GER**, is the term given to the spilling of fluids from the stomach upwards into the esophagus (throat) and possibly all the way up and out of the mouth. The **lower esophageal sphincter,** which is a muscle ring, allows swallowed contents headed down the esophagus to enter into the stomach, but prevents acid-drenched stomach contents from making their way back up. The spilling upward of stomach contents, or reflux, is attributed to a weak esophageal sphincter and this is often treated as something abnormal that needs medicating. The reality is that 70% or more of infants have "weak" lower esophageal sphincters, depending upon who is defining it. This is not an error; it is normal. Infants have sphincters that are weaker than they will have as children. Possibly this loose sphincter is a protective means of preventing infants from being overfed at any one feeding and of allowing them to easily rid themselves of anything that does not agree with them.

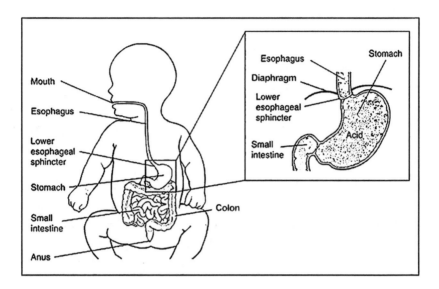

Milk (human, formula, or cow) is quite alkaline, as opposed to acidic, and baby tummies themselves are low in acid, compared to child or adult stomachs. Half of all young infants visibly spit up at least once per day. Even more babies experience silent reflux, which is when stomach contents spill only partway up the throat and go down again without coming out of baby's mouth. Most infant reflux is not highly acidic and likely not uncomfortable nor damaging to esophageal tissues.

Acid reflux that causes burning chest pain in adults is known as heartburn. If a child's crying tends to occur 10 to 40 minutes after eating, and is greater when lying down after a meal, he may be experiencing such heartburn pain.

The term gastroesophageal reflux *disease*, or **GERD**, is intended to represent extreme reflux cases that cause frequent heartburn pain, breathing problems, or poor growth in infants. In such cases, doctors have concern over potential damage to the esophageal tissues—damage that can lead to worse consequences over time. Whereas simple reflux is common in babies, authoritative sources report that only one in 300 infants actually has GERD. According to common medical guidelines, only GERD requires treatment with drugs, yet the number of infants receiving some kind of acid-reducing medication is about 15 to 25 times higher than this amount.

A baby with actual GERD will exhibit a few or more of these symptoms:
- Frequent spitting up or vomiting
- Frequent coughing or gagging
- Excess crying and fussing, especially after meals and when lying down

- Hoarse sounding cries
- Wheezing or trouble breathing
- Slow heartbeat
- Arching backward
- Bad breath
- Acid damage to teeth
- Difficulty sleeping
- Waking with screams
- Poor feeding
- Poor weight gain

Is Colic Caused by Parental Care Practices?

Hundreds of studies have researched prolonged crying in babies. Some studies have found differences in crying dependent upon the kinds of caring provided by the caretakers, and other studies have found no such correlations. The preponderance of studies agree that, on average, babies around the world cry equally as often, but those who are kept close to their caretakers and are responded to quickly do not cry for as long. Studies distinguish this crying, however, from the very prolonged and frustrated cries of colic.

Research has well demonstrated that colic occurs chiefly in industrialized regions. Studies in the United States and Canada have reported that between 15 and 25% of young babies experience colicky crying. Sixteen percent of babies in a large Brazilian city were reported to display colic, as were 20% in the capital of Iran. On the other hand, 8% of mothers reported excessive crying in a Nigerian study, but none of these Nigerian infants may have fit the strict definition for colic. Rates of colic also appear to be lower in more recently industrialized regions than in those with longstanding development. Though the picture may be gradually changing, a 1994 study of infants in South Korea found less crying, and more holding provided, than seen in Western studies; the study did not find that any babies fit the standard definition for colic. In 2009, a 1% incidence of colic was reported in Shanghai. These regional findings suggest possible colic links to breastfeeding rates (with breastfeeding quite high and colic negligible in Asian regions), maternal diets, or cultural practices. When these same peoples are third generation, or higher, citizens of the United States, however, their rates of infant distress more closely match U.S. averages; these findings eliminate genetics as a possible explanation for differences around the world.

Studies in emerging nations find more colic in infants who are not breastfed, which demonstrates a dietary or an attention factor with colic. In industrialized nations, where the frequencies of colic and reflux are much higher overall, less difference is seen in the rates between formula-fed and breastfed babies, although reports do find reflux less often in breastfed babies. It appears that breastfeeding mothers with more traditional, less westernized customs and diets and with more responsive infant care practices, present less cause for infant colic.

Is it Lactose Intolerance?

Cow milk protein allergies are quite common in infants. Lactose intolerance is something entirely different. Primary lactose intolerance—in which a child is born unable to make lactase enzyme, which is needed to digest the milk sugar, lactose—is exceedingly *rare* in babies. Lactose is a milk sugar meant only for babies: baby humans, baby cows, and all baby mammals. Before the advent of lactose-free formulas, only a couple of genera-

Cow milk protein allergies are quite common in infants. Lactose intolerance is something entirely different.

tions ago, no gene for true lactose intolerance from birth could have been passed on, as a baby would not survive without being able to tolerate mother's milk. Nearly all mammals lose lactase enzyme production as they grow up. This occurs because lactose is naturally only found in milk, the food that mammals make for their babies. The persistent production of lactase enzyme throughout one's life is a uniqueness that has developed over the millennia among humans of Northern European descent, as they learned to survive in cold regions by drinking the milk of cows that could turn scrub into nutritious calories. Most of these Caucasian adults are uniquely able to digest lactose, and thus consume milk products, for most of their lives.

As a result of intestinal irritation due to an infection or a food reaction in baby's digestive system, lactase enzyme production can be *temporarily* reduced. This can lead to excess gas for a period of time, which can increase crying. Some doctors may do testing for lactase enzyme during such a time and proclaim a child to be lactose intolerant. But, once recovered from illness or freed of foods to which they are reacting, a baby's lactase enzyme production will quickly return. If their breastfeeding mom is a super milk-maker, a few babies may take in excess amounts of high-lactose foremilk, also causing gas and associated fussiness if their lactase enzyme production doesn't keep up. Block feedings typically can resolve this situation, as described in Chapter 8.

Some formula-fed babies are needlessly switched to lactose-free formula in response to colic. Remember that lactose is a healthy sugar for most babies. A child will respond better to a formula with hydrolyzed (partly broken down) milk proteins, with alternate proteins (soy formula), or to a formula made from simple amino acids instead of cow milk proteins. Many lactose-free formulas are also hydrolyzed, so improvement is seen with the switch, and the diagnosis of lactose intolerance wrongly remains. Cow milk protein allergy (also known as milk protein intolerance or sensitivity) is the proper diagnosis.

One study added lactose back into the diets of milk allergic babies who were given lactose-free hydrolyzed formula for 2 months. After another 2 months with the addition of lactose, the babies' flora exhibited healthier lactobacilli and bifidobacteria populations and fewer undesirable bacteria. Such an improved floral balance could help reduce infections and help to reduce allergic reactions over time.

An even worse recommendation is made on occasion, also from a misunderstanding of lactose. Incorrectly thinking that lactose intolerance is the issue, some doctors call for a breastfeeding mother of a colicky or refluxing baby to switch to feeding a lactose-free formula. Taking a baby away from the healing and immune-protective properties of mother's milk makes no sense; all that is needed is an adjustment in the way baby is nursed or an adjustment to mother's diet to eliminate cow milk proteins or other allergens.

Other Possible Causes of Colic and Reflux

Some professionals have proposed that colic is generally the result of poor **neural regulation** of responses to external stimuli. Such a thing sounds reasonable, although it still begs for a causative factor, given the connections between colic and industrialized living. It *is* known that some people have genes for greater pain sensation than others, and it's reasonable for this to be a factor. But the strong links between colic and food reactions tend to dim neurological theories for most cases.

The strong links between colic and food reactions tend to dim neurological theories for most cases.

Over-feeding can cause excess spitting up in babies. This can happen when the hole in the nipple of baby's bottle is too large or when caretakers strongly encourage a baby to finish a bottle after he's had enough. Oversupply in a breastfeeding mother can occasionally have the same result. These causes of spitting up can be easily sleuthed and easily remedied with smaller nipple holes or smaller feeds for bottle-fed infants or with block feeding for nursing babies.

Many lactation professionals report that tongue-tie can occasionally mimic reflux, as gagging and coughing may occur during feeding. These reactions can also result from other problems with baby's *latch technique*. Painful nipples are most likely part of the picture in these situations, and a lactation consultation is in order.

> *Cruciferous vegetables, onions, spicy foods, chocolate, and caffeine are also known to cause fussiness in some nurslings.*

It's well known that a portion of young babies react with a little gas or colicky symptoms when their breastfeeding mothers consume **cruciferous vegetables**, such as broccoli, cauliflower, and cabbage. Onions, spicy foods, chocolate, and caffeine are also known to cause fussiness in some nurslings. These particular reactions generally do not fit a picture of food allergy; they typically do not seem driven by an inflammatory process or accompanied by other allergy or delayed sensitivity-type symptoms, such as rashes or green poops. Cows eat foods that may cause this same kind of reaction in babies who consume cow milk or possibly milk formulas. There is just something about these particular vegetables that, when passed through mother's milk, can sometimes cause extra gas in immature intestines. The caffeine effect is more obvious, and spicy foods may actually burn a little. All of these effects occur only in a portion of babies, and most moms have no reason to worry about eating any of these foods. A mom who is feeling frustrated with a colicky baby can observe her own infant's responses to these foods. Even if some of baby's symptoms seem linked to any of these, most likely mom doesn't need to avoid the foods altogether. Most babies who are affected by cruciferous vegetables, caffeine, or spicy foods are only bothered by bigger doses. Only a few may be sensitive to smaller exposures. Tolerance of these foods in mom's milk should develop after some weeks or months.

Sometimes medical imaging studies performed on a refluxing baby reveal that baby has a **hiatal hernia**. Typically, the esophagus meets the stomach at an opening through the diaphragm, where the lower esophageal sphincter normally lies. With a hiatal hernia, a bit of stomach has pushed up through the diaphragm. This elevates and weakens the sphincter and enlarges the opening in the diaphragm. Although a hiatal hernia is seen more often with GER than without, its mere presence should not call for any kind of treatment and, unless it is large, it is likely not the key cause of reflux.

Rarely, a baby with episodes of inconsolable crying, with or without vomiting, could be experiencing **migraines**. Researchers have found that children who suffer from migraine headaches are more than 6 times as likely to have suffered from colic as babies. It's difficult to prove whether infants actually experience headaches. Until recently, medical doctors have been fed the standard lore that it's not possible. From the 1940s through the 1980s, medicine typically purported that young infants do not feel pain, but this ridiculous mindset has been well overturned, showing even early fetal responses to pain. This migraine association could also simply mean that the same triggers that cause headaches in a child caused colic during infancy. Other than hormonal cycles in females during and after puberty, food sensitivities are known to be the most common triggers for migraines, although the most common migraine foods differ from the usual intestinal offenders. Chemical food additives, fragrances, and other chemical exposures can also be triggers.

Exposure to **cigarette smoke** is known to cause or aggravate infant colic and reflux. Baby may also be sensitive to fragrances in his caretaker's cologne, antiperspirant, or skin care products. Many skin care ingredients can also absorb into mom's system and end up in her milk. These may need consideration when a fussy baby is tough to diagnose.

H. pylori

Doctors once thought that stomach acid would prevent any bacteria from living inside a stomach. Around 1990, it was determined that the bacterium *Helicobacter pylori* lives in many human stomachs and that it is associated with the development of peptic ulcers (sores in the stomach or first part of intestine). Now researchers have found that possibly hundreds of bacterial species can be found in healthy human stomachs. Because infant stomachs are less acidic, it's possible, or even probable, that baby tummies entertain whole microbiomes of their own. The balance of these bacteria can certainly have health-promoting as well as deleterious effects.

When first studied, H. *pylori* was always thought to be bad, yet the picture is much fuzzier today. Its presence has been linked to lower levels of asthma and obesity. Now it's known to exist in approximately half of young tummies in the world, yet peptic ulcers are rare in children. What about colic and reflux? Whereas colic studies find H. *pylori* presence in more colicky tummies than those of happier babies, eradication of this bacterium has been shown to increase actual reflux in children. Whereas its presence is associated with an increased

Whereas colic studies find H. pylori presence in more colicky tummies than those of happier babies, eradication of this bacterium has been shown to increase actual reflux in children.

risk of gastric cancer (although this cancer is not a high risk and occurs in older adults), it's also linked to decreased risks of esophageal cancer and inflammatory bowel disease. *H. pylori* is present in well over two-thirds of tummies throughout much of Asia, where colic is practically unknown, but it's found in fewer than 10% of U.S. stomachs today.

I'm not interested in jumping on the *H. pylori*–colic bandwagon and would certainly not recommend attempting antibiotic eradication. The flora balance in stomachs—young or old—is far from being understood. Rather than trying to target *H. pylori*, it's best to focus on removing any irritating foods and to work on general gut health.

The Main Cause of Colic and Reflux

Whether calling it colic, GER, or GERD, studies confirm that the majority of excessively fussy babies are suffering from sensitivity reactions to one or more foods in their diet.

In each of four separate studies, reflux and colic were significantly reduced in *100%* of babies when cow milk proteins were completely removed from their diets. With such findings, it's difficult to deny cow milk proteins as the basis of most colic and reflux. These studies used **amino acid infant formulas** to provide totally cow milk-free diets. Also known as **elemental formulas**, these are made from simple pieces of proteins that immune systems won't react to.

In contrast to these four studies, some researchers use **hydrolyzed milk formulas** and then report lower percentages of babies recovering from colic or reflux. Although these formulas are promoted as hypoallergenic, many allergic babies still react to the traces of intact milk proteins that remain in hydrolyzed formulas, as the hydrolysis, or breakdown of cow proteins, is not complete.

Cows also eat many foods that are common allergens to babies, such as grasses (grains), corn, and soy, and some even receive wheat. Few people consider it, but these food proteins passed in cow milk could be the cause for some children to react to milk and milk formulas. Whether it's the actual milk proteins, or other proteins from the cow's diet—either way, milk avoidance is the key.

Some babies with excessive spitting up—and other GERD symptoms of chronic cough, feeding refusal, and poor weight gain—are found, upon biopsy, to have many white blood cells in their esophageal tissues of the type known to be associated with allergies. These cells are known as eosinophils, and such a baby will be diagnosed with **eosinophilic esophagitis (EE)**. Some medical sources describe EE as a cause of GERD, others GERD as a cause of EE, and others call them two different entities with all of the same symptoms. Like other GERD diet studies in infants, a small Baltimore study of formula-fed GERD babies with EE found improvement in 100% of those given amino acid formula to eliminate exposure to cow milk proteins. A large study in Philadelphia found significant improvement in 98% of children with EE when milk proteins were removed. In both of these studies, the number of eosinophils in the esophageal membranes greatly reduced after weeks on the milk-free diet.

Most of the studies discussed above involved formula-fed babies. Researchers in one study gave amino acid formula to babies who were previously being breast-fed. This is not a recommended move, however. The use of elemental formula makes for clear-cut studies to scientifically prove the possibilities. This does not mean that a breastfeeding mother would actually want to make this switch. Of course, not every food-allergic person needs to live on expensive and unnatural elemental formula. Babies receiving solid foods or breastmilk can certainly continue to do so with the simple elimination of cow milk proteins or other foods to which they react. Amino acid formulas are very expensive, may have some detrimental effects, and are composed entirely from artificial building blocks. In addition, amino acid formulas contain no whole-food qualities, have only one form of each vitamin, are not well-accepted by babies, and do not have the healing, anti-inflammatory, and immune-providing factors that breastmilk has, nor the prebiotics, superior fatty acid content, and antioxidant qualities of both breastmilk and healthy solid foods.

With such findings, it's difficult to deny cow milk proteins as the basis of most colic and reflux.

Any elemental formulas available in the United States today also contain traces of corn proteins (from the corn syrup solids) and, therefore, are not actually 100% hypoallergenic for all babies. If mother's milk is available, a baby with colic, GER, EE, GERD, or other food allergy symptoms will do far better to remain breastfeeding while mother simply eliminates one or a few foods from her diet.

Hypothetically, any foreign milk proteins can cause reactions in babies, leaving goat milk suspect as well as cow. Many other foods, especially soy and gluten, are also common offenders. Often a formula-fed baby's symptoms will improve when milk formula is replaced by soy formula, but some will soon develop a sensitivity to soy as well.

It is known for certain that intact cow milk proteins from mother's diet can be passed through her breastmilk, and a portion of babies react to them—possibly those who've already had some gastrointestinal (GI) insults or those with high genetic allergic potential. Research that studied finding and eliminating offending foods from a breastfeeding mother's diet showed beneficial results for babies. One study eliminates several common allergens from mothers' diets and measures a 37% improvement in their babies. The results from such a trial would be much greater if all allergens were specifically determined for each infant. Just like the additional solid-food diet for a breast or formula-feeding baby, the diet of a breastfeeding mother needs to be tailored to her own infant's sensitivities. A trial of removing only cow milk is recommended by a multitude of sources as a first effort, and often may be all that is needed. Consider that breastfeeding mothers, or any adult humans, do not require milk in their diets any more than grown cows do. If milk elimination is not enough, then a more complete elimination diet can be performed, adding foods back one at a time and watching for reactions.

The clinical experiences of those who assist breastfeeding mothers with this kind of effort reveal very significant improvements in symptoms associated with most colicky and refluxing infants when diets are conscientiously determined and consistently followed. Breastfeeding moms who choose to undergo elimination diets for the benefit of their colicky nursling often receive an extra bonus—they find improvements in their own intestinal health.

When a breastfeeding mother of a food-allergic baby is offered elemental formula, she can certainly use it. She can use it to make smoothies for herself to easily supplement her hypoallergenic diet designed to benefit her nursling.

The reasons that food sensitivities may develop, and the methods for discovering and treating food reactions and healing the gut, are discussed in Chapters 15 and 16.

Medicating Crying Babies

There once was a day when various kinds of sedatives, narcotics, and antispasm medications were regularly prescribed for fussy babies. Regardless of the kind of drug, its chief action was sedation and, on occasion, the ramifications of such use were dire. The unhealthy side effects of these drugs fortunately became widely recognized, and these prescriptions have mostly stopped.

Bentyl (*dicyclomine*) is one drug still occasionally prescribed today. It's been shown to be effective in calming (sedating) crying babies but can also have serious side effects. Another common GERD medication still prescribed today is **Reglan** (**metmoclopramide**). This drug is meant to speed up the emptying of the stomach so there is less opportunity for reflux. Studies generally find that Reglan does reduce stomach contents, but they cannot prove any reduction in the symptoms of colic or GER for which this drug was prescribed. Over two million prescriptions of Reglan-type medications are dispensed per year to U.S. children. Reglan is associated with frequent mild side effects, and prolonged use is known to pose a risk for serious, permanent neurologic disorders.

Antacid Drugs

Traditional antacid medications such as **Zantac** (**ranitidine**) and **Tagamet** (**cimetidine**) have long been used to decrease acid secretions in babies suspected of suffering from GERD, with some reductions in babies' symptoms. These are still widely used today. Unfortunately, the beneficial effect from these medications can diminish over time, some children suffer headaches from these drugs, and other side effects occasionally occur.

These older antacid drugs are actually more than antacids. They are histamine blockers. Just as allergy pills block histamine reactions to airborne allergens, Zantac and Tagamet block intestinal histamine receptors that instigate many delayed-type food allergy reactions. Often prescribed with acid in mind, histamine blocking drugs may actually reduce the cause of the reflux by reducing the initiation of food reactions.

Proton Pump Inhibitor Drugs

An expensive new breed of antacid drugs, known as **proton pump inhibitors**, or **PPI drugs**, entered the scene about 20 years ago and soon GERD diagnoses grew by leaps and bounds, with 4 to 8% of infants receiving PPI drugs today. Common PPI drug names include Prilosec (omeprazole), Prevacid (lansoprazole), and Nexium (esomeprazole).

Separate, large 2010 and 2011 reviews of the studies both state that PPI drugs are no more effective than placebos in reducing GERD-associated symptoms in infants and that infant safety studies are lacking.

With a large number of babies receiving PPI drugs for GERD diagnoses, we could assume that these have been found to be effective in relieving the various symptoms for which they are prescribed. Remarkably, they have not. A large number of studies, including some by the PPI drug industry itself, have shown no consistent consensus as to what the definition of GERD is, what the diagnostic criteria for GERD are, and how these symptoms relate to damage of the esophagus or to other serious concerns. There is also no evidence that diagnostic tests used are able to predict damage from reflux or benefit from medication, and evidence is considered *weak*, at best, that PPI drugs are effective for reducing symptoms in crying, fussing, vomiting, and poorly sleeping infants. Separate, large 2010 and 2011 reviews of the studies both state that PPI drugs are no more effective than placebos in reducing GERD-associated symptoms in infants and that infant safety studies are lacking.

PPI drugs may reduce the acidity found in babies' tummies, but this reduction does not correlate to a reduction in infants' symptoms—this has been known for many years. Even though a large international pediatric gastroenterology organization released guidelines in 2009, based upon over 600 research studies, and called for limiting the use of these drugs in infants, there is no evidence of a decrease in prescribing. If rare erosive damage is certain to be occurring in an infant's esophagus from acidity, PPI drugs generally *do* promote healing.

When prescribed PPI drugs for their crying, fussing, and poorly sleeping infant, some parents do report gradual improvements over time. Hopefully, a few babies are responding positively to the medications, but colic, reflux, and other such symptoms tend to reduce gradually on their own over the first many months. Many parents simply hope that the prescribed drugs are providing some kind of health benefit as they go about trying to find other means to reduce their baby's symptoms. If antacid drugs are truly benefiting the infant, fussing after meals should quickly diminish. The acidity of stomach contents reduces within hours after giving a traditional antacid drug and within a day of giving a PPI. Babies heal very quickly, so any pain from damaged throat membranes should go away in a few days, in all but the most severe of cases, after acid levels are reduced.

A sudden withdrawal from PPI drugs will cause a child to have a rebound response of increased acid, with increased crying and fussing as a result. A baby's symptoms worsening with withdrawal of antacid drugs does not indicate that the medications were helping. Any time a child *does* need to be removed from antacid drugs, the withdrawal should be performed very gradually and probably with some support from calcium and magnesium buffering, such as with Mylanta, during the process.

In addition to their questionable benefit, there are concerns over harmful effects from antacid drugs. Acid exists in babies' tummies for a purpose, of course. Not only does it aid in the digestion of food, but it also helps to protect against bacterial infections in the digestive tract. Babies on these medications may face an increased risk for infections and may experience some bone weakening due to reduced absorption of minerals.

In the absence of better information and physician guidance, and fed by advertising and misinformation on the Internet, distressed parents take their concerns to doctors, who very frequently comply and prescribe acid-suppressing medications for symptoms and signs that, in most cases, are not GERD . . . We are medicalizing normality.
—Eric Hassall, MD, FACG, Children's Hospital, Cincinnati, OH

Other Measures for Colic and Reflux

For breast or bottle-fed babies, **smaller, more frequent feeds** may help reduce reflux. Milk and formula act like antacids, soothing the throat and tummy. Little bits going down can be soothing, whereas larger amounts at once can cause reflux.

When prescribed, calcium- and magnesium-containing **antacid liquids** can provide short-term but immediate relief for a burning reflux and do not interrupt the immune provisions of breastmilk the way that any iron- or protein-containing food or supplement does. Calcium slows stools down a bit whereas magnesium speeds them up. Thus, these two buffering minerals balance each other out when taken together. Though available over the counter, these minerals can alter a child's electrolyte balance, so more than very occasional usage should be monitored by a physician. Excessive buffering can also lead to a yeasty diaper rash.

Many studies have been performed to see whether the use of **probiotics** can help to reduce infant colic. *Lactobacillus reuteri* has gained the most attention. Some studies have shown some improvement with supplements of this bacterium in breastfed babies; others have not. Formulas containing probiotics have not shown benefits. I have not seen any studies with high quality probiotics given to formula-fed infants, as opposed to the probiotics companies are able to put into canned, powdered infant formula that sits unrefrigerated on store shelves. Such studies are needed. Basically, it comes down to this: probiotics are clearly not the cure for colic and reflux, but they *are* shown to be a useful component of a full effort toward healing baby's gut. In fact, the one study that showed high benefits from *L. reuteri* supplements given to breastfed babies also included mother's avoidance of cow milk in the process.

Aloe vera gel, found in drinkable versions, can speed healing of irritated digestive tissues. The **latex** of aloe, found in aloe vera *juice*, acts as a laxative and irritant and is not recommended for use in children.

Gripe water is a term out of the 1800s. It's a liquid typically given by dropper for infant colic and reflux. Early gripe waters tended to contain significant amounts of alcohol, which did soothe some babies and had detrimental effects in some babies. Even tiny amounts of alcohol can be very toxic to infants and toddlers. Traditional and modern gripe waters may contain significant amounts of sugar, which is well known to soothe babies, but is certainly not ideal for regular colic treatment, and "cures" nothing. Various combinations of herbal extracts are sold or made in homes as gripe water today.

Various **herbs** used as teas or in gripe waters used by mothers today include **marshmallow root, slippery elm, chamomile, dill, fennel,** and **ginger**. All of these have been shown in studies (not necessarily in infants) to act as tissue protectants that soothe digestive membranes and/or speed their healing. Some are thought to reduce spasms of the digestive tract as well. Chamomile is known to have relaxing and antioxidant qualities. **Deglycerized licorice (DGL)** has been shown to reduce the release of stomach acid. Studies on various herbal tea combinations report reduced crying in many colicky infants. One study that compared herbs to a reduction of milk proteins found better results from the milk allergen relief, but measurable relief from the herbs. Small amounts of these herbs as teas may soothe baby and help reduce the burn from acid in an infant beyond a few months who is already receiving any formula or solid foods. Large doses of fennel have occasionally led to breast development in babies.

Breastmilk has potent anti-inflammatory and healing factors, and an exclusively breastfed baby doesn't need other remedies. When a breastfeeding mother consumes most of these herbs, however, they may pass through her milk and should be safe even with newborns. Several studies have measured the transfer of flavorful compounds to breastmilk and have found wide variation among the various compounds; therefore, many components of many herbs are known to pass but practitioners don't necessarily know which herbs will pass in greater or lesser quantities. Fennel is probably the most studied herb in terms of colic relief. At least certain components of fennel have been shown to pass through breastmilk. Fennel can also increase breastmilk production, so it is not an infant colic remedy choice for a mother with oversupply.

Star anise tea is a traditional colic tea that has been shown to be potentially toxic and should not be used. A strong, home-brewed **mint tea** may contain an oil that can be quite toxic.

Some herbal colic products are formulated as **essential oils** that are rubbed into baby's skin. These should usually be diluted with a simpler oil. Studies suggest moderate benefits from essential oils of **chamomile**, **dill**, **fennel**, **ginger**, **lavender**, and **lemon balm**. **Sesame oil** massage has been shown to help induce sleep in infants.

Considered quite safe, **simethicone drops** (Mylicon, Infacol) are still promoted today in baby supply stores for colic and infant gas even though studies have shown for 30 years that they work no better than placebos.

Thickening

A common recommendation for babies who spit up excessively or who are thought to be crying due to unseen reflux is thickening of their feed. Parents are frequently advised to add baby cereal and some other concoctions to formula or to breastmilk in a bottle. Thickening agents add low-nutrition calories, reducing the amount of high-nutrition feed baby receives. Whether these provide real benefit is controversial, and sometimes they increase coughing. Studies show some reduction in spitting up among formula-fed infants drinking thickened feeds, but studies also show that silent reflux continues with thickening.

Breastmilk has an enzyme that digests cereals and thus thickening breast-milk with rice cereal is not effective. It's just as well, as adding any protein- or iron-containing product to breastmilk is the same thing as starting solid foods, which interfere with breastmilk's immune provisions—not a beneficial move for a young, fussy infant. Again, it's controversial as to whether babies truly benefit from thickening feeds, even if some reduction in visible reflux is seen.

A xanthan gum product called Simply Thick was used in NICUs for several years with breastfeeding premature babies, who typically have great reflux challenges. This product was discontinued because of links to many cases of necrotizing enterocolitis, which is a serious intestinal inflammation that can occur when anything is added to mother's milk for preemies. For this reason, instead of many babies continuing with valuable mother's milk, these preemies have been switched to formula over the years so that they could obtain thickened feeds to reduce reflux. Formula also increases the risk of necrotizing enterocolitis, so I personally fail to find the logic in that move.

Soothing Colicky Babies

Studies suggest that the old reflux advice of raising the head of baby's bed is not actually beneficial, but some parents report advantages from elevating baby's head and shoulders using a *wedge pillow* under baby's head and torso. *Carrying baby upright* for 20 or 30 minutes after feeding may reduce reflux and gas and can be helpful with baby's mood. Baby may find relief in light bouncing while held this way. Greater bouncing can increase reflux, if that's baby's source of pain, but it can help to move air through baby's intestines, providing some relief to a gassy baby. Colicky babies and those suffering from reflux will often sleep better when worn in wraps. Carrying provides the added benefit of encouraging release of baby's comforting, pain-relieving, and health-promoting hormone, oxytocin.

Colicky babies and those suffering from reflux will often sleep better when worn in wraps.

Some parents sense greater comfort in their colicky infants with the sitting position in a car seat carrier, but studies do not show overall benefits from this position and report reflux worsening in some infants. **Rocking** provides general comforting to babies. When rocking arms are unavailable, a windup or **electric swing** can help lull an uncomfortable baby off to sleep. Some fussy babies benefit from **vibrating chairs**. Vibrating action can override pain signals and break up gas bubbles.

Babies are designed to be settled and regulated by **sucking** action. Comfort nursing, or sucking on a finger or pacifier, can bring pain relief to baby when she's not too upset to try. **Skin-to-skin contact** leads to increased soothing hormone releases, as do hugs and squeezes. Infant **massage** can be helpful for infants, incorporating the diluted essential oils mentioned above. **Singing**, soft words, or shushing like the sound of blood rushing through the placenta can all be soothing, and baby will sense your empathy. If a baby or child is crying from a frustration or upset, distraction isn't always the best advice, but if his tears are from pain, **distraction** techniques can be very kind, if they help.

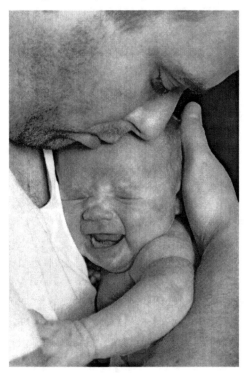

The Ramifications of Colic and Its Care

Doctors say that babies outgrow colic, often intimating that parents are to just allow their babies to cry their little hearts out and are to find a way to live through all the crying themselves, while they wait until it all somehow fades away. One problem with this theory is that a very large portion of colicky and refluxing babies are reacting to foods in their diet and often these food reactions don't entirely go away; the symptoms just change over time. Even if a baby does outgrow her food sensitivities or other cause for colic, wouldn't it be nicer if all could enjoy those first months more?

According to one study, 10% of infants who have experienced colic continue to have these same symptoms after a year. Additionally, many infants who "grow out" of colic, as defined by the sign of prolonged crying, actually just *grow in* to new symptoms, generally gastrointestinal related. Sometimes it's decades before such symptoms become extreme enough to lead the now adult to seek treatment and acquire a diagnosis, but the syndrome has probably been lightly festering for all of those years, and the greater illness could have been preventable.

A good portion of older children and adults suffering from bowel diseases, diabetes, asthma, constipation, and other maladies started out as colicky babies, spitting-up babies, or babies with other food intolerance symptoms. Finding and resolving issues early on may not only bring more peace and comfort to the lives of the new or growing family but also prevent further illness and suffering for the life of the child.

Such "preventive care" always has one drawback; we often never know what we may have prevented, if anything. But when allergies, arthritis, asthma, celiac disease, diabetes, inflammatory bowel diseases, irritable bowel syndrome, food allergies, or other such problems already run in a family, parents may have greater surety that their early efforts will be worthwhile and bring greater health to their child's future.

We must certainly look for other reasons besides diet for colic in any given infant. Sometimes no amount of effort can determine a source of distress, but all colicky babies deserve to have a chance for relief from their apparent discomfort, if possible. Until reasonable efforts have been made, I do not ascribe to the common medical paradigm of simply waiting until a baby outgrows her fits of crying.

Some Final Thoughts

Both infants and parents need emotional support when colic causes frequent and prolonged crying and fussiness. Babies' cries are designed to get and keep the attention of their parents, who are under the influence of parenting hormones, and they're meant to cause the parents to powerfully desire to do something about the cries. When the crying baby cannot be consoled, prolonged crying can be very taxing to caregivers. Parents should seek some support from relatives, other parents, friends, or a visiting nanny. Sometimes unwanted advice and judgments can only add more stress for caretakers of a colicky baby. If it doesn't work to remember that these intrusive comments only come from caring positions based upon instinctual desires to help, parents may need to be firm about choosing who visits, when, and for how long.

14

Gut Health and Autoimmune Diseases

Autism, Celiac, Diabetes, and More

Diabetes is appearing in more and more children every year, and it's popping up in children with less and less genetic risk. Many other childhood autoimmune diseases—such as autism, celiac disease, and Crohn's disease—are also exhibiting ever-rising rates, and this same phenomenon is likely true for all of them. Children are facing an increasing amount of environmental challenges in the womb, during birth, and during infancy. Exposures to toxins, interferences in the birth process, and drug provisions are all escalating and are producing greater and greater rates of chronic diseases in our children—even those with low genetic susceptibilities.

Some aspects of interfering with optimal floral development in young infants and some of the ramifications were introduced in Chapter 3, "Messing with the Microbiome." The floral environment is known to exercise a powerful influence on the gut barrier and on immune system functions. A one-cell layer is all that separates the food and bacteria inside the intestines from the immune system tissues beneath the membrane surfaces and from potential access to the bloodstream. Floral disruptions decrease the strength of this barrier and allow various immune system reactions that were not meant to be.

Young infants naturally possess slightly "leaky" intestinal walls that are intended to pass valuable antibodies and other healthy factors from mother's milk into baby's bloodstream. This should not be a problem when healthy floral defenses behave properly and when only intended human milk elements pass through. So many things can challenge this optimal scenario, however. This chapter more deeply explores the strong impacts that early gut health factors can have on the potentials for development of autoimmune diseases that have become far too common. Chapters 15 and 16 will discuss how to work toward healing such disruptions in hopes of reducing future disease.

Childhood Diabetes

In childhood **type 1**, or insulin-dependent **diabetes**, cells in the pancreas that develop insulin—which manages blood sugar levels—are destroyed by the child's own immune system. This lifelong disease leads to a need to inject insulin daily and predisposes a person to many other serious health risks. **Type 2 diabetes**—once called adult-onset diabetes—now occurs at increasingly younger ages. In this insulin-resistant diabetes, blood sugar levels can become dangerously high as insulin loses its effectiveness.

Since 1960, the portion of U.S. citizens diagnosed with diabetes (both type 1 and type 2) has grown 7 times, from 1 to 7%.

Like so many other chronic disorders in the industrialized world, diabetes incidence has grown tremendously over the last decades. Since 1960, the portion of U.S. citizens diagnosed with diabetes (both type 1 and type 2) has grown 7 times, from 1 to 7%. This includes one in every 400 children under the age of 20.

Diabetes and Feeding Babies

A study of children who were genetically susceptible to type 1 diabetes found that those who expressed high levels of IgG antibodies to cow milk proteins as infants—who were experiencing significant milk protein intolerance reactions—later developed diabetes. Pre-diabetes antibodies can be found in some infants younger than 3 months old. As the amounts and kinds (there are four main kinds of pre-diabetes milk antibodies) of these antibodies increase, so does the child's risk of developing diabetes in the years to come.

For approximately 30 years, it's been known that the early introduction of milk formula in infants correlates with a higher rate of development of childhood diabetes. Breastfeeding mothers' cow milk consumption does not appear to be a factor; breastfeeding appears to remain protective, regardless. Certain immune system reactions, which fight against particular cow milk proteins, can lead a child's body to then react to similar cells in her own pancreas, creating type 1 diabetes.

Early introductions of soy formula and of cereals also lead to increased development of diabetes.

Examinations of early milk consumption and childhood diabetes around the world help to confirm the links. Finland has the highest rate of childhood type 1 diabetes in the world. They are also by far the greatest milk consumers around the globe. China is among the lowest in the world in both milk consumption and diabetes. A graph of diabetes rates around the world would rather closely resemble a graph of milk consumption by country—more so than other possible correlations, such as country wealth, prenatal care, or breastfeeding levels. Correlation is not causation, but more interesting evidence exists.

Iceland's low rate of childhood diabetes contradicts this milk correlation as Icelanders' milk consumption is relatively high. It turns out that certain cows create milk proteins that are known to cause fewer immune reactions in humans than those from the most commonly found cows, and most milk products consumed by Icelandic infants come from these less allergenic cows.

The connection between early cow milk feeding and diabetes risk becomes less clear, however, as it's been shown that early introductions of soy formula and of cereals also lead to increased development of diabetes. It seems as though the early introduction of any foreign proteins not naturally found in human milk has a gut-disturbing effect that, when combined with a genetic propensity, can lead to the development of diabetes. Hydrolyzed or even amino acid formulas also increase diabetes risk, although less so than standard milk formulas do. Apparently, the *absence* of the gut health that exclusive breastmilk can provide is a sure factor in a portion of cases of childhood diabetes. A 2012 review of studies confirms that receiving breastmilk for only a short duration, or not at all, increases the risk of developing childhood diabetes.

Diabetes and Other Gut Health Factors

As discussed in Chapter 3, a reasonable hypothesis exists about hygiene and children's intestinal flora. A popular example compares Finnish children to genetically similar children just across the Russian border. The Russian Karelian children have greater natural exposures to microbes, and they suffer far less type 1 diabetes (1/6th the rate). They have lower rates of other autoimmune diseases as well. As you may have suspected, plenty of other studies also link less diverse and more undesirable gut flora to childhood type 1 diabetes development. Poor childhood flora is also linked to the development of obesity, which can lead to greater type 2 diabetes. In addition to direct studies of microbiomes in children with diabetes, examinations of factors known to hinder healthy childhood flora also suggest strong links between childhood diabetes and early gut health.

> *Examinations of factors known to hinder healthy childhood flora suggest strong links between childhood diabetes and early gut health.*

I demonstrated earlier, in Chapter 2, that cesarean birth leads to the establishment and long-term maintenance of less desirable intestinal flora. A large review of studies found that being born by cesarean section leads to a 20% increased risk of developing childhood-onset type 1 diabetes.

A large Netherlands study compared the amount of antibiotics, antifungals, and antivirals used among children who then developed diabetes versus those who did not. This 2014 paper reported finding greater use of anti-infectives among children who later developed diabetes and also greater use of serious second-line and third-line antibiotics. The study consideration is that children progressing toward diabetes are weaker and become ill more often. Although barely mentioned in this study's discussion, I find a different explanation quite possible: the diabetes developments were resultant from the destruction of gut flora by the drugs chosen for those children and by the number of times that drugs were given. Second- and third-line antibiotics are broader spectrum and more toxic to flora than first. A Finnish study found significantly more development of diabetes in children after greater use of these strong drugs and correlated the drug usage directly to the diabetes, although a Dutch study found no such association.

Causes of Autism and ADHD

Autism-related symptom complexes diagnosed as Asperger's, Rett syndrome, and pervasive developmental disorder are referred to as falling on the autism spectrum or as **autism spectrum disorders (ASDs)**. The U.S. CDC estimates that about one in every 68 children today displays the behaviors associated with ASD. This number had been reported as one in 500 in 1995 and one in 5,000 in 1975. Many genes are found to be more common among ASD children, but not every child with any such genetics develops autism-related symptoms and not every child classified as autistic shows the predominantly characteristic genes; large variation exists within the genetic findings among ASD children. Even in view of changes in diagnostic practices over the years, the enormous increases in ASDs make it obvious that more is involved than merely genes.

Attention deficit disorder (ADD) and **attention deficit hyperactivity disorder (ADHD)** are related in many ways to ASDs, with many overlaps in symptoms, genes, environmental factors that affect them, and in responses to certain treatments. Between 3 and 7% of children are diagnosed with ADHD in the United States today. In both ASDs and ADHD, 4 times as many boys are labeled as girls. For nearly every environmental factor suggested in an ASD study—from toxin exposures to food reactions to prenatal factors—you can find a corresponding ADHD study with a similar finding.

Evidence points toward most cases along the autism spectrum as resulting from interactions between various genetic factors and assorted environmental exposures during the most sensitive neurodevelopmental stages before birth and during early infancy. Early twin studies had professionals quite convinced that autism was a completely genetic disorder. More recently, improved sibling studies partly contradict these findings. Reflecting many newer reports, a 2014 analysis of all children born in Sweden over a 25-year period confirms that—in addition to genetics—environmental factors are responsible for, on average, 50% of the cause of ASDs.

Among environmental toxins with stronger evidential links are phthalate plasticizers, Tylenol (acetaminophen, paracetamol) exposure, certain heavy metals, various solvents, air pollutants, and pesticides. Fetal perfume exposure and other less known possibilities are suggested in individual studies. Other known precipitating factors include premature birth, older maternal age, maternal nutrition factors, an infection or autoimmune irregularity in mother during pregnancy, or an infection or irregular immune reaction in a young child. Suffice it to say that there is no one cause of ASDs. Likely countless combinations of conditions have led to each different autism-related case that has developed among children.

ASDs, ADHD, and Gastrointestinal Disorders

Whereas ASDs and ADHD are known for brain alterations and their associated behavior patterns, connections to gastrointestinal disorders are frequently reported. A large review of studies on gastrointestinal (GI) findings among ASD children reported that these children experience over 4 times as many general GI complaints, with nearly quadruple the diarrhea and constipation as children not on the spectrum. Such complaints amount to some 40 to 50% of all ASD children. A large study found nearly triple the constipation experienced in ADHD children as those without a behavioral diagnosis, and another large study reported triple the rate of diarrhea as well. Individual studies often report that children with the greatest severity of autism exhibit the greatest amounts of GI disorders.

A number of doctors argue that common diarrhea, constipation, and other GI symptoms associated with ASDs are only behavioral *results*. Clear verification exists that emotional states can affect digestive functioning. Sufficient science also confirms that many health factors and many environmental factors can affect both the intestinal tract and the brain at the same time. Today, however, studies have found a significant preponderance of genes known for GI disorders among ASD children with GI symptoms. The question should no longer be whether GI disorders are a part of ASDs but whether we can use this knowledge to help this subset of ASD children.

J. Wright summarizes an autism genetics study from S. Walker on SFARI:

> *Overall gene expression patterns in the autism cells are . . . more similar to cells from people with one of the two inflammatory [bowel] disorders, but are not a perfect match with either. For example, small intestine cells from people with autism share 1,381 altered genes with Crohn's disease and 1,071 with ulcerative colitis; 587 genes overlap with both disorders. However, as many as 1,231 genes from cells in the small intestine and 1,011 from cells in the large intestine are abnormally expressed only in people with autism.*

New research has discovered the mechanism by which inflammation creates openings in the blood-brain barrier—allowing effects on the brain from various hormones and immune factors—effects which typically are not meant to happen. Poor gut health is one common source of chronic inflammation in the body. As demonstrated in the section on the gut-brain axis, in Chapter 2, considerable evidence suggests that early infant flora balance influences brain development and individual behavior, for better or for worse. Many studies, especially using mice, describe these early brain effects as permanent, but current researchers are attempting to learn whether improvements in flora and other gut health factors may be able to lessen any negative effects.

Breastfeeding studies provide clues that, in a subset of children, gut health combines with genetics in the development of ASDs and ADHD. Researchers show double the number of these behavioral disorders developing in children who were not breastfed (a known impairment to gut health) compared to those who were—even compared to siblings who were breastfed. Another clue about gut involvement is that autistic children are consistently shown to have a large portion of undesirable intestinal florae. These factors are not the *results* of disordered behavior; they belong on the causative side of the equation.

Regardless of what factors may have been involved in a child's development of behavioral symptoms, it can certainly be useful to explore interventions that may help some autistic and ADHD children, with gut health being a clear target.

Dietary Intervention/ for Behavioral Di/order/

Foods and food additives appear to be significant environmental factors for a sizeable portion of ASD and ADHD children. Powerful correlations between active intestinal food reactions and temporarily altered child behavior have been documented by many researchers for decades and have been observed thousands of times over by families of food allergic children.

It's quite possible that—without their consumption of offending foods—they have no ADHD.

Many parents report that their ASD children's symptoms and functioning improve through dietary interventions, especially when focusing on milk proteins and gluten. An Italian study found a preponderance of milk and gluten antibodies in ASD children compared to those not on the spectrum. Numerous studies and several study reviews have been performed with diets free of milk and gluten in attempt to reduce symptoms in autistic children. When researchers look at numbers of random ASD children avoiding these foods, consistent improvements are not being measured. It's become clear that this kind of random exclusion of milk and gluten—and only milk and gluten—is not an across-the-board autism cure. Diets need to be tailored to each child's specific food reactions. Improvements are not going to be exhibited if a child is still reacting to some other foods or additives. Some children are not reacting to milk and gluten at all, and some are not reacting to any foods.

Other studies and reviews do reveal that a subset of ASD children suffer from GI conditions related to food reactions. When high quality elimination diets are performed to discover exactly what foods a child reacts to, significant results are measured with avoidance of these foods. Among ASD children, these reactions are typically not IgE antibody related, and studies have found that blood testing for IgG antibodies is not a good predictor of actual reactions either. Elimination dieting is the key. In addition to the common food allergens, artificial food dyes and various other food additives, such as benzoates, present statistically significant results in many studies and reviews—more so with ADHD but also in some autism studies.

Looking at the connections between allergies and behavior from a different angle, a U.S. national survey of over 27,500 children found that children who suffered from one or more allergic disorders (including asthma, hay fever, and food allergy) were 5 times more likely to be labeled with ADHD.

Research showing improved child behavior with allergen elimination typically continues on to demonstrate return of behavioral symptoms with re-introduction of such foods or food additives. These studies not only help us to learn how to help behaviorally disordered children, but they also act to confirm that intestinal reactions to foods do indeed lead to behavioral symptoms in a substantial subset of children. The behavioral links are so strong in many ADHD children that it's quite possible that—without their consumption of offending foods—they have no ADHD.

Interestingly, many studies of dietary links summarize that if medication treatments for a child's autism or ADHD symptoms fail, elimination dieting is worth a try. Wouldn't it make more sense to try it the other way around? It seems more reasonable to determine how much, if any, progress can be made by exploring whether a child exhibits actual intestinal, behavioral, or other reactions to milk or gluten, other foods, or to food colorings or additives. In these cases, the opportunity may exist for improved behavioral symptoms with avoidance of potentially offending foods, possibly reducing or eliminating the question of medication.

Because of distinct floral differences found between children on the spectrum and those not, as discussed in Chapter 2, the use of probiotics and other gut healing efforts could also be of benefit. A large review of studies involving nutritional efforts to treat autism found good evidence that regular high dose supplementation with probiotics may be helpful. Research on mice supports these findings and provides suggested mechanisms. Probiotic supplements can change the floral balance, reduce toxicities, strengthen gut barriers, and otherwise improve gut health, all of which have demonstrated effects on brain functioning. *Bacteroides fragilis* and the standard lactobacilli and bifidobacteria, including *Bifidobacterium infantis*, are the most commonly mentioned beneficial probiotics in autism studies.

Omega-3 fatty acid deficiencies are quite common in ASD and ADHD children, for unexplained reasons. One large survey by San Diego medical researchers found 13 times the number of cases of autism with regression in children who were raised on infant formula without omega-3 supplementation versus those who were breastfed. That number of autism cases was only double for those who had received formula *with* DHA versus those who had been breastfed. Supplementing known ASD or ADHD children with this important nutrient has shown benefits in some studies.

Celiac Disease and Early Gut Health

Celiac disease (CD) is the name given to one particular presentation of food sensitivity to gluten proteins. The gluten proteins of concern are found in wheat, rye, and barley, and somewhat in oats. A CD diagnosis is given when certain antibodies to these glutens are found upon blood testing and when a certain kind of damage is found in the intestinal linings. Children with CD will often experience pale, smelly diarrhea. Like other food reactions, the inflammatory response causes damage to the intestinal linings. The particular kind of damage that's strongly associated with CD is known as **villous atrophy**. The villi are tiny fingerlike projections that cover intestinal linings, increasing the surface area and providing specialized cells for absorption of nutrients. Atrophy, or destruction, of these villi interferes greatly with the absorption of nutrients.

It's difficult to quote a percentage of population affected by CD because diagnosis is greatly inadequate. Researchers in Spain performed blood tests on a large segment of population and found celiac disease to exist among one in 70 children and one in 350 adults. Because CD is thought to never go away, the difference between these rates represents the growing incidence of CD over the decades.

The saga of the Finnish and Russian children reveals that, with the same genetic heritage, Finnish children experience 5 times the rate of CD as the Russian Karelian. This one example makes it clear that, like other autoimmune diseases, there is more to the development of CD than just genes.

A large Italian study reported that antibiotic use in the first year after birth increased the risk of developing CD by 24%; a particular antibiotic, cephalosporin, increased the risk by 42%. Independent of antibiotic usage, the study measured a doubling of CD development in children who experienced gastrointestinal infections during their first year. As demonstrated in Chapter 4, breastfed babies suffer fewer than half as many intestinal infections as those receiving any formula, suggesting that breastfeeding should be a protective factor against CD.

Several studies also report an increased risk of CD development in children who were born by cesarean section, further supporting the powerful factor of early flora establishment in regards to the development of autoimmune diseases. Researchers have found this link to be most powerful in C-sections performed without labor, as opposed to emergency cesareans. Immune factors are actively passed to the baby during labor. There is a need for researchers to further investigate the distinction between pre- and postlabor cesareans in respect to their effects on other autoimmune diseases in order to see what more can be learned about the active passage of antibodies in terms of children's long-term health.

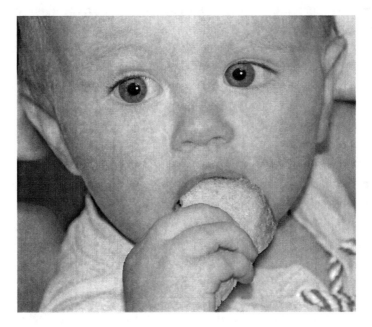

In several studies, a strong correlation has been reported between breastfeeding and the timing of gluten introduction to a child. A review of studies reports that it's not clear as to whether breastfeeding reduces the lifetime risk of developing CD. It's shown to at least delay the development of CD by one or two decades if small portions of gluten are introduced while a child is still breastfeeding and not receiving formula and if breastfeeding continues for at least 2 or 3 months after gluten introduction. Breastfeeding helps the digestive system to establish tolerance of foods as they are introduced. Many studies conclude that the optimal timing to introduce gluten-containing foods to babies, to reduce the risk of CD, is between 4 and 7 months. Because exclusive breastfeeding is known to be optimal until at least 6 months, then 6 or 7 months of age may be the time to begin small doses of cereals, at least in a child suspected of having a genetic risk for CD. However, I don't find enough reason to push grain introduction in response to these studies, before you feel your child is really ready for it.

Many children have other kinds of reactions to glutens or reactions to other forms of proteins in wheat. These children will not have positive blood test findings for CD, but they still have inflammatory reactions to wheat. Also, many vulnerable children who manage to evade CD during childhood eventually develop it at some point during adulthood. Evidence is mounting about negative effects of glutens, and the lectins associated with them, on the intestinal tract and throughout the body for a large segment of the population, at least in the cases of genetically susceptible or otherwise vulnerable systems. Contrary to the recommendations of the breastfeeding-related studies mentioned above, many nutrition experts recommend a delay of 2 years or more before feeding grains to infants, and a growing number of experts question whether grains are healthy for any of us.

A significant portion of CD children are found to have continued symptoms, weight loss, and tissue destruction even with excellent avoidance of gluten.

A significant portion of CD children are found to have continued symptoms, weight loss, and tissue destruction even with excellent avoidance of gluten. Most of these children are found to also react to cow milk proteins, with similar GI destruction. Villous atrophy is typically designated as a sign of celiac disease, but it's also seen in some milk-reacting and other-food-reacting children. A small Italian study found strong inflammatory reactions to cow milk proteins in 50% of the CD children studied. Test elimination and subsequent challenge with cow milk should be performed in every CD child who does not show excellent resolution of symptoms with gluten avoidance alone.

Inflammatory Bowel Diseases

Inflammatory bowel diseases (Crohn's disease and ulcerative colitis), often associated with bloody diarrhea and poor weight gain, have climbed to affect one in 1,000 children under 20 years of age in the United States. In North Carolina, the incidence more than doubled in only 10 years, between 1996 and 2006.

A high sugar and low fiber diet, sure to impede gut health, is known to promote the development of IBD. Chapter 3 demonstrates that breastfeeding has a powerful impact on the prevention of IBD. In a large U.S. study, exposure to antibiotics was found to correlate in a dose-dependent manner with the risk of developing IBD. The greatest impact was from antibiotic exposure during the first year, with five and a half times the risk of developing IBD.

> *The greatest impact was from antibiotic exposure during the first year, with five and a half times the risk of developing IBD.*

Overlap of Autoimmune Disorders

Autoimmunity occurs when components of our immune system attack certain cells within our own body. Interruptions in gut floral balance and impairments of gut barriers allow proteins to improperly pass through the intestinal walls into the bloodstream where their inappropriate presence can incite unwanted immune reactions.

Childhood vulnerability to autoimmune disorders has definitely climbed over the decades, along with increases in many environmental factors that take advantage of genetic susceptibilities. As greater disease development is occurring with lesser genetic distinctions, frequent overlap of autoimmune disorders is now occurring as well. Analyses tend to find overlaps of disorders in 5 to 10% of children affected by autoimmune diseases.

For instance, an Arab study found 5.5% of diabetic children to have celiac disease and an Iraqi study found celiac disease in 11% of diabetic patients. Studies also report that 10 to 20% of diabetic children eventually develop autoimmune thyroid disorders.

Thyroid disorders, juvenile rheumatoid arthritis, and allergies are all seen at higher rates among children with CD. An inordinate amount of ADHD symptomatology is found in children with untreated CD, and behavior symptoms are found to improve with gluten avoidance.

Autistic children develop diabetes at an elevated rate. We've discussed gluten involvement in ASDs, although this may often be distinct from CD. Finally, autoimmune thyroid disease has doubled among autistic children with regression.

Some Final Thoughts

The drastic increases in autoimmune diseases demonstrate that genes are only a portion of these disease pictures. Many early dietary factors, drug and toxin exposures, and birthing procedures—among other environmental elements—can have large impacts on our children's lifelong health. We may have less choice over some of these factors, but it's clear that efforts to support early gut health can pay off well.

Along with those preventive efforts that are feasible to any given family, an important step is clearly to sleuth the causes of GI symptoms that a child may exhibit. Lastly, if you take anything at all from this chapter, remember that the discovery and avoidance of any food reactions can decrease the development of many diseases to which a child has any genetic predisposition.

Food Sensitivities and the Gut

Understanding, Detecting, and Treating

The percentage of children who suffer from food reactions has escalated in industrialized nations over the past many decades. As an example, a New York study found a four-fold increase of life-threatening peanut reactions in children just between 1990 and 2006. Food sensitivities are beginning to grow across African and Asian nations where they once were minimal, as these peoples adopt more westernized diets and habits.

As demonstrated throughout this book, food reactions are often at the root of many chronic digestive problems, such as constipation and diarrhea, and are also linked to the development of autoimmune diseases, such as diabetes and Crohn's disease. In turn, a mix of genetic predispositions and increasing, gut-insulting environmental misfortunes—from toxin exposures to birth interferences to antibiotic usage—are at the core of the development of food allergies. Avoidance of foods that cause unpleasant symptoms, which are indicative of inflammation in the body, is important for preventing further disease. At the same time, food sensitivity symptoms can be heeded as warning signs that baby's gut may need some healing attention.

Around 6% of babies reportedly suffer immediate-type food allergies. Although a majority of medical sources relay that food allergies are generally outgrown over time, the American Academy of Allergy, Asthma and Immunology reports on their website that 8% of children from 3 to 18 years of age suffer food allergies. Aside from immediate-type food allergies, many more babies and children suffer delayed-type food reactions, which typically involve the intestines, skin, and/or behavior. Between immediate-, delayed-, and mixed-type reactions, 15 to 25% of infants and young children are affected by food hypersensitivity reactions of some kind.

Why All These food Allergies?

Although genes, and hence ancestry, are part of the picture about whether or not a child may develop food allergies, it's the child's siblings, parents, aunts, uncles, and possibly grandparents who hold the most clues, as opposed to older relatives. More than likely, your grandparents or great-grandparents (age 75 and over) did not suffer from food allergies or many of the other disorders covered in this book. Over the last 60 or more years, such disorders have grown enormously, and the pace of their expansion speeds up every decade.

It's not uncommon for babies to be born with some kinds of genetic suscep-tibilities for allergies, diabetes, intestinal diseases, behavioral disorders, or other chronic disorders, but generally, one or more environmental assaults are required to turn many vulnerabilities into diseases. Why is this happening at such an accel-erated rate? I remind you that these disorders are chiefly found in industrialized nations, and they become more numerous as emerging nations westernize. What are these environmental assaults? The significance of early floral development can't be understated. A diverse balance of healthy gut bacteria promotes effec-tive intestinal membrane barriers that do not allow unwanted proteins to leak across. Modern birthing and feeding interventions, and early antibiotic usage, are strongly linked to establishment of undesirable flora and increases in many disorders. We can assume that untoward results also occur from factors such as pollution, pesticides, plasticizers, and an enormous array of other chemicals that have crept into industrialized lives. To this list, let's add vast adulterations of foods and a general deterioration of diets. Who knows what other elements play roles?

In addition to allergies and sensitivities to foods and food additives, asthma, sneezing-type airborne allergies, and skin sensitivities to all kinds of agents have also been rising. Although airborne allergies are traditionally thought to be uncommon in infants, they are appearing more often in younger children. These allergies can also amplify the intensity of food reactions in a baby, and a baby who has significant food reactions is quite likely to develop asthma, allergic skin reactions, and airborne allergies as he grows.

On top of these findings and suspicions, the new science of epigenetics teaches that not only can mother's accumulated pre-pregnancy exposures affect her babies while in her womb, but both parents' exposures prior to reproducing can actually alter some gene expressions in their children—and in their children's children.

Kinds of Food Reactions

The most well-known kind of allergic reaction involves **IgE antibodies**— immune system factors that, in allergic people, react quickly to the presence of allergens—such as eaten peanuts or airborne pollen—by prompting inflammatory responses. IgE food reactions, also referred to as **immediate reactions,** occur within seconds to one hour after consuming a food. Reactions can include any of the symptoms of swelling and itching of the tongue and throat, difficulty breathing, wheezing, reddening and swelling of the face, developing hives, running or stuffy nose, vomiting, and experiencing tummy pain. Immediate allergies are usually easy to suspect because the reactions occur soon after the offending food is eaten. IgE allergies are diagnosed medically by finding IgE antibodies to particular foods via a blood test or by observing swelling in response to a skin test.

Some children suffer life-threatening IgE reactions known as **anaphylactic shock**. In these episodes, breathing becomes dangerously restricted and blood pressure drops. Rapid medical attention is required. An injection of epinephrine can reverse this reaction. Today, school office closets are full of *EpiPens*, which are used to administer epinephrine in the case that a child is exposed to an allergen in school.

Non-IgE reactions are delayed reactions, beginning two hours to 2 days, or occasionally 3 days, after the food exposure.

Many other kinds of unwanted reactions to foods occur that do not involve IgE antibodies. **Non-IgE reactions** are **delayed reactions**, beginning two hours to 2 days, or occasionally 3 days, after the food exposure, often making it difficult to ascertain the cause of symptoms when they occur. Some children experience mixed IgE and non-IgE reactions. Their symptoms begin quickly but can still last for several days.

Initially, any kind of hypersensitivity reaction to a food was called a food allergy. Around 1970, tests were becoming available for the measurement of IgE antibodies. This generation also had renewed excitement about psychology as a prevalent medical science. After these developments, and for quite some time, an over-reaction to a food was only considered a "true immune system reaction" if IgE antibodies could be measured. Because they could not be documented with laboratory tests and did not provoke quick and obvious responses, most other food reactions could no longer be called allergies. They were relegated to the field of psychology—as being in the head. In the case of infants, the mental condition would be in the mother's head.

Cow or goat milk protein sensitivities are often mistakenly thought of as lactose intolerance. Any rashes, itching, breathing difficulties, or constipation in response to milk consumption are reactions to proteins—not intolerance of lactose.

Today, most allergists continue to restrict their vision to IgE reactions, with delayed reactions being abrogated to gastrointestinal (GI) specialists, who are only beginning to have widespread recognition of this growing phenomenon. You will still hear a lot of talk about intestinal reactions being "not a true immune reaction," in a tone that discounts the symptom complaints. However, food reactions go way beyond simple IgE reactions. Responses from all kinds of immune system factors are measured in advanced research laboratories that study delayed food reactions. For instance, it's well known that T cells mediate many non-IgE food sensitivity reactions. Additionally, measurable rises or drops are found to occur in all kinds of immune system components. The following are some of the immune components involved: several interleukins, tumor necrosis factor alpha, transforming growth factor beta, interferon gamma, and other inflammatory cytokines; IgG, IgA, and IgM antibodies; and platelet-activating factors.

Typically, food reactions are thought of as occurring in response to food proteins, but reactions to various chemicals in foods are common as well. Uncharacteristic reactions that occur in some people in response to various drugs are examples of **chemical sensitivities**. The most common food chemical sensitivities are to added sulfite preservatives, various food colorings, or to high levels of salicylates or histamines found naturally in certain foods.

Lactose intolerance does not involve any kind of immune system factors—such as antibodies, mast cells, or T cells—and the only symptoms revolve around gas and diarrhea. It should not be likened to a food allergy at all. Lactose intolerance is simply an insufficiency of the enzyme needed to digest the milk sugar lactose. Temporary lactose intolerance can occur in irritated infant intestines, but long-term lactose intolerance is rarely found in young children.

Cow or goat milk protein sensitivities are often mistakenly thought of as lactose intolerance. Any rashes, itching, breathing difficulties, or constipation in response to milk consumption are reactions to proteins—not intolerance of lactose. Both milk protein reactions and lactose intolerance can cause abdominal pain, diarrhea, and gas, but most babies and children who develop symptoms from milk formula, or from cow or goat milk consumption, are actually reacting to proteins in these milks, not to lactose.

Some call non-IgE food reactions "food intolerances." This is common, and I use the term as well, but this can be confusing because some medical sources define intolerance as the lacking of an enzyme, such as with lactose intolerance and lack of the lactase enzyme. This makes the term "milk intolerance" non-descript because a person can't know whether it's milk sugar or milk proteins that are the problem. To confuse matters even more, the term "dairy" product is often used to mean a lactose-containing food. A product could be labeled as "non-dairy" because it contains no lactose, but it can be full of milk proteins.

Naming Food Reactions

As medical awareness over delayed food reactions increases, the number of specific diagnostic terms for them grows. We have no reason to worry ourselves with finding an exact title for any given child's sensitivities, but physicians often have this goal, even though it sometimes means taking a tissue biopsy and even though, in every case, elimination dieting is the gold standard for diagnosis and allergen avoidance is the treatment.

Among these food reaction diagnostic terms is food protein-induced gastroesophageal reflux disease, which is self-explanatory, as is cow's milk protein sensitive enteropathy. The label, *food protein-induced enterocolitis syndrome* (**FPIES**), is given to any severe form of delayed food reaction that includes diarrhea and vomiting. Food protein-induced procto-colitis (FPIP) is diagnosed when the reaction occurs further down, in the colon, causing blood in the stools. Eosinophilic gastrointestinal disorders are often mixed IgE and non-IgE and include eosinophilic esophagitis (EE),

Not every child who reacts to wheat fits into the diagnostic criteria for celiac disease, which include the finding of certain IgG antibodies in the blood.

which was covered in Chapter 13, eosinophilic gastroenteritis, and eosinophilic proctitis. For the most part, only children with extreme reactions are given any of these specific titles. Eosinophil disorders are typically only diagnosed after a tissue biopsy, based upon the number of eosinophil cells seen in an area. This number will, of course, go up and down with allergen exposures and avoidances.

Not every child who reacts to wheat fits into the diagnostic criteria for celiac disease, which include the finding of certain IgG antibodies in the blood. Some children have an immediate-type IgE allergy to wheat, and their symptoms come quickly. When delayed wheat sensitivity is seen, but testing comes up negative for the specific antibodies described in CD, parents will want to determine whether their child is actually sensitive to all gluten-containing products (wheat, rye, barley, and maybe oats) or only to wheat. This will distinguish them as **non-celiac gluten sensitive**, or simply wheat intolerant.

Intestinal Food Reactions: The Chief Causes of Colic and Reflux

IgE food allergies usually receive good medical attention and diagnosis, and sometimes these are severe enough that they require a medical prescription for epinephrine. Although delayed reactions are more common, they are more difficult to sleuth and well-informed attention for delayed reactions is more challenging to find. They also involve the intestines, so are the focus of this book.

As said, intestinal reactions are delayed, starting some 2 to 48 hours after exposure to the food and possibly lasting for a few days. Babies suffering delayed reactions to foods can exhibit:

- prolonged or frequent bouts of distressful crying (colic)
- arching of back while crying
- bouts of great irritability
- feeding refusals or fussy nursing
- reflux, spitting up, or vomiting
- poor weight gain
- poor sleep/sleeplessness
- waking with screams
- rashes on the face or body, or certain diaper rashes
- excess smelly gas
- green stools
- light blood in stools
- bright red ring around anus (sometimes called allergy ring)
- diarrhea, constipation, or both

- chronic sinus congestion
- frequent ear infections
- tantrums or periods of hyperactivity
- bedwetting (after potty training)

Skin Rashes and the Intestines

Most of the common symptoms of food reactions have been discussed in earlier chapters. Rashes are another predominant symptom. Delayed skin symptoms are more common than immediate. Skin reactions can be found over any part of the body. Skin swelling, itching, redness, hives, or visible rashes occur in roughly half of children with food sensitivities, and food reactions are found in 50 to 80% of children who exhibit atopic dermatitis or eczema.

The term **eczema** is most commonly used for various itchy baby and child rashes other than specific rashes recognized as, say, measles or hives, or specific kinds of diaper rash. When assumed to be allergic in nature, the term **atopic dermatitis** is sometimes used. Redness, swelling, and itchiness can occur quickly after exposure to a food, especially around the face, and this can linger as a rash. Or, itchy and visibly rough eczema rashes can form within a day to 3 days after consumption of a food. This skin can become dry, cracked, and tender. Sometimes the rash is blistery or even pus-filled. Delayed skin responses to food allergens occur when food proteins leak into the bloodstream through irritated, damaged, or just highly vulnerable intestinal membranes, and incite inflammatory reactions in the bloodstream that become expressed through areas of the skin.

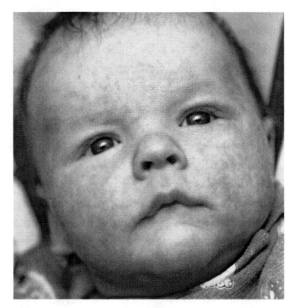

Red, raised, itchy *hives* can also occur quickly after a food exposure, although a few children experience delayed and lasting hives from consumption of offending foods. The occasional young child will exhibit thickly scaled patches in more defined shapes and be diagnosed with **psoriasis**. This too is frequently associated with delayed food reactions, particularly to gluten. Large regions of red, itchy, blistery skin may be labeled by doctors as **dermatitis herpetiformis** (not related to herpes)—a rash commonly seen with celiac disease.

> *Many food-sensitive children maintain some level of waxing and waning eczema or psoriasis due to other irritations and then experience noticeable worsening of rashes after certain food exposures.*

A child whose skin is genetically more sensitive may develop eczema rashes in reaction to cigarette smoke, pollen, dust mites, laundry detergent residues, furniture fabrics, or even certain kinds of clothing, although responses to pollen and dust are thought to be less common in young infants. Of course, gut health can be a factor in any sensitivity reaction. Many food-sensitive children maintain some level of waxing and waning eczema or psoriasis due to other irritations and then experience noticeable worsening of rashes after certain food exposures.

Facial rashes are sometimes due to direct contact with foods (**contact dermatitis**), but other times they are delayed responses after food allergens have provoked the gut. The same is true for **diaper rashes**. Quite often, a rash in the diaper area occurs from direct contact with stool containing offending foods. Typically this can be recognized because the irritated skin areas are exactly those that were touching poop in the diaper. Delayed food allergies can also lead to generalized rashes in the diaper area—just as with any body parts. Wherever they occur, delayed rashes will typically have a rather symmetrical pattern. Of course, diaper rashes have many other causes, including chafing, heat, and excess time spent being wet. **Yeasty** diaper rashes occur from an imbalance in intestinal flora. Often a result of antibiotic exposure, this condition can also result from irritation caused by food reactions. In the case of yeast, local treatment is valuable in addition to addressing gut flora damages. A bright red ring directly around the anus, or an **allergy ring**, is not officially a rash but *is* a skin signal that irritation is occurring inside the rectum—and probably farther up as well.

During research studies, many children with eczema or similar rashes are found to have damaged intestinal linings—the kind of inflammation and damage seen to result from food reactions—even when food reactions had not been suspected. One Russian study found intestinal inflammation or more serious intestinal membrane degradation (villous atrophy) in all study children diagnosed with atopic dermatitis. This is the kind of damage that allows proteins to leak across the intestinal membranes, leading to immune reactions in the blood that can be exhibited as rashes. Such damage reduces optimal absorption of nutrients, and the chronic inflammation can predispose a child to the development of autoimmune disorders. Parents should know that, although it may seem that rashes on babies are only unattractive vanity issues or simply itchy annoyances, rashes likely represent more insidious damage happening inside the child's intestines, and this damage can bring other health ramifications.

As mentioned later in this chapter, skin patch tests may be partly useful for finding out what foods could be causing rashes. Efforts to discover the triggers for a child's rashes can help to reduce or prevent the uncomfortable and unhealthy condition.

Treatment of rashes with steroids does nothing to eliminate the causes of the condition, and regular use of **steroid creams** or pills can have some serious consequences for a child, including weakening of bones, hormonal disturbances, and cataract formation over the eyes. Alternatively, gentle, skin-nourishing creams can be used to moisturize itchy skin and reduce the discomfort.

Food Sensitivities and Behavior

There is no doubt that pain in an infant or child can alter their behavior in many ways. In addition to the direct emotional responses a child can display in reaction to discomfort, the brain—and hence behavior—can be affected chemically by food intolerance reactions.

Both IgE and non-IgE food reactions bring about inflammatory responses, which include the involvement of mast cells and histamines. Researchers have discovered various manners by which such inflammation in the body can lead to slight interruptions of the **blood-brain barrier (BBB)**. An impaired BBB may allow various hormones or inflammatory factors to pass directly into the brain, altering behavior. Other researchers describe routes by which inflammatory factors can have influence over brain pathways without directly crossing the BBB. In addition to these mechanisms, scientists have mapped out direct brain responses to stress. They have found that stress—which can result from the pain of a food reaction—can cause the activation of brain mast cells and the release of histamines directly inside the brain. Via any of these routes, food reactions can lead directly to behavior-modifying brain responses. Any of these various brain effects can result in altered behaviors, such as immense irritability and prolonged crying. These children can display easily triggered moods, hyperactivity, reduced attention, tantrum-throwing, and even bouts of laughing or euphoria.

Epilepsy has been found to occur nearly 3 times as often in children with food allergies. This finding alone serves to demonstrate that food reactions can and do affect the brain. It is well known that migraine headaches are frequently the result of consumption of offending foods, even in young children—a clear example of foods in the body affecting the other side of the BBB.

Diagnosing Delayed Food Reactions

Although some delayed reactions are actually mixed reactions that include IgE antibody involvement, IgE antibody tests will generally be negative and are seldom worth performing in a child who suffers delayed food reactions. **IgG antibody blood tests** can be somewhat helpful in children over two years of age, although both positive and negative findings need to be confirmed with food challenges anyway. These tests are believed to be of lesser value in younger children.

In testing for food reactions, if the child has been avoiding the suspected allergen for some time, the testing is quite likely to turn out negative.

The finding of villous atrophy upon examination of a biopsy tissue sample is considered diagnostic of celiac disease, after specific blood tests are performed. This destruction of the tiny fingerlike villi, which create the absorptive surface of the intestines, is also occasionally found with other food reactions. At times, those who are diagnosed with CD receive follow-up biopsies in order to determine the success of gluten avoidance. Some children are labeled as non-responsive to the gluten elimination diet when damage continues to be seen. Clearly, in such cases, elimination dieting should be implemented to look for other foods potentially causing the malabsorption-causing damage.

In celiac disease testing and any other blood, skin, or biopsy testing for food reactions, if the child has been avoiding the suspected allergen for some time, the testing is quite likely to turn out negative. The longer a food is avoided, the lower the antibody levels in the body will become. This also means that a child may not display the physical symptoms to a food, which he has been avoiding, upon re-introduction. It may take two, three, or more exposures to the food for symptoms to return, depending upon the intensity of the sensitivity.

Finding the Offending Foods

Available IgG antibody tests may diagnose a portion of non-IgE food reactions, in children over two years, but with a large number of false positives and false negatives. **Patch tests**, a longer acting kind of skin test, may produce positive results for some food-reacting children who also develop rashes. These tests are also not highly reliable, however. Researchers have found that certain **stool tests** and **blood eosinophil counts** can give clues as to whether a child is suffering from inflammatory reactions or can demonstrate that he is recovering from his gut inflammation

> *No consistent blood, skin, or stool test exists for diagnosing and documenting delayed-type food reactions.*

due to successful elimination. These tests give no information about specific foods involved and, again, are not highly accurate. For the most part, no consistent blood, skin, or stool test exists for diagnosing and documenting delayed-type food reactions, outside of highly equipped research laboratories and the use of biopsy samples of intestinal tissues. Even biopsies, demanded by some doctors, do not provide information as to what foods are offending the gut; they only demonstrate that some kind of damage is occurring—that is, if the biopsy correctly samples the actual affected portion of the intestinal tract during a time that the child is actually reacting. Food reactions can occur exclusively in the esophagus, stomach, upper or lower small intestine, in a portion of the large intestine, or in the rectum. Doctors call elimination dieting, followed by subsequent food challenging, the gold standard in diagnosing food sensitivities. I agree.

IgG blood tests or skin patch tests may be partly useful when ample food elimination trials have been performed without fully clear results and parents are looking for more clues. Positive laboratory tests can give ideas as to what foods parents may wish to eliminate and challenge. *Negative results mean nothing.* It's entirely possible that the child is reacting to foods that do not show up in any blood or skin tests.

Sometimes, babies seem to be able to detect—by taste or by smell—the presence of an irritating food in mother's milk or in a formula. Babies are far more responsive to odors than adults are and far more in tune with their own physiology. Many mothers report that their babies will fuss at or reject the breast when they have consumed a food to which the baby has been known to react. This is not surprising. Adults hold some of this instinctual capacity as well, although complicated multi-ingredient, highly seasoned foods reduce our natural ability.

We've also learned to simply ignore any such signals. It may behoove parents to pay attention to such indications from their infants.

Regardless of pressure that you may be experiencing, please consider that you do not need to put your child through uncomfortable and expensive (and not highly accurate) tests just to prove your child's food sensitivities to your doctor or others. Only use these as tools to complement food elimination efforts, if you feel the need.

Food Eliminations and Health

Doctors frequently hear messages from their education sources—which are often associated with food and dairy industries—that food eliminations can cause serious nutritional deficiencies, particularly with cow milk avoidance, even though doctors are largely—if not completely—unaware of what their patients *do* eat (beyond early infancy), with or without food eliminations. A child does not need to be able to consume every food available in order to have a balanced diet. Humans survived from their inception until 7,500 years ago without consuming the milk of another animal. A billion Asians (known for long lives) live without milk today, as do other large populations. Paleo diet promoters believe that grains are not beneficial to us. Many healthy people in the world have diets that consist of barely more than a handful of different foods, and many others get by without ever consuming French fries, hamburgers, or milk shakes.

Humans survived from their inception until 7,500 years ago without consuming the milk of another animal.

Japanese researchers recently examined a large number of schoolchildren who avoided milk, eggs, and/or wheat for an extended period of time due to food allergies from infancy. They found significantly lower overweight and obesity among these children, without any increase in underweight, meaning that food-avoiding children were far more likely to have healthy weights. Although greater attention to the child's diet overall possibly led to healthier feeding practices for these children, floral imbalances—known to result *from* food reactions as well as play a role in their cause—have been shown to contribute to obesity. The chronic inflammation caused by chronic food intolerance reactions has also been connected to increased risks for obesity.

In the industrialized world, under-feeding is probably the least of our problems. Appropriate diet is the great concern. Twelve percent of young U.S. children are considered obese and one quarter of children and adolescents are considered overweight. Overweight and obesity are life-shortening risk factors that raise risks for diabetes, heart disease, and many more maladies throughout life.

Beginning the Elimination Diet

We have arrived at the heart of diagnosing food intolerance—does an ingested food provoke symptoms in the child or not? The only way to tell is to first eliminate all foods that are causing any symptoms so that the child reaches a comfortable, symptom-free state. Only now can the effects of any food exposures be accurately recognized. The goal is to eliminate any potentially offending foods so that the child's digestive system recovers from inflammation and damage, and the child's symptoms go away. Once this point is achieved, the child is then "challenged" with each of the eliminated foods, one at a time, and watched for the return of symptoms.

If a child is breastfeeding, the mother needs to remove the foods from her diet. The process may take about two days longer, as the foods need time to leave her system in order to be out of her milk. Then the foods need time to leave the nursling's system. If the baby is also eating solid foods, these need to be tailored along with mom's eliminations.

A child receiving formula and solid foods will require a switch in formula and elimination of all milk ingredients in other foods, along with any other desired food eliminations. Formula information is provided further down in this chapter.

The *easiest elimination effort* is to remove only the most suspect foods, in hopes that the child does not have sensitivities to other foods as well. Because cow milk proteins are the most common offenders, researchers and child health professionals recommend a trial elimination of all milk ingredients first. Parents may wish to eliminate a few more of the next most common allergens in order to increase their chances of having all offending foods removed. The *top food allergens* are reported to be cow milk, eggs, soy, wheat, peanuts, tree nuts, fish, and shellfish. The next most common allergen that finds its way into many baby foods, especially infant formulas, is corn. Over

If a food is not 100% avoided during the elimination trial, the food can trigger symptoms and cause the entire elimination trial to be in vain.

time, children with strong cow milk sensitivities often develop reactions to beef. Certainly, any other foods that are suspected should be removed from the child's diet during this trial as well. If the child's symptoms are more behavioral in nature, remember that food additives are often implicated. A simple whole-foods diet—avoidance of most prepared foods—is the easy answer here.

When a child is highly sensitized to a particular food, often it can take only trace amounts to cause symptoms. If a food is not 100% avoided during the elimination trial, the food can trigger symptoms and cause the entire elimination trial to be in vain.

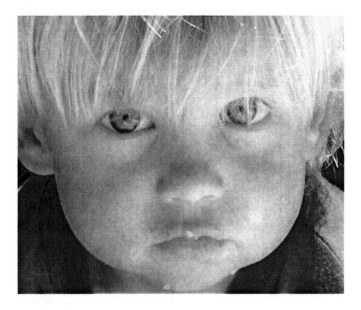

Complete milk elimination means you will need to read ingredients of every package and to avoid whey, casein, caseinate, cream, lactose (because it can be tainted with milk proteins), hydrolyzed protein (when protein source is not specified), and "natural flavor" (which can often be hydrolyzed milk protein—a source of MSG). Of course, butter, cream, ice cream, cheese, and yogurt must be avoided as well. Ghee butter is highly purified of proteins, but traces *do* remain and *do* cause problems for the most milk-sensitive people. Ghee can confuse a milk elimination diet. Some products are labeled as dairy free. This terminology traditionally refers only to the milk sugar, lactose. In fact, these "dairy-free" products often contain high amounts of milk proteins—either casein or whey—the very things you want to avoid.

If you decide **to avoid wheat,** it makes the most sense to avoid all gluten-containing grains; this means also avoiding barley and rye. Many gluten-intolerant individuals also react to oats. Some food products contain vague words like "starch," or "hydrolyzed starch," and "modified food starch." Avoid these as well. Starch can be wheat or corn, and natural flavor can possibly be a wheat product. If you want to know exactly what these ingredients are, call the company. Kamut and spelt are promoted as alternatives to wheat, but they're *still* wheat. On the other hand, buckwheat is not wheat and can be a good grain substitute.

Carrying Out Challenges

After suspect foods are meticulously eliminated, baby will often require only 2 or 3 days before he is looking and feeling better and symptoms of concern go away. If this does not occur, give it a few more days. If a child has suffered extensive intestinal damage, he may need a little longer before he begins to feel better, even after all offending agents have been successfully removed. If the child is quite constipated, a little natural laxative effort may be needed in order to unclog his system and for improvement in stooling to be seen.

Once the child reaches a comfortable, nearly symptom-free baseline, food reintroductions can begin. If this state is not achieved within 5 or 10 days, a more complete elimination diet will be needed.

If your child has ever displayed symptoms that suggest she could experience anything approximating anaphylactic shock, food reintroductions need to occur under medical supervision.

If your child has ever displayed any symptoms that suggest she could experience anything approximating anaphylactic shock, food reintroductions need to occur under medical supervision. Often, symptoms can be more extreme upon reintroduction of a food that had been consumed regularly and then avoided for some time. This is because the body learns over time to partly compensate for the negative effects regularly occurring from that food. With avoidance of the food, these compensatory mechanisms go away, and nothing occurs to cushion the blow when the food is first reintroduced. Past symptoms that suggest danger in performing food introductions at home include any itching or swelling in or around the mouth, any difficulty swallowing, and any wheezing or other difficulty breathing.

The opposite of this heightened reaction can also happen, in the case of milder sensitivities. Antibody levels drop with avoidance and symptoms may only reoccur after 2 or 3 reintroductions.

Assuming that your child's symptoms are mild immediate reactions or are entirely delayed reactions, you may begin reintroductions. Provide an average dosage of the food that you are most eager to return to your child's diet. If no symptoms occur in a few hours, provide a larger dose.

Again, if your child seems fine after a few more hours, provide a third dose. Try to fit three doses into one day or day and a half. If the child's reaction is going to be intense, it will probably occur before the third introduction. If you are dealing with slower-forming reactions, such as rashes, this larger amount of potential allergens in a short period should provide a significant enough response that, when it does occur, it is recognizable—if the child is indeed sensitive to that food.

> **If you are watching for rashes, you may need to wait 72 hours.**

If the chief food sensitivity symptoms you are looking to appease are colic, reflux, and/or diarrhea, 24 to 48 hours should be ample time for symptoms to appear. If you are watching for rashes, you may need to wait 72 hours. If you are looking for constipation, the number of days you wait will depend, of course, upon your child's usual stool intervals. You can feed the food in question for the second and third day, while you wait, but it will take longer to clear the food from the child's body, for the next challenge, if a reaction does occur.

> **The more consistent you can be with long-term, complete avoidances of foods known to offend, the healthier your child's intestines can become and the better his chances are of eventually losing some or all of his food intolerances and of avoiding further disease developments down the road.**

If you feel you have waited an adequate amount of time after introducing a food and if your child exhibits no symptoms, you can assume your child is not reactive to this food and you can therefore begin introducing another food. Of course, if a food does cause symptoms, keep this food 100% out of his diet until the rest of your food trials are complete. Further down the road, after all of your elimination diet trials are completed, you may decide to determine whether your child can tolerate minute doses of an offending food or not. Typically, the more consistent you can be with long-term, complete avoidances of foods known to offend, the healthier your child's intestines can become and the better his chances are of eventually losing some or all of his food intolerances and of avoiding further disease developments down the road.

The Complete Elimination Diet

If you're unable to produce a significant improvement in your child's symptoms with a one- or several-food elimination, your best option is to undergo an extensive elimination diet. You will bring your diet (if nursing) and your child's diet (if on solid foods) down to only a few foods that are seldom found to cause reactions in children.

Before doing this, you can try one more trick. If you suspect a food that is only consumed in small and non-daily amounts, try providing a few large doses of this food in one day to see if baby's symptoms are noticeably worse. This method doesn't always work if the child is already experiencing considerable food reactions, but it may be worth a try.

Nursing moms need not fret about this food elimination effort because, more often than not, they find relief from their own nagging intestinal symptoms during this process. As the food allergy tendency is genetic, this makes sense. Nursing moms can be comforted that breastfed children suffer less milk allergy and fewer other food allergies, in addition to their reduced risks for other illnesses. Also, there is no greater reward than to find an end to frequent bouts of crying and sleeplessness in a child. Mom's elimination diet efforts are worth it.

Below is a chart of foods ranked according to their tendency to cause reactions in children. Additionally, both you and your child will be far less likely to react to foods that have almost never been in your diets in the first place. Unless the food is similar to foods you regularly consume—such as grapefruit, which is quite similar to oranges and other citrus fruits—you or your child should not have had an opportunity to develop sensitivity to it. Unsurprisingly, the most common allergens for children are largely those foods that are most often fed to babies. Researchers are not certain, but some evidence suggests that a baby can be sensitized to a food during his last few months in the womb. For these reasons, you may want to seek out fruits, vegetables, and other foods that are unusual to you and your child.

Both you and your child will be far less likely to react to foods that have almost never been in your diets in the first place.

Yes, choices in an extensive elimination diet are not immediately about optimal nutrition. Some less nutrient-dense foods may be needed for their low-allergen potential during the early elimination process, but they help to pave a pathway to improved health for your child.

For instance, although cold-pressed oils contain more nutrients, standard cooking oils have been treated at such a high heat that any allergens are destroyed. These commercial oils are the place to start when selecting foods to consume during an elimination diet. Even a severely peanut allergic child can supposedly consume commercial peanut oil safely. These processed oils still contain the variety of essential fatty acids that are essential nutrients, and they provide filling calories that are wanted when reducing the variety of foods in a diet. Another example is that dark-colored fruits contain the most intense antioxidants whereas fruits that are nearly white inside tend to pose less allergen challenge. White sugar and starchy grains provide some fullness and satisfaction in the elimination diet, although the nutrients of more whole-food options will be missed for a while.

Remember that the elimination diet is only a temporary effort, and it does not prevent mom and/or baby from consuming as many calories as desired. As described earlier, it's truly not that difficult to have a well-balanced diet with a limited number of foods, although this low-allergen diet does require substituting some less nutritious options for some more nutritious options.

Choose foods chiefly from the "seldom" column in the chart and maybe one to three foods from the "low" column. If you are vegetarian, you'll need to choose proteins from the "low" column. The fewer foods you include in the elimination diet, the better chance you have of successfully eliminating all foods that your child is reacting to.

Choose one or two fruits and two or three vegetables. A starchy vegetable, such as yam, can provide some of the filling that is typically acquired from grains, and yams are nutrient-packed (and are a different food from more allergenic sweet potatoes). Choose a couple of protein sources, such as a meat, poultry, a bean, teff, or quinoa. Include a few fatty acid sources—fats and oils from meat, turkey, coconut, and cooking oils—using oil and vinegar to dress up some baby lettuce. This diet will cover all needed basic nutrients and calories. Round out your menu with a tapioca and *real* maple syrup treat, made with nourishing hemp milk or anti-inflammatory coconut milk. Hypoallergenic multi-vitamin and mineral supplements can be added if you have concern about nutrients, but if vitamin supplements are a challenge to provide, know that the body can depend on its own nutrient stores for some time, except for vitamin C. Vitamin C supplements often come from the common allergen citrus. Basic ascorbic acid is a better option right now.

The allergy potential of foods for children

High	Medium	Medium	Low	Seldom
DAIRY				
casein/whey cow milk egg white	butter cheese cream	egg yolk goat milk yogurt	ghee goat cheese	
MEAT/FISH				
cod shellfish sole	beef chicken pork	tuna salmon	turkey	buffalo lamb
NUTS/SEEDS				
brazil nut hazelnut walnut	almond cashew chocolate flax	mustard pecan sesame seed sunflower seed	carob coconut flax seed	hemp milk poppy seed
GRAINS				
corn wheat	barley buckwheat Kamut	rice rye spelt	millet oat quinoa teff	amaranth arrowroot poi tapioca
FRUITS				
grapefruit lemon lime orange raspberry strawberry tangerine	apple banana blackberry blueberry cherry fig grape guava	kiwi loquat mango melon nectarine peach pineapple	apricot cranberry date papaya prune raisin *Medium category fruits cooked/dried*	lychee fruit pear persimmon rhubarb star fruit
LEGUMES				
peanut soy	kidney bean lima bean miso	peas tofu	green bean lentil white bean	
VEGETABLES				
celery spinach tomato	avocado bell pepper black pepper cabbage cucumber garlic ginger	mushroom onion radish squash sweet potato white potato	asparagus beet broccoli Brussels sprouts carrot cauliflower leafy greens	baby lettuce iceberg lettuce turnip yam
OIL/VINEGAR/SUGARS				
	cold pressed oils balsamic vinegar corn syrup honey	virgin olive oil cider vinegar molasses	coconut/palm oils rice vinegar cane sugar agave nectar	refined oils distilled vinegar beet sugar maple sugar or syrup

Palmer, L. F. *Baby Poop.* 2015

Elimination Diet for the Formula-Fed Child

A trial switch from milk formula to a soy formula is one option. Occasionally a baby will do well with soy formula intially, only to develop intolerance to it over time. Some infant milk formulas, such as Good Start and Gentlease, are lightly **hydrolyzed**. This means that their cow milk proteins are partly broken down to be more easily digested. Most allergic babies will still react to these formulas. *Extensively hydrolyzed infant formulas*—such as Alimentum, standard Nutrimigen, and Pregestimil—do not contain whole cow milk at all. They contain bovine casein, one kind of protein extracted from cow milk. This cow protein is then extensively broken down by enzymes into smaller pieces so that allergic babies' systems are less apt to recognize them as allergens.

> **A significant portion of allergic babies still react to the remaining traces of cow milk proteins in hydrolyzed formulas.**

These formulas are labeled hypoallergenic, but this is misleading. The hydrolysis process is not complete and some intact protein pieces remain in hydrolyzed formulas. A significant portion of allergic babies still react to the remaining traces of cow milk proteins in hydrolyzed formulas. Such babies can then be fed **amino acid formulas**, such as EleCare, Neocate, or Nutrimigen AA, also referred to as **elemental formulas**. These are not made from cow milk proteins but rather only from basic amino acids, which are the building blocks of proteins. The amino acids should not incite allergic reactions. A few babies still have problems with some other ingredients in amino acid formulas, but most babies accustomed to formula-feeding are able to tolerate them well.

After Elimination Dieting

In most cases, you will see a reduction in your child's symptoms after an extensive elimination diet, and now you can begin reintroducing foods one at a time and watching for any kind of reactions. After you have found the culprit foods, 100% avoidance of these ingredients will allow your child (and hence, her caretakers) to remain more comfortable and will allow her intestines to heal.

A vulnerable infant's very first inflammatory food reactions can create leaky gut opportunities that allow the formation of reactions to new foods, creating multiple food intolerances. If your child has reacted to multiple foods, avoidance of foods that currently irritate her intestines may help to reduce the development of reactions to even more foods later on. In a multiple-food-sensitive child—once you have discovered which foods your child reacts to—rotation of the non-reactive foods in her diet may be beneficial rather than feeding the same foods for days in a row. Provide one or two fruits, one grain or starch, one protein, and one vegetable on one day. Give different fruits, grains, proteins, and vegetables the next day, and another set of foods for a third day. In this manner, you can create a 3 to 5 day *rotation diet* in order to reduce the chances of developing significant antibodies to additional foods. Sometimes foods to which a child only mildly reacts can be successfully incorporated in the diet in this fashion, as long as reactions are not occurring.

If you desire, you can re-test avoided foods after 6 months or a year, but know that, although a first exposure may not bring on symptoms, multiple exposures may. It's better to keep a child less sensitized to foods so that accidental exposures are not a large problem. Most families find that when they have not had any "accidents" for a long time—because they do happen as the elimination learning curve can be challenging—their child may be ready for a trial reintroduction.

The following chapter on gut health describes methods that can be added to diligent food eliminations in attempt to improve the health of your child's gut. The goal is to reduce the gut's tendency toward food reactions and help to prevent the development of other autoimmune diseases for which your child may have a genetic predilection.

If extensive and precise food eliminations do not bring about improvements in your child, and patch or blood IgE and IgG tests give no clues, be sure you've also examined other exposures your child encounters, such as fragrances, animals, body care products, and cleaning products in the home. In chemically sensitive children, such agents can intensify food reactions. Finally, you may resolve that the source of baby's symptoms is not a product of determinable food or other environmental exposure. Depending upon the severity of symptoms, you may wish to return to your pediatrician for other kinds of testing. Other gut healing efforts, as described in the following chapter, may still be a worthy effort that could bring on some positive results.

Why is Cow Milk such a Common Allergen?

I've long pondered why it is that one particular food—cow milk—is responsible for such a great number of protein reactions in children, and even adults. First, it seems to make sense that it's because milk formula is the first food given to so many babies, but cow milk seems to be a chief culprit for breastfeeding babies as well, even though they are exposed to a wide spectrum of foods in

mother's diet. It's also common for a child who is switched to goat milk to eventually develop reactions to the goat milk proteins as well.

Some claim that raw cow or goat milks do not pose allergic challenges but, although they have healthy benefits, they still contain the same milk proteins to which allergic individuals react. The milk qualities that are intended to provide easy passing of milk proteins through gut barriers in the young are actually more intact in raw milks. Animal allergy studies demonstrate greater allergic reactions to raw milks than to processed milks because heating breaks down some of the proteins and some other milk properties.

Here's what happens. Animal milks have proteins that are quite similar to human milk proteins; they are similar, but not identical. All milks are designed to buffer the digestive system—preserving the structure of many of milk's proteins—and to allow certain milk proteins to pass right through a child's intestinal membrane barriers. Intestinal barriers are meant to prevent bacteria and other food proteins from passing through, into the bloodstream, but milk has valuable antibodies and other agents that are meant to pass into baby's bloodstream. As long as these are human proteins, there is no problem. The similarity in design of animal milks to human milk causes animal milk proteins to pass these barriers. In a child predisposed to an over-reactive immune system—or in a damaged intestinal environment made more vulnerable to the passing of proteins and less able to maintain tolerance— trouble occurs when these "look-alike" proteins appear. They can cause an uproar in various immune surveillance systems. Local inflammation occurs in the intestinal walls and reactions can also occur throughout the rest of the body. Although the biochemical

All milks are designed to buffer the digestive system—preserving the structure of many of milk's proteins—and to allow certain milk proteins to pass right through a child's intestinal membrane barriers.

details are a little different, I liken this occurrence to that from a blood transfusion with the wrong type of blood. The blood components are quite similar, but not identical, and this sets off alarms. When "look-alike" cow proteins pass through baby's gut walls instead of human proteins, the immune system can react negatively to the imposters. These irritated intestinal walls are then more prone to leak other proteins through, which increases the likelihood of baby developing sensitivities to other foods.

To go along with this theory, egg white is the second most common allergen in children. If you think about it, egg white is practically chicken milk. It contains similar proteins to human milk—proteins designed to feed the growing chick.

I have to add here that it's not healthy for children to drink large amounts of animal milk daily—even if they have no reactions to it and even if delightfully fresh raw organic milk. The first and most important negative effect that commonly occurs in children consuming more than 2 or 3 servings of dairy a day is iron deficiency anemia—which has many negative ramifications. When a significant portion of a child's calories come from milk, other nutritional deficiencies can occur as well because cow milk is quite low

When "look-alike" cow proteins pass through baby's gut walls, the immune system can react negatively to the imposters. These irritated intestinal walls are then more prone to leak other proteins through, which increases the likelihood of baby developing sensitivities to other foods.

in vitamins C and K and in the minerals manganese, magnesium, copper, and zinc. Cow milk also has no fiber. Vitamins A and D are added to liquid milk, but other milk products are low in these. In addition to these limited nutrients, goat milk is also seriously low in folic acid.

On top of all this, even though calcium levels are quite high, the excessively high levels of phosphorous in cow or goat milk, along with the high levels of animal protein, actually cause leaching of calcium out of a child's body. Lack of vitamin K and boron, an inadequate magnesium to calcium ratio, and some other important factors prevent milk calcium from being absorbed and utilized well. Infant formulas correct for most of these factors. When animal milk is the chief source of dietary calcium, a larger overall calcium intake is required (reflected in the U.S. RDA). What about those who consume no milk? Studies do not find higher numbers of bone fractures among vegans. After breastmilk or formula ends, vegetables, legumes, and exercise are of high importance for building strong bones.

Can Allergies be Prevented?

You may have heard study reports that the avoidance of major allergens by mother—both during the last trimester of pregnancy and during the first months of breastfeeding—may be partly successful for preventing diet-related colic and reflux in susceptible newborns. Other studies have not confirmed these findings. Studies

report some allergy prevention by feeding hydrolyzed formulas to susceptible formula-fed infants as soon as formula is being started. Infants considered susceptible would be those with at least one parent or a sibling who has food or airborne allergies, or a digestive disease. The idea is that these children should be less likely to develop allergies after typical allergens are later introduced to their diets.

The results of all these studies are weak and variable because genetics and early exposure are only two pieces of the food-reaction puzzle. Maternal nutrition before and during pregnancy, maternal stress during pregnancy, infant drug exposures in-utero and during and after birth, speed of access to mother's breast after birth, place and mode of birth, home environmental factors, the family's microbiota, and a wide variety of potential toxin exposures—such as pesticides, plasticizers, pollutants and food additives—are all parts of the puzzle.

One thing that most prevention studies do tend to agree on is that exclusive breastfeeding for the first 4 to 6 months, and then continued breastfeeding after solid foods begin, reduces a child's risk of developing food allergies, eczema, asthma, and airborne allergies. For other health reasons, the latest recommendations for solid food introductions are for after 6 months.

Of those who developed early sensitivity to cow milk proteins in mother's milk, upon examination of records, all were found to have been unknowingly exposed to cow milk formula in the newborn nursery.

Although not always the case, one cause of infant sensitivities to cow milk proteins in breastfeeding mother's milk is accidental early exposure to cow milk formula. An important Dutch study looked at a number of breastfeeding newborns. Of those who developed early sensitivity to cow milk proteins in mother's milk, upon examination of records, all were found to have been unknowingly exposed to cow milk formula in the newborn nursery. An earlier Swedish study had this same conclusion. These studies were performed in 1976 and 1984, before the current explosion of such sensitivities. Infants likely have more reasons to react to foreign proteins in mothers' milks today. Let's hope that nurseries are more conscientious today about respecting breastfeeding mothers' instructions to feed no formula.

You may hear an occasional report that food avoidances do not prevent food allergies. This means that avoidance from the start may not prevent the later development of sensitivities to the particular foods avoided, once they are introduced. If and when a sensitivity *does* develop, then food avoidance is the key to preventing frequent inflammatory reactions and the poor health that can follow.

Good floral balance appears to help prevent food and other kinds of allergies. A preponderance of animal and human studies demonstrate that possessing a wide variety of healthy gut flora is linked to fewer allergies overall.

Some Final Thoughts

Interruptions in the junctions between the barrier cells lining intestinal walls—commonly called a leaky gut—lead to increased permeability toward whole and incompletely digested proteins and allow these proteins inappropriate access to immune cells deeper in the intestinal lining and to the bloodstream. Not only does this condition allow for the establishment of immune system sensitivities to foods—and allow for the actual food reactions to occur upon future exposures to those foods—but this condition also *results from* intestinal inflammatory reactions to foods. Hence, a cycle of damage, exposure, and further damage occurs. This intestinal damage is even found in most cases of eczema, in many behavioral conditions, in eosinophilic esophagitis, and in diabetes. Conditions such as these may appear to be local afflictions but actually involve the health of the gut. Avoidance of foods that lead to reactions is important to allow the intestines to heal in an effort to reduce future illness.

Healing Baby's Gut for Lifelong Health

Why Give a Poop about the Intestines?

People would generally prefer not to think much about their child's poop, or the organs that create and store it. We've learned now, though, about the huge populations of microscopic creatures maintained within and the tremendous impact their makeup and diversity can have on baby's overall health. We've seen that the appearance and behavior of stools can provide key clues about baby's wellbeing.

The quality of a child's diet, her flora, and other gut health factors can influence the frequency and severity of infections suffered. Intestinal infections can occasionally be devastating, especially in those born too early or too small. When gut health impedances lead to frequent infections, these infections can create an environment that's ripe for further disorders.

Guided by baby's symptoms and reactions, we can determine whether dietary factors are impeding a baby's health, and we can reduce chronic inflammation by detecting and avoiding food allergens—reducing risks for later autoimmune and other disease developments in the process. Common symptoms in infants—such as colic, reflux, green stools, and diarrhea—generally signify food intolerances. There's still more to the picture though. Food sensitivities are a loss of normally expected tolerance, and many known factors contribute to this condition—such as antibiotic usage, early formula feeding, infections, and even birthing interventions and locations. Left unchecked, food intolerance becomes a self-perpetuating cycle that can lead to further health problems. Except when strongly genetic, this loss of tolerance is itself only a symptom—an indicator that intestinal healing is needed.

35% of Americans aged 20 years or older today have pre-diabetes and this number grows each year.

Beyond the common childhood autoimmune diseases discussed in Chapter 14—diabetes, autism, celiac disease, and inflammatory bowel diseases—more and rarer autoimmune diseases can develop as a child matures. The seeds for these can be planted during infancy and the risk is increased when poor gut health is persistent throughout childhood and beyond. Decades into a child's life, we could see lupus, myasthenia gravis, multiple sclerosis, rheumatoid arthritis, thyroiditis, uveitis (an eye condition), myocarditis, and other more rare disorders. Autoimmune disorders of neurological bases are often seen to develop with celiac disease. In later decades, Alzheimer's disease and some cancers are illnesses that begin through the same pathways and are reduced by the same gut health efforts as all others discussed. I bring these up only because they are largely preventable by beginning during infancy—actually at, and even before, birth.

There's still more. It's known today that gut flora play quite a role in obesity and, of course, nutrition does as well. Chronic inflammation can occur with food allergies or an otherwise unhealthy gut and is linked to obesity, as is early formula feeding. Obesity combines with autoimmune tendencies to drive diabetes risks higher. Additionally, later heart disease is strongly linked to early programming, with not only early obesity being a risk factor but also chronic inflammation from frequent food intolerance reactions.

Although all these diseases have genetic components, we see genetic factors becoming less and less necessary for the development of such disorders. Even a body with a clean genetic slate (if such a thing exists) is going to find a way to express itself with disease when enough chronic inflammation, nutritional deficiency, or floral destruction is maintained for long enough periods of time.

In terms of numbers, diabetes accounts for the major portion of autoimmune diseases in the industrialized world. Although the prevalence among children is small, 12% of Americans between the ages of 45 and 64 are diagnosed with diabetes (type 1 and type 2 combined)—and 22% above that age—with the seeds being most often planted in early childhood. In view of greatly accelerating rates, and in the absence of some large national health campaign, when today's children reach these decades, the portion of the population affected by diabetes will be unthinkable. If these numbers are not disconcerting enough, consider that 35% of Americans aged 20 years or older today have pre-diabetes and this number, too, grows each year.

Another health and life-threatening disorder that you may not have even heard of, non-alcoholic fatty liver disease, is found in 17% of older teenagers today and in one third of adults over 20.

To help prevent your child from joining any of these statistics, gut healing and ongoing gut health efforts are worthwhile, particularly if your child expresses any of the symptoms of concern discussed throughout this book, has been exposed early to antibiotic drugs, has had early exposure to formula feeding, or has experienced multiple gastrointestinal (GI) infections.

Besides caring for illnesses and avoiding non-tolerated foods, much more can be done in attempt to bring baby from a state of reduced symptoms toward a state of optimal gut health.

Basic Nutrition

So much more could be written on child nutrition; it's a book in itself. I'd like to touch on some highlights that I find important. Early infant nutrition is easy because we know that breastmilk contains the right amounts of everything a baby needs. When mother practices optimal nutrition herself, she can feel confident that her milk is supercharged with nutrients. Although infant formulas are missing immune support factors, prebiotics, probiotics, enzymes, and certain fatty acids, they approximate the vitamins and minerals in breastmilk and provide the basic calories and nutrients that infants need to survive.

Studies show that it's best to avoid starting any formula or solid food supplements for breastfed babies until after 6 months. This doesn't mean that solids need to be started *at* 6 months. I've met many exclusively breastfed babies who simply preferred the best for much longer than 6 months. Breastmilk, as an exclusive diet for a toddler, has no nutritional deficits. (Studies suggesting differently are performed on populations with greatly under-nourished mothers.)

Fewer studies exist about starting solids sooner versus later in formula-fed babies. Their flora has already transitioned to the more challenging adult-type microbes so floral protection is not a reason to delay solids when formula has already been fed. Nutritious solids after 4 months may provide some relief from hard-to-digest formula proteins. They can provide fiber and extra antioxidants as well. The digestive enzymes in some formula-fed babies may not be ready this early, so observation of their handling of solids, including analysis of what comes out, is useful.

Traditional starter foods in the Western world—such as white rice, oats, and bananas—have far fewer nutrients than either breastmilk or formula, and grains may be irritating or allergy-inducing. Although sweetened puddings are found on

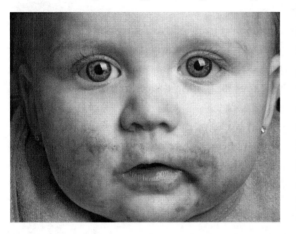

baby food shelves, there is no reason to provide sugary foods. Quinoa is a healthy grain-alternative. Dark vegetables provide a wide spectrum of valuable nutrients and fibers, and should be the focus of solid foods for all children. Avocados are ideal for the additional healthy oils they provide. When desired, poultry can be a nutritious and low-allergen food. Salmon and tuna are healthy when tolerated. Also when tolerated, beans and nut butters are highly nutrient packed.

Juices create a taste for sweets and provide far too much sugar without the fruit fiber, which is so valuable for feeding healthy flora and slowing sugar absorption. Fruits are certainly healthier. When extra liquid is desired to balance the fiber in a child's solid food diet, water or unsweetened (or barely sweetened) herbal teas are perfect choices. Sugar-sweetened and artificially sweetened drinks are only negatives.

In order to achieve appropriate nutrition for infant formulas, cow milk proteins and calcium are reduced to avoid taxing the kidneys and to make room for adequate levels of other necessary nutrients—all of which are added in. Follow-on formulas marketed for babies over 6 months are only cheaper versions of infant formulas. They are promoted as higher in protein and calcium, but these are not purposeful advantages; rather, they are simply money-saving moves for the manufacturers. The higher calcium competes with iron absorption, so extra iron is added to these, but excess iron can be highly oxidizing. A recent German study demonstrated that babies fed higher portions of protein, within generally accepted levels, were two and a half times as likely to be obese at 6 years of age as lower-protein-fed babies, with no difference in height. Additional studies show other disadvantages to a higher protein diet in infancy. Stick with infant formulas.

As mentioned in the previous chapter, cow or goat milk products—which are preferably not fed before a year—should be limited to two or three servings per day, if fed at all. This will make room for all the other nutrients that are important to child nourishment and that are not found in animal milks—such as several B vitamins; vitamins C, E, and K (liquid milks are fortified with vitamins A and D but other milk products are not); fiber; antioxidants; and iron and other minerals (besides calcium and phosphorous). Organic raw and fermented milks can provide beneficial probiotics for the child who does not react negatively to animal milks.

It's quite popular today to try following some specific eating plan. It's apparent, however, that people can be robust and healthy when eating vegan (no meat or dairy products) or eating paleo (high in meats, low in grains). The healthier diet is likely somewhere in-between these. Infants are designed to live on human milk, which is an animal product, and to do so for their first several years when the majority of brain development occurs. A strict vegan diet, without breastmilk, is not nutritionally ideal for an infant or toddler.

Probiotic Supplements: What Can They Do?

Factors such as cesarean birth, a long delay before first colostrum feeding at breast, birth to a mother taking antibiotics, and the microbial environment of a large hospital can all lead to less-than-optimal floral development in the newborn and can result in more negative outcomes later on. Infants receiving formula early can also face greater intestinal health challenges. Antibiotics cause a major blow to anyone's intestinal floral balance. Studies show that the younger the antibiotic exposure occurs, the longer the detrimental results last. Multiple exposures in early childhood are of course more damaging than a single exposure. These studies were discussed in Chapter 3. Although various researchers describe a certain degree of these early, negative consequences as "permanent," other studies describe improvements in symptoms and in floral makeup with regular probiotic supplementation.

Probiotic supplements are capsules, liquids, or powders containing specific strains of beneficial bacteria, or a beneficial yeast. Beneficial gut flora secrete all kinds of active acids that fight unwanted bacteria, reduce inflammation, and improve the health of the surrounding flora. Probiotic supplements can act in this manner as well, on a dose-dependent basis.

Although fermented foods are useful builders of flora, a discussion of probiotic supplements is important: firstly, because they can be given even to newborn infants whereas other foods cannot and, secondly, because there is a large amount of research on probiotic supplements and little, to date, on fermented foods. I use this research to represent the benefits that would also be derived from other sources of flora. Healthy probiotic bacteria are numerous in fermented foods, which—when a child is old enough or for lactating mom—are excellent options for boosting a healthy microbiota.

Contrary to early medical complaints, it's been well established that ample portions of most probiotic strains do survive digestion. Infant tummies are less acidic than adult stomachs and thus even more likely to be friendly to passing probiotics. Flora and probiotic supplements have been highly researched in infants, although there's still much to learn. Improvement of gut flora with probiotics requires regular usage over an extended period of time, but probiotics are your best bet for improving a damaged microbiome or for amending one that had a tough start.

Healthy probiotic bacteria are numerous in fermented foods, which—when a child is old enough or for lactating mom—are excellent options for boosting a healthy microbiota.

Several studies have provided evidence that colonies of supplemented bacterial strains can take hold in the intestines. This occurrence appears to depend upon the strain taken, the manner in which it is taken, the regularity, the dosage used, the child's diet, and other unknown factors. Appropriate **prebiotics**—which are particular fruit and vegetable fibers or oligosaccharides from human milk—need to be readily available in the gut to feed the probiotics. The establishment in the gut of new probiotic colonies is actually only one of many means by which probiotics provide benefits and is not necessarily the chief goal. In fact, a few research studies are performed with "killed" probiotics and even these provide measurable benefits. This is at least partly a result of helpful acids and bacteriocins (agents that kill unwanted bacteria) found inside the bacterial cells.

An important Baltimore study gave *Lactobacillus plantarum* and prebiotic fructo-oligosaccharides to breastfed newborns for 7 days. By the third day, the researchers were able to measure the supplemented bacterium in the infants' stools. Six months after the 7-day supplementation, one third of babies still had this strain in their stools. It was not found in the infants who received placebos. Possibly even more important, the babies who had received this one strain of probiotic bacteria were found, at 4 weeks, to have a much greater diversity of other healthy bacteria and fewer negative bacteria than the placebo babies.

Actions of probiotic supplements, according to detailed studies, include the following:

- increasing protective mucus coating of intestinal mucous membranes,
- releasing bacteriocins—substances that kill unwanted bacteria,
- blocking sites along membranes to prevent attachment by unwanted bacteria,
- reducing gut membrane permeability (reduction of leaky gut),
- activating gut immune cells that attack disease-causing microbes,
- increasing the action of other protective immune agents,
- preventing the release of inflammatory factors,
- supporting the growth of other beneficial bacterial strains, and
- establishing colonies of the supplemented strain.

Through these mechanisms and more, fortification of a child's microbiome via probiotic supplements can limit leaking of proteins and lessen a child's tendency to react allergically to foods and additives, thus reducing colic, reflux, eczema, behavior swings, constipation, and other symptoms. Probiotic supplementation can reduce intestinal inflammation and, for a damaged microbiome, it can help to lessen the number of intestinal infections and to speed illness recoveries.

Probiotic Studies in Infants

If a probiotic supplement is able to reduce food allergies, eczema, or colic in children, then it must be doing so by improving the health of the gut flora, gut barriers, and/or the intestinal immune system.

According to a 2007 review, covering both breastfed and formula-fed infants, studies that showed the most promise for reducing eczema in susceptible babies used *Lactobacillus rhamnosus*. This review found less response in formula-fed infants, but some reduction in eczema was shown. A Russian study successfully used the species *Bifidobacterium lactis* and *Streptococcus thermophilus* (a good guy, even though the name sounds scary), in addition to elimination dieting, for infants who were allergic to cow milk. Significant decreases in constipation, diarrhea, and colic were seen after 4 weeks of treatment. A 2014 Iranian study performed since the most recent study reviews gave breastfed infants a mix of *L. casei*, *L. rhamnosus*, *S. thermophilus*, *B. breve*, *L. acidophilus*, *B. infantis*, and *L. bulgaricus*, along with a prebiotic; researchers saw a large improvement in infant colic.

Polish researchers reviewed the available studies on L. *reuteri* and found the use of this probiotic to reduce colic in breastfed and partly formula-fed infants but not in fully formula-fed babies. One well-controlled Italian study using this species to treat both breast- and formula-fed newborns found crying to be nearly cut in half and reflux cut by one third. An analysis of infants' florae at the end of a similar trial found increased levels of other beneficial bacteria in the babies who had improved during probiotic usage.

Weaning, meaning the first introductions of non-breastmilk feeds, can be a time of increased illness. Swedish scientists provided L. *paracasei* to infants in their first cereal at 4 months and continued this supplementation for 9 additional months. They measured strong improvements in the children's T-cell profiles—immune cells that help to regulate food tolerance and immune protection—and improvements in some other immune system factors as well. These same researchers performed an 8-year followup on the children who had received probiotics for 9 months as infants. Unfortunately, they measured no long-lasting effects of their treatment. The Kim study in the chart below did, however, measure continued eczema benefits at 12 months when breastfeeding mothers used probiotics from pre-birth until 6 months.

Although no harm is done, a few babies react with mild negative symptoms when probiotics are started.

Many other studies demonstrate that the regular addition of a health-promoting bacterium helps to improve the overall microbiome balance. It appears that probiotic benefits may be somewhat lasting but, understandably, are not permanent. Treatment should continue for as long as you desire significant benefits. Probiotics are clearly useful as part of a full gut-healing plan.

Many variables exist in probiotic studies, thus the results in many studies are modest, although some are strongly positive. Because of mixed findings, some medical reports conclude that there is no reason to recommend probiotic supplementation until extensive evidence is presented. The psychology works in reverse, however, when the research is performed by formula companies. They typically fail to show any substantial benefits from probiotic-enhanced infant formulas, but they go ahead and add probiotics to their products anyway.

Reviews also consistently conclude that safety concerns don't exist with probiotic supplements in infants, children, or adults. To me, this leaves little reason *not* to try some form of flora boosting when a baby has challenges or when early infant care doesn't go entirely as planned. Although no harm is done, a few babies react with mild negative symptoms when probiotics are started. Health practitioners describe that these instances may represent a die-off of bad bacteria. As long as a child does not appear allergic to the ingredients in a supplement (such as beef gelatin capsules or a milk source), simply reducing the dose, and later increasing it gradually, may be a good option for some.

Below are more findings about some specific probiotic strains.

Specific probiotic strains and benefits shown in children

Probiotic	Benefit	Trials
B. bifidum, B. lactis, and L. acidophilus	Lasting reduction in eczema in breastfed infants when mother supplemented before and after birth	Kim (2010) RDBPCT
B. lactis and S. thermophilus	Reduced constipation, diarrhea, and colic in cow milk allergic infants	Ivakhnenko (2013) RPCT
B. longum with L. paracasei or with L. rhamnosus	Reduced infant eczema when mother takes during pregnancy and breastfeeding	Rautava (2012) RDBPCT
L. acidophilus	Reduced eczema in children	Torii (2011) RDBPCT
L. fermentum plus prebiotic	Reduced overall infectious diseases in formula-fed children by 30%	Maldonado (2012) RDBPCT
L. paracasei	Strongly improved intestinal immune cell profiles in breastfed children beginning cereal at 4 months	West (2012) RDBPCT
L. reuteri	Reduced colic in infants who were breastfed >50%	Urbanska (2014) Review
L. reuteri	32 hours shorter infectious diarrhea in hospitalized children over 3 months of age	Szajewska (2014) Review
L. reuteri with L. rhamnosus	Stabilized intestinal barrier and reduced GI symptoms in children with eczema	Rosenfeldt (2004) RDBPCT
L. rhamnosus GG	Reduced eczema in high risk infants and children treated directly or through treating mother	Betsi (2008) Review
L. rhamnosus	Reduced eczema in susceptible babies, less response in formula fed than in breastfed	Osborn (2007) Review
L. rhamnosus GG	1 day shorter infectious diarrhea	Szajewska 2013 Review
S. boulardii (a yeast)	1 day shorter infectious diarrhea, reduced antibiotic-associated diarrhea in children	Vandenplas (2013) Review

Note: RDBPCT = Randomized, double-blinded, placebo-controlled trial; Review = Review of available, well-designed trials

Prebiotics, Probiotics, and Infant Formulas

As said, studies on probiotic-supplemented formulas do not report favorable results. I believe that it's difficult to maintain potency of a bacterium in a processed and canned infant formula product that needs to sit on shelves for long periods of time. Studies using direct provision of probiotic supplements to formula-fed infants appear to have somewhat more success. Fresh probiotics provided from the home refrigerator may be superior to those in canned formulas. These are my recommendation for formula-fed infants, along with prebiotics or vegetables, depending on the baby's age. There is no reason to avoid a formula with probiotics added but also no reason to expect much benefit from it.

Fresh probiotics provided from the home refrigerator are my recommendation for formula-fed infants, along with prebiotics or vegetables.

More importantly, many formulas contain little to feed beneficial flora. Cow milk contains less than 1/1000th the amount of prebiotic oligosaccharides as human milk, and many formulas use only the protein portions of milk. Soy fiber is usually removed from soy formulas. Many formulas contain lactose, and lactose *does* feed some healthy flora. Other cow milk formulas, and soy formulas, use corn syrup or other simple sugars instead of lactose. These sugars are mostly broken down and absorbed before reaching the colon and, if portions do reach the colon, simple sugars are found to feed less desirable flora. An infant consuming only lactose-free infant formula, with no supplemental breastmilk, fruits, or vegetables, is acquiring almost nothing to optimally feed healthy flora. Flora *can* survive on proteins (via putrefaction), but many potentially toxic substances are produced by this process.

Formula companies have been working with additions of prebiotics to infant formulas. The prebiotics in breastmilk include around 200 different, complicated oligosaccharides—something that would be pretty difficult to match. Studies on the addition of one or two kinds of simple prebiotics to infant formulas have shown certain beneficial results, along with occasional less desirable (non-harmful) effects, but the most recent review of the studies reports that no beneficial effects have been proven for additions of prebiotics, probiotics, or combinations of these (known as synbiotics). Research in this area appears to have slowed down, although infant formulas are available today with added prebiotics.

Efforts have been made, with the use of probiotic supplements, to reduce infections in formula-fed infants. A Spanish study gave breastmilk-derived

Lactobacillus fermentum, plus a prebiotic, to formula-fed children. A 30% reduction in total infectious diseases was measured, but without any reduction in fevers experienced. Belgium reviewers of multiple probiotic studies found the evidence, in terms of preventing infectious GI illnesses in formula-fed infants, to be only modest but found the evidence for respiratory infections to be somewhat stronger. Probiotic supplementation may make up for part of the protection gap experienced by babies who receive formula, and the addition of prebiotics can make this more likely.

Probiotics during Antibiotic Exposure

Probiotics should definitely be provided during any exposure to antibiotic drugs, for breastfed or formula-fed infants, for breastfeeding moms, and for the whole family. Research reviews find the strongest probiotic evidence in relation to prevention of antibiotic-related diarrhea. Studies show, on average, a 40% reduction in the diarrhea that frequently attends or follows antibiotic usage. If probiotics are successfully reducing this drug-related diarrhea, then they must be competing with some of the dangerous flora that antibiotic usage often promotes. Probiotic supplementation should also be maintained for a long period of time after antibiotic usage has ended, in attempt to restore the health and diversity of the microbiome. Some of the probiotics that showed promise in such studies include species from the *Bifidobacterium*, *Lactobacillus*, *Saccharomyces*, and *Streptococcus* genera.

As well as wiping out many healthy bacterial colonies and allowing the growth of unwanted opportunistic bacteria, antibiotic usage is well-known to encourage overgrowth of the fungus *Candida*—not only in lady parts but also in the digestive tract. Chronic use of reflux medicines and pain and fever reducers (NSAIDs) also encourages GI *Candida* growth. Excess *Candida* colonization is sometimes found in areas of intestinal damage associated with chronic intestinal inflammation. *Candida* then promotes further inflammation and reduces the intestine's ability to heal. Researchers gave a supplement with

Probiotics should be provided during any exposure to antibiotic drugs.

multiple probiotic strains and fructo-oligosaccharides to critically ill hospitalized children who were receiving broad spectrum antibiotics. Those receiving probiotics had one third less gastrointestinal *Candida* colonization. Of course, continuation of this therapy should reduce fungal colonization even more.

Providing Probiotics

Probiotic powders can be shaken into infant formula, stirred into pumped breastmilk, or inserted into baby's mouth with a finger and then washed down with a couple gulps at the breast or bottle. Alternatively, tiny bits at a time can be placed onto mother's nipple as baby breastfeeds. Liquid forms of pediatric probiotics are also available. Probiotic supplements maintain their potency best when kept refrigerated.

In terms of strain choices, quality products are designed to provide strains that have been found helpful. Look for species you are interested in, such as *Lactobacillus reuteri* and *L. rhamnosus*, but don't worry too much about which strains are present. Research always points toward a wide diversity of beneficial strains living in the gut as being optimal. Selecting a probiotic product with many different species is probably the best option, or even selecting two different products in order to increase the variety of the strains. If you are selecting a product for a baby who receives only formula, look for one that contains prebiotics as well, or select an additional prebiotic product.

Studies show probiotic benefits to be dose related. Quality brands provide formulations and dosage recommendations that they feel to be effective. Reportedly, the minimum dose found to be effective in infants and children is from one million to one billion CFU (colony forming units) daily. (These may be labeled as 10^6 and 10^9 CFU.) Some studies with the best results, showing good outcomes even with short-term treatments, have used 10 billion to 100 billion CFUs per day. It's best to divide the dosage into two to four provisions per day.

If your baby reacts to cow milk, you can find probiotics that are milk free. If you don't look specifically for a milk-free product, it will have been grown on milk. Although many other food products that use the term "dairy-free" are actually just lactose free and contain milk proteins, this term—when found on probiotic products—does appear to mean "milk-free."

A breastfeeding mother can take probiotic supplements herself and this may lead to a greater balance of beneficial flora being provided through her milk. Ample studies demonstrate positive alterations in breastmilk flora or in infant responses when mothers take probiotics.

Many practitioners advise to take probiotics on an empty stomach, but I disagree. Probiotics need to be fed. Don't take them with a Coke, but do take probiotics with a bit of vegetables or fruit, or with a prebiotic supplement such as inulin or fructo-oligosaccharides. Even mixed with a meal, the probiotics will find their way to their targets. Mom's own floral balance, and thus that of her milk, will improve when she also takes other gut health measures.

For mom or the older child, fermented foods, such as yogurt and sauerkraut, also contain beneficial flora and are beneficial means of keeping one's microbiome strong. Non-dairy yogurts are available for milk-sensitive children. Another natural means of consuming healthy flora is eating unwashed or lightly rinsed organic fruits and vegetables. If your food was grown in healthy soil, thereby coated with health-promoting bacteria, your barely rinsed organic food is a great source of beneficial flora.

Herbal and Nutritional Supplements

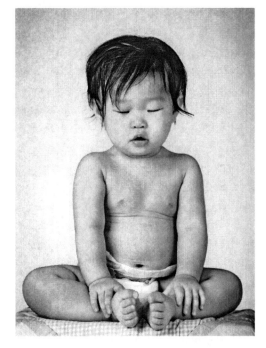

Many dietary substances are shown to have valuable healing qualities. Many nutritional supplements can be considered for breastfeeding moms and for breastfeeding babies who are already eating solid foods. For babies who receive any formula, dietary supplements can be given by 4 to 6 months, and some parents may choose to give tiny sips of strong herbal teas, or possibly infant vitamin C drops, sooner than this. Probiotic supplements can be given to younger infants, even newborns, and are well-studied in preterm infants.

As long as a baby is exclusively receiving breastmilk, with no formula, baby foods, iron supplements, or other additions (besides water), he is benefiting from a vast and uninhibited array of GI infection protection, anti-inflammatory agents, healthy flora, and other factors to promote and maintain gut health. Once any irritants are removed, an exclusively breastfed gut should heal well, with the possible addition of probiotics directly to baby to boost recovery from any assaults, such as antibiotic usage or frequent food reactions. Studies have shown that free iron (which is found in almost every food or herb), foreign proteins, and even simple starches partly interfere with the protection that exclusive breastmilk provides. For these reasons, there is no need for the provision of herbs or other nutritional supplements directly to an exclusively breastfeeding baby.

At least some fragrant portions of some herbs, when consumed by breastfeeding mothers, have been proven to pass into breastmilk. Little study has been performed on this, but it's likely that most portions of most herbs are passed on.

> *There is no need for the provision of herbs or other nutritional supplements directly to an exclusively breastfeeding baby.*

You may want to also follow some of the recommendations below when caring for a breastfeeding baby who is also receiving solid foods, iron supplements, or formula supplements.

The omega-3 fatty acids, **DHA** and **EPA**, are highly important to intestinal health. They can help to reduce allergies in infants, reduce intestinal inflammation, and promote intestinal healing. These fatty acids have been deficient in modern diets for quite some time. Naturally found in fish oil, especially salmon, and in organ meats, the body can also make DHA and EPA from the fatty acid ALA—which is found in some green vegetables and in more significant quantities in flax seed and walnuts. It's been found that babies do not generate optimal levels of DHA for themselves. Adults who do not eat fish have also been found to suffer from inadequate DHA and EPA. These omega-3 fatty acids have always been in breastmilk but, when mothers consume healthy doses of these, they can increase the amounts they pass in their milk, to baby's benefit. Vegan versions are available if desired.

Many infant formulas have begun adding DHA—and ARA—another important fatty acid found in breastmilk. Unfortunately, they have not found as much benefit as hoped for from formulas supplemented with manufactured versions of these. Additionally, a portion of infants respond to this ingredient with diarrhea and vomiting, possibly as a result of the unnatural form that is produced and possibly as a result of remaining traces of the chemical hexane used in the manufacturing process. Natural DHA supplements are available in infant and child versions and are advisable for children who do not receive the majority of their nourishment from breastmilk.

Modern diets have dropped what has negatively come to be known as "meat by-products." "Meat" sold today is all muscle tissue that contains ample protein, vitamin B12, and minerals to feed our muscles, but other tissues in our bodies use nutrients found in—well, other tissues. Eye and liver are packed with omega-3 fatty acids. Tongue and intestinal linings are packed with connective tissues that our digestive system is made from. Cartilage from joints also contains these valuable connective tissue components such as chondroitin, glucosamine, hyaluronan, MSM, and gelatin—nutrients that are not only essential for joint development but also for growth and repair of intestinal membranes. The earliest humans consumed nutrient-packed soups made by boiling all portions of meat. Man flourished this way until the 1800s.

At the turn of the 21st century, The Weston A. Price Foundation brought back the wisdom of **bone broths**, and paleo diet enthusiasts are strengthening the trend. To support this with science, many studies investigate the utility of one or two cartilage components at a time, such as chondroitin or glucosamine, and document their merit in the healing of intestinal and other tissues. The full spectrum of these is certainly more beneficial. Many who seek gut healing today are re-confirming the value of bone broths. For those interested, some of the connective tissue ingredients mentioned above can be obtained in vegan joint support supplements.

For babies receiving solid foods, **cabbage** is an ideal healing aid for intestines. It's been shown to help heal ulcers and other digestive irritations, and it provides fiber to feed healthy flora. Fermented cabbage, or sauerkraut, adds good doses of probiotics to this prebiotic and gut-healing food. Cabbage can cause some excess gassiness. Building up the dosage gradually gives gut flora time to adapt to the digestive needs of cabbage.

Chamomile and **ginger** are two herbs that have been demonstrated to have anti-inflammatory, membrane-protecting, and intestinal-healing effects, and are gentle for children. These can be provided in teas. **Mastic gum** is thought to help protect the linings of the stomach and intestines. This tree resin has been demonstrated to hold a wide variety of GI healing properties including defense against unwanted microbes and anti-inflammatory, antioxidant, and anti-cancer qualities. The powder from capsules can be added to a child's nourishment. **Curcumin**, the active component in the spice turmeric, is not only powerfully antioxidant and anti-inflammatory but also has been shown to be quite valuable against inflammatory bowel

For babies receiving solid foods, cabbage is an ideal healing aid for intestines.

diseases and other serious GI problems. It's been studied in children, proving to be effective and well tolerated. Mom can easily take curcumin supplements, but the taste of the powder is pretty strong for young children, beyond typical curry-seasoning amounts. **Chinese medicine** and **Ayurvedic medicine** also have many herbs with gut healing effects that are not only proven by time, but today, most of these have undergone scientific safety and effectiveness studies.

Vitamin C has antioxidant power and is known to assist in tissue healing. Often liquid forms can be found with additional **bioflavonoids**. Most vitamin C supplements are derived from citrus, as are bioflavonoids. If a child is sensitive to citrus, then simple ascorbic acid can be found, possibly with added **rose hips** for extra antioxidant potency. Most doctors would not object to vitamin C supplements for infants only two or three months old.

The amino acid **glutamine**—which does not have the negative properties of free glutamates like MSG—has long been supplemented in preterm infants with the intention of speeding intestinal maturation and healing. Study results on glutamine supplementation are quite mixed, and a 2012 review suggests that its effectiveness has not been solidly proven. Since this review, one well-designed 2014 study demonstrated improvement in intestinal barrier protection in Brazilian children. Many practitioners still have faith in glutamine supplements. It simply takes more than one nutrient to heal a gut. Glutamine may provide benefits when combined with other nutritional healing efforts. Upcoming studies need to be watched.

When serious healing of digestive system tissues is needed, **aloe vera gel** (not whole juice, not latex-containing) has been shown to be quite anti-inflammatory and healing for intestinal tissues. Today, many filtered aloe juices are sold with the latex portions removed. Some medical sources advise against oral aloe use in children, but most concerns focus on the latex portion of whole aloe juice, which is used to treat adult constipation and which is not desirable for use in children. Surveys reveal widespread use of oral aloe gel or filtered juice for intestinal healing in children. Non-toxicity has been shown through animal tests, and a history of moderate use in children has failed to reveal any negative effects, outside of rare allergic reactions.

Healing Mom, the Family, and the Home

Mother's nutrition is important before pregnancy, during pregnancy, and while creating milk for her baby. As learned elsewhere in this chapter, breast-feeding mother can take many nutritional steps in effort to pass more healing factors through her milk. Lessons about flora are also important for mother because her flora supports her immune system while housing the developing baby, and baby's own flora is initiated by exposure to mom's—some before birth and then, importantly, during vaginal birth.

While sharing the same home, mom, dad, and siblings' florae all influence baby's floral balance. Keeping everyone's flora optimal improves baby's gut health. Studies show that plants inside the home improve the health of the home microbiome and can positively influence human health. Likewise, a home with a pet that goes outside and comes back in promotes healthier flora in those living in the home and reduces allergies in the children. The same, of course, would be true for humans who go out and play in the dirt. If a child has already developed an allergy to the family pet, however, the pet needs to find a new home. Chronic inflammation from frequent immune reactions is what we want to avoid.

Sunshine, Dirt, and Play

Concerns over skin cancer have led to 50 years of vitamin D deficiency for the majority of those in industrialized nations. We now know that this has increased our susceptibilities for illnesses ranging from the flu to breast cancer and has weakened our bones. Children have been just as affected as adults. When a breastfeeding mother does not acquire the sunshine or the supplemental vitamin D that is important for her own health, then sun exposure for her infant can make up for the lower amount her milk may provide.

Vitamin D is vital to intestinal growth and repair and to immune protection. Vitamin D supplementation or good dietary intake is especially important in the winter for most people. Those with darker skin and living in more Northern latitudes need to pay more attention to obtaining sun exposure and consuming vitamin D. This vitamin can be obtained from fish consumption. If the animals are raised outside in the sun, eggs and animal fats (including whole cow milk) should contain vitamin D as well, but almost all are raised indoors.

Sunshine provides other health-promoting benefits besides the UV rays that promote vitamin D production in the skin, and these other benefits are not dependent upon the time of day. When skin is exposed to blue and green light, which are parts of white sunlight, the processing of bile is promoted. Many modern studies demonstrate other healing benefits from other various portions of white light. Daily bright light is also known to improve emotional wellbeing, and inadequate amounts of daylight are said to lead to seasonal affective disorder. The pineal gland, in the center of our brain, is fed messages about light and dark from the eyes and creates health-promoting hormones that help regulate our daily rhythms, including digestive cycles. Complete darkness at night is just as important to the pineal gland as light during the day, so that it will create optimal levels of the health-promoting, antioxidant, and inflammation-reducing hormone melatonin.

> *Complete darkness at night is just as important to the pineal gland as light during the day.*

Chapter 3 presented the importance of childhood exposure to probiotic- and bacteriophage-filled **dirt**. Babies naturally sample the flora in their environment by touching and crawling and then putting their hands into their mouths. Although we prefer to avoid such exposures when cold or flu viruses are near, or when the dog has worms, such exposures are otherwise healthy. Play is, of course, of high value to intellectual and emotional development in children and the best play can be outdoors with sunshine (or raindrops), plants, and dirt.

Responsive Care and Child Health

Like adults, stress in babies and children interferes with many facets of health. Regular responsive affectionate care has been well shown to reduce stress and to provide greater emotional and physical health for children and the adults they will become. Skin-to-skin contact especially promotes the release of the hormone oxytocin, which improves emotional wellbeing, boosts the immune system, reduces risks for heart disease, and even improves digestion and absorption of nutrients. It's especially important to remember that babies' brains and immune systems do not turn off at night; they need as much responsive affection as they do during the day.

Some Final Thoughts

It's difficult to even imagine how the health and diversity of millions of colonies of thousands of species of tiny microbes play far more crucial roles in a baby's health—and that of the adult she will become—than anything we will ever see with our eyes. Baby's first hours, days, and months from birth have the most important influence. The diet of mother and the activities of the entire family all affect a child's floral wellbeing. Healing mother's gut and providing a non-sterile environment are two important steps in improving baby's gut health. Prebiotics and probiotics can help diversify the flora and strengthen the immune protection it provides the child, especially when antibiotic exposure or other damage occurs. Good nutrition and effective nutritional supplements support gut healing. Along with avoidance of irritating foods, these steps reduce intestinal inflammation and pave the way for gut recovery that can, in turn, promote greater food tolerance, strengthen overall membrane barrier function, enhance nutrient absorption, increase infection resistance—and help prevent future disease developments.

Messages in the diaper can provide major clues for caretakers about the infant's wellbeing. Based upon these clues, this book suggests steps that parents can take to optimize the comfort, health, and longevity of their child.

Endnotes

1 Why the Poop

Baby's Vulnerable Gut

Vighi, G., et al. Allergy and the gastrointestinal system. *Clin Exp Immunol* 153, Suppl. 1 (Sep 2008): 3–6.

Industrialization and Disease

Kassebaum, N. J., et al. Global, regional, and national levels and causes of maternal mortality during 1990-2013: A systematic analysis for the Global Burden of Disease Study 2013. *Lancet* pii (May 2014): S0140–6736(14)60696-6.

"The world factbook—country comparison: Maternal mortality rate," Central Intelligence Agency, accessed July 14, 2014, https://www.cia.gov/library/publications/the-world-factbook/rankorder/2223rank.html

"The world factbook—country comparison: Infant mortality rate," Central Intelligence Agency, accessed July 14, 2014, https://www.cia.gov/library/publications/the-world-factbook/rankorder/2091rank.html

"Committing to child survival: A promise renewed," Unicef, accessed July 12, 2014, http://www.unicef.org/lac/Committing_to_Child_Survival_APR_9_Sept_2013.pdf

Spiegelman, M., & Marks, H.H. Age and sex variations in the prevalence and onset of diabetes mellitus. *Am J Public Health Nations Health* 36, no. 1 (Jan 1946): 26–33.

Ogden, C. L., et al. Prevalence of childhood and adult obesity in the United States, 2011-2012. *JAMA* 311, no. 8 (Feb 2014): 806–14.

"Summary health statistics for U.S. children: National health interview survey, 2011," Center for Disease Control and Prevention, accessed July 14, 2014, http://www.cdc.gov/nchs/data/series/sr_10/sr10_254.pdf

Perrin, J. M., et al. The increase of childhood chronic conditions in the United States. *JAMA* 297, no. 4 (2007): 2755–2759.

"Methiicillin resistant D Aureus infection rates: United States and other countries," Center for Disease Dynamics, Economics & Policy, accessed July 10, 2014, http://www.cddep.org/tools/methicillin_resistant_D_aureus_infection_rates_united_states_and_other_countries

Industrialized Nutrition

Okada Y., et al. Trans fatty acids in diets act as a precipitating factor for gut inflammation? *J Gastroenterol Hepatol* 28, Suppl. 4, (Dec 2013): 29–32.

Kloetzel M., et al. Trans fatty acids affect cellular viability of human intestinal Caco-2 cells and activate peroxisome proliferator-activated receptors. *Nutr Cancer* 65, no. 1 (2013): 139–46.

Hofmanová, J., et al. Interaction of dietary fatty acids with tumour necrosis factor family cytokines during colon inflammation and cancer. *Mediators Inflamm* 2014 (2014): 848632.

2 It's Alive

Gut Flora Work to Complete Baby's Nutrition

Kurokawa, K., et al. Comparative metagenomics revealed commonly enriched gene sets in human gut microbiomes. *DNA Res* 14, no. 4 (Aug 2007): 169–81.

Sears, C. L. A dynamic partnership: Celebrating our gut flora. *Anaerobe* 11, no. 5 (Oct 2005): 247–51.

Turroni, F., et al. Human gut microbiota and bifidobacteria: From composition to functionality. *Antonie Van Leeuwenhoek* 94, no. 1 (2008): 35–50.

Wostmann, B.S., et al. Dietary intake, energy metabolism, and excretory losses of adult male germfree Wistar rats. *Lab Anim Science* 33, no. 1 (Feb 1983): 46–50.

Yatsunenko, T., et al. Human gut microbiome viewed across age and geography. *Nature* 486, no. 7402 (May 2012): 222–7.

Flora and Fermentation

Jiang, T., et al. Gas production by feces of infants. *J Pediatr Gastroenterol Nutr* 32, no. 5 (May 2001): 534–41.

Detoxifying

Rowland, I. R., et al. Effects of diet on mercury metabolism and excretion in mice given methylmercury: Role of gut flora. *Arch Environ Health* 39, no. 6 (Nov–Dec 1984): 401–8.

Sobko, T., et al. Gastrointestinal bacteria generate nitric oxide from nitrate and nitrite. *Nitric Oxide* 13, no. 4 (Dec 2005): 272–8.

Flora Provide Valuable Immune Protection

Bucci, V., et al. The evolution of bacteriocin production in bacterial biofilms. *Am Nat* 178, no. 6 (Dec 2011): E162–73.

Fanaro, S., et al. Intestinal microflora in early infancy: Composition and development. *Acta Paediatr Suppl.* 91, no. 441 (Sep 2003): 48–55.

Ganal, S. C., et al. Priming of natural killer cells by nonmucosal mononuclear phagocytes requires instructive signals from commensal microbiota. *Immunity* 37, no. 1 (Jul 2012): 171–86.

Hooper, L.V., et al. Interactions between the microbiota and the immune system. *Science* 336, no. 6086 (Jun 2012): 1268–73.

Gut-Brain Axis: Flora Influence Baby's Brain

Al-Asmakh, M., et al. Gut microbial communities modulating brain development and function. *Gut Microbes* 3, no 4 (Jul 2012): 366–73.

Bravo, J. A., et al. Ingestion of Lactobacillus strain regulates emotional behavior and central GABA receptor expression in a mouse via the vagus nerve. *Proc Natl Acad Sci USA* 108, no. 38 (Sep 2011): 16050–5.

Diaz Heijtz, R., et al. Normal gut microbiota modulates brain development and behavior. *Proc Natl Acad Sci USA* 108, no. 7 (Feb 2011): 3047–52.

Grenham, S., et al. Brain-gut-microbe communication in health and disease. *Front Physiol* 2, no. 94 (Dec 2011): 94.

Tillisch, K., et al. Consumption of fermented milk product with probiotic modulates brain activity. *Gastroenterology* 144, no. 7 (Jun 2013): 1394–401, e1–4.

Establishment of Flora in the Newborn

Fanaro, S., et al. Intestinal microflora in early infancy: Composition and development. *Acta Paediatr Suppl* 91, no. 114 (Sep 2003): 48–55.

Hamzelou, J. A dusty home may influence a baby's gut. *New Scientist* 2862 (Apr 30 2012).

Jiménez, E., et al. Is meconium from healthy newborns actually sterile? *Res Microbiol* 159, no. 3: 187–93.

Penders, J., et al. Factors influencing the composition of the intestinal microbiota in early infancy. *Pediatrics* 118, no. 2 (Aug 2006): 511–21.

Establishment of Flora after Cesarean Section

Biasucci, G., et al. Cesarean delivery may affect the early biodiversity of intestinal bacteria. *J Nutr* 138, no. 9 (Sep 2008): 1796S–1800S.

Cho, C. E. and M. Norman. Cesarean section and development of the immune system in the offspring. *Am J Obstet Gynecol* 208, no. 4 (Aug 2012): 249–54.

Grönlund, M. M., et al. Fecal microflora in healthy infants born by different methods of delivery: Permanent changes in intestinal flora after cesarean delivery. *J Pediatr Gastroenterol Nutr* 28, no. 1 (Jan 1999): 19–25.

Koplin, J., et al. Is caesarean delivery associated with sensitization to food allergens and IgE-mediated food allergy: A systematic review. *Pediatr Allergy Immunol* 19, no. 8 (Dec 2008): 682–7.

Laubereau, B., et al., & GINI Study Group. Caesarean section and gastrointestinal symptoms, atopic dermatitis, and sensitisation during the first year of life. *Arch Dis Child* 89, no. 11 (Nov 2004): 993–7.

Thavagnanam, S., et al. A meta-analysis of the association between Caesarean section and childhood asthma. *Clin Exp Allergy* 38, no. 4 (Apr 2008): 629–33.

van Nimwegen, F. A., et al. Mode and place of delivery, gastrointestinal microbiota, and their influence on asthma and atopy. *J Allergy Clin Immunol* 128, no. 5: 948–55, e1–3.

Continued Establishment of Flora in the Infant

Azad, M. B., et al., & CHILD Study Investigators. Gut microbiota of healthy Canadian infants: Profiles by mode of delivery and infant diet at 4 months. *CMAJ* 185, no. 5 (Mar 2013): 385–94.

Fujimura, K. E., et al. House dust exposure mediates gut microbiome Lactobacillus enrichment and airway immune defense against allergens and virus infection. *Proc Natl Acad Sci U S A*. 2013 Dec 16.

Hesselmar, B., et al. Pacifier cleaning practices and risk of allergy development. *Pediatrics* 131, no. 6 (Jun 2013): e1829–37.

Flora of a Lifetime

Caporaso, J. G., et al. Moving pictures of the human microbiome. *Genome Biol* 12, no. 5 (2011): R50.

Lee, S. M., et al. Bacterial colonization factors control specificity and stability of the gut microbiota. *Nature* 501, no. 7467 (Sep 2013): 426–9.

3 Messing with the Microbiome

Good Efforts Gone Bad

Acton, D. S., et al. Intestinal carriage of Staphylococcus aureus: How does its frequency compare with that of nasal carriage and what is its clinical impact? *Eur J Clin Microbiol Infect Dis* 278, no. 2 (Feb 2009):115–27.

Blaser, M. J., & Falkow, S. What are the consequences of the disappearing human microbiota? *Nat Rev Microbiol* 9, no. 12 (Dec 2009): 887–94.

Bogaert, D., et al. Colonisation by Streptococcus pneumoniae and Staphylococcus aureus in healthy children. *Lancet* 263, no. 9424 (Jun 2004): 1871–2.

Brouwer, M. C., et al. Epidemiology, diagnosis, and antimicrobial treatment of acute bacterial meningitis. *Clin Microbiol Rev* 23, no. 3 (Jul 2010): 467–92.

Chowdhary, S. & Puliyel, J. Incidence of pneumonia is not reduced by pneumococcal conjugate vaccine. *Bull World Health Organ* 86, no. 10 (Oct 2008): A.

David, M. Z., & Daum, R. S. Community-associated methicillin-resistant Staphylococcus aureus: Epidemiology and clinical consequences of an emerging epidemic. *Clin Microbiol Rev* 23, no. 3 (Jul 2010): 616–87.

Eisler P. Dangerous MRSA bacteria expand into communities. *USA Today* (Dec16, 2013). Accessed Feb 20, 2015. "2011 … U.S. Agency for Healthcare Research and Quality. The data suggest those hospitalizations resulted in nearly 23,000 deaths."

Evans, R. The silent epidemic: CA-MRSA and HA-MRSA. *American Academy of Orthopedic Surgeons* 7, no. 12 (May 2008). Accessed Dec 13, 2012.

"FDA Contributing to Fight Against Polio. FDA Consumer Health Information," U.S. Food & Drug Administration (April 2013). http://www.fda.gov/downloads/ForConsumers/ConsumerUpdates/UCM349441.pdf

Hayward, A., et al. Increasing hospitalizations and general practice prescriptions for community-onset staphylococcal disease, England. *Emerg Infect Dis* 14, no. 5 (May 2008): 720–6.

Klein, E., et al. Hospitalizations and deaths caused by methicillin-resistant Staphylococcus aureus, United States, 1999-2005. *Emerg Infect Dis* 13, no. 12 (Dec 2007): 1840–6.

Klevens, R. M., et al. Invasive methicillin-resistant Staphylococcus aureus infections in the United States. *JAMA* 298, no. 15 (Oct 2007): 1763–71.

Ladhani, S. N. Two decades of experience with the Haemophilus influenzae serotype b conjugate vaccine in the United Kingdom. *Clin Ther* 34, no. 2 (Feb 2012): 385–99.

Lindberg, E., et al. Long-time persistence of superantigen-producing Staphylococcus aureus strains in the intestinal microflora of healthy infants. *Pediatr Res* 48, no. 6 (Dec 2000): 741–7.

Lysenko, E. S., et al. The role of innate immune responses in the outcome of interspecies competition for colonization of mucosal surfaces. *PLoS Pathog* 1, no. 1 (Sep 2005): e1.

Morita, J. Y., et al. Association between antimicrobial resistance among pneumococcal isolates and burden of invasive pneumococcal disease in the community. *Clin Infect Dis* 35, no. 4 (Aug 2002): 420–7.

Park, B., et al. Role of Staphylococcus aureus catalase in niche competition against Streptococcus pneumoniae. *J Bacteriol* 190, no. 7 (Apr 2008): 2275–8.

Pulido M. & Sorvillo F. Declining invasive pneumococcal disease mortality in the United States, 1990-2005. *Vaccine* 28, no.4 (Jan 22, 2009): 889-92. (Figure 1 shows increase in rate of decline after introduction of vaccine.)

Regev-Yochay, G., et al. Association between carriage of Streptococcus pneumoniae and Staphylococcus aureus in Children. *JAMA* 292, no. 6 (Aug 2004): 716–20.

Shaban, L., & Siam, R. Prevalence and antimicrobial resistance pattern of bacterial meningitis in Egypt. *Ann Clin Microbiol Antimicrob* 8 (Sep 2009): 26.

Thigpen, M. C., et al. Bacterial meningitis in the United States, 1998-2007. *N Engl J Med* 364, no. 21 (May 2011): 2016–25.

van Gils, E. J., et al. Effect of seven-valent pneumococcal conjugate vaccine on Staphylococcus aureus colonisation in a randomised controlled trial. *PLoS One* 6, no. 6 (Jun 2011): e20229.

Vesterlund, S., et al. Staphylococcus aureus adheres to human intestinal mucus but can be displaced by certain lactic acid bacteria. *Microbiology* 152, Pt. 6, (Jun 2006): 1819–26.

Antibiotics: Friend and Foe

"Battle of the bugs: Fighting antibiotic resistance." U.S. Food & Drug Administration, last modified August 17, 2011. Accessed November 16, 2012, http://www.fda.gov/drugs/resourcesforyou/consumers/ucm143568.htm

Fouhy, F., et al. High-throughput sequencing reveals the incomplete, short-term recovery of infant gut microbiota following parenteral antibiotic treatment with ampicillin and gentamicin. *Antimicrob Agents Chemother* 56, no. 11 (Nov 2012): 5811–20.

Jakobsson, H. E., et al. Short-term antibiotic treatment has differing long-term impacts on the human throat and gut microbiome. *PLoS One* 24, no. 3 (Mar 2010): e9836.

Ranji, S. R., et al. Interventions to reduce unnecessary antibiotic prescribing: A systematic review and quantitative analysis. *Med Care* 46, no. 8 (Aug 2008): 847–62.

Antibiotic Over-Usage

Clair, E., et al. Effects of Roundup(®) and glyphosate on three food microorganisms: Geotrichum candidum, Lactococcus lactis subsp. cremoris and Lactobacillus delbrueckii subsp. bulgaricus. *Curr Microbiol* 64, no. 5 (May 2012): 486–91.

Gaur, A. H., et al. Provider and practice characteristics associated with antibiotic use in children with presumed viral respiratory tract infections. *Pediatrics* 115, no. 3 (Mar 2005): 635–41.

Graham, J. P., et al. Growth promoting antibiotics in food animal production: An economic analysis. *Public Health Rep* 122, no. 1 (Jan–Feb 2007):79–87.

Greene, S. K., et al. Distribution of multidrug-resistant human isolates of MDR-ACSSuT Salmonella Typhimurium and MDR-AmpC Salmonella Newport in the United States, 2003–2005. *Foodborne Pathog Dis* 5, no. 5 (Oct 2008): 669–80.

Jernberg, C., et al. Long-term impacts of antibiotic exposure on the human intestinal microbiota. *Microbiology* 156, Pt. 11 (Nov 2010): 3216–23.

Joly, C., et al. Impact of chronic exposure to low doses of chlorpyrifos on the intestinal microbiota in the Simulator of the Human Intestinal Microbial Ecosystem (SHIME) and in the rat. *Environ Sci Pollut Res Int* 20, no. 5 (May 2013): 2726–34.

Krüger, M., et al. Glyphosate suppresses the antagonistic effect of Enterococcus spp. on \ \ \ \ botulinum. *Anaerobe* 20 (Apr 2013): 74–8.

Manson, J. M., et al. A clonal lineage of VanA-type Enterococcus faecalis predominates in vancomycin-resistant Enterococci isolated in New Zealand. *Antimicrob Agents Chemother* 47, no. 1: 204–10.

Rosenfeld, R. M., & Kay, D. Natural history of untreated otitis media. *Laryngoscope* 113, no. 10 (Oct 2003): 1645–57.

Sonderholm, J. "Use of antibiotics in food animals (not for circulation outside the CGD working group)." Center for Global Development, June 30, 2008. Accessed November 15 2012, http://www.cgdev.org/doc/drug%20 resistance/Veterinary_use_of_antibiotics.pdf

Spurling, G. K., et al. Delayed antibiotics for respiratory infections. *Cochrane Database Syst Rev* 18, no. 3 (Jul 2007): CD004417.

Threlfall, E. J., et al. Spread of resistance from food animals to man--the UK experience. *Acta Vet Scand Suppl* 93 (2000): 63–8; discussion 68–74.

Williamson, I. Otitis media with effusion in children. *Clin Evid Online* (Aug 2007), pii: 0502.

Antibiotics Given to Laboring Moms

Aloisio, I., et al. Influence of intrapartum antibiotic prophylaxis against group B Streptococcus on the early newborn gut composition and evaluation of the anti-Streptococcus activity of Bifidobacterium strains. *Appl Microbiol Biotechnol* 98, no. 13 (Jul 2014): 6051–60.

Ashkenazi-Hoffnung, L., et al. The association of intrapartum antibiotic exposure with the incidence and antibiotic resistance of infantile late-onset serious bacterial infections. *Clin Pediatr* (Phila) 50, no. 9 (Sep 2011): 827–33.

Brocklehurst, P., et al. Antibiotics for treating bacterial vaginosis in pregnancy. *Cochrane Database Syst Rev* 1 (Jan 2013): CD000262.

Byington, C. L., et al. Serious bacterial infections in febrile infants younger than 90 days of age: The importance of ampicillin-resistant pathogens. *Pediatrics* 111, no. 5 Pt. 1 (May 2003): 964–8.

Cohain, J. S. Long-term symptomatic group B streptococcal vulvovaginitis: Eight cases resolved with freshly cut garlic. *Eur J Obstet Gynecol Reprod Biol* 146, no. 1 (Sep 2009): 110–1.

Conde-Agudelo, A., & Díaz-Rossello, J. L. Kangaroo mother care to reduce morbidity and mortality in low birthweight infants. *Cochrane Database Syst Rev* 4 (Apr 2014): CD002771.

Dermer, P., et al. A history of neonatal group B streptococcus with its related morbidity and mortality rates in the United States. *J Pediatr Nurs* 19, no. 5 (Oct 2004): 357–63.

Glasgow, T. S., et al. Association of intrapartum antibiotic exposure and late-onset serious bacterial infections in infants. *Pediatrics* 116, no. 3 (Sep 2005): 696–702.

"Group B Strep Infection in Newborns," Centers for Disease Control and Prevention, last modified November 18, 2010, accessed March 16, 2012, http://www.cdc.gov/groupbstrep/about/newborns-pregnant.html

Hantoushzadeh, S., et al. Comparative efficacy of probiotic yoghurt and clindamycin in treatment of bacterial vaginosis in pregnant women: A randomized clinical trial. *J Matern Fetal Neonatal Med* 25, no. 7 (Jul 2012): 1021–4.

Manzoni, P., et al. Prevention of nosocomial infections in neonatal intensive care units. *Am J Perinatol* 30, no. 2 (Feb 2013): 81–8.

Mohammadzadeh, F., et al. Comparing the therapeutic effects of garlic tablet and oral metronidazole on bacterial vaginosis: A randomized controlled clinical trial. *Iran Red Crescent Med J*. 16, no 7 (Jul 2014): e19118.

Ohlsson, A., & Shah, V. S. Intrapartum antibiotics for known maternal Group B streptococcal colonization. *Cochrane Database Syst Rev* 6 (Jun 2014): CD007467.

Petersen, E. E., et al. Efficacy of vitamin C vaginal tablets in the treatment of bacterial vaginosis: A randomised, double blind, placebo controlled clinical trial. *Arzneimittelforschung* 61, no. 4 (2011): 260–5.

Shane, A. L., & Stoll, B. J. Neonatal sepsis: Progress towards improved outcomes. *J Infect* 68, Suppl 1 (Jan 2014): S24–32. doi:10.1016/j.jinf.2013.09.011

Stoll, B. J., et al. Early onset neonatal sepsis: The burden of group B Streptococcal and E. coli disease continues. *Pediatrics* 127, no. 5 (May 2011): 817–26.

Toltzis, P. Colonization with antibiotic-resistant Gram-negative bacilli in the neonatal intensive care unit. *Minerva Pediatr* 55, no. 5 (Oct 2003): 385–93.

Wolf, J. H. Low breastfeeding rates and public health in the United States. *Am J Public Health* 93, no. 12 (Dec 2003): 2000–10.

Epidemic Results

Benson, L., et al. Changing epidemiology of Clostridium difficile-associated disease in children. *Infect Control Hosp Epidemiol* 28, no. 11 (Nov 2007): 1233–5.

Cloud, J. & Kelly, C. P. Update on Clostridium difficile associated disease. *Curr Opin Gastroenterol* 23, no. 1 (Jan 2007): 4–9.

Kelly, C. R., et al. Fecal microbiota transplantation for relapsing Clostridium difficile infection in 26 patients: Methodology and results. *J Clin Gastroenterol* 46, no. 2 (Feb 2012): 145–9.

Khanna, S., et al. Outcomes in community-acquired Clostridium difficile infection. *Aliment Pharmacol Ther* 35, no. 5 (Mar 2012): 613–8.

Lessa F. C., et al. Burden of Clostridium difficile infection in the United States. *N Engl J Med* 372, no. 9 (Feb 26, 2015): 825-34.

Pituch, H. Clostridium difficile is no longer just a nosocomial infection or an infection of adults. *Int J Antimicrob Agents* 33, Suppl 1 (Mar 2009): S42–5.

Startling Treatment for a Serious Epidemic

Brandt, L. J., et al. Long-term follow-up of colonoscopic fecal microbiota transplant for recurrent Clostridium difficile infection. *Am J Gastroenterol* 107, no. 7 (Jul 2012): 1079–87.

Mattila, E., et al. Fecal transplantation, through colonoscopy, is effective therapy for recurrent Clostridium difficile infection. *Gastroenterology* 142, no. 3 (Mar 2012): 490–6.

Evil E. coli

Bizzarro, M. J., et al. Changing patterns in neonatal Escherichia coli sepsis and ampicillin resistance in the era of intrapartum antibiotic prophylaxis. *Pediatrics* 121, no. 4 (Apr 2008): 689–96.

Cohen, M. B., et al. Prevalence of diarrheagenic Escherichia coli in acute childhood enteritis: A prospective controlled study. *J Pediatr* 146, no. 1 (Jan 2005): 54–61.

" infection: Symptoms," WebMD, last modified June 14, 2010, http://www.webmd.com/a-to-z-guides/e-coli-infection-symptoms

Early Flora, Allergies, and Asthma

Abrahamsson, T. R., et al. Low diversity of the gut microbiota in infants with atopic eczema. *J Allergy Clin Immunol* 129, no. 2 (Feb 2012): 434–40, e1–2.

Almqvist, C., et al. Antibiotics and asthma medication in a large register-based cohort study: Confounding, cause and effect. *Clin Exp Allergy* 42, no. 1 (Jan 2012): 104–11.

Bisgaard, H., et al. Reduced diversity of the intestinal microbiota during infancy is associated with increased risk of allergic disease at school age. *J Allergy Clin Immunol* 128, no. 3 (Sep 2011): 646–52, e1–5.

Chu, K. M., et al. Childhood helminth exposure is protective against inflammatory bowel disease: A case control study in South Africa. *Inflamm Bowel Dis* 19, no. 3 (Mar 2013): 614–20.

Jensen, E. T., et al. Early life exposures as risk factors for pediatric eosinophilic esophagitis. *J Pediatr Gastroenterol Nutr* 57, no. 1 (Jul 2013):67–71.

Johansson, M. A., et al. *Early colonization with a group of Lactobacilli decreases the risk for allergy at five years of age despite allergic heredity.* PLoS One 6, no. 8 (2011): e23031.

Kondrashova, A., et al. The 'hygiene hypothesis' and the sharp gradient in the incidence of autoimmune and allergic diseases between Russian Karelia and Finland. *APMIS* 121, no. 6 (Nov 2012): 478–93.

Mårild, K., et al. Antibiotic exposure and the development of coeliac disease: A nationwide case-control study. BMC Gastroenterol 13 (Jul 2013): 109.

Penders, J., et al. Gut microbiota composition and development of atopic manifestations in infancy: The KOALA Birth Cohort Study. Gut 56, no. 5 (May 2007): 661–7.

Risnes, K. R., et al. Antibiotic exposure by 6 months and asthma and allergy at 6 years: Findings in a cohort of 1,401 US children. Am J Epidemiol 173, no. 3 (Feb 2011): 310–8.

Russell, S. L., et al. Early life antibiotic-driven changes in microbiota enhance susceptibility to allergic asthma. EMBO Rep 13, no. 5 (May 2012): 440–7.

Sobko, T., et al. Neonatal sepsis, antibiotic therapy and later risk of asthma and allergy. Paediatr Perinat Epidemiol 24, no. 1 (Jan 2010): 88–92.

Early Flora, Obesity, and Diabetes

Ajslev, T. A., et al. Childhood overweight after establishment of the gut microbiota: The role of delivery mode, pre-pregnancy weight and early administration of antibiotics. Int J Obes (Lond) 35, no. 4 (Apr 2011): 522–9.

Diamant, M., et al. Do nutrient-gut-microbiota interactions play a role in human obesity, insulin resistance and type 2 diabetes? Obes Rev 12, no. 4 (Apr 2011): 272–81.

Everard, A., et al. Cross-talk between Akkermansia muciniphila and intestinal epithelium controls diet-induced obesity. Proc Natl Acad Sci U S A. 110, no. 22 (May 2013): 9066–71.

Kalliomäki, M., et al. Early differences in fecal microbiota composition in children may predict overweight. Am J Clin Nutr 87, no. 3 (Mar 2008): 534–8.

Million, M., & Raoult, D. The role of the manipulation of the gut microbiota in obesity. Curr Infect Dis Rep 15, no. 1 (Feb 2013): 25–30.

Neu, J., et al. The intestinal microbiome: Relationship to type 1 diabetes. Endocrinol Metab Clin North Am 39, no. 3 (Sep 2010): 563–71.

Owen, C. G., et al. Does breastfeeding influence risk of type 2 diabetes in later life? A quantitative analysis of published evidence. Am J Clin Nutr 84, no. 5 (Nov 2006): 1043–54.

Patelarou, E., et al. Current evidence on the associations of breastfeeding, infant formula, and cow's milk introduction with type 1 diabetes mellitus: A systematic review. Nutr Rev 70, no. 9 (Sep 2012): 509–19.

Qin, J., et al. A metagenome-wide association study of gut microbiota in type 2 diabetes. Nature 490, no. 7418 (Oct 2012): 55–60.

Reinhardt, C., et al. Intestinal microbiota during infancy and its implications for obesity. J Pediatr Gastroenterol Nutr 48, no. 3 (Mar 2009): 249–56.

Trasande, L., et al. Infant antibiotic exposures and early-life body mass. Int J Obes 37, no. 1 (Aug 2012): 16–23.

Vaarala, O. Is the origin of type 1 diabetes in the gut? Immunol Cell Biol 90, no. 3 (Mar 2012): 271–6.

Vrieze, A., et al. Transfer of intestinal microbiota from lean donors increases insulin sensitivity in individuals with metabolic syndrome. Gastroenterology 143, no. 4 (Oct 2012): 913–916, e7.

Flora and Autism

Finegold, S. M., et al. Microbiology of regressive autism. Anaerobe 18, no. 2 (Apr 2012): 260–2.

Martirosian, G., et al. Fecal lactoferrin and Clostridium spp. in stools of autistic children. Anaerobe 17, no. 1 (Feb 2011): 43–5.

Parracho, H. M., et al. Differences between the gut microflora of children with autistic spectrum disorders and that of healthy children. J Med Microbiol 54, Pt. 10 (Oct 2005): 987–91.

Williams, B. L., et al. Application of novel PCR-based methods for detection, quantitation, and phylogenetic characterization of Sutterella species in intestinal biopsy samples from children with autism and gastrointestinal disturbances. MBio 3, no. 1 (Jan 2012). pii: e00261–11.

Flora, Colic and Reflux

Savino, F., et al. Antagonistic effect of Lactobacillus strains against gas-producing coliforms isolated from colicky infants. BMC Microbiol 11 (Jun 2011): 157.

Antibiotics and Inflammatory Bowel Disease

Economou, M., & Pappas, G. New global map of Crohn's disease: Genetic, environmental, and socioeconomic correlations. Inflamm Bowel Dis 14, no. 5 (May 2008): 709–20.

Hutfless, S., et al. Prenatal and perinatal characteristics associated with pediatric-onset inflammatory bowel disease. Dig Dis Sci 57, no. 8 (Aug 2012): 2149–56.

Kronman, M. P., et al. Antibiotic exposure and IBD development among children: A population-based cohort study. Pediatrics 130, no. 4 (Oct 2012): e794–803.

Shaw, S. Y., et al. Association between early childhood otitis media and pediatric inflammatory bowel disease: An exploratory population-based analysis. J Pediatr 162, no. 3 (Oct 2012): 510–514.

Thoughts on Choosing Our Microbial Friendships

Dinwiddie, M. T., et al. Recent evidence regarding triclosan and cancer risk. *Int J Environ Res Public Health* 11, no. 2 (Feb 2014): 2209–17.

4 The Poop on Breastmilk

Beattie, L. M., & Weaver, L. T. Mothers, babies and friendly bacteria. *Arch Dis Child Fetal Neonatal Ed* 96, no. 3 (May 2011): F160–3.

Romond, M. B., et al. Does the intestinal bifidobacterial colonisation affect bacterial translocation? *Anaerobe* 14, no.1 (Feb 2008): 43–8.

Romond, M. B., et al. Intestinal colonization with bifidobacteria affects the expression of galectins in extraintestinal organs. *FEMS Immunol Med Microbiol* 55, no. 1 (Jan 2009): 85–92.

Tsay, T. B., et al. Gut flora enhance bacterial clearance in lung through toll-like receptors 4. *J Biomed Sci* 18 (Sep 2011): 68.

In the Beginning

Cabrera-Rubio, R., et al. The human milk microbiome changes over lactation and is shaped by maternal weight and mode of delivery. *Am J Clin Nutr* 96 (Sep 2012): 544–51.

Jost, T., et al. Vertical mother-neonate transfer of maternal gut bacteria via breastfeeding. *Environ Microbiol* (Aug 2013).

Koren, G. Therapeutic drug monitoring principles in the neonate. National Academy of Clinical Biochemistry. *Clin Chem* 43, no. 1 (Jan 1997): 222–7.

Regulation

Baughcum, A.E., et al. Maternal feeding practices and beliefs and their relationships to overweight in early childhood. *J Dev Behav Pediatr* 22, no. 6 (Dec 2001): 391–408.

Beck, K.L. et al. Comparative proteomics of human and macaque milk reveals species-specific nutrition during post-natal development. *J Proteome Res.* (Mar 2015).

Dundar, N.O., et al. Longitudinal investigation of the relationship between breast milk leptin levels and growth in breast-fed infants. *J Pediatr Endocrinol Metab* 18, no. 2 (Feb 2005): 181–7.

Heinig, M. J., & Dewey, K. G. Health effects of breast feeding for mothers: A critical review. *Nutr Res Rev* 10, no. 1 (Jan 1997): 35–56.

Mehta, R., & Petrova A. Biologically active breast milk proteins in association with very preterm delivery and stage of lactation. *J Perinatol* 31, no. 1 (Jan 2011): 58–62.

Palmer, L. F. *Baby Matters*, San Diego, CA: BabyReference, 2015.

Sánchez, C. L., et al. The possible role of human milk nucleotides as sleep inducers. *Nutr Neurosci* 12, no. 1 (Feb 2009): 2–8.

Satter, E. The feeding relationship: Problems and interventions. *J Pediatr* 117, no. 2 Pt. 2 (Aug 1990): S181–9.

Antibodies from Mother

Agrawal, S., et al. Comparative study of immunoglobulin G and immunoglobulin M among neonates in caesarean section and vaginal delivery. *J Indian Med Assoc* 94, no. 2 (Feb 1996): 43–4.

Leuridan, E., et al. Early waning of maternal measles antibodies in era of measles elimination: Longitudinal study. *BMJ* 340 (May 2010): c1626.

Savilahti, E., et al. Serum immunoglobulins in preterm infants: Comparison of human milk and formula feeding. *Pediatrics* 72, no. 3 (Sep 1983): 312–6.

Broncho-Entero-Mammary Pathway

"How breastfeeding transfers immunity to babies," *Science Daily*, October 27, 2008. Retrieved from http://www.sciencedaily.com/releases/2008/10/081026101713.htm

Albesharat, R., et al. Phenotypic and genotypic analyses of lactic acid bacteria in local fermented food, breast milk and faeces of mothers and their babies. *Syst Appl Microbiol* 34, no. 2 (Apr 2011): 148–55.

Brandtzaeg, P. Mucosal immunity: Integration between mother and the breast-fed infant. *Vaccine* 21, no. 24 (Jul 2003): 3382–8.

Chirico, G., et al. Antiinfective properties of human milk. *J Nutr* 138, no. 9 (Sep 2008): 1801S–1806S.

Densmore, L., & Pflueger, S. M. Using interphase fluorescence in situ hybridization (I-FISH) to detect the transfer of infant cells during breastfeeding. *J Hum Lact* 24, no. 4 (Nov 2008): 401–5.

Donnet-Hughes, A., et al. Potential role of the intestinal microbiota of the mother in neonatal immune education. *Proc Nutr Soc* 69, no. 3 (Aug 2010): 407–15.

Morteau, O., et al. An indispensable role for the chemokine receptor CCR10 in IgA antibody-secreting cell accumulation. *J Immunol* 181, no. 9 (Nov 2008): 6309–15.

Nathavitharana, K. A., et al. IgA antibodies in human milk: Epidemiological markers of previous infections? *Arch Dis Child Fetal Neonatal Ed* 71, no. 3 (Nov 1994): F192–7.

Van de Perre, P. Transfer of antibody via mother's milk. *Vaccine* 21, no. 24 (Jul 2003): 3374–6.

Yu, X., et al. Neutralization of HIV by milk expressed antibody. *J Acquir Immune Defic Synd* 62, no. 1 (Jan 2013): 10–6.

More Health Protection from Human Milk

Ballard, O. & Morrow, A. L. Human milk composition: Nutrients and bioactive factors. *Pediatr Clin North Am* 60, no. 1 (Feb 2013): 49–74.

Bode, L., & Jantscher-Krenn, E. Structure-function relationships of human milk oligosaccharides. *Adv Nutr* 3, no. 3 (May 2012): 383S–91S.

Chirico, G., et al. Antiinfective properties of human milk. *J Nutr* 138, no. 9 (Sep 2008): 1801S–1806S.

Newburg, D. S. Neonatal protection by an innate immune system of human milk consisting of oligosaccharides and glycans. *J Anim Sci* 87, no. 13 Suppl (Apr 2009): 26–34.

Lactoferrin, Iron, and Infant Protection

Gerstley, J. R., et al. Some factors influencing the fecal flora of infants. *Am J Dis Child* 43, no. 3 (Mar 1932): 555–565.

Formula Supplementing and Floral Health

Artym, J., & Zimecki, M. The role of lactoferrin in the proper development of newborns. *Postepy Hig Med Dosw (Online)* 58 (2005): 421–32.

Brown, E. W., & Bosworth A. W. Studies of infant feeding VI. A bacteriological study of the feces and the food of normal babies receiving breast milk. *Am J Dis Child* 23 (1922): 243.

Bullen, C. L., et al. The effect of "humanised" milks and supplemented breast feeding on the faecal flora of infants. *J Med Microbiol* 10, no. 4 (Nov 1977): 403–13.

Cantani, A., & Micera, M. Neonatal cow milk sensitization in 143 case-reports: Role of early exposure to cow's milk formula. *Eur Rev Med Pharmacol Sci* 9, no. 4 (Jul–Aug 2005): 227–30.

Gerstley, J. R, et al. Some factors influencing the fecal flora of infants. *Am J Dis Child* 43 (1932): 555.

Høst, A., et al. A prospective study of cow's milk allergy in exclusively breast-fed infants. Incidence, pathogenetic role of early inadvertent exposure to cow's milk formula, and characterization of bovine milk protein in human milk. *Acta Paediatr Scand* 77, no. 5 (Sep 1988): 663–70.

Penn, A. H., et al. Digested formula but not digested fresh human milk causes death of intestinal cells in vitro: Implications for necrotizing enterocolitis. *Pediatr Res* 72, no. 6 (Dec 2012): 560–7.

Walker, M. *Just one bottle won't hurt, or will it?* Retrieved from http://www.health-e-learning.com/articles/JustOneBottle.pdf

Wharton, B. A., et al. Faecal flora in the newborn: Effect of lactoferrin and related nutrients. *Adv Exp Med Biol* 357 (1994): 91–8.

More about Iron

Lozoff, B., et al. Iron-fortified vs low-iron infant formula: Developmental outcome at 10 years. *Arch Pediatr Adolesc Med* 166, no. 3 (Mar 2012): 208–15.

Oski, F. A., & Landaw, S. A. Inhibition of iron absorption from human milk by baby food. *Am J Dis Child* 134, no. 5 (May 1980): 459–60.

Siimes, M. A., et al. Exclusive breast-feeding for 9 months: Risk of iron deficiency. *J Pediatr* 104, no. 2 (Feb 1984): 196–9.

Sullivan, P. B. Cows' milk induced intestinal bleeding in infancy. *Arch Dis Child* 68, no. 2 (Feb 1993): 240–5.

Tawia, S. Iron and exclusive breastfeeding. *Breastfeed Rev* 20, no. 1 (Mar 2012): 35–47.

About Formula and Other Breastmilk Substitutes

Lecce, J. G., & King, M. W. Rotaviral antibodies in cow's milk. *Can J Comp Med* 46, no. 4 (Oct 1982): 434–6.

"The cost of feeding," *Kansas State Board of Health.* Circa 1920.

Measurable impact

Howie, P. W., et al. Protective effect of breast feeding against infection. *BMJ* 300, no. 6716 (Jan 1990): 11–6.

Breastmilk, Diarrhea and Gastroenteritis

Chien, P. F., & Howie, P. W. Breast milk and the risk of opportunistic infection in infancy in industrialized and nonindustrialized settings. *Adv Nutr Res* 10 (2001): 69–104. [2.7 times the diarrhea in formula fed.]

Dewey, K. G. et al. Differences in morbidity between breast-fed and formula-fed infants. *Journal of Pediatrics* (Davis, USA) 126, no. 5, pt. 1 (May 1995): 696–702. [Double the diarrhea for formula fed U.S. infants.]

Duijts, L. et al. Prolonged and exclusive breastfeeding reduces the risk of infectious diseases in infancy. *Pediatrics* 126, no. 1 (Jul 2010): e18–25. [2.5 times the risk for formula fed.]

Escuder, M. M. et al. Impact estimates of breastfeeding over infant mortality. *Rev Saude Publica* 37, no. 3 (Jun 2003): 319–25. [15 times the diarrheal death rate for formula fed in Brazil.]

Fisk, C. M. et al., & Southampton Women's Survey Study Group. Breastfeeding and reported morbidity during infancy: Findings from the Southampton Women's Survey. *Matern Child Nutr* 7, no. 1 (Jan 2011): 61–70.

Fu, Z. et al. Exclusive breastfeeding and growth of infants under 4 months in China. *Wei Sheng Yan Jiu* (Center for Public Health Information, Chinese Academy of Preventive Medicine) 29, no. 5 (Sep 2000): 275–8. [2.8 times the diarrhea for formula fed in China.]

Golding, J. et al. Gastroenteritis, diarrhoea and breast feeding. *Early Human Development* 49, suppl. (Oct 1997): S83–103. [Average triple risk diarrhea in formula fed.]

Gutland, A. Rotavirus vaccine cuts deaths of Mexican babies from diarrhoea by 40%. *BMJ* 340 (Jan 2010): c511. doi:10.1136/bmj.c511

Hlavaty, T. et al. Smoking, breastfeeding, physical inactivity, contact with animals, and size of the family influence the risk of inflammatory bowel disease: A Slovak case–control study. *Unit Eur Gast J* 1, no. 2 (Apr 2013): 109–119. [2.7 times the Crohn's disease for <6 months breastfeeding.]

Ip, S. et al. A summary of the Agency for Healthcare Research and Quality's evidence report on breastfeeding in developed countries. *Breastfeed Med* 4, Suppl. 1 (Oct 2009): S17–30. [2.8 times the risk for formula fed.]

Ip, S. et al. Breastfeeding and maternal and infant health outcomes in developed countries. *Evid Rep Technol Assess* (Full Rep), 153 (Apr 2007): 1–186.

Lamberti, L. M. et al. Breastfeeding and the risk for diarrhea morbidity and mortality. *BMC Public Health* 11, Suppl. 3 (Apr 2011): S15. [Meta-analysis finding 10.5 times the risk of diarrheal deaths for formula fed in developing nations.]

"LCWK7. Infant, neonatal, and postneonatal deaths, percent of total deaths, and mortality rates for the 15 leading causes of infant death by race and sex: United States, 2010," Centers for Disease Control & National Center for Health Statistics, accessed December 9, 2012, http://www.cdc.gov/nchs/data/dvs/LCWK7_2010.pdf

Maranhão, H. S. et al. The epidemiological and clinical characteristics and nutritional development of infants with acute diarrhoea, in north-eastern Brazil. *Ann Trop Med Parasitol* 102, no. 4 (Jun 2008): 357–65. [10 times diarrhea for formula fed in Brazil.]

Monterrosa, E. C. et al. Predominant breast-feeding from birth to six months is associated with fewer gastrointestinal infections and increased risk for iron deficiency among infants. *J Nutr* 138, no. 8 (Aug 2008): 1499504.

Raisler, J. et al. Breast-feeding and infant illness: A dose-response relationship? *Am J Public Health* 89, no. 1 (Jan 1999): 25–30. [1.8 times the diarrhea for formula fed in U.S.]

Sachdev, H. P. et al. Does breastfeeding influence mortality in children hospitalized with diarrhoea? *Journal of Tropical Pediatrics* 37, no. 6 (Dec 1991): 275–9. [6 times the diarrheal death rate for formula fed in India.]

Scariati, P. D. et al. A longitudinal analysis of infant morbidity and the extent of breastfeeding in the United States. *Pediatrics* 99, no. 6 (Jun 1997): E5. [1.8 times the diarrhea for formula fed in U.S.]

Vernacchio, L. et al. Diarrhea in American infants and young children in the community setting: incidence, clinical presentation and microbiology. *Pediatr Infect Dis J* 25 no. 1 (Jan 2006): 2–7.

Yoon, P. W. Effect of not breastfeeding on the risk of diarrheal and respiratory mortality in children under 2 years of age in Metro Cebu, The Philippines. *American Journal of Epidemiology* 143, no. 11 (Jun 1996): 1142–8. [9 times the diarrheal deaths for formula fed in Philippines.]

Other Intestinal Health

Krogh, C., et al. Bottle-feeding and the risk of Pyloric Stenosis. *Pediatrics* 130, no. 4 (Oct 2012) :e943–9.

Tunc, V. T, et al. Factors associated with defecation patterns in 0-24-month-old children. *Eur J Pediatr* 167, no. 12 (Dec 2008): 1357–62.

Gearry, R. B., et al. Population-based cases control study of inflammatory bowel disease risk factors. *J Gastroenterol Hepatol* 25, no. 5 (Feb 2010): 325–33.

Hansen, T. S., et al. Environmental factors in inflammatory bowel disease: A case-control study based on a Danish inception cohort. *J Crohns Colitis* 5, no. 6 (Dec 2011): 577–84.

Akobeng, A. K., et al. Effect of breast feeding on risk of coeliac disease: A systematic review and meta-analysis of observational studies. *Arch Dis Child* 91, no. 1 (Jan 2006): 39–43.

Johnson, B., et al. Sociodemographic and dietary risk factors for natural infant intussusception in the United States. *J Pediatr Gastroenterol Nutr* 51, no. 4 (Oct 2010): 458–63.

Barclay, A. R., et al. Systematic review: Tthe role of breastfeeding in the development of pediatric inflammatory bowel disease. *J Pediatr* 155, no. 3 (Sep 2009): 421–6.

Sullivan, S., et al. An exclusively human milk-based diet is associated with a lower rate of necrotizing enterocolitis than a diet of human milk and bovine milk-based products. *J Pediatr* 156, no. 4 (Apr 2010): 562–7.e1.

More Breastfeeding Impact

Bachrach, V. R., et al. Breastfeeding and the risk of hospitalization for respiratory disease in infancy: A meta-analysis. *Arch Pediatr Adolesc Med* 157, no. 3 (Mar 2003): 237–43.

Chantry, C. J., et al. Full breastfeeding duration and associated decrease in respiratory tract infection in US children. *Pediatrics* 117, no. 2 (Feb 2006): 425–32.

Hauck, F. R., et al. Breastfeeding and reduced risk of sudden infant death syndrome: A meta-analysis. *Pediatrics* 128, no. 1 (Jul 2011): 103–10.

Eidelman, A. I., et al. Breastfeeding and the use of human milk, from the Academy of Pediatrics. *Pediatrics* 129, no. 3 (Mar 2012): e827–e841.

Patelarou, E., et al. Current evidence on the associations of breastfeeding, infant formula, and cow's milk introduction with type 1 diabetes mellitus: A systematic review. *Nutr Rev* 70, no. 9 (Sep 2012): 509–19.

Owen, C. G., et al. Does breastfeeding influence risk of type 2 diabetes in later life? A quantitative analysis of published evidence. *Am J Clin Nutr* 84, no. 5 (Nov 2006): 1043–54.

Abrahams, S. W., et al. Breastfeeding and otitis media: A review of recent evidence. *Curr Allergy Asthma Rep* 11, no. 6 (Dec 2011): 508–12.

Breastfeeding Success

Lee, M. "High estrogen levels while breastfeeding." *Livestrong.com.* Last modified August 16, 2013, http://www.livestrong.com/article/500552-high-estrogen-levels-while-breastfeeding/#ixzz2INXSmdMV

Rudel, R. A., et al. Environmental exposures and mammary gland development: State of the science, public health implications, and research recommendations. *Environ Health Perspect* 119, no. 8 (Aug 2011): 1053–61.

Tan, S. W., et al. The endocrine effects of mercury in humans and wildlife. *Crit Rev Toxicol* 39, 3 (2009): 228–69.

5 First Poops

Meconium Timing

Ameh, N., & Ameh, E. A. Timing of passage of first meconium and stooling pattern in normal Nigerian newborns. *Ann Trop Paediatr* 29, no 2. (Jun 2009): 129–33.

Bekkali, N., et al. Duration of meconium passage in preterm and term infants. *Arch Dis Child Fetal Neonatal Ed* 93, no. 5 (Sep 2008): F376–9.

Chih, T. W. et al. Time of the first urine and the first stool in Chinese newborns. *Zhonghua Min Guo Xiao Er Ke Yi Xue Hui Za Zhi* 32, no. 1 (Jan 1991): 17–23.

Clark, D. A. Times of first void and first stool in 500 newborns. *Pediatrics* 60, no. 4 (Oct 1977): 457–9.

Omoigberale, A. I., & Okolo, A. A. Time of passage of first stools (meconium) and serum levels of calcium and magnesium in Nigerian neonates (African neonates). *Niger J Clin Pract* 12, no. 1 (Mar 2009): 54–7.

Meconium and Baby's Microbiome

Bercik, P., et al. The intestinal microbiota affect central levels of brain-derived neurotropic factor and behavior in mice. *Gastroenterology* 141, no. 2(Aug 2011): 599-609, e1–3.

Gosalbes, M. J., et al. Meconium microbiota types dominated by lactic acid or enteric bacteria are differentially associated with maternal eczema and respiratory problems in infants. *Clin Exp Allergy* 43, no. 2 (Feb 2013): 198–211.

Hamzelou, J. Babies are born dirty, with a gutful of bacteria. *New Scientist* 2860 (Apr 2012): 6–7.

Hansen, C. H., et al. Patterns of early gut colonization shape future immune responses of the host. *PLoS One* 7, no. 3: e34043.

Jiménez, E., et al. Isolation of commensal bacteria from umbilical cord blood of healthy neonates born by cesarean section. *Curr Microbiol* 54, no. 4 (Oct 2005): 270–4.

Meconium Concerns

Aguilar, A. M., & Vain, N. E. The suctioning in the delivery room debate. *Early Hum Dev* 87, Suppl. 1 (Mar 2011): S13–5.

Evans, A. Neonatal resuscitation with intact umbilical cord. *Midwifery Today Int Midwife* 102 (Summer 2012): 42–3.

Hofmeyr, G. J. What (not) to do before delivery? Prevention of fetal meconium release and its consequences. *Early Hum Dev* 85, no. 10, (Oct 2009): 611–5.

Kelleher, J., et al. Oronasopharyngeal suction versus wiping of the mouth and nose at birth: A randomised equivalency trial. *Lancet* 328, no. 9889 (Jul 2013): 326–30.

Matonhodze, B. B., et al. Labor induction and meconium: In vitro effects of oxytocin, dinoprostone and misoprostol on rat ileum relative to myometrium. *J Perinat Med* 30, no. 5 (2002): 405–10.

Velaphi, S., & Vidyasagar, D. The pros and cons of suctioning at the perineum (intrapartum) and post-delivery with and without meconium. *Semin Fetal Neonatal Med* 13, no. 6 (Dec 2008): 375–82.

First Feedings

Dollberg, S., et al. A comparison of intakes of breast-fed and bottle-fed infants during the first two days of life. *J Am Coll Nutr*. 20, no. 3 (Jun 2001): 209–11.

Santoro, W., Jr., et al. Colostrum ingested during the first day of life by exclusively breastfed healthy newborn infants. *J Pediatr* 156, no. 1 (Jan 2010): 29–32.

Zangen, S., et al. Rapid maturation of gastric relaxation in newborn infants. *Pediatr Res* 50, no. 5 (Nov 2001): 629–32.

Initial Weight Loss

Bullen, C. L., et al. The effect of "humanised" milks and supplemented breast feeding on the faecal flora of infants. *J Med Microbiol* 10, no. 4 (Nov 1977): 403–13.

Caglar, M. K., et al. Risk factors for excess weight loss and hypernatremia in exclusively breast-fed infants. *Braz J Med Biol Res* 39, no. 4 (Apr 2006): 539–44.

Chantry, C. J., et al. Excess weight loss in first-born breastfed newborns relates to maternal intrapartum fluid balance. *Pediatrics* 127, no 1 (Jan 2011): e171–9.

Chen, C. F., et al. Influence of breast-feeding on weight loss, jaundice, and waste elimination in neonates. *Pediatr Neonatol* 52, no. 2 (Apr 2011): 85-92.

Davanzo, R., et al. Breastfeeding and neonatal weight loss in healthy term infants. *J Hum Lact* 29, no. 1 (Feb 2013): 45–53.

Grossman, X., et al. Neonatal weight loss at a US Baby-Friendly Hospital. *J Acad Nutr Diet* 112, no. 3 (Mar 2012): 410–3.

Macdonald, P. D., et al. Neonatal weight loss in breast and formula fed infants. *Arch Dis Child Fetal Neonatal Ed* 88, no. 6 (Nov 2003): F472–6.

Noel-Weiss, J., et al. An observational study of associations among maternal fluids during parturition, neonatal output, and breastfed newborn weight loss. *Int Breastfeed J* 9 (Aug 2011): 9.

Preer, G. L., et al. Weight loss in exclusively breastfed infants delivered by cesarean birth. *J Hum Lact* 28, no. 2 (May 2012): 153–8.

Next Poops

den Hertog, J., et al. The defecation pattern of healthy term infants up to the age of 3 months. *Arch Dis Child Fetal Neonatal Ed* 97, no. 6 (Nov 2012): F465–70.

Hyams, J. S., et al. Effect of infant formula on stool characteristics of young infants. *Pediatrics* 95, no. 1 (Jan 1995): 50–4.

Newman, J., & Kernman, E. "Is My Baby Getting Enough?" International Breastfeeding Center, 2009. http://tiny.cc/ks3h9w

Tunc, V. T., et al. Factors associated with defecation patterns in 0-24-month-old children. *Eur J Pediatr* 167, no. 12 (Dec 2008): 1357–62.

Jaundice and First Poops

Alex, M., & Gallant, D. P. Toward understanding the connections between infant jaundice and infant feeding. *J Pediatr Nurs* 23, no. 6 (Dec 2008): 429–38.

Christensen, T., et al. Cells, bilirubin and light: Formation of bilirubin photoproducts and cellular damage at defined wavelengths. *Acta Paediatr* 83, no. 1 (Jan 1994): 7–12.

Crofts, D. J., et al. Assessment of stool colour in community management of prolonged jaundice in infancy. *Acta Paediatr* 88, no. 9 (Sep 1999): 969–74

Deshpande, P., et al. "Breast milk jaundice." Medscape, last modified May 18, 2012. http://emedicine.medscape.com/article/973629-overview#a0104

Horsfall, L. J., et al. Gilbert's syndrome and the risk of death: A population-based cohort study. *J Gastroenterol Hepatol* 28, no. 10 (May 2013):1643–7.

Laforgia, N., et al. Neonatal hyperbilirubinemia and Gilbert's syndrome. *J Perinat Med* 30, no. 2 (2002): 166–9.

Markel, S.G., & Palmer, L. F. What Your Pediatrician Doesn't Know Can Hurt Your Child. Dallas: BenBella, 2010.

Nicoll, A., et al. Supplementary feeding and jaundice in newborns. Acta Paediatr Scand 75, no. 5 (Sep 1982): 759–61.

Philipp, B. L., et al. Breastfeeding information in nursing textbooks needs improvement. *J Hum Lact* 23, no. 4 (Nov 2007): 345–9.

Philipp, B. L., et al. Breastfeeding information in pediatric textbooks needs improvement. *J Hum Lact* 20, no. 2 (May 2004): 206–10.

Roll, E. B., & Christensen, T. Formation of photoproducts and cytotoxicity of bilirubin irradiated with turquoise and blue phototherapy light. *Acta Paediatr* 94, no. 10 (Oct 2005): 1448–54.

Shekeeb Shahab, M., et al. Evaluation of oxidant and antioxidant status in term neonates: A plausible protective role of bilirubin. *Mol Cell Biochem* 317, no. 1–2, (Oct 2008): 51–9.

Soldi, A., et al. Neonatal jaundice and human milk. *J Matern Fetal Neonatal Med* 24, Suppl. 1 (Oct 2011): 85–7.

Weinberger, B., et al. Effects of bilirubin on neutrophil responses in newborn infants. *Neonatology* 103, no. 2 (2013): 105–11.

6 Preemie Poops

Supporting Optimal Care

"Find Facilities," Baby-Friendly USA, accessed May 5, 2013, http://www.babyfriendlyusa.org/find-facilities

Conde-Agudelo, A., & Díaz-Rossello, J. L. Kangaroo mother care to reduce morbidity and mortality in low birthweight infants. *Cochrane Database Syst Rev* 4 (2014): CD002771.

DelliFraine, J., et al. Cost comparison of baby friendly and non-baby friendly hospitals in the United States. *Pediatrics* 127, no. 4 (Apr 2011): e989–94.

Labbok, M. H. Global baby-friendly hospital initiative monitoring data: Update and discussion. *Breastfeed Med* (Aug 2012): 210–22.

Palmer, L. F. *Baby Matters*, San Diego, CA: BabyReference, 2015.

Renfrew, M. J., et al. Breastfeeding promotion for infants in neonatal units: A systematic review and economic analysis. *Health Technol Assess* 13, no 40 (Aug 2009): 1–146, iii–iv.

"Baby Friendly Hospital Initiative," United Nations International Children's Emergency Fund, accessed May 5, 2013, http://www.unicef.org/programme/breastfeeding/baby.htm

It's All about the Intestines

Ghandehari, H., et al., & H2MF Study Group. An exclusive human milk-based diet in extremely premature infants reduces the probability of remaining on total parenteral nutrition: A reanalysis of the data. *BMC Res Notes* 5 (Apr 2012): 188.

Necrotizing Enterocolitis

Arslanoglu, S., et al., & World Association of Perinatal Medicine Working Group on Nutrition. Donor human milk in preterm infant feeding: Evidence and recommendations. *J Perinat Med* 38, no. 4 (Jul 2010): 347–51. [Donor milk is preferred supplement when inadequate mother's milk, reducing infections and NEC, and improving long term outcomes.]

Boyd, C. A., et al. Donor breast milk versus infant formula for preterm infants: Systematic review and meta-analysis. *Arch Dis Child Fetal Neonatal Ed* 92, no. 3 (May 2007): F169–75. [Review shows that donor milk brings slower growth but 79 % reduced NEC.]

Corpeleijn, W. E., et al. Intake of own mother's milk during the first days of life is associated with decreased morbidity and mortality in very low birth weight infants during the first 60 days of life. *Neonatology* 102, no. 4 (2012): 276–81.

Quigley, M. A., et al. Formula milk versus donor breast milk for feeding preterm or low birth weight infants. *Cochrane Database Syst Rev* 17, no. 4 (Oct 2007): CD002971. [Review reports donor milk brings slower growth but 60% reduced rate of NEC versus formula. States only limited data available on fortified human milk.]

Schanler, R. J., et al. Randomized trial of donor human milk versus preterm formula as substitutes for mothers' own milk in the feeding of extremely premature infants. *Pediatrics* 116, no. 2 (Aug 2005): 400–6. [Mother's milk reduced infections and hospital stay versus donor milk or preterm formula]

Schulzke, S. M., et al. Neurodevelopmental outcomes of very-low-birth-weight infants with necrotizing enterocolitis: A systematic review of observational studies. *Arch Pediatr Adolesc Med* 161, no. 6 (Jun 2007): 583–90.

Shah, T. A., et al. Hospital and neurodevelopmental outcomes of extremely low-birth-weight infants with necrotizing enterocolitis and spontaneous intestinal perforation. *J Perinatol* 32, no. 7 (Jul 2012): 552–8.

Sisk, P. M., et al. Early human milk feeding is associated with a lower risk of necrotizing enterocolitis in very low birth weight infants. *J Perinatol* 27, no. 7 (Jul 2007) :428–33. [Eighty-three percent reduced NEC with high amounts of human milk versus low.]

Sullivan, S., et al. An exclusively human milk-based diet is associated with a lower rate of necrotizing enterocolitis than a diet of human milk and bovine milk-based products. *J Pediatr* 156, no. 4 (Apr 2010): 562–7. [Ninety per-cent fewer NEC cases when all human milk with human-based fortifier vs. formula with cow-derived fortifier.]

Fortify Human Milk?

Anderson, J. W., et al. Breast-feeding and cognitive development: A meta-analysis. *Am J Clin Nutr* 70, no. 4 (Oct 1999): 525–35. [Significantly higher IQs for breastfed children.]

Andres, A., et al. Developmental status of 1-year-old infants fed breast milk, cow's milk formula, or soy formula. *Pediatrics* 129, no. 6 (Jun 2012): 1134–40. [Cognitive advantage for term infants breastfed over soy formula fed.]

Brion, M. J., et al. What are the causal effects of breastfeeding on IQ, obesity and blood pressure? Evidence from comparing high-income with middle-income cohorts. *Int J Epidemiol* 40, no. 3 (Jun 2011): 670–80. [Takes a different approach to removing potential confounding causes, reconfirming strength of breastfeeding in promoting IQ and heart health indicators.]

Dusick, A. M., et al. Growth failure in the preterm infant: Can we catch up? *Semin Perinatol* 27, no. 4 (Aug 2003): 302–10. [Earlier preterms have slower growth. States that breastfed require fortification but the only reason given is growth before 9 months. No developmental deficits and no reduced head circumference are found in breastmilk-fed.]

Ehrenkranz, R. A., et al. Growth in the neonatal intensive care unit influences neurodevelopmental and growth outcomes of extremely low birth weight infants. *Pediatrics* 117, no. 4 (Apr 2006): 1253–61. [Improved neurodevelopment with faster growth in likely, chiefly, formula-fed infants. No considerations/comparisons made of human milk in diets.]

Faerk, J., et al. Diet, growth, and bone mineralization in premature infants. *Adv Exp Med Biol* 501 (2001): 479–83. [Fully human milk-fed preemies experienced slightly slower growth and lesser early bone mineral content but no reduction in head circumference; an indicator of brain development.]

Fewtrell, M. S. Does early nutrition program later bone health in preterm infants? *Am J Clin Nutr* 94, no. 6 (Dec 2011): 1870S–1873S.

Forman, M. R., et al. Through the looking glass at early-life exposures and breast cancer risk. *Cancer Invest* 23, no. 7 (2005): 609–24.

Funkquist, E. L., et al. Growth and breastfeeding among low birth weight infants fed with or without protein enrichment of human milk. *Ups J Med Sci* 111, no. 1 (2006): 97–108. [Preemies with cow-derived protein fortifier added to their mother's milk grew faster initially, had more illnesses, and had poorer later breastfeeding, whereas full breastfeeding led to later growth improvement.]

Gross, S. J. Bone mineralization in preterm infants fed human milk with and without mineral supplementation. *J Pediatr* 111, no. 3 (Sep 1987): 450–8.

Jimenez-Chillaron, J. C., & Patti, M. E. To catch up or not to catch up: Is this the question? Lessons from animal models. *Curr Opin Endocrinol Diabetes Obes* 14, no. 1 (Feb 2007): 23–9.

Kramer, M. S., et al., & Promotion of Breastfeeding Intervention Trial Study Group. Breastfeeding and child cognitive development: New evidence from a large randomized trial. *Arch Gen Psychiatry* 65, no. 5 (May 2008): 578–84. ["...strong evidence that prolonged and exclusive breastfeeding improves children's cognitive development."]

Lucas, A., et al. Breast milk and subsequent intelligence quotient in children born preterm. *Lancet* 339, no. 8788 (Feb 1992): 261–4. [At age 8, IQ advantages remained in children who received breastmilk as premature infants, averaging 8 points, after accounting for factors of mother's education, choice of feeding, and other potential confounders.]

Lucas, A., & Cole, T. J. Breast milk and neonatal necrotising enterocolitis. *Lancet* 336, no. 8730 (Dec 1990): 1519–23. [In babies fed only formula, NEC occurred 6-10 times more often than in human milk alone. Of preemies over 30 weeks, NEC was 20 times more with formula vs. human milk.]

Morley, R., & Lucas, A. Randomized diet in the neonatal period and growth performance until 7.5-8 y of age in preterm children. *Am J Clin Nutr* 73, no. 3 (Mar 2000): 822–8. [Preterm diet of formula versus unfortified donor breastmilk had no influence on final size at 18 mos or 8 years, nor head circumference.]

O'Connor, D. L., et al. Growth and development of premature infants fed predominantly human milk, predominantly premature infant formula, or a combination of human milk and premature formula. *J Pediatr Gastroenterol Nutr* 37, no. 4 (Oct 2003): 437–46. ["...despite a slower early growth rate, human milk-fed low birth weight infants have development at least comparable to that of infants fed nutrient-enriched formula." In this study, even head circumferences were slightly less in human milk fed, although cognitive indicators were better.]

Patel, A. L., et al. Impact of early human milk on sepsis and health-care costs in very low birth weight infants. *J Perinatol* 33, no. 7 (Jul 2013): 514–9. [The more human milk, the lower the risk of sepsis.]

Premji, S., et al. Does amount of protein in formula matter for low-birthweight infants? A Cochrane systematic review. *J Parenter Enteral Nutr* 30, no. 6 (Nov-Dec 2006): 507–14. [Preemies receiving higher amounts of protein grew faster but: "This benefit could not be weighed against the adverse consequences of elevated blood urea nitrogen levels and increased metabolic acidosis and neurodevelopmental abnormalities."]

Quigley, M. A., et al. Breastfeeding is associated with improved child cognitive development: A population-based cohort study. *J Pediatr* 160, no. 1 (Jan 2012): 25–32. [Improved cognitive abilities in 5 y.o. children who were born preterm, when fed breastmilk.]

Schanler, R. J. Outcomes of human milk-fed premature infants. *Semin Perinatol* 35, no. 1 (Feb 2011): 29–33. [Human milk-fed infants have improved motor and mental development, IQ, vision, and adolescent body composition, and reduced metabolic syndrome, over formula fed.]

Singhal, A., et al. Breastmilk feeding and lipoprotein profile in adolescents born preterm: Follow-up of a prospective randomised study. *Lancet* 363, no. 9421 (May 2004): 1571–8. [Teens born prematurely had less atherosclerosis if fed donor human milk rather than preterm formula.]

Singhal, A., et al. Early nutrition and leptin concentrations in later life. *Am J Clin Nutr* 75, no. 6 (Jun 2002): 993–9. [Preemies growing faster on enriched preterm formula showed greater leptin levels (propensity for obesity) as teens than those fed donor human milk.]

Singhal, A., et al. Low nutrient intake and early growth for later insulin resistance in adolescents born preterm. *Lancet* 361, no. 9363 (Mar 2003): 1089–97. [Slower growth diets for preterm infants led to fewer diabetes risk factors in teens.]

Vohr, B. R., et al. Beneficial effects of breast milk in the neonatal intensive care unit on the developmental outcome of extremely low birth weight infants at 18 months of age. *Pediatrics* 118, no. 1 (Jul 2006): e115–23. [Five IQ points higher for preterm infants receiving >80% breastmilk, versus none.]

Studying Fortifiers

Colaizy, T. T., et al. Growth in VLBW infants fed predominantly fortified maternal and donor human milk diets: A retrospective cohort study. *BMC Pediatr* 12 (Aug 2012): 124. [University of Iowa]

Fallon, E. M. et al; American Society for Parenteral and Enteral Nutrition (A.S.P.E.N.) Board of Directors, A.S.P.E.N. clinical guidelines: Nutrition support of neonatal patients at risk for necrotizing enterocolitis. *J Parenter Enteral Nutr* 36, no. 5 (Sep 2012): 506–23.

Kuschel, C. A., & Harding, J. E. Multicomponent fortified human milk for promoting growth in preterm infants. *Cochrane Database Syst Rev* 1 (2004): CD000343. [Cow-derived fortifiers produced short term weight gain, no evidence of other benefits, and no proof that harm does not occur.]

Lambert, D. K., et al. Fulminant necrotizing enterocolitis in a multihospital healthcare system. *J Perinatol* 32, no. 3 (Mar 2012): 194–8. [Utah]

Rozé, J. C., et al. The apparent breastfeeding paradox in very preterm infants: Relationship between breast feeding, early weight gain and neurodevelopment based on results from two cohorts, EPIPAGE and LIFT. *BMJ Open* 2, no. 2 (Apr 2012): e000834.

Simpson, C. D., et al. Trends in cause-specific mortality at a Canadian outborn NICU. *Pediatrics* 126, no. 6 (Dec 2010): e1538–44.

Fortifiers Made from Human Milk

Cristofalo, E. A., et al. Randomized trial of exclusive human milk versus preterm formula diets in extremely premature infants. *J Pediatr* 163, no. 6 (Dec 2013): 1592–1595.

Lee, M. L., telephone call with author, Dec 16, 2013.

Probiotics for Preemies

AlFaleh, K., & Anabrees, J. Probiotics for prevention of necrotizing enterocolitis in preterm infants. *Cochrane Database Syst Rev* 4 (2014): CD005496.

Benor, S., et al. Probiotic supplementation in mothers of very low birth weight infants. *Am J Perinatol* 31, no. 6 (Jun 2014): 497–504.

Ofek Shlomai, N., et al. Probiotics for preterm neonates: What will it take to change clinical practice? *Neonatology* 105, no. 1 (2014): 64–70.

Some Final Thoughts

Ganapathy, V., et al. Costs of necrotizing enterocolitis and cost-effectiveness of exclusively human milk-based products in feeding extremely premature infants. *Breastfeed Med* 7, no. 1 (Feb 2012): 29–37. [Fortifying mother's milk with human-derived fortifiers rather than cow-derived is cost-effective because of reduced NEC treatment costs.]

7 The Character of Poop

How Often?

Arias, A., et al. Educating parents about normal stool pattern changes in infants. *J Pediatr Health Care* 15, no. 5 (Sep-Oct 2001): 269–74.

den Hertog, J., et al. The defecation pattern of healthy term infants up to the age of 3 months. *Arch Dis Child Fetal Neonatal Ed* 97, no. 6 (Nov 2012): F465–70.

Hyams, J. S., et al. Effect of infant formula on stool characteristics of young infants. *Pediatrics* 95, no. 1 (Jan 1995): 50–4.

Tunc, V. T., et al. Factors associated with defecation patterns in 0-24-month-old children. *Eur J Pediatr* 167, no. 12 (Dec 2008): 1357–62. [Turkey]

Those Growth Charts

Dewey, K. G., et al. Do exclusively breast-fed infants require extra protein? *Pediatr Res* 39, no. 2 (Feb 1996): 303–7.

Dewey, K. G., et al. Growth of breast-fed and formula-fed infants from 0 to 18 months: The DARLING Study. *Pediatrics* 86, no. 6 Pt 1 (Jun 1992): 1035–41.

Kramer, M. S., & Kakuma, R. Optimal duration of exclusive breastfeeding. *Cochrane Database Syst Rev* 8 (Aug 2012): CD003517.

Vafa, M., et al. Relationship between breastfeeding and obesity in childhood. *J Health Popul Nutr* 30, no. 3 (Sep 2012): 303–10.

8 The Color of Poop

Colorful Bile

Kay, I. T., et al. The formation in vitro of stercobilin from bilirubin. *J Biol Chem* 238 (Mar 1963): 1122–3.

Boron, W. F., & Boulpaep, E. L. *Medical Physiology, 2nd Edition* (Philadelphia: Saunders, 2011), 988–91.

Green Poop in a Breastfed Baby

den Hertog, J., et al. The defecation pattern of healthy term infants up to the age of 3 months. *Arch Dis Child Fetal Neonatal Ed* 97, no. 6 (Nov 2012): F465–70.

Lloyd, B., et al. Formula tolerance in postbreastfed and exclusively formula-fed infants. *Pediatrics* 103, no. 1 (Jan 1999): E7.

Mizuno, K., et al. Is increased fat content of hindmilk due to the size or the number of milk fat globules? *Int Breastfeed J* 4 (2009): 7.

Woolridge, M.W., & Fisher, C. Colic, "overfeeding", and symptoms of lactose malabsorption in the breast-fed baby: A possible artifact of feed management? *Lancet* 2, no. 8607 (Aug 1988): 382–4.

Unexpected Yellow Poop

Horsfall, L.J., et al. Gilbert's syndrome and the risk of death: A population-based cohort study. *J Gastroenterol Hepatol* 28, no. 10 (Oct 2013): 1643–7.

Laforgia, N., et al. Neonatal hyperbilirubinemia and Gilbert's syndrome. *J Perinat Med* 30, no. 2 (2002): 166–9.

Orange Poop

Oceana. *Oceana Study Reveals Seafood Fraud Nationwide*. http://oceana.org/sites/default/files/National_Seafood_Fraud_Testing_Results_Highlights_FINAL.pdf, 2013.

Gray to White Poop

Ziegler, E. E. Adverse effects of cow's milk in infants. *Nestle Nutr Workshop Ser Pediatr Program* 60 (2007): 185–96; discussion 196–9.

Black Poop

Rolig, A. S., et al. The degree of Helicobacter pylori-triggered inflammation is manipulated by preinfection host microbiota. *Infect Immun* 81, no. 5 (May 2013): 1382–9.

Yang, I., et al. Survival in hostile territory: The microbiota of the stomach. *FEMS Microbiol Rev* 37, no. 5 (Sep 2013): 736–61.

Red in Poop

Arvola, T., et al. Rectal bleeding in infancy: Clinical, allergological, and microbiological examination. *Pediatrics* 117, no. 4 (Apr 2006): e760–8.

Xanthakos, S.A., et al. Prevalence and outcome of allergic colitis in healthy infants with rectal bleeding: A prospective cohort study. *J Pediatr Gastroenterol Nutr* 41, no. 1 (Jul 2005): 16–22.

Ziegler, E. E., et al. Cow milk feeding in infancy: Further observations on blood loss from the gastrointestinal tract. *J Pediat* 116, no. 1 (Jan 1990): 11–8.

Port Wine Purple Poop

James, M. F. & Hift, R. J. Porphyrias. *Br J Anaesth* 85, no. 1 (Jul 2000): 143–53.

9 Loose Poop

Should You Call the Doctor

Alam, N. H., & Ashraf, H. Treatment of infectious diarrhea in children. *Paediatr Drugs* 5, no. 3 (2003): 151–65.

Mayo Clinic Staff. "Dehydration: Symptoms." Mayo Clinic, last modified Jan 7, 2011. http://www.mayoclinic.com/health/dehydration/DS00561/DSECTION=symptoms

Teething and Diarrhea

Ramos-Jorge, J., et al. Prospective longitudinal study of signs and symptoms associated with primary tooth eruption. *Pediatrics* 128, no. 3 (Sep 2011): 471–6.

Juice Diarrhea

Perman. J. A. Digestion and absorption of fruit juice carbohydrates. *J Am Coll Nutr* 15, no. 5 Suppl (Oct 1996): 12S–17S.

Fructose Diarrhea

Gibson, P. R., et al. Review article: Fructose malabsorption and the bigger picture. *Aliment Pharmacol Ther* 25, no. 4 (Feb 2007): 349–63.

Latulippe, M. E., & Skoog, S. M. Fructose malabsorption and intolerance: Effects of fructose with and without simultaneous glucose ingestion. *Crit Rev Food Sci Nutr* 51, no. 7 (Aug 2011): 583–92.

Breastmilk Supply and Diarrhea

West, D. "What is the difference between foremilk and hindmilk." La Leche League Intl., last modifed Jul 31, 2008. http://www.llli.org/faq/foremilk.html

Diarrhea after a Cold, Pulling on Ear

Cantekin, E. I., et al. Antimicrobial therapy for otitis media with effusion ('secretory' otitis media). JAMA 266, no. 23 (Dec 1991): 3309–17.

van Zon, A., et al. Antibiotics for otitis media with effusion in children. *Cochrane Database Syst Rev* 9 (Sep 2012): CD009163.

Venekamp, R. P., et al. Antibiotics for acute otitis media in children. *Cochrane Database Syst Rev* 31 (Jan 2013): CD000219.

Autism

Chaidez, V., et al. Gastrointestinal problems in children with autism, developmental delays or typical development. *J Autism Dev Disord* (2013).

Wang, L. W., et al. The prevalence of gastrointestinal problems in children across the United States with autism spectrum disorders from families with multiple affected members. *J Dev Behav Pediatr* 32, no. 5 (Jun 2011): 351–60.

Norovirus and Rotavirus Infections

Ansari, S. A., et al. Survival and vehicular spread of human rotaviruses: Possible relation to seasonality of outbreaks. *Rev Infect Dis* 13, no. 3 (May–Jun 1991): 448–61.

Center for Disease Control and Prevention. "Vaccine Safety: Rotavirus." Last modified October 21, 2013. http://www.cdc.gov/vaccinesafety/vaccines/rotavsb.html

Dennehy, P. H., et al. Detection of rotavirus RNA in hospital air samples by polymerase chain reaction (PCR). *Pediatric Research* 43 (1998): 143–143.

Desai, R., et al. All-cause gastroenteritis and rotavirus-coded hospitalizations among US children, 2000-2009. *Clin Infect Dis* 55, no. 4 (Aug 2012): e28–34.

Desai, R., et al. Trends in intussusception: Associated deaths among US infants from 1979–2007. *J Pediatr* 160, no. 3 (Mar 2012): 456–60.

Donato, C. M., et al. Identification of strains of RotaTeq rotavirus vaccine in infants with gastroenteritis following routine vaccination. *J Infect Dis* 206, no. 3 (Aug 2012): 377–83.

Duijts, L., et al. Prolonged and exclusive breastfeeding reduces the risk of infectious diseases in infancy. *Pediatrics* 126, no. 1 (July 2010): e18–25.

Eidelman, A. I., & Schanler, R. J. Breastfeeding and the use of human milk. Section on Breastfeeding. *Pediatrics* 129, no. 3 (Mar 2012): e827–41.

Gastañaduy, P. A., et al. Gastroenteritis hospitalizations in older children and adults in the United States before and after implementation of infant rotavirus vaccination. JAMA 310, no. 8 (Aug 2013): 851–3.

Gordon, S. "CDC: Rotavirus vaccine cuts kids' hospitalization rates." US Today News, last modified Sept 11, 2011. http://usatoday30.usatoday.com/news/health/story/health/story/2011-09-22/Rotavirus-vaccine-cuts-kids-hospitalization-rates/50514052/1

Gulland, A. Rotavirus vaccine cuts deaths of Mexican babies from diarrhoea by 40%. BMJ 340 (Jan 2010): c511.

Hall, A. J., et al. Norovirus disease in the United States. *Emerg Infect Dis* 19, no. 8 (Aug 2013): 1198–205.

Ip, S., et al. A summary of the Agency for Healthcare Research and Quality's evidence report on breastfeeding in developed countries. *Breastfeed Med* 4, Suppl 1 (Oct 2009): S17–30.

Ip, S., et al. Breastfeeding and maternal and infant health outcomes in developed countries. *Evid Rep Technol Assess* 153 (Apr 2007): 1–186.

Lamberti, L. M., et al. Breastfeeding and the risk for diarrhea morbidity and mortality. *BMC Public Health* 11, Suppl 3 (Apr 2011): S15.

Prince, D. S., et al. Aerosol transmission of experimental rotavirus infection. *Pediatr Infect Dis* 5, no. 2 (Mar-Apr 1986): 218–22.

Quigley, M. A., et al. Breastfeeding is associated with improved child cognitive development: A population-based cohort study. *J Pediatr* 160, no. 1 (Jan 2012): 25–32.

Tate, J. E., et al. Uptake, impact, and effectiveness of rotavirus vaccination in the United States: Review of the first 3 years of postlicensure data. *Pediatr Infect Dis J* 30, Suppl 1 (Jan 2011): S56–60.

Weinberg, G. A., et al. Detection of novel rotavirus strain by vaccine postlicensure surveillance. *Emerg Infect Dis* 19, no. 8 (Aug 2013): 1321–3.

Wikswo, M. E., et al. "Clinical profile of children with norovirus disease in rotavirus vaccine era." *Emerging Infectious Diseases* 19, no. 10 (Oct 2013). http://wwwnc.cdc.gov/eid/article/19/10/13-0448_article.htm

E. coli

Gothefors, L., et al. Breast feeding and biological properties of faecal E. coli strains. *Acta Paediatr Scand* 64, no. 6 (Nov 1975): 807–12.

Wold, A. E., & Adlerberth, I. Breast feeding and the intestinal microflora of the infant: Implications for protection against infectious diseases. *Adv Exp Med Biol* 478 (2000): 77–93.

10 Caring for Loose Poop

Oral Rehydration

Bajait, C., & Thawani V. Role of zinc in pediatric diarrhea. *Indian J Pharmacol* 43, no. 3 (May 2011): 232–5.

Diggins, K. C. Treatment of mild to moderate dehydration in children with oral rehydration therapy. *J Am Acad Nurse Pract* 20, no. 8 (Aug 2008): 402–6.

King, C. K., et al., & Centers for Disease Control and Prevention. Managing acute gastroenteritis among children: Oral rehydration, maintenance, and nutritional therapy. *MMWR Recomm Rep* 52, RR-16 (Nov 2003): 1–16.

Larson, C. E. Safety and efficacy of oral rehydration therapy for the treatment of diarrhea and gastroenteritis in pediatrics. *Pediatr Nurs* 26, no. 2 (Mar/Apr 2000): 177–9.

Munos, M. K., et al. The effect of oral rehydration solution and recommended home fluids on diarrhoea mortality. *Int J Epidemiol* 39, Suppl 1(Apr 2010): i75–87.

Pie cik-Lech, M., et al. Review article: The management of acute gastroenteritis in children. *Aliment Pharmacol Ther* 37, no. 3 (Feb 2013): 289–303.

Spandorfer, P. R., et al. Oral versus intravenous rehydration of moderately dehydrated children: A randomized, controlled trial. *Pediatrics* 115, no. 2 (Feb 2005): 295–301.

Fluids and the Exclusively Breastfeeding Baby

Marín Gabriel, M. A., et al. Analgesia with breastfeeding in addition to skin-to-skin contact during heel prick. *Arch Dis Child Fetal Neonatal Ed* 98, no. 6 (Nov 2013): F499–F503.

"Rehydration, Pediatriac," Scott and White Healthcare, last modified March 11, 2013 http://www.sw.org/HealthLibrary?page=Rehydration,%20Pediatric

Shah, P. S., et al. Breastfeeding or breast milk for procedural pain in neonates. *Cochrane Database Syst Rev* 12 (Dec 2012): CD004950.

Oral Rehydration Solutions

Ziegler, E. E. Adverse effects of cow's milk in infants. *Nestle Nutr Workshop Ser Pediatr Program* 60 (2007): 185–96; discussion 196-9.

Fevers and Sick Children

Adair, S. M. Pacifier use in children: A review of recent literature. *Pediatr Dent* 25, no 5 (Sep/Oct 2003): 449–58.

Gormally, S., et al. Contact and nutrient caregiving effects on newborn infant pain responses. *Dev Med Child Neurol* 43, no. 1 (Jan 2001): 28–38.

Harding, C. An evaluation of the benefits of non-nutritive sucking for premature infants as described in the literature. *Arch Dis Child* 94, no. 8 (Aug 2009): 636–40.

Hauck, F. R., et al. Do pacifiers reduce the risk of sudden infant death syndrome? A meta-analysis. *Pediatrics* 116, no. 5 (Nov 2005): e716–23.

Medoff-Cooper, B., & Ray, W. Neonatal sucking behaviors. *Image J Nurs Sch* 27, no. 3 (Fall 1995): 195–200.

Nelson, A. M. A comprehensive review of evidence and current recommendations related to pacifier usage. *J Pediatr Nurs* 27, no. 6 (Dec 2012): 690–9.

Soszy ski, D. The pathogenesis and the adaptive value of fever. *Postepy Hig Med Dosw* 57, no. 5 (2003): 531–54.

Fevers and Pain Medications

Bárzaga Arencibia, Z., & Choonara, I. Balancing the risks and benefits of the use of over-the-counter pain medications in children. *Drug Saf* 35, no. 12 (Dec 2012): 1119–25.

Baumann, R. J., & Duffner, P. K. Treatment of children with simple febrile seizures: The AAP practice parameter. American Academy of Pediatrics. *Pediatr Neurol* 23, no. 1 (Jul 2000): 11–7.

Bertuola, F., et al. Association between drug and vaccine use and acute immune thrombocytopenia in childhood: A case-control study in Italy. *Drug Saf* 33, no. 1 (Jan 2010): 65–72.

Bianciotto, M., et al.; Italian Multicenter Study Group for Drug and Vaccine Safety in Children. Drug use and upper gastrointestinal complications in children: A case-control study. *Arch Dis Child* 98, no. 3 (Mar 2013): 218–21.

Carey, J. V. Literature review: Should antipyretic therapies routinely be administered to patients with [corrected] fever? *J Clin Nurs* 19, no. 17–18 (Sep 2010): 2377–93.

Casteels-Van Daele, M., et al. Reye syndrome revisited: A descriptive term covering a group of heterogeneous disorders. *Eur J Pediatr* 159, no. 9 (Sep 2000): 641–8.

Civen, R., et al. The incidence and clinical characteristics of herpes zoster among children and adolescents after implementation of varicella vaccination. *Pediatr Infect Dis J* 28, no. 11 (Nov 2009): 954–9.

Doran, T. F., et al. Acetaminophen: More harm than good for chickenpox? *J Pediatr* 114, no. 6 (Jun 1989): 1045–8.

Eyers, S., et al. The effect on mortality of antipyretics in the treatment of influenza infection: Systematic review and meta-analysis. *J R Soc Med* 103, no. 10 (Oct 2010): 403–11.

Ferrandiz-Pulido, C., & Garcia-Patos, V. A review of causes of Stevens-Johnson syndrome and toxic epidermal necrolysis in children. *Arch Dis Child* 98, no. 12 (Jul 2013): 998–1003.

Goldman, R. D. Efficacy and safety of acetaminophen versus ibuprofen for treating children's pain or fever: A meta-analysis. *J Pediatr* 146, no. 1 (Jan 2005): 142–3.

Good, P. Did acetaminophen provoke the autism epidemic? *Altern Med Rev* 14, no. 4 (Dec 2009): 364–72.

Greisman, L. A., & Mackowiak, P. A. Fever: Beneficial and detrimental effects of antipyretics. *Curr Opin Infect Dis* 15, no. 3 (Jun 2002): 241–5.

Jefferies, S., et al. Systematic review and meta-analysis of the effects of antipyretic medications on mortality in Streptococcus pneumoniae infections. *Postgrad Med J* 88, no. 1035 (Jan 2012): 21–7.

Kiekkas, P. Fever treatment in critical care: When available evidence does not support traditional practice. *Nurs Crit Care* 17, no. 1 (Jan–Feb 2012): 7–8.

Kluger, M. J., et al. The adaptive value of fever. *Infect Dis Clin North Am* 10, no. 1 (Mar 1996): 1–20.

Kuehn, B. M. FDA: Acetaminophen may trigger serious skin problems. *JAMA* 310, no. 8 (Aug 2013): 785.

Mikaeloff, Y., et al. Nonsteroidal anti-inflammatory drug use and the risk of severe skin and soft tissue complications in patients with varicella or zoster disease. *Br J Clin Pharmacol* 65, no. 2 (Feb 2008): 203–9.

Misurac, J. M., et al. Nonsteroidal anti-inflammatory drugs are an important cause of acute kidney injury in children. *J Pediatr* 162, no. 6 (Jun 2013): 1153–9, 1159.e1.

Moulis, G., et al.; French Association of Regional Pharmacovigilance Centers. Drug-induced immune thrombocytopenia: A descriptive survey in the French PharmacoVigilance database. *Platelets* 23, no. 6 (2012): 490–4.

Offringa, M., & Newton, R. Prophylactic drug management for febrile seizures in children. *Cochrane Database Syst Rev* 4 (Apr 2012): CD003031.

Orlowski, J. P., et al. Is aspirin a cause of Reye's syndrome? A case against. *Drug Saf* 25 (2002): 225–231.

Plaisance, K. I., et al. Effect of antipyretic therapy on the duration of illness in experimental influenza A, Shigella sonnei, and Rickettsia rickettsii infections. *Pharmacotherapy* 20, no. 12 (Dec 2000): 1417–22.

Plaisance, K. I., & Mackowiak, P. A. Antipyretic therapy: Physiologic rationale, diagnostic implications, and clinical consequences. *Arch Intern Med* 160, no. 4 (Feb 2000): 449–56.

Prescott, L. F. Effects of non-narcotic analgesics on the liver. *Drugs* 32, Supple 4 (1986): 129–47.

Rosenbloom, E., et al. Do antipyretics prevent the recurrence of febrile seizures in children? A systematic review of randomized controlled trials and meta-analysis. *Eur J Paediatr Neurol* 17, no. 6 (May 2013): 585–8.

Schrör, K. Aspirin and Reye syndrome: A review of the evidence. *Paediatr Drugs* 9, no. 3(2007): 195–204. Review.

Souyri, C., et al.; French Network of Pharmacovigilance Centres. Severe necrotizing soft-tissue infections and nonsteroidal anti-inflammatory drugs. *Clin Exp Dermatol* 33, no. 3 (May 2008): 249–55.

Titchen, T., et al. Adverse drug reactions to nonsteroidal anti-inflammatory drugs, COX-2 inhibitors and paracetamol in a paediatric hospital. *Br J Clin Pharmacol* 59, no. 6 (Jun 2005): 718–23.

Tolman, K. G. Hepatotoxicity of non-narcotic analgesics. *Am J Med* 105, no. 1B (Jul 1998): 13S–19S.

Varicella, herpes zoster and nonsteroidal anti-inflammatory drugs: Serious cutaneous complications. *Prescrire Int* 19, no. 106 (Apr 2010): 72–3.

Wickens, K., et al.; New Zealand Asthma and Allergy Cohort Study Group. The effects of early and late paracetamol exposure on asthma and atopy: A birth cAhort. *Clin Exp Allergy* 41, no. 3 (Mar 2011): 399–406.

Wiegand, T. J., et al.; Toxicology Investigators Consortium Case Registry Investigators. The Toxicology Investigators Consortium Case Registry: The 2011 experience. *J Med Toxicol* 8, no. 4 (Dec 2012): 360–77.

Other Medications

Alam, N. H., & Ashraf, H. Treatment of infectious diarrhea in children. *Paediatr Drugs* 5, no. 3 (2003): 151–65.

Colletti, J. E. Are antiemetics still contraindicated for gastroenteritis in children? Solid evidence now supports the safe use of ondansetron. *Evid Based Nurs* 15, no. 2 (Apr 2012): 46–7.

Fedorowicz, Z., et al. Antiemetics for reducing vomiting related to acute gastroenteritis in children and adolescents. *Cochrane Database Syst Rev* 9 (Sep 2011): CD005506.

Ford, A. C., et al. Adverse events with bismuth salts for Helicobacter pylori eradication: Systematic review and meta-analysis. *World J Gastroenterol* 15, no. 48 (Dec 2008): 7361–70.

Freedman, S. B., et al. Treatment of acute gastroenteritis in children: An overview of systematic reviews of interventions commonly used in developed countries. *Evid Based Child Health* 8, no. 4 (Jul 2013): 1123–37.

Leung, A. K., & Robson, W. L. Acute gastroenteritis in children: Role of anti-emetic medication for gastroenteritis-related vomiting. *Paediatr Drugs* 9, no. 3 (2007): 175–84.

Manteuffel, J. Use of antiemetics in children with acute gastroenteritis: Are they safe and effective? *J Emerg Trauma Shock* 2, no. 1 (Jan 2009): 3–5.

Szajewska, H., & Dziechciarz, P. Gastrointestinal infections in the pediatric population. *Curr Opin Gastroenterol* 26, no. 1 (Jan 2010): 36–44.

Turck, D. Prevention and treatment of acute diarrhea in infants. *Arch Pediatr* 14, no. 11 (Nov 2007): 1375–8.

Caring for Antibiotic-Caused Diarrhea

"Fecal microbiota transplant for relapsing Clostridium difficile infection in adults and children using a frozen encapsulated inoculum," Clinical Trials.gov, last modified August 6, 2013. http://clinicaltrials.gov/show/NCT01914731

"Fecal transplant pill knocks out recurrent C. diff infection," Science Daily, October 4, 2013. http://www.sciencedaily.com/releases/2013/10/131004105253.htm

Högenauer, C., et al. Mechanisms and management of antibiotic-associated diarrhea. *Clin Infect Dis* 27, no. 4 (Oct 27): 702–10.

Reisinger, E. C., et al. Diarrhea caused by primarily non-gastrointestinal infections. *Nat Clin Pract Gastroenterol Hepatol* 2, no. 5 (May 2005): 216–22.

Rohlke, F., & Stollman, N. Fecal microbiota transplantation in relapsing Clostridium difficile infection. *Therap Adv Gastroenterol* 5, no. 6 (Nov 2012): 403–20.

Schröder, O., et al. Antibiotic-associated diarrhea. *Z Gastroenterol* 44, no. 2 (Feb 2006): 193–204.

Tummy Tamers

Al-Hashem, F. H. Gastroprotective effects of aqueous extract of Chamomilla recutita against ethanol-induced gastric ulcers. *Saudi Med J* 31, no. 11 (Nov 2010): 1211–6.

Ankri, S., & Mirelman, D. Antimicrobial properties of allicin from garlic. *Microbes Infect* 1, no. 2 (Feb 1999): 125–9.

Duarte, C. M., et al. Effects of Chamomilla recutita (L.) on oral wound healing in rats. *Med Oral Patol Oral Cir Bucal* 16, no. 6 (Sep 2011): e716–21.

Ezz El-Arab, A. M., et al. Effect of dietary honey on intestinal microflora and toxicity of mycotoxins in mice. *BMC Complement Altern Med* 6 (Mar 2006): 6.

Fujisawa, H., et al. Antibacterial potential of garlic-derived allicin and its cancellation by sulfhydryl compounds. *Biosci Biotechnol Biochem* 73, no. 9 (Sep 2009): 1948–55.

Haniadka, R., et al. A review of the gastroprotective effects of ginger (Zingiber officinale Roscoe). *Food Funct* 4, no. 6 (Jun 2013): 845–55.

Herbal remedies for dyspepsia: Peppermint seems effective. *Prescrire Int* 17, no. 95 (Jun 2008): 121–3.

Karuppiah, P., & Rajaram, S. Antibacterial effect of Allium sativum cloves and Zingiber officinale rhizomes against multiple-drug resistant clinical pathogens. *Asian Pac J Trop Biomed* 2, no. 8 (Aug 2012): 597–601.

Langmead, L., & Rampton, D. S. Review article: Herbal treatment in gastrointestinal and liver disease--benefits and dangers. *Aliment Pharmacol Ther* 15, no. 9 (Sep 2001): 1239–52.

McKay, D. L., & Blumberg, J. B. A review of the bioactivity and potential health benefits of peppermint tea (Mentha piperita L.). *Phytother Res* 20, no. 8 (Aug 2006): 619–33.

Sasaki, J., et al. Antibacterial activity of garlic powder against Escherichia coli O-157. *J Nutr Sci Vitaminol* (Tokyo) 45, no. 6 (Dec 1999): 785–90.

Probiotics

Abrahamsson, T. R., et al. Probiotic lactobacilli in breast milk and infant stool in relation to oral intake during the first year of life. *J Pediatr Gastroenterol Nutr* 49, no. 3 (Sep 2009): 349–54.

Cucchiara, S., et al. New therapeutic approach in the management of intestinal disease: Probiotics in intestinal disease in paediatric age. *Dig Liver Dis* 34, Suppl 2 (Sep 2002): S44–7.

Eren, M., et al. Clinical efficacy comparison of Saccharomyces boulardii and yogurt fluid in acute non-bloody diarrhea in children: A randomized, controlled, open label study. *Am J Trop Med Hyg* 82, no. 3 (Mar 2010): 488–91.

Guandalini, S. Probiotics for prevention and treatment of diarrhea. *J Clin Gastroenterol* 45, Suppl. (Nov 2011): S149–53.

Guarino, A., et al. Probiotics as prevention and treatment for diarrhea. *Curr Opin Gastroenterol* 25, no. 1 (Jan 2009): 18–23.

Szajewska, H., et al. Meta-analysis: Lactobacillus GG for treating acute gastroenteritis in children—updated analysis of randomised controlled trials. *Aliment Pharmacol Ther* 38, no. 5 (Sep 2013): 467–76.

Vandenplas, Y., et al. Probiotics and prebiotics in pediatric diarrheal disorders. *Expert Opin Pharmacother* 14, no. 4 (Mar 2013): 397–409.

Zwoli ska-Wcisło, M., et al. Are probiotics effective in the treatment of fungal colonization of the gastrointestinal tract? Experimental and clinical studies. *J Physiol Pharmacol* 57, Suppl 9 (Nov 2006): 35–49.

Preventing Spread of Infectious Diarrhea

Aiello, A. E., et al. Consumer antibacterial soaps: Effective or just risky? *Clin Infect Dis* 45, Suppl 2 (Sep 2007): S137–47.

Andersen, B. M., et al. Floor cleaning: Effect on bacteria and organic materials in hospital rooms. *J Hosp Infect* 71, no 1 (Jan 2009): 57–65.

Baban, B., et al. Use of a new, simple, laboratory method for screening the antimicrobial and antiviral properties of hand sanitizers. *Am J Dent* 25, no. 6 (Dec 2012): 327–31.

Bedoux, G., et al. Occurrence and toxicity of antimicrobial triclosan and by-products in the environment. *Environ Sci Pollut Res Int* 19, no. 4 (May 2012): 1044–65.

Burton, M., et al. The effect of handwashing with water or soap on bacterial contamination of hands. *Int J Environ Res Public Health* 8, no. 1 (Jan 2011): 97–104.

Dann, A. B. & Hontela, A. Triclosan: Environmental exposure, toxicity and mechanisms of action. *J Appl Toxicol* 31, no. 4 (May 2011): 285–311.

Edmonds, S. L., et al. Effectiveness of hand hygiene for removal of Clostridium difficile spores from hands. *Infect Control Hosp Epidemiol* 34, no. 3 (Mar 2013): 302–5.

Goldenberg, J. Z., et al. Probiotics for the prevention of Clostridium difficile-associated diarrhea in adults and children. *Cochrane Database Syst Rev* 5 (May 2013): CD006095.

Jabbar, U., et al. Effectiveness of alcohol-based hand rubs for removal of Clostridium difficile spores from hands. *Infect Control Hosp Epidemiol* 31, no. 6 (Jun 2010): 565–70.

Magee, P. Antiseptic drugs and disinfectants. *Side Eff Drugs Annu* 21, (1998): 254–256.

Oughton, M. T., et al. Hand hygiene with soap and water is superior to alcohol rub and antiseptic wipes for removal of Clostridium difficile. *Infect Control Hosp Epidemiol* 31, no. 10 (Oct 2009): 939–44.

Rhoades, J., et al. Oregano essential oil as an antimicrobial additive to detergent for hand washing and food contact surface cleaning. *J Appl Microbiol* 115, no. 4 (Oct 2013): 987–94.

Steinmann, J., et al. Comparison of virucidal activity of alcohol-based hand sanitizers versus antimicrobial hand soaps in vitro and in vivo. *J Hosp Infect* 82, no. 4 (Dec 2012): 277–80.

Todd, E. C., et al. Outbreaks where food workers have been implicated in the spread of foodborne disease. Part 10. Alcohol-based antiseptics for hand disinfection and a comparison of their effectiveness with soaps. *J Food Prot* 73, no. 11 (Nov 2010): 2128–40.

Zhang, L., et al. Protection by face masks against Influenza A(H1N1)pdm09 Virus on trans-Pacific passenger aircraft, 2009. *Emerg Infect Dis* 19, no. 9 (Sep 2013).

Feeding the Sick Child on Solid Foods

Jirapinyo, P., et al. High-fat semielemental diet in the treatment of protracted diarrhea of infancy. *Pediatrics* 86, no. 6 (Dec 1990): 902–8.

11 Hard Poop

"Childhood constipation just as serious as asthma," *Science Daily*, Nov 28, 2008, accessed Nov 8, 2013. http://www.sciencedaily.com/releases/2008/11/081126122319.htm

Is It Constipation?

Arnaud, M. J. Mild dehydration: A risk factor of constipation? *Eur J Clin Nutr* 57, Suppl 2 (Dec 2003): S88–95.

Burgers, R., et al. Functional defecation disorders in children: Comparing the Rome II with the Rome III criteria. *J Pediatr* 161, no. 4, (Oct 2012): 615–20.e1.

Soiling: Your Child Has Accidents in His Pants

Price, K. J., & Elliott, T. M. What is the role of stimulant laxatives in the management of childhood constipation and soiling? *Cochrane Database Syst Rev* 3 (2001): CD002040.

Functional Constipation

Image: "Bathroom Reading," by Jay Ryness, https://www.flickr.com/photos/jbird/19650368/, 2005. *Fotor.com.* License: creativecommons.org/licenses/by/2.0/.

Dietary Causes

Corkins, M. R. Are diet and constipation related in children? *Nutr Clin Pract* 20, no. 5 (Oct 2005): 536–9.

Crowley, E. T., et al. Does milk cause constipation? A crossover dietary trial. *Nutrients* 5, no. 1 (Jan 2013): 253–66.

Dehghani, S. M., et al. The role of cow's milk allergy in pediatric chronic constipation: A randomized clinical trial. *Iran J Pediatr* 22, no. 4 (Dec 2012): 468–74.

El-Hodhod, M. A., et al. Cow's milk allergy related pediatric constipation: Appropriate time of milk tolerance. *Pediatr Allergy Immunol* 21, no. 2 (Mar 2010): e407–12.

Heine, R. G. Allergic gastrointestinal motility disorders in infancy and early childhood. *Pediatr Allergy Immunol* 19, no. 5 (Aug 2008): 383–91.

Irastorza, I., et al. Cow's-milk-free diet as a therapeutic option in childhood chronic constipation. *J Pediatr Gastroenterol Nutr* 51, no. 2 (Aug 2010): 171–6.

Philichi, L. When the going gets tough: Pediatric constipation and encopresis. *Gastroenterol Nurs* 31, no. 2 (Mar-Apr 2008): 121–30. doi:10.1097/01.SGA.0000316531.31366.27

Syrigou, E. I., et al. Food allergy-related paediatric constipation: The usefulness of atopy patch test. *Eur J Pediatr* 170, no. 9 (Sep 2011): 1173–8.

Botulism

McMaster, P., et al. A taste of honey. *J Paediatr Child Health* 36, no. 6 (Dec 2000): 596–7.

Spika, J. S., et al. Risk factors for infant botulism in the United States. *Am J Dis Child* 143, no. 7 (Jul 1989): 828–32.

Tanzi, M. G., & Gabay, M. P. Association between honey consumption and infant botulism. *Pharmacotherapy* 22, no. 1 (Nov 2002): 1479–83.

Constipation and Iron-Fortified Formulas

Hermoso, M., et al. The effect of iron on cognitive development and function in infants, children and adolescents: A systematic review. *Ann Nutr Metab* 59, no. 2–4 (Dec 2011): 154–65.

Hyams, J. S., et al. Effect of infant formula on stool characteristics of young infants. *Pediatrics* 95, no. 1 (Jan 1995): 50–4.

Lozoff, B., et al. Iron-fortified vs low-iron infant formula: Developmental outcome at 10 years. *Arch Pediatr Adolesc Med* 166, no. 2 (Mar 2012): 208–15.

Moy, R. J. Iron fortification of infant formula. *Nutr Res Rev* 13, no. 2 (Dec 2000): 215–27.

Nelson, S. E., et al. Lack of adverse reactions to iron-fortified formula. *Pediatrics* 82, no. 3 (Mar 1988): 360–4.

Oski, F. A., et al. Iron-fortified formulas and gastrointestinal symptoms in infants: A controlled study. *Pediatrics* 66, no. 2 (Aug 1980): 168–170.

12 Caring for Constipation and Withholding

Bongers, M. E., et al. Long-term prognosis for childhood constipation: Clinical outcomes in adulthood. *Pediatrics* 126, no. 1 (Jul 2010): e156–62.

van Ginkel, R., et al. Childhood constipation: Longitudinal follow-up beyond puberty. *Gastroenterology* 125, no. 2 (Aug 2003): 357–63.

Physical Measures First

Anders, E. F., et al. Acupuncture for treatment of hospital-induced constipation in children: A retrospective case series study. *Acupunct Med* 30, no. 4 (Dec 2012): 258–60.

Arslan, G. G., & Eser, I. An examination of the effect of castor oil packs on constipation in the elderly. *Complement Ther Clin Pract* 17, no. 1 (Feb 2011): 58–62.

Broide, E., et al. Effectiveness of acupuncture for treatment of childhood constipation. *Dig Dis Sci* 46, no. 6 (Jun 2001): 1270–5.

Coccorullo, P., et al. Novel and alternative therapies for childhood constipation. *J Pediatr Gastroenterol Nutr* 48, Suppl. 2 (Apr 2009): S104–6.

Culbert, T. P., & Banez, G. A. Integrative approaches to childhood constipation and encopresis. *Pediatr Clin North Am* 54, no. 6 (Dec 2007): 27–47.

Liem, O., et al. Novel and alternative therapies for childhood constipation. *Curr Gastroenterol Rep* 9, no. 3 (Jun 2007): 214–8.

Nurko, S. Advances in the management of pediatric constipation. *Curr Gastroenterol Rep* 2, no. 3 (Jun 2000): 234–40.

Tarsuslu, T., et al. The effects of osteopathic treatment on constipation in children with cerebral palsy: A pilot study. *J Manipulative Physiol Ther* 32, no. 8 (Oct 2009): 648–53.

Waring, R. H. Report on Absorption of magnesium sulfate (Epsom salts) across the skin. *Epsom Salt Council, & School of Biosciences*, University of Birmingham, UK.

Natural Oral Laxatives

"Aloe," last modified March 12, 2014, http://www.nlm.nih.gov/medlineplus/druginfo/natural/607.html

"Aloe," RXList, accessed November 28, 2013, http://www.rxlist.com/aloe-page2/supplements.htm#SafetyConcerns

Bolla, G., & Sartore, G. The psyllium fibre for the treatment of functional constipation in children. *Pediatr Med Chir* 30, no. 3 (May–Jun 2008): 146–8.

Castillejo, G., et al. A controlled, randomized, double-blind trial to evaluate the effect of a supplement of cocoa husk that is rich in dietary fiber on colonic transit in constipated pediatric patients. *Pediatrics* 118, no. 3 (Sep 2006): e641–8.

Francavilla, R., et al. Effect of lactose on gut microbiota and metabolome of infants with cow's milk allergy. *Pediatr Allergy Immunol* 23, no. 5 (Aug 2012): 420–7.

Godding, E. W. Laxatives and the special role of senna. *Pharmacology* 36, Suppl. 1 (1988): 230–6.

Grzeskowiak, Ł., et al. The impact of perinatal probiotic intervention on gut microbiota: Double-blind placebo-controlled trials in Finland and Germany. *Anaerobe* 18, no. 1 (Feb 2012): 7–13.

Hannan, M. A., et al. Maternal milk concentration of zinc, iron, selenium, and iodine and its relationship to dietary intakes. *Biol Trace Elem Res* 127, no. 1 (Jan 2009): 6–15.

Loening-Baucke, V., et al. Fiber (glucomannan) is beneficial in the treatment of childhood constipation. *Pediatrics* 113, no. 3 Pt. 1 (Mar 2004): e259–64.

McRorie, J. W., et al. Psyllium is superior to docusate sodium for treatment of chronic constipation. *Aliment Pharmacol Ther* 12, no. 5 (May 1998): 491–7.

Quitadamo, P., et al. A randomized, prospective, comparison study of a mixture of acacia fiber, psyllium fiber, and fructose vs polyethylene glycol 3350 with electrolytes for the treatment of chronic functional constipation in childhood. *J Pediatr* 161, no. 4 (Oct 2012): 710–5.e1.

Sanz, Y. Gut microbiota and probiotics in maternal and infant health. *Am J Clin Nutr* 94, 6 Suppl (Dec 2011): 2000S–2005S.

Sondheimer, J. M., & Gervaise, E. P. Lubricant versus laxative in the treatment of chronic functional constipation of children: A comparative study. *J Pediatr Gastroenterol Nutr* 1, no. 2 (1982): 223–6.

Stacewicz-Sapuntzakis, M. Dried plums and their products: Composition and health effects—an updated review. *Crit Rev Food Sci Nutr* 53, no. 12 (2013): 1277–302.

Tatsuki, M., et al. Serum magnesium concentration in children with functional constipation treated with magnesium oxide. *World J Gastroenterol* 17, no. 6 (Feb 2011): 779–83.

Williams, C. L., & Bollella, M. Is a high-fiber diet safe for children? *Pediatrics* 96, no. 5 Pt. 2 (Nov 1995): 1014–9.

Medical Laxatives

Clausen, M. R., & Mortensen, P. B. Lactulose, disaccharides and colonic flora. Clinical consequences. *Drugs* 53, no. 6 (Jun 1997): 930–42.

Constipation Guideline Committee of the North American Society for Pediatric Gastroenterology, Hepatology and Nutrition. Evaluation and treatment of constipation in infants and children: Recommendations of the North American Society for Pediatric Gastroenterology, Hepatology and Nutrition. *J Pediatr Gastroenterol Nutr* 43, no. 3 (Sep 2006): e1–13.

Daniel, K. T. "The poop on Miralax." Accessed Nov 21 2013. http://drkaayladaniel.com/the-poop-on-miralax/

FDA. "Drug safety oversight board meeting," Accessed November 21, 2013. http://www.fda.gov/AboutFDA/CentersOffices/OfficeofMedicalProductsandTobacco/CDER/ucm171059.htm

Empire State Consumer Project Inc. "Citizen petition to investigate polyethylene glycol 3350 product safety for use with pediatric patients." June 3, 2012. http://www.elsevierbi.com/~/media/Supporting%20Documents/The%20Tan%20Sheet/20/28/Polyethylene_glycol_citizen_petn_120603.pdf

Food and Drug Administration. "Potential signals of serious risks/new safety information identified by the adverse event reporting system (AERS) between October–December 2011." Last modified October 31, 2013. http://www.fda.gov/Drugs/GuidanceComplianceRegulatoryInformation/Surveillance/AdverseDrugEffects/ucm295585.htm

Gattuso, J. M., & Kamm, M. A. Adverse effects of drugs used in the management of constipation and diarrhoea. *Drug Saf* 10, no. 1 (Jan 1994): 47–65.

Gordon M., et al. Cochrane Review: Osmotic and stimulant laxatives for the management of childhood constipation (Review). *Evid Based Child Health* 8, no. 1 (Jan 2013): 57–109.

Khalif, I. L., et al. Alterations in the colonic flora and intestinal permeability and evidence of immune activation in chronic constipation. *Dig Liver Dis* 37, no. 11 (Nov 2005): 838–49.

McClung, H. J., & Potter, C. Rational use of laxatives in children. *Adv Pediatr* 51 (2004): 231–62.

Pijpers, M. A., et al. Currently recommended treatments of childhood constipation are not evidence based: A systematic literature review on the effect of laxative treatment and dietary measures. *Arch Dis Child* 94, no. 2 (Feb 2009): 117–31.

Salminen, S., & Salminen, E. Lactulose, lactic acid bacteria, intestinal microecology and mucosal protection. *Scand J Gastroenterol Suppl* 222 (1997): 45–8.

Tabbers, M. M., et al. Nonpharmacologic treatments for childhood constipation: Systematic review. *Pediatrics* 128, no. 4 (Oct 2011): 753–61.

Tarumi, Y., et al. Randomized, double-blind, placebo-controlled trial of oral docusate in the management of constipation in hospice patients. *J Pain Symptom Manage* 45, no. 1 (Jan 2013): 2–13.

Vitalone, A., et al. Surveillance of suspected adverse reactions to herbal products used as laxatives. *Eur J Clin Pharmacol* 68, no. 3 (Mar 2012): 231–8.

Xing, J. H., & Soffer, E. E. Adverse effects of laxatives. *Dis Colon Rectum* 44, no. 8 (Aug 2001): 1201–9.

Treating from the Bottom

Hansen S. E., et al. Safety and efficacy of milk and molasses enemas compared with sodium phosphate enemas for the treatment of constipation in a pediatric emergency department. *Pediatr Emerg Care* 27, no. 12 (Dec 2011): 1118–20.

Moses, S. "Pediatric constipation notebook." Accessed December 2, 2013. http://www.fpnotebook.com/gi/peds/PdtrcCnstptnMngmnt.htm

Schmitt, B. "Enemas: How to give." Accessed December 2, 2013. http://www.summitmedicalgroup.com/library/pediatric_health/hhg_enema_home/

Wallaker, K., et al. Milk and molasses enemas: Clearing things up. *J Emerg Nurs* (2013).

The Evolution of a Withholder

Blum, N. J., et al. During toilet training, constipation occurs before stool toileting refusal. *Pediatrics* 113, no. 6 (Jun 2004): e520–2.

Indiana University Health. "Constipation and your child." Accessed December 3, 2013. http://iuhealth.org/images/ril-doc-upl/Handout%20-%20Constipation_and_Your_Child.pdf

Bowel Training

Image: "Beginning Reader," by Andre Chinn, https://www.flickr.com/photos/andrec/442877596/, 2007. *Fotor.com*. License: creativecommons.org/licenses/by/2.0/.

13 The Poop on Colic and Reflux

What is Colic?

Palmer, L. F. *Baby Matters*, San Diego, CA: BabyReference, 2015.

Reflux: The New Colic

Campanozzi, A., et al. Prevalence and natural history of gastroesophageal reflux: Pediatric prospective survey. *Pediatrics* 123, no. 3 (Mar 2009): 779–83.

Chen, I. L., et al. Proton pump inhibitor use in infants: FDA reviewer experience. *J Pediatr Gastroenterol Nutr* 54, no. 1 (Jan 2012): 8–14.

Nelson, S. P., et al. Pediatric gastroesophageal reflux disease and acid-related conditions: trends in incidence of diagnosis and acid suppression therapy. *J Med Econ* 12, no. 4 (2009): 348–55.

Nelson, S. P., et al. Prevalence of symptoms of gastroesophageal reflux during infancy. A pediatric practice-based survey. Pediatric Practice Research Group. *Arch Pediatr Adolesc Med* 151, no. 6 (Jun 1997): 569–72.

14 Gut Health and Autoimmune Disease

Liu, Z., et al. Tight junctions, leaky intestines, and pediatric diseases. *Acta Paediatr* 94, no. 4 (Apr 2005): 386–93.

Childhood Type 1 Diabetes

CDC. "National diabetes statistics report, 2014: Estimates of diabetes and its burden in the United States," accessed June 10, 2014, http://www.cdc.gov/diabetes/pubs/statsreport14/national-diabetes-report-web.pdf

Diabetes and Feeding Babies

Antvorskov, J. C., et al. Dietary gluten and the development of type 1 diabetes. *Diabetologia* (May 2014).

Birgisdottir, B. E., et al. Lower consumption of cow milk protein A1 beta-casein at 2 years of age, rather than consumption among 11- to 14-year-old adolescents, may explain the lower incidence of type 1 diabetes in Iceland than in Scandinavia. *Ann Nutr Metab* 50, no. 3 (2006): 177–83.

Buschard, K. What causes type 1 diabetes? Lessons from animal models. *APMIS* 132, Suppl. (Jul 2011): 1–19.

"Current Worldwide Total Milk Consumption per capita," Charts Bin, 2007 data, http://chartsbin.com/view/1491

Dahl-Jørgensen, K.et al. Relationship between cows' milk consumption and incidence of IDDM in childhood. *Diabetes Care* 14, no. 11 (Nov 1991): 1081–3.

Efstathiou, E., & Skordis, N. "Altering trends in the epidemiology of type 1 diabetes mellitus in children and adolescents." In *Type 1 Diabetes: Complications, Pathogenesis, and Alternative Treatments*, edited by. Chih-Pin Liu. (InTech, 2011).

Gyula, S., et al. "Diabetes in the young: A global perspective, global trends in childhood type 1 diabetes." International Diabetes Federation, accessed June 2010, http://www.idf.org/sites/default/files/Diabetes_in_the_Young.pdf

Luopajärvi, K., et al. Enhanced levels of cow's milk antibodies in infancy in children who develop type 1 diabetes later in childhood. *Pediatr Diabetes*. 9, no. 5 (Oct 2008): 434–41.

Monetini, L. et al; IMDIAB Group. Bovine beta-casein antibodies in breast- and bottle-fed infants: Their relevance in Type 1 diabetes. *Diabetes Metab Res Rev* 17, no. 1 (Jan-Feb 2001): 51–4.

Patelarou, E., et al. Current evidence on the associations of breastfeeding, infant formula, and cow's milk introduction with type 1 diabetes mellitus: A systematic review. *Nutr Rev* 70, 9 (Sep 2012): 509–19.

Savilahti, E., & Saarinen, K. M. Early infant feeding and type 1 diabetes. *Eur J Nutr* 48, no. 4 (Jun 2009): 243–9.

Strotmeyer, E. S., et al. Infant diet and type 1 diabetes in China. *Diabetes Res Clin Pract* 65, no. 3 (Sep 2004): 283–92.

Tuomilehto, J. The emerging global epidemic of type 1 diabetes. *Curr Diab Rep* 13, no. 6 (Dec 2013): 795–804.

Virtanen, S. M., & Knip, M. Nutritional risk predictors of beta cell autoimmunity and type 1 diabetes at a young age. *Am J Clin Nutr* 78, no. 6 (Dec 2003): 1053–67.

Wasmuth, H. E., & Kolb, H. Cow's milk and immune-mediated diabetes. *Proc Nutr Soc* 59, no. 4 (Nov 2000): 573–9.

Diabetes and Other Gut Health Factors

Beyan, H., et al. Guts, germs, and meals: The origin of type 1 diabetes. *Curr Diab Rep* 12, no. 5 (Oct 2012): 456–62.

Cardwell, C. R., et al. Caesarean section is associated with an increased risk of childhood-onset type 1 diabetes mellitus: A meta-analysis of observational studies. *Diabetologia* 51, no. 5 (May 2008): 726–35.

CDC's Division of Diabetes Translation. "Long-term trends in diagnosed diabetes." October 2011. http://www.cdc.gov/diabetes/statistics/slides/long_term_trends.pdf

Fazeli Farsani, S., et al. Anti-infective medication use before and after the onset of type 1 diabetes in children and adolescents: A population-based cohort study. *Antimicrob Agents Chemother* (Jun 2014).

Hviid, A., & Svanström, H. Antibiotic use and type 1 diabetes in childhood. *Am J Epidemiol* 169, no. 9 (May 2009): 1079–84.

Kilkkinen, A., et al. Use of antimicrobials and risk of type 1 diabetes in a population-based mother-child cohort. *Diabetologia* 49, no. 1 (Jan 2006): 66–70.

Soyucen, E., et al. Differences in the gut microbiota of healthy children and those with type 1 diabetes. *Pediatr Int* 56, no. 3 (Jun 2014): 336–43.

Vaarala, O. Is the origin of type 1 diabetes in the gut? *Immunol Cell Biol* 90, no. 3 (Mar 2012): 271–6.

Zipris, D. The interplay between the gut microbiota and the immune system in the mechanism of type 1 diabetes. *Curr Opin Endocrinol Diabetes Obes* 20, no. 4 (Aug 2013): 265–70.

Causes of Autism and ADHD

Bagasra, O., et al. Role of perfumes in pathogenesis of autism. *Med Hypotheses* 80, no. 6 (Jun 2013): 795–803.

Bauer, A. Z., & Kriebel, D. Prenatal and perinatal analgesic exposure and autism: An ecological link. *Environ Health* 12 (May 2013): 41.

Chopra, V., et al. Association between phthalates and attention deficit disorder and learning disability in U.S. children, 6-15 years. *Environ Res* 128 (Jan 2014): 64–9.

Cooper, M., et al. Antenatal acetaminophen use and attention-deficit/hyperactivity disorder: An interesting observed association but too early to infer causality. *JAMA Pediatr* 168, no. 4 (Apr 2014): 306–7.

Ghanizadeh, A. Acetaminophen may mediate oxidative stress and neurotoxicity in autism. *Med Hypotheses* 78, no. 2 (Feb 2012): 351.

Grandjean, P., & Landrigan, P. J. Neurobehavioural effects of developmental toxicity. *Lancet Neurol* 13, no. 3 (Mar 2014): 330–8.

Leavey. A., et al. Gestational age at birth and risk of autism spectrum disorders in Alberta, Canada. *J Pediatr* 162, no. 2 (Feb 2013): 361–8.

Liew, Z., et al. Acetaminophen use during pregnancy, behavioral problems, and hyperkinetic disorders. *JAMA Pediatr* 168, no. 4 (Apr 2014): 313–20.

Lyall, K., et al. Maternal lifestyle and environmental risk factors for autism spectrum disorders. *Int J Epidemiol* 43, no. 2 (Apr 2014): 443–64.

Rossignol, D. A., et al. Environmental toxicants and autism spectrum disorders: A systematic review. *Transl Psychiatry* 4 (Feb 2014): e360.

Sandin, S., et al. Advancing maternal age is associated with increasing risk for autism: A review and meta–analysis. *J Am Acad Child Adolesc Psychiatry* 51, no. 5 (May 2012): 477–486.e1.

Sandin, S., et al. The familial risk of autism. *JAMA* 311, no. 17 (May 2014): 1770–7.

Shelton, J. F., et al. Neurodevelopmental disorders and prenatal residential proximity to agricultural pesticides: The CHARGE study. *Environ Health Perspect* (Jun 2014).

Singh, G. K., et al. Mental health outcomes in US children and adolescents born prematurely or with low birthweight. *Depress Res Treat* 2013 (2013): 570743.

Tarver, J., et al. Attention-deficit hyperactivity disorder (ADHD): An updated review of the essential facts. *Child Care Health Dev* (2014).

Theoharides, T. C., et al. Focal brain inflammation and autism. *J Neuroinflammation* 10 (Apr 2013): 46.

ASDs, ADHD, and Gastrointestinal Disorders

Chaidez, V., et al. Gastrointestinal problems in children with autism, developmental delays or typical development. *J Autism Dev Disord* 44, no. 5 (May 2014): 1117–27.

Finegold, S. M. State of the art; microbiology in health and disease. Intestinal bacterial flora in autism. *Anaerobe* 17, no. 6 (Dec 2011): 367–8.

Kang, V., et al. Gastrointestinal dysfunction in children with autism spectrum disorders. *Autism Res* (Apr 2014).

Lopez-Ramirez, M. A., et al. MicroRNA-155 negatively affects blood-brain barrier function during neuroinflammation. *FASEB J* 28, no. 6 (Jun 2014): 2551–2565.

McElhanon, B. O., et al. Gastrointestinal symptoms in Autism Spectrum Disorder: A meta-analysis. *Pediatrics* (Apr 2014).

McKeown, C., et al. Association of constipation and fecal incontinence with attention-deficit/hyperactivity disorder. *Pediatrics* 132, no. 5 (Nov 2013): e1210–5.

Mimouni-Bloch, A., et al. Breastfeeding may protect from developing attention-deficit/hyperactivity disorder. *Breastfeed Med* 8, no. 4 (Aug 2013): 363–7.

Schieve, L. A., et al. Concurrent medical conditions and health care use and needs among children with learning and behavioral developmental disabilities, National Health Interview Survey, 2006-2010. *Res Dev Disabil* 33, no. 2 (Mar-Apr 2012): 467–76.

Schultz, S. T., et al. Breastfeeding, infant formula supplementation, and Autistic Disorder: The results of a parent survey. *Int Breastfeed J* 1 (Sep 2006): 16.

Wang, L. W., et al. The prevalence of gastrointestinal problems in children across the United States with autism spectrum disorders from families with multiple affected members. *J Dev Behav Pediatr* 32, no. 5 (Jun 2011): 351–60.

Wright, J. "Genetics: Gene expression altered in autism gut," Simons Foundation Autism Research Initiative, accessed June 11, 2014, http://sfari.org/news-and-opinion/in-brief/2013/genetics-gene-expression-altered-in-autism-gut.

Walker, S. J., et al. Identification of unique gene expression profile in children with regressive autism spectrum disorder (ASD) and ileocolitis. *PLoS One* 8, no. 3 (2013): e58058.

Williams, B. L., et al. Impaired carbohydrate digestion and transport and mucosal dysbiosis in the intestines of children with autism and gastrointestinal disturbances. *PLoS One* 6, no. 9 (2011): e24585.

Dietary Interventions for Behavioral Disorders

Alanazi, A. S. The role of nutraceuticals in the management of autism. *Saudi Pharm J* 21, no. 3 (Jul 2013): 233–243.

Arnold, L. E., et al. Artificial food colors and attention-deficit/hyperactivity symptoms: Conclusions to dye for. *Neurotherapeutics* 9, no. 3 (Jul 2012): 599–609.

Brown, A. C., & Mehl-Madrona, L. Autoimmune and gastrointestinal dysfunctions: Does a subset of children with autism reveal a broader connection? *Expert Rev Gastroenterol Hepatol* 5, no. 4 (Aug 2011): 465–77.

Campbell, D. B., et al. Distinct genetic risk based on association of MET in families with co-occurring autism and gastrointestinal conditions. *Pediatrics* 123, no. 3 (Mar 2009): 1018–24.

de Magistris, L., et al. Antibodies against food antigens in patients with autistic spectrum disorders. *Biomed Res Int* 2013 (2013): 729349.

de Theije, C. G., et al. Food allergy and food-based therapies in neurodevelopmental disorders. *Pediatr Allergy Immunol* 25, no. 3 (May 2014): 218–26.

Field, S. S. Interaction of genes and nutritional factors in the etiology of autism and attention deficit/hyperactivity disorders: A case control study. *Med Hypotheses* 82, no. 6 (Jun 2014): 654–61.

Garg, N., & Silverberg, J. I. Association between childhood allergic disease, psychological comorbidity, and injury requiring medical attention. *Ann Allergy Asthma Immunol* 112, no. 6 (Jun 2014): 525–32.

Gilbert, J. A., et al. Toward effective probiotics for autism and other neurodevelopmental disorders. *Cell* 155, no. 7 (Dec 2013): 1446–8.

Hsiao, E. Y., et al. Microbiota modulate behavioral and physiological abnormalities associated with neurodevelopmental disorders. *Cell* 155, no. 7 (Dec 2013): 1451–63.

Jyonouchi, H. Autism spectrum disorders and allergy: Observation from a pediatric allergy/immunology clinic. *Expert Rev Clin Immunol* 6, no. 3 (May 2010): 397–411.

Kanarek, R. B. Artificial food dyes and attention deficit hyperactivity disorder. *Nutr Rev* 69, no. 7 (Jul 2011): 385–91.

Kawicka, A., & Regulska-Ilow, B. How nutritional status, diet and dietary supplements can affect autism. A review. *Rocz Panstw Zakl Hig* 64, no. 1 (2013): 1–12.

Marí-Bauset, S., et al. Evidence of the gluten-free and casein-free diet in autism spectrum disorders: A systematic review. *J Child Neurol* (2014).

Millichap, J. G., & Yee, M. M. The diet factor in attention-deficit/hyperactivity disorder. *Pediatrics* 129, no. 2 (Feb 2012): 330–7.

Nigg, J. T., et al. Meta-analysis of attention-deficit/hyperactivity disorder or attention-deficit/hyperactivity disorder symptoms, restriction diet, and synthetic food color additives. *J Am Acad Child Adolesc Psychiatry* 51, no. 1 (Jan 2012): 86–97.e8.

Pelsser, L. M., et al. Effects of a restricted elimination diet on the behaviour of children with attention-deficit hyperactivity disorder (INCA study): A randomised controlled trial. *Lancet* 377, no. 9764 (Feb 2011): 494–503.

Pelsser, L. M., & Buitelaar, J. K. Favourable effect of a standard elimination diet on the behavior of young children with attention deficit hyperactivity disorder (ADHD): A pilot study. *Ned Tijdschr Geneeskd* 146, no. 52 (Dec 2002): 2543–7. Dutch. Erratum in *Ned Tijdschr Geneeskd* 147, no. 52 (Dec 2003): 2612.

Sonuga-Barke, E. J. et al; European ADHD Guidelines Group. Nonpharmacological interventions for ADHD: Systematic review and meta-analyses of randomized controlled trials of dietary and psychological treatments. *Am J Psychiatry* 170, no. 3 (Mar 2013): 275–89.

Stevens, L. J., et al. Dietary sensitivities and ADHD symptoms: Thirty-five years of research. *Clin Pediatr (Phila)* 50, no. 4 (Apr 2011): 279–93.

Stevens, L. J., et al. Mechanisms of behavioral, atopic, and other reactions to artificial food colors in children. *Nutr Rev* 71, no. 5 (May 2013): 268–81.

Wang, Y., & Kasper, L. H. The role of microbiome in central nervous system disorders. *Brain Behav Immun* 38C (May 2014): 1–12.

Celiac Disease and Early Gut Health

Cabrera-Chávez, F., & de la Barca, A. M. Bovine milk intolerance in celiac disease is related to IgA reactivity to alpha- and beta-caseins. *Nutrition* 25, no. 6 (Jun 2009): 715–6.

Canova, C., et al. Association of maternal education, early infections, and antibiotic use with celiac disease: A population-based birth cohort study in Northeastern Italy. *Am J Epidemiol* 180, no. 1 (Jul 2014): 76–85.

Chmielewska, A., et al. Celiac disease: Prevention strategies through early infant nutrition. *World Rev Nutr Diet.* 108 (2013): 91–7.

Decker, E., et al. Cesarean delivery is associated with celiac disease but not inflammatory bowel disease in children. *Pediatrics* 125, no. 6 (Jun 2010): e1433–40.

Freed, D. L. Do dietary lectins cause disease? *BMJ* 318 (Apr 1999): 1023–4.

Guandalini, S. The influence of gluten: Weaning recommendations for healthy children and children at risk for celiac disease. *Nestle Nutr Workshop Ser Pediatr Program* 60 (2007): 139–51.

Kristjánsson, G., et al. Mucosal reactivity to cow's milk protein in coeliac disease. *Clin Exp Immunol* 147, no. 3 (Mar 2007): 449–55.

Mårild, K., et al. Antibiotic exposure and the development of coeliac disease: A nationwide case-control study. *BMC Gastroenterol* 13 (Jul 2013): 109.

Mariné, M., et al. The prevalence of coeliac disease is significantly higher in children compared with adults. *Aliment Pharmacol Ther* 33, no. 4 (Feb 2011): 477–86.

Savilahti, E. Food-induced malabsorption syndromes. *J Pediatr Gastroenterol Nutr* 30, Suppl (2000): S61-6.

Szajewska, H., et al., & PREVENTCD Study Group. Systematic review: Early infant feeding and the prevention of coeliac disease. *Aliment Pharmacol Ther* 36, no. 7 (Oct 2012): 607–18.

Inflammatory Bowel Diseases

Abramson, O., et al. Incidence, prevalence, and time trends of pediatric inflammatory bowel disease in Northern California, 1996 to 2006. *J Pediatr* 157, no. 2 (Aug 2010): 233–239.e1.

Bruce, A., et al. Mode of delivery and risk of inflammatory bowel disease in the offspring: Systematic review and meta-analysis of observational studies. *Inflamm Bowel Dis* 20, no. 7 (Jul 2014): 1217–26.

Kappelman, M. D., et al. Recent trends in the prevalence of Crohn's disease and ulcerative colitis in a commercially insured US population. *Dig Dis Sci* 58, no. 2 (Feb 2013): 519–25.

Kronman, M. P., et al. Antibiotic exposure and IBD development among children: A population-based cohort study. *Pediatrics* 130, no. 4 (Oct 2012): e794–803.

Overlap of Autoimmune Disorders

Al-Sinani, S., et al. Prevalence of celiac disease in Omani children with type 1 diabetes mellitus: A cross sectional study. *Oman Med J* 28, no. 4 (Jul 2013): 260–3.

Buysschaert, M. Coeliac disease in patients with type 1 diabetes mellitus and auto-immune thyroid disorders. *Acta Gastroenterol Belg* 66, no. 3 (Jul 2003): 237–40.

Bybrant, M. C., et al. High prevalence of celiac disease in Swedish children and adolescents with type 1 diabetes and the relation to the Swedish epidemic of celiac disease: A cohort study. *Scand J Gastroenterol* 49, no. 1 (Jan 2014): 52–8.

Kohane, I. S., et al. The co-morbidity burden of children and young adults with autism spectrum disorders. *PLoS One* 7, no. 4 (2012): e33224.

Kota, S. K., et al. Clinical profile of coexisting conditions in type 1 diabetes mellitus patients. *Diabetes Metab Syndr* 6, no. 2 (Apr-Jun 2012): 70–6.

Levy-Shraga, Y., et al. Type 1 diabetes in pre-school children: Long-term metabolic control, associated autoimmunity and complications. *Diabet Med.* 29, no. 10 (Oct 2012): 1291–6.

Mansour, A. A., & Najeeb, A. A. Coeliac disease in Iraqi type 1 diabetic patients. *Arab J Gastroenterol* 12, no. 2 (Jun 2011): 103–5.

Molloy, C. A., et al. Familial autoimmune thyroid disease as a risk factor for regression in children with Autism Spectrum Disorder: A CPEA Study. *J Autism Dev Disord* 36, no. 3 (Apr 2006): 317–24.

Niederhofer, H., & Pittschieler, K. A preliminary investigation of ADHD symptoms in persons with celiac disease. *J Atten Disord* 10, no. 2 (Nov 2006): 200–4.

Niederhofer, H. Association of attention-deficit/hyperactivity disorder and celiac disease: A brief report. *Prim Care Companion CNS Disord* 13, no. 3 (2011).

Nousen, E. K., et al. Unraveling the mechanisms responsible for the comorbidity between metabolic syndrome and mental health disorders. *Neuroendocrinology* 98, no. 4 (2013): 254–66.

Pi tkowska, E., & Szalecki, M. Autoimmune thyroiditis in children and adolescents with type 1 diabetes. *Pediatr Endocrinol Diabetes Metab* 17, no. 4 (2011): 173–7.

Sattar, N., et al. Celiac disease in children, adolescents, and young adults with autoimmune thyroid disease. *J Pediatr* 158, no. 2 (Feb 2011): 272–5.e1

Størdal, K., et al. Epidemiology of coeliac disease and comorbidity in Norwegian children. *J Pediatr Gastroenterol Nutr* 57, no. 4 (Oct 2013): 467–71.

Tyler, C. V., et al. Chronic disease risks in young adults with autism spectrum disorder: Forewarned is forearmed. *Am J Intellect Dev Disabil* 116, no. 5 (Sep 2011): 371–80.

15 Food Sensitivites and the Gut

Ho, M. H., et al. Clinical spectrum of food allergies: A comprehensive review. *Clin Rev Allergy Immunol* 46, no. 3 (Jun 2014): 225–40.

American Academy of Allergy, Asthma & Immunology. "Allergy statistics," accessed March 5, 2014, http://www.aaaai.org/about-the-aaaai/newsroom/allergy-statistics.aspx

Allen, K. J., & Martin, P. E. Clinical aspects of pediatric food allergy and failed oral immune tolerance. *J Clin Gastroenterol* 44, no. 6 (Jul 2010): 391–401.

Boye, J. I. Food allergies in developing and emerging economies: Need for comprehensive data on prevalence rates. *Clin Transl Allergy* 2, no. 1 (Dec 2012): 25.

Kung, S. J., et al. Food allergy in Africa: Myth or reality? *Clin Rev Allergy Immunol* 46, no. 3 (Jun 2014): 241–9.

Lin, R. Y., et al. Increasing anaphylaxis hospitalizations in the first 2 decades of life: New York State, 1990–2006. *Ann Allergy Asthma Immunol* 101, no. 4 (Oct 2008): 387–93.

Prescott, S. L., et al. A global survey of changing patterns of food allergy burden in children. *World Allergy Organ J* 6, no. 1 (Dec 2013): 21.

Why All These Food Allergies?

Chahine, B. G., & Bahna, S. L. The role of the gut mucosal immunity in the development of tolerance versus development of allergy to food. *Curr Opin Allergy Clin Immunol* 10, 4 (Aug 2010): 394–9.

Fogarty, A. What have studies of non-industrialised countries told us about the cause of allergic disease? *Clin Exp Allergy* (May 2014).

Kunisawa, J., & Kiyono, H. Aberrant interaction of the gut immune system with environmental factors in the development of food allergies. *Curr Allergy Asthma Rep* 10, no. 3 (May 2010): 215–21.

Suderman, M., et al. Conserved epigenetic sensitivity to early life experience in the rat and human hippocampus. *Proc Natl Acad Sci U S A.* 109, Suppl. 2 (Oct 2012): 17266–72.

Kinds of Food Reactions

Bohle, B. T lymphocytes and food allergy. *Mol Nutr Food Res* 48, no. 6 (Nov 2004): 424–33.

Ho, M. H., et al. Clinical spectrum of food allergies: A comprehensive review. *Clin Rev Allergy Immunol* (Nov 2012).

Johansson, S. G. The history of IgE: From discovery to 2010. *Curr Allergy Asthma Rep* 11, no. 2 (Apr 2011): 173–7.

Morita, H., et al. Gastrointestinal food allergy in infants. *Allergol Int* 62, no. 3 (Sep 2013): 297–307.

Paajanen, L., et al. Increased IFN-gamma secretion from duodenal biopsy samples in delayed-type cow's milk allergy. *Pediatr Allergy Immunol* 16, no. 5 (Aug 2005): 439–44.

Sütas, Y., et al. Late onset reactions to oral food challenge are linked to low serum interleukin-10 concentrations in patients with atopic dermatitis and food allergy. *Clin Exp Allergy* 30, no. 8 (Aug 2000): 1121–8.

Skin Rashes and the Intestines

Atherton, D. J. Diagnosis and management of skin disorders caused by food allergy. *Ann Allergy* 53, no. 6 Pt. 2 (Dec 1984): 623–8.

Breuer, K., et al. Late eczematous reactions to food in children with atopic dermatitis. *Clin Exp Allergy* 34, no.. 5 (May 2004): 817–24.

Kaimal, S., & Thappa, D. M. Diet in dermatology: Revisited. *Indian J Dermatol Venereol Leprol* 76, no. 2 (Mar 2010): 103–15.

Kwon, J., et al. Characterization of food allergies in patients with atopic dermatitis. *Nutr Res Pract* 7, no. 2 (Apr 2013): 115–21.

Majamaa, H., & Isolauri, E. Evaluation of the gut mucosal barrier: Evidence for increased antigen transfer in children with atopic eczema. *J Allergy Clin Immunol* 97, no. 4 (Apr 1996): 985–90.

Niggemann, B., et al. Outcome of double–blind, placebo-controlled food challenge tests in 107 children with atopic dermatitis. *Clin Exp Allergy* 29, no. 1 (Jan 1999): 91–6.

Noh, G., & Lee, J. H. Revision of immunopathogenesis and laboratory interpretation for food allergy in atopic dermatitis. *Inflamm Allergy Drug Targets* 11, no. 1 (Feb 2012): 20–35.

Rokaite, R., & Labanauskas, L. Gastrointestinal disorders in children with atopic dermatitis. *Medicina (Kaunas)* 41, no. 10 (2005): 837–45.

Sazanova, N. E., et al. Immunological aspects of food intolerance in children during first years of life. *Pediatriia* 3 (1992): 14–8.

Tan, T. H., et al. The role of genetics and environment in the rise of childhood food allergy. *Clin Exp Allergy* 42, no. 1 (Jan 2012): 20–9.

Werfel, T. Skin manifestations in food allergy. *Allergy* 56, Suppl 67 (2001): 98–101.

Werfel, T., et al. Eczematous reactions to food in atopic eczema: Position paper of the EAACI and GA2LEN. *Allergy* 62, 7 (Jul 2007): 723–8.

Food Sensitivities and Behavior

Abbott, N. J. Inflammatory mediators and modulation of blood-brain barrier permeability. *Cell Mol Neurobiol* 20, no. 2 (Apr 2000): 131–47.

Costa-Pinto, F. A., & Basso, A. S. Neural and behavioral correlates of food allergy. *Chem Immunol Allergy* 98 (2012): 222–39.

Engelhardt, B. Molecular mechanisms involved in T cell migration across the blood-brain barrier. *J Neural Transm* 113, no. 4 (Apr 2006): 477–85.

Esposito, P., et al. Acute stress increases permeability of the blood-brain-barrier through activation of brain mast cells. *Brain Res* 888, no. 1 (Jan 2001): 117–127.

Lopez-Ramirez, M. A., et al. MicroRNA-155 negatively affects blood-brain barrier function during neuroinflammation. *FASEB J* 28, no. 6 (Jun 2014): 2551–2565.

Millichap, J. G., & Yee, M. M. The diet factor in pediatric and adolescent migraine. *Pediatr Neurol* 28, no. 1 (Jan 2003): 9–15.

Schilling, L., & Wahl, M. Opening of the blood-brain barrier during cortical superfusion with histamine. *Brain Res* 653, no. 1–2 (Aug1994): 289–96.

Silverberg, J. I., et al. Allergic disease is associated with epilepsy in childhood: A US population-based study. *Allergy* 69, no. 1 (Jan 2014): 95–103.

Diagnosing Delayed Food Reactions

Fluge, G., & Aksnes, L. Influence of cow's milk proteins and gluten on human duodenal mucosa in organ culture. *J Pediatr Gastroenterol Nutr* 11, no. 4 (Nov 1990): 481–8.

Patey-Mariaud De Serre, N., et al. Etiological diagnosis of villous atrophy. *Ann Pathol* 21, no. 4 (Aug 2001): 319–33.

Finding the Offending Foods

Cudowska, B., & Kaczmarski, M. Atopy patch test in the diagnosis of food allergy in children with gastrointestinal symptoms. *Adv Med Sci* 55, no. 2 (2010): 153–60.

Hochwallner, H., et al. Patients suffering from non-IgE-mediated cow's milk protein intolerance cannot be diagnosed based on IgG subclass or IgA responses to milk allergens. *Allergy* 66, no. 9 (Sep 2011): 1201–7.

Lipozenci , J. & Wolf, R. The diagnostic value of atopy patch testing and prick testing in atopic dermatitis: Facts and controversies. *Clin Dermatol* 28, no. 1 (Jan–Feb 2010): 38–44.

Saarinen, K. M., et al. Markers of inflammation in the feces of infants with cow's milk allergy. *Pediatr Allergy Immunol* 13, no. 3 (Jun 2002): 188–94.

Turjanmaa, K. "Atopy patch tests" in the diagnosis of delayed food hypersensitivity. *Allerg Immunol* 34, no. 3 (Mar 2002): 95–7.

Food Eliminations and Health

Luo, X., et al. Association between obesity and atopic disorders in Chinese adults: An individually matched case-control study. *BMC Public Health* 8 (Jan 2013): 12.

Mukaida, K., et al. The effect of past food avoidance due to allergic symptoms on the growth of children at school age. *Allergol Int* 59, no. 4 (Dec 2010): 369–74.

Kotzampassi, K., et al. Obesity as a consequence of gut bacteria and diet interactions. *ISRN Obes* 2014 (2014): 651895.

Beginning the Elimination Diet

Vandenplas, Y., et al., & North American Society for Pediatric Gastroenterology Hepatology and Nutrition (NASPGHAN), European Society for Pediatric Gastroenterology Hepatology and Nutrition (ESPGHAN). Pediatric gastroesophageal reflux clinical practice guidelines: Joint recommendations of the NASPGHAN and the ESPGHAN. *J Pediatr Gastroenterol Nutr* 49, no. 4 (Oct 2009): 498–547.

Elimination Diet for the Formula-fed Child

Hill, D. J., et al. The efficacy of amino acid-based formulas in relieving the symptoms of cow's milk allergy: A systematic review. *Clin Exp Allergy* 37, no. 6 (Jun 2007): 808–22.

Why is Cow Milk such a Common Allergen?

Image: "Garrett Likes the Bookcase," by Heather, https://www.flickr.com/photos/rowdyharv/5979227466/, 2011. *Fotor.com*. License: creativecommons.org/licenses/by/2.0/.

Hodgkinson, A. J., et al. Effect of raw milk on allergic responses in a murine model of gastrointestinal allergy. *Br J Nutr* 112, 3 (Aug 2014): 390–7.

Ho-Pham, L. T., et al. Vegetarianism, bone loss, fracture and vitamin D: A longitudinal study in Asian vegans and non-vegans. *Eur J Clin Nutr* 66, no. 1 (Jan 2012): 75–82.

Høst, A. Cow's milk protein allergy and intolerance in infancy: Some clinical, epidemiological and immunological aspects. *Pediatr Allergy Immunol* 5, Suppl. 5 (1994): 1–36.

Krigbaum, W. R., & Kügler, F. R. Molecular conformation of egg-white lysozyme and bovine alpha-lactalbumin in solution. *Biochemistry* 9, no. 5 (Mar 1970): 1216–23.

Loss, G., et al., & GABRIELA study group. The protective effect of farm milk consumption on childhood asthma and atopy: The GABRIELA study. *J Allergy Clin Immunol* 128, no. 4 (Oct 2011): 766–773.e4.

Palmer, L. F. *Baby Matters*, San Diego, CA: BabyReference, 2015.

Restani, P., et al. Cross-reactivity between mammalian proteins. *Ann Allergy Asthma Immunol* 89, no. 6 Suppl. 1 (Dec 2002): 11–5.

Shandilya, U. K., et al. Effect of thermal processing of cow and buffalo milk on the allergenic response to caseins and whey proteins in mice. *J Sci Food Agric* 93, no. 9 (Jul 2013): 2287–92.

Smith, A. M. Veganism and osteoporosis: A review of the current literature. *Int J Nurs Pract* 12, no. 5 (Oct 2006): 302–6.

Can Allergies Be Prevented?

Fleischer, D. M., et al. Primary prevention of allergic disease through nutritional interventions. *J Allergy Clin Immunol Pract* 1, no. 1 (Jan 2013): 29–36.

Gigante, G., et al. Role of gut microbiota in food tolerance and allergies. *Dig Dis* 29, no. 6 (2011): 540–9.

Greer, F. R., et al., & American Academy of Pediatrics Committee on Nutrition, & American Academy of Pediatrics Section on Allergy and Immunology. Effects of early nutritional interventions on the development of atopic disease in infants and children: The role of maternal dietary restriction, breastfeeding, timing of introduction of complementary foods, and hydrolyzed formulas. *Pediatrics* 121, no. 1 (Jan 2008): 183–91.

Høst, A., et al. A prospective study of cow's milk allergy in exclusively breast-fed infants: Incidence, pathogenetic role of early inadvertent exposure to cow's milk formula, and characterization of bovine milk protein in human milk. *Acta Paediatr Scand* 77, no. 5 (Sep 1988): 663–70.

Kramer, M. S. Breastfeeding and allergy: The evidence. *Ann Nutr Metab* 59, Suppl. 1 (2011): 20–6.

Lodge, C. J., et al. Overview of evidence in prevention and aetiology of food allergy: A review of systematic reviews. *Int J Environ Res Public Health* 10, no. 11 (Nov 2013): 5781–806.

Marini, A., et al. Effects of a dietary and environmental prevention programme on the incidence of allergic symptoms in high atopic risk infants: Three years' follow-up. *Acta Paediatr Suppl* 414 (May 1996): 1–21.

Stintzing, G., & Zetterström, R. Cow's milk allergy, incidence and pathogenetic role of early exposure to cow's milk formula. *Acta Paediatr Scand* 68, no. 3 (May 1979): 383–7.

Some Final Thoughts

Katzka, D. A., et al. Small intestinal permeability in patients with eosinophilic oesophagitis during active phase and remission. *Gut* (2014): pii: gutjnl–2013–305882.

Vaarala, O. The gut as a regulator of early inflammation in type 1 diabetes. *Curr Opin Endocrinol Diabetes Obes* 18, no. 4 (Aug 2011): 241–7.

16 Healing Baby's Gut for Lifelong Health

Why Give a Poop about the Intestines?

Amarasekera, M., et al. Nutrition in early life, immune-programming and allergies: The role of epigenetics. *Asian Pac J Allergy Immunol* 31, no. 3 (Sep 2013): 175–82.

Bhargava, P., & Mowry, E. M. Gut microbiome and multiple sclerosis. *Curr Neurol Neurosci Rep* 14, no. 10 (Oct 2014): 492.

"Diabetes Public Health Resource: Percentage of civilian, noninstitutionalized population with diagnosed diabetes, by age, United States, 1980–2011," Centers for Disease Control and Prevention, accessed July 27, 2014, last modified March 28, 2013. http://www.cdc.gov/diabetes/statistics/prev/national/figbyage.htm

Garg, N., & Silverberg, J. I. Association between childhood allergic disease, psychological comorbidity, and injury requiring medical attention. *Ann Allergy Asthma Immunol* 112, no. 6 (Jun 2014): 525–32.

Ghezzi, A., & Zaffaroni M. Neurological manifestations of gastrointestinal disorders, with particular reference to the differential diagnosis of multiple sclerosis. *Neurol Sci* 22, Suppl 2 (Nov 2001): S117–22.

Imai, C. M., et al. Associations between infant feeding practice prior to six months and body mass index at six years of age. *Nutrients* 6, no. 5 (Apr 2014): 1608–17.

Luo, X., et al. Association between obesity and atopic disorders in Chinese adults: An individually matched case-control study. *BMC Public Health* 8, no. 3 (Jan 2013): 12.

Schwimmer, J. B., et al. Prevalence of fatty liver in children and adolescents. *Pediatrics* 118, no. 4 (Oct 2006): 1388–93.

Yamakawa. M., et al. Breastfeeding and obesity among schoolchildren: A nationwide longitudinal survey in Japan. *JAMA Pediatr* 167, no. 10 (Oct 2013): 919–25.

Basic Nutrition

Palmer, L. F. *Beyond Breastmilk*. Feb 13, 2013. http://www.BabyReference.com /beyond-breastmilk/

Saavedra, J. M., et al. Lessons from the feeding infants and toddlers study in North America: What children eat, and implications for obesity prevention. *Ann Nutr Metab* 62, Suppl 3 (2013): 27–36.

Weber, M., et al.; European Childhood Obesity Trial Study Group. Lower protein content in infant formula reduces BMI and obesity risk at school age: Follow-up of a randomized trial. *Am J Clin Nutr* 99, no. 5 (May 2014): 1041–51.

Zivkovic, A. M., & Barile, D. Bovine milk as a source of functional oligosaccharides for improving human health. *Adv Nutr* 2, no. 3 (May 2011): 284–9.

Probiotic Supplements: What Can They Do?

Antigoni, M. "Probiotics in pediatrics: Properties, mechanisms of action, and indications," in *Probiotics*, ed. Everlon C. Rigobelo (Croatia: InTech, 2012)

Awad, H., et al. Comparison between killed and living probiotic usage versus placebo for the prevention of necrotizing enterocolitis and sepsis in neonates. *Pak J Biol Sci* 13, no. 6 (Mar 2010): 253–62.

Gibson, G. R., et al. Final technical report for FSA project ref G01022. An evaluation of probiotic effects in the human gut: Microbial aspects. Mar 22, 2005. http://multimedia.food.gov.uk/multimedia/pdfs/probioticreport.pdf

Panigrahi, P., et al. Long-term colonization of a Lactobacillus plantarum synbiotic preparation in the neonatal gut. *J Pediatr Gastroenterol Nutr* 47, no. 1 (Jul 2008): 45–53.

Peng, G. C., & Hsu, C. H. The efficacy and safety of heat-killed Lactobacillus paracasei for treatment of perennial allergic rhinitis induced by house-dust mite. *Pediatr Allergy Immunol* 16, no. 5 (Aug 2005): 433–8.

Sherman, P. M., et al. Unraveling mechanisms of action of probiotics. *Nutr Clin Pract* 24, no. 1 (Feb-Mar 2009): 10–4.

Probiotic Studies in Infants

Indrio, F., et al. Prophylactic use of a probiotic in the prevention of colic, regurgitation, and functional constipation: A randomized clinical trial. *JAMA Pediatr* 168, no. 3 (Mar 2014): 228–33.

Ivakhnenko, E. S., & Nian'kovski , S. L. Effect of probiotics on the dynamics of gastrointestinal symptoms of food allergy to cow's milk protein in infants. *Georgian Med News* 219 (Jun 2013): 46–52.

Kianifar, H., et al. Synbiotic in the management of infantile colic: A randomised controlled trial. *J Paediatr Child Health* (Jun 2014).

Osborn, D. A., & Sinn, J. K. Probiotics in infants for prevention of allergic disease and food hypersensitivity. *Cochrane Database Syst Rev* 4 (Oct 2007): CD006475.

Roos, S., et al. 454 pyrosequencing analysis on faecal samples from a randomized DBPC trial of colicky infants treated with Lactobacillus reuteri DSM 17938. *PLoS One* 8, no. 2 (2013): e56710.

Urbanska, M., & Szajewska, H. The efficacy of Lactobacillus reuteri DSM 17938 in infants and children: A review of the current evidence. *Eur J Pediatr* (May 2014).

West, C. E., et al. Probiotic effects on T-cell maturation in infants during weaning. *Clin Exp Allergy* 42, no. 4 (Apr 2012): 540–9.

West, C. E., et al. Probiotics in primary prevention of allergic disease: Follow-up at 8-9 years of age. *Allergy* 68, no. 8 (Aug 2013): 1015–20.

Probiotic Chart

Betsi, G. I., et al. Probiotics for the treatment or prevention of atopic dermatitis: A review of the evidence from randomized controlled trials. *Am J Clin Dermatol* 9, no. 2 (2008): 93–103.

Ivakhnenko, E. S., & Nian'kovskii, S. L. Effect of probiotics on the dynamics of gastrointestinal symptoms of food allergy to cow's milk protein in infants. *Georgian Med News* 219 (Jun 2013): 46–52.

Kwon, J., et al. Characterization of food allergies in patients with atopic dermatitis. *Nutr Res Pract* 7, no. 2 (Apr 2013): 115–21.

Maldonado, J., et al. Human milk probiotic Lactobacillus fermentum CECT5716 reduces the incidence of gastrointestinal and upper respiratory tract infections in infants. *J Pediatr Gastroenterol Nutr* 54, no. 1 (Jan 2012): 55–61.

Osborn, D. A., & Sinn, J. K. Probiotics in infants for prevention of allergic disease and food hypersensitivity. *Cochrane Database Syst Rev* 17, no. 4 (Oct 2007): CD006475.

Rautava, S., et al. Maternal probiotic supplementation during pregnancy and breast-feeding reduces the risk of eczema in the infant. *J Allergy Clin Immunol* 130, no. 6 (Dec 2012): 1355–60.

Rosenfeldt, V., et al. Effect of probiotics on gastrointestinal symptoms and small intestinal permeability in children with atopic dermatitis. *J Pediatr* 145, no. 5 (Nov 2004): 612–6.

Szajewska, H., et al. Meta-analysis: Lactobacillus GG for treating acute gastroenteritis in children - updated analysis of randomised controlled trials. *Aliment Pharmacol Ther* 38, no. 5 (Sep 2013): 467–76.

Szajewska, H., et al. Meta-analysis: Lactobacillus reuteri strain DSM 17938 (and the original strain ATCC 55730) for treating acute gastroenteritis in children. *Benef Microbes* 5, no. 3 (Sep 2014): 285–93.

Torii, S., et al. Effects of oral administration of Lactobacillus acidophilus L-92 on the symptoms and serum markers of atopic dermatitis in children. *Int Arch Allergy Immunol* 154, no. 3 (2011): 236–45.

Urba ska, M., & Szajewska, H. The efficacy of Lactobacillus reuteri DSM 17938 in infants and children: A review of the current evidence. *Eur J Pediatr* (May 2014).

Vandenplas, Y., et al. Probiotics and prebiotics in infants and children. *Curr Infect Dis Rep* 15, no. 3 (Jun 2013): 251–62.

West, C. E., et al. Probiotic effects on T-cell maturation in infants during weaning. *Clin Exp Allergy* 42, no. 4 (Apr 2012): 540–9.

Prebiotics, Probiotics, and Infant Formulas

Maldonado, J., et al. Human milk probiotic Lactobacillus fermentum CECT5716 reduces the incidence of gastrointestinal and upper respiratory tract infections in infants. *J Pediatr Gastroenterol Nutr* 54, no. 1 (Jan 2012): 55–61.

Mugambi, M. N., et al. Synbiotics, probiotics or prebiotics in infant formula for full term infants: A systematic review. *Nutr J* 11 (Oct 2012): 81.

Osborn, D. A., & Sinn J. K. Prebiotics in infants for prevention of allergy. *Cochrane Database Syst Rev* 28 (Mar 2013): CD006474.

Rao, S., et al. Prebiotic supplementation in full-term neonates: A systematic review of randomized controlled trials. *Arch Pediatr Adolesc Med* 163, no. 8 (Aug 2009): 755–64.

Vandenplas, Y., et al. Probiotics and prebiotics in infants and children. *Curr Infect Dis Rep* 15, no. 3 (Jun 2013): 251–62.

Williams, T., et al. Tolerance of infant formulas containing prebiotics in healthy, term infants. *J Pediatr Gastroenterol Nutr* (Jul 2014).

Probiotics during Antibiotic Exposure

Brzozowski, T., et al. Influence of gastric colonization with Candida albicans on ulcer healing in rats: Effect of ranitidine, aspirin and probiotic therapy. *Scand J Gastroenterol* 40, no. 3 (Mar 2005): 286–96.

Hempel, S., et al. Probiotics for the prevention and treatment of antibiotic-associated diarrhea: A systematic review and meta-analysis. *JAMA* 307, no. 18 (May 2012): 1959–69.

Kumamoto, C. A. Inflammation and gastrointestinal Candida colonization. *Curr Opin Microbiol* 14, no. 4 (Aug 2011): 386–91.

Kumar, S., et al. Evaluation of efficacy of probiotics in prevention of candida colonization in a PICU: A randomized controlled trial. *Crit Care Med* 41, no. 2 (Feb 2013): 565–72.

Weichert, S., et al. The role of prebiotics and probiotics in prevention and treatment of childhood infectious diseases. *Pediatr Infect Dis J* 331, no. 8 (Aug 2012): 859–62.

Zwoli ska-Wcisło, M., et al. Are probiotics effective in the treatment of fungal colonization of the gastrointestinal tract? Experimental and clinical studies. *J Physiol Pharmacol* 57, Suppl 9 (Nov 2006): 35–49.

Providing Probiotics

Guandalini, S. Probiotics for prevention and treatment of diarrhea. *J Clin Gastroenterol* 45, Suppl (Nov 2011): S149–53.

Szajewska, H., et al. Meta-analysis: Lactobacillus GG for treating acute gastroenteritis in children: Updated analysis of randomised controlled trials. *Aliment Pharmacol Ther* 38, no. 5 (Sep 2013): 467–76.

Szajewska, H., et al. Probiotics in gastrointestinal diseases in children: Hard and not-so-hard evidence of efficacy. *J Pediatr Gastroenterol Nutr* 42, no. 5 (May 2006): 454–75.

Thum, C., et al. Can nutritional modulation of maternal intestinal microbiota influence the development of the infant gastrointestinal tract? *J Nutr* 142, no. 1 (Nov 2012): 1921–8.

Uenishi, T., et al. Role of foods in irregular aggravation of skin lesions in children with atopic dermatitis. *J Dermatol* 35, no. 7 (Jul 2008): 407–12.

Herbal and Nutritional Supplements

Al-Hashem, F. H. Gastroprotective effects of aqueous extract of Chamomilla recutita against ethanol-induced gastric ulcers. *Saudi Med J* 31, no. 11 (Nov 2010): 1211–6.

Andersen, F. A. Final report on the safety assessment of Aloe Andongensis Extract, Aloe Andongensis Leaf Juice, aloe Arborescens Leaf Extract, Aloe Arborescens Leaf Juice, Aloe Arborescens Leaf Protoplasts, Aloe Barbadensis Flower Extract, Aloe Barbadensis Leaf, Aloe Barbadensis Leaf Extract, Aloe Barbadensis Leaf Juice,aloe Barbadensis Leaf Polysaccharides, Aloe Barbadensis Leaf Water, Aloe Ferox Leaf Extract, Aloe Ferox Leaf Juice, and Aloe Ferox Leaf Juice Extract. *Int J Toxicol* 26 Suppl 2 (2006): 1–50.

Bak, Y. K., et al. Effects of dietary supplementation of glucosamine sulfate on intestinal inflammation in a mouse model of experimental colitis. *J Gastroenterol Hepatol* 29, no. 5 (May 2014): 957–63.

Brahmbhatt, V, et al. Protective effects of dietary EPA and DHA on ischemia-reperfusion-induced intestinal stress. *J Nutr Biochem* 24, no. 1 (Jan 2013): 104–11.

Carvalho, C. A., et al. Evaluation of antiulcerogenic activity of aqueous extract of Brassica oleracea var. capitata (cabbage) on Wistar rat gastric ulceration. *Arq Gastroenterol* 48, no. 4 (Oct–Dec 2011): 276–82.

Deters, A., et al. N-Acetyl-D-glucosamine oligosaccharides induce mucin secretion from colonic tissue and induce differentiation of human keratinocytes. *J Pharm Pharmacol* 60, no. 2 (Feb 2008): 197–204.

D'Vaz, N., et al. Fish oil supplementation in early infancy modulates developing infant immune responses. *Clin Exp Allergy* 42, no. 8 (Aug 2012): 1206–16.

EkçI, B., et al. The effect of omega-3 fatty acid and ascorbic acid on healing of ischemic colon anastomoses. *Ann Ital Chir* 82, no. 6 (Nov–Dec 2011): 475–9.

Haniadka, R., et al. A review of the gastroprotective effects of ginger (Zingiber officinale Roscoe). *Food Funct* 4, no. 6 (Jun 2013): 845–55.

Langmead, L.., & Rampton, D. S. Review article: Herbal treatment in gastrointestinal and liver disease: Benefits and dangers. *Aliment Pharmacol Ther* 15, no. 9 (Sep 2001): 1239–52.

Li, J., et al. Intakes of long-chain omega-3 (n-3) PUFAs and fish in relation to incidence of asthma among American young adults: The CARDIA study. *Am J Clin Nutr* 97, no. 1 (Jan 2013): 173–8.

Lima, A. A., et al. Effects of glutamine alone or in combination with zinc and vitamin A on growth, intestinal barrier function, stress and satiety-related hormones in Brazilian shantytown children. *Clinics* (Sao Paulo) 69, no. 4 (2014): 225–33.

Mansour, G., et al. Clinical efficacy of new aloe vera- and myrrh-based oral mucoadhesive gels in the management of minor recurrent aphthous stomatitis: A randomized, double-blind, vehicle-controlled study. *J Oral Pathol Med* 43, no. 6 (Jul 2014): 405–9.

Paraschos, S., et al. Chios gum mastic: A review of its biological activities. *Curr Med Chem* 19, no. 14 (2012): 2292–302.

Cornucopia Institute. "Questions and answers about DHA/ARA and infant formula." Accessed August 18, 2014. http://cornucopia.org/DHA/DHA_QuestionsAnswers.pdf

Rajasekaran, S. A. Therapeutic potential of curcumin in gastrointestinal diseases. *World J Gastrointest Pathophysiol* 2, no. 1 (Feb 2011): 1–14.

Ravanti, L., & Kähäri, V. M. Matrix metalloproteinases in wound repair (review). *Int J Mol Med* 6, no. 4 (Oct 2000): 391–407.

Rodríguez Rodríguez, E., et al. Aloe vera as a functional ingredient in foods. *Crit Rev Food Sci Nutr* 50, no. 4 (Apr 2010): 305–26.

Shi, L., et al. In vitro and in vivo studies on matrix metalloproteinases interacting with small intestine submucosa wound matrix. *Int Wound J* 9, no. 1 (Feb 2012): 44–53.

Suskind, D. L., et al. Tolerability of curcumin in pediatric inflammatory bowel disease: A forced-dose titration study. *J Pediatr Gastroenterol Nutr* 56, no. 3 (Mar 2013): 277–9.

van den Elsen, L. W., et al. n-3 Long-chain PUFA reduce allergy-related mediator release by human mast cells in vitro via inhibition of reactive oxygen species. *Br J Nutr* 190, no. 10 (May 2013): 1821–31.

Volpi, N., et al. Role, metabolism, chemical modifications and applications of hyaluronan. *Curr Med Chem* 16, no. 14 (2009): 1718–45.

Wagner, J. V., et al. Glutamine supplementation for young infants with severe gastrointestinal disease. *Cochrane Database Syst Rev* (Jul 2012): CD005947.

Healing Mom, the Family, and the Home

Berg, G., et al. Beneficial effects of plant-associated microbes on indoor microbiomes and human health? *Front Microbiol* 5, (Jan 2014): 15.

Fujimura, K. E., et al. House dust exposure mediates gut microbiome Lactobacillus enrichment and airway immune defense against allergens and virus infection. *Proc Natl Acad Sci USA* 111, no. 2 (Jan 2014): 805–10.

Gern, J. E., et al. Effects of dog ownership and genotype on immune development and atopy in infancy. *J Allergy Clin Immunol* 113, no. 2 (Feb 2004): 307–14.

Sunshine, Dirt, and Play

Fitzgerald, M., et al. Red/near-infrared irradiation therapy for treatment of central nervous system injuries and disorders. *Rev Neurosci* 24, no. 2 (2013): 205–26.

Kühne, H., et al. Vitamin D receptor regulates intestinal proteins involved in cell proliferation, migration and stress response. *Lipids Health Dis* 13 (Mar 2014): 51.

Lindqvist, P. G., et al. Avoidance of sun exposure is a risk factor for all-cause mortality: Results from the Melanoma in Southern Sweden cohort. *J Intern Med* 276, no. 1 (Jul 2014): 77–86.

Nilforoushzadeh, M. A., et al. Macroscopic effect of blue light cure on wound healing in NMRI mice NMRI. *Adv Biomed Res* 3 (Mar 2014): 106.

Yang, L., et al. Ultraviolet exposure and mortality among women in Sweden. *Cancer Epidemiol Biomarkers Prev* 20, no 4 (Apr 2011): 683–90.

Responsive Care and Child Health

Palmer, L. F. *Baby Matters*, San Diego, CA: BabyReference, 2015.

Glossary

AAP American Academy of Pediatrics. A large segment of pediatricians belong to this medical organization involved in policy making and continued education.

acetaminophen Tylenol, paracetamol, APAP. Widely used over-the-counter pain and fever reducer, also found in some prescription medications.

ADHD *See* attention deficit hyperactivity disorder.

allergen More appropriately called an antigen. An agent, such as pollen or peanuts, that stimulates an excessive immune system response in vulnerable (allergic) individuals.

allergy A hypersensitivity or excessive immune reaction to a food, pollen, or other exposure whereby one will exhibit certain excessive symptoms not exhibited by most individuals. In the strict usage of the term, an allergy is a response by IgE antibodies in the body, resulting in symptoms such as hives, difficulty breathing, or a runny nose. In a looser sense of the term, allergy can include any non-normal physical reaction, such as intestinal symptoms of diarrhea and green stools in reaction to certain foods.

aloe vera gel Pulp from the leaves of the aloe vera plant. Drinkable gel, can speed healing of irritated digestive tissues, is sold formulated without the latex portion of aloe, and should not be confused with aloe vera juice, which contains the latex portion of the leaves. The latex portion can irritate the intestinal walls or cause diarrhea and is typically used to treat constipation. Leaves crushed directly from the plant would contain both the healing pulp and the stool-softening latex.

aloe vera juice Commercial aloe vera juice is intended to contain the latex portion of aloe plant leaves. Aloe latex is used as a laxative. Juice made at home from crushed aloe leaves would contain both the healing pulp and the stool-softening latex.

aloe vera latex A certain portion of aloe vera leaves that is found commercially in products labeled as aloe vera juice or aloe latex. Typically used to treat constipation, latex can irritate intestinal walls or cause diarrhea.

amino acid infant formula Also known as elemental formula. An infant feeding formula designed for infants who are highly intolerant of or allergic to foreign (non-human milk) proteins and who do not have access to human milk. Rather than containing whole protein sources, such as cow milk or soy, amino acid formulas are made from simple pieces of proteins (amino acids) that immune systems typically don't react to.

anaphylactic Anaphylactic reaction, anaphylactic shock, or anaphylaxis. A severe hypersensitivity reaction to an allergen, involving symptoms such as swelling of the tongue and lips, difficulty breathing, dropping blood pressure, and hives; typically initiated by IgE antibodies.

anemia A deficiency in the ability of the blood to carry enough oxygen to the tissues of the body. Among other things, iron, folic acid, and vitamin B12 are required to create red blood cells and the hemoglobin within them—the oxygen carrying portion of red blood cells. Insufficient iron leads to "iron deficiency anemia." Some other anemias are vitamin B12 deficiency anemia and folic acid deficiency anemia.

antibody A component of the immune system, also known as immunoglobulin, abbreviated as Ig. Antibodies are proteins found in the blood and other sites in the body that identify and neutralize foreign invaders (antigens) such as bacteria or viruses. In a sensitized individual, antibodies may attack certain food proteins, pollens, or other allergens/antigens. Antibody-antigen interactions typically instigate a cascade of other immune system responses and resultant symptoms.

antioxidant A substance that reduces oxidation of other substances. A certain amount of oxidation is necessary to body functioning, but it can also be damaging. Popular antioxidants are vitamin C, selenium, and grape seed extract (resveratrol).

ARA Arachidonic acid. An important omega-6 fatty acid found in the diet and in breastmilk and found to be low in standard infant formulas. The body can create this fatty acid from other dietary fats, but it is thought that this ability is low in infants, so ARA is currently an additive in many formulas.

ASDs *See* autism spectrum disorders.

asthma Attacks of wheezing, coughing, and shortness of breath caused by mucus accumulation and swelling of airways. Asthma attacks can be set off by all kinds of irritants such as smoke, allergens, exercise, and cold viruses.

atopic Allergic, as a result of or prone to allergies. Atopic dermatitis, meaning allergic rashes, is another term used for eczema, even though eczema may not always be allergic in nature.

attention deficit hyperactivity disorder (ADHD) A set of behavioral symptoms, such as lack of attention and excessive activity, classified as a specific disorder. A wide range of expressions among children is classified as such, from what many might call a normal, highly active child, to one who is strongly impaired in ability to learn. Related in many ways to autism spectrum disorders, with many overlaps in symptoms, genes, related environmental factors, and with responses to certain treatments.

autism A disorder of brain development showing symptoms of repetitive actions, poor verbal and non-verbal communication abilities, and impaired social interactions.

autism spectrum disorders (ASDs) Autism-related symptom complexes including those diagnosed as Asperger's, Rett syndrome, and pervasive developmental disorder.

Baby Friendly Hospital Initiative A set of guidelines created by WHO and UNICEF as a global effort to create hospital practices that protect, promote, and support breastfeeding.

bacteriocins Antibiotic-type factors created by friendly flora that kill off specific undesirable strains of bacteria.

bacteriophages A huge spectrum of tiny viruses that live among the gut bacteria and play roles in supporting and maintaining the bacterial colonies. They can be likened to the protective flora of bacteria.

Bifidobacteria A genus of bacteria widely found in the intestinal tract, certain species of which are considered very probiotic, or beneficial.

bile A digestive fluid released into the small intestine, when food is present, to aid in the digestion of fats. Bile is dark green to yellowish brown, is made in the liver, stored in the gallbladder, and contributes most of the color of stool.

bilirubin A yellow product of the breakdown of hemoglobin from red blood cells. When excess bilirubin builds up in the body, a yellow tint to the skin and eyes occurs, known as jaundice. Commonly elevated after birth, bilirubin likely provides powerful antioxidant protection to the newborn.

bismuth An element used in treatment of intestinal irritations. It is most commonly combined with aspirin to form bismuth salicylate, a substance used in medications for antibacterial and anti-inflammatory actions. It can combine with sulfur in saliva or in the colon and create a harmless black salt that can color the tongue or stools black.

block feeding A breastfeeding pattern used to help compensate for oversupply issues that are causing ongoing problems for a baby. Consists of restricting baby to one breast for a certain block of time before allowing baby to nurse on the other breast.

blood-brain barrier (BBB) A barrier between the circulating blood and the fluids of the brain that allows only a very limited and controlled spectrum of substances to pass through.

BRAT diet Stands for bananas, rice, applesauce, and plain toast. A bland diet often recommended for diarrhea or upset stomach.

breastfeeding jaundice A jaundice, or yellowing of the skin, in newborns named as such because it is associated with breastfeeding. Implicated as being caused by breastfeeding, it's actually caused by too little breastfeeding, which leads to too little stooling, such that bilirubin products are not being quickly removed by stool.

breastmilk jaundice A jaundice, or yellowing of the skin, in breastfed babies that occurs a little later than breastfeeding jaundice, sometime after the first week. Shown to be common and harmless, and possibly beneficial, as bilirubin is a powerful antioxidant.

broncho-entero-mammary pathway A pathway through which mother's body detects infective agents that her baby is exposed to and then supplies specifically tailored antibodies through her milk. It has been shown that certain cells (dendritic cells) carry bacterial samples directly from the intestines to the breasts, through the lymphatic system. Certain antibody producing cells (B lymphocytes) travel through the lymph system to the breasts as well.

CDC Centers for Disease Control and Prevention. U.S. government agency intended to protect public health and safety through provision of information about the prevention of accidents and disease.

celiac disease The name given to one particular presentation of food sensitivity to gluten proteins, accompanied by damage to intestinal linings.

Clostridium difficile *C. diff.* A bacterium that can cause significant diarrheal illness in babies and elderly, frequently caused by antibiotic usage or exposure to hospital care.

closure Ultimate tightening of cell junctions in intestinal linings, which more greatly limits the passage of proteins through intestinal walls. Occurs as gradual transition, especially from around 4 to 9 months. Considered significant by 6 months of age, at which time it's considered safer to introduce some formula or other foods.

colic Infant colic. Excessive crying in a baby for no serious medical cause. Strictly defined as crying for more than three hours a day for three days a week for at least three weeks.

colitis Irritation (inflammation) of the large intestine, which can result from infection or other disease. Studies show that in infants and young children, the most common cause of colitis is sensitivity to cow's milk protein, soy, or other allergens.

colon *See* large intestine.

colostrum First product of mother's breasts provided in first days after birth before transitioning to full milk. A thick yellowish fluid available from breasts after giving birth and expressible for some time before birth. Has important immune factors and dense nutrition for the baby.

constipation Technically defined as 3 or fewer bowel movements per week for 3 or more weeks, but this definition is not appropriate for infants. For infants, a better definition for constipation is when stools are much less frequent than usual and are also hard and painful and/or very difficult to expel. Typically caused by ignoring signals that it's time to poop, or defecate. Also occurs as a result of hypersensitivity reactions to foods or from high iron in the diet.

Crohn's disease A type of inflammatory bowel disease (IBD). A disorder of the small and/or large intestine accompanied by diarrhea, weight loss, poor nutrient absorption, and sometimes rectal bleeding. *See also* inflammatory bowel disease.

cystic fibrosis A hereditary disease that presents itself in infancy as unusually thick mucus in the lungs and digestive juices in the intestines. These thickened secretions cause frequent lung infections and poor digestion and absorption of nutrients.

cytokines A class of a large number of various small proteins, found in the blood and other areas of the body, that help to control and perform actions of the immune system, regulating various inflammatory responses.

delayed reaction A mostly non-IgE reaction. A type of sensitivity reaction to foods or other allergens that occurs slowly. Abnormal physical reactions to certain agents, usually foods, involving intestinal symptoms, slowly developing rashes, and occasionally mood changes, as opposed to immediate-type reactions such as mouth swelling, restricted breathing, and hives.

dermatitis A general term for any kind of inflammatory skin condition: a rash. Atopic dermatitis, meaning allergic rash, is another term for eczema, even though eczema may not always be allergic in nature.

DHA Docosahexaenoic acid. An important omega-3 fatty acid found in fish oil and in breastmilk and found to be low in standard infant formulas. The body can create this fatty acid from other dietary fats, but it is thought that this ability is low in infants and some others. Some formulas are currently adding this ingredient but without much beneficial result being reported. DHA is especially anti-inflammatory, heart protective, and brain building.

diabetes *See also* type 1 diabetes, type 2 diabetes, gestational diabetes. Diabetes mellitus. A group of disorders that lead to prolonged periods of harmful high blood sugar. Long-term diabetes can lead to many kinds of damage in the body including nerve pain, blindness, loss of limbs, and heart disease. Mild and possibly moderate forms may be controlled with diet and exercise but typically diabetics are treated with the blood sugar controlling hormone insulin.

EC *See* elimination communication.

E. coli *Escherichia coli.* A bacterium found as a predominant part of the normal flora in children and adults and in infants who receive any formula or solid foods. Certain strains of E. coli, different from those normally found in the body, cause illness with diarrhea, sometimes bloody and sometimes with vomiting.

eczema Atopic dermatitis. A persistent skin rash. Some eczema may be simply a condition of dry skin, but most is allergic in nature. Most infant eczema is associated with delayed reactions to certain foods in the child's diet or in the diet of the breastfeeding mother.

elemental formula *See* amino acid formula.

elimination communication (EC) A method used by some parents to begin a progression toward appropriate toilet use from early infancy. EC involves using cues and intuition to recognize when a child is ready to urinate or stool.

elimination diet A dietary means of determining foods that might be causing troubling symptoms in a person by means of eliminating suspect foods in the diet to see whether symptoms subside. The term usually implies that one will later re-challenge suspected foods to see whether symptoms return.

enema Injection of fluid into lower bowel by the squirting of fluid into the rectum via a bulb inserted into the anus, generally for the purpose of relieving constipation.

entero-mammary pathway *See* broncho-entero-mammary pathway.

eosinophil Kind of immune system cell. One type of white blood cell that battles parasites and is also involved in creating allergic reactions and asthma attacks.

eosinophilic esophagitis (EE) A high concentration in esophageal tissues of eosinophils, which are allergy-associated immune system cells arriving as a result of allergic reaction to foods, causing swelling of the throat, difficulty swallowing, and vomiting.

eosinophilic gastroenteritis A high concentration of eosinophils in stomach and/or intestinal tissues. They are allergy-associated immune system cells arriving as a result of allergic reaction to foods and causing stomach and/or intestinal swelling, inflammation, and distress.

EPA Eicosapentaenoic acid. An important omega-3 fatty acid found in fish oil and breastmilk. The body can create this fatty acid from other dietary fats, but it is thought that this ability is low in infants. EPA is not currently considered important to add to infant formulas because it is not found in the brain.

fatty acids Chief building blocks of fats that come in many different types with different functions in the body.

fermentation Specifically, fermentation by intestinal flora. The manner by which intestinal bacteria and fungi digest carbohydrates and some other food products via breaking them down into fatty acids and gases.

ferritin A protein in the body that binds to iron and provides iron storage, especially in the liver, spleen, muscles, and bone marrow. While exclusively breastfed babies born full term seldom develop iron deficiency anemia, they commonly have low iron stores, indicated by a low serum ferritin finding. This provides for reduced susceptibility to infection.

flora The friendly microbes, chiefly bacteria, that normally live on and in the body, throughout the digestive tract, and chiefly in the large intestine. *E. coli*, bifidobacteria, and lactobacillus are examples. Normal flora help break down some undigested materials, create healthy fatty acids, create some vitamins, help prevent the growth of harmful bacteria, and help to regulate the intestines in many other ways.

foremilk The first portions of breastmilk that come out of the breasts during a nursing or pumping session. Foremilk is higher in lactose than the later hindmilk. In actuality, two kinds of milk—foremilk and hindmilk—are not made; rather, it's a gradual transition from sugary milk to high fat milk. These terms are simply used for descriptive purposes.

foremilk-hindmilk imbalance It's thought that frequent small snacks can cause baby to obtain high quantities of high-lactose foremilk, which causes baby to have symptoms—such as green stools, gassiness, and fussiness—due to higher doses of lactose sugar than available lactase enzyme levels can handle.

functional A disorder is medically labeled as functional when doctors are unable to find any measurable differences or signs such as laboratory results or examination findings. A functional cause may be neurological, hormonal, or a low level immune reaction. The term is interpreted by many to mean that the cause is psychological or psychosomatic.

gastritis Inflammation and irritation of the stomach. May result from food allergy, infection, or possibly from a chronic gastric floral imbalance.

gastroenteritis Irritation (inflammation) of the stomach and/or small intestine as a result of infection or other agent, generally resulting in diarrhea. Gastroenteritis typically equates with infectious diarrhea, but the term is also combined in eosinophilic gastroenteritis, which is an allergic inflammation. Other food reactions, stress reactions, and floral imbalances may also be responsible for gastroenteritis symptoms.

gastroesophageal reflux (GER) Reflux. In adults, often termed acid reflux or heartburn. The term given to the spilling of fluids from the stomach upwards into the esophagus (throat) and possibly all the way up and out of the mouth. This is a common occurrence for a large percentage of infants, and the fluids are often less acidic than in adults. Reflux may be exhibited in babies as spitting up, vomiting, or coughing, and sometimes fussiness or other signs of pain.

gastroesophageal reflux disease (GERD) Reflux disease. A serious condition of chronic spilling upward of stomach contents into the throat and often out the mouth or nose. Chronically refluxed acid can cause damage to esophageal tissues and, in infants, great irritability, feeding difficulties, poor sleep, and sometimes weight loss.

GBS Group B strep.

GER *See* gastroesophageal reflux.

GERD *See* gastroesophageal reflux disease.

gestational diabetes When a pregnant woman who was not previously diabetic develops high blood sugar. Many possible risks occur, particularly to the fetus. Frequently treatable by dietary management. *See also* diabetes.

Gilbert's syndrome Hereditary condition that brings on mild bouts of jaundice and itchiness throughout life and is a little known genetic quirk that actually affects 3 to 7% of Americans. People with Gilbert's syndrome have reduced activity in an enzyme that helps in the clearing of bilirubin from the bloodstream, which has been found to extend the lifespan of people with Gilbert's syndrome.

glycerin suppositories Soft, capsule-shaped and -sized tablets containing the slippery, sugar-like compound, glycerin. They're intended to be inserted just inside the anus to provide soothing lubrication for hard stools. Pediatric suppositories are commonly prescribed by physicians and are available over the counter for parents who've gotten the okay.

gripe water A liquid mixture of various herbs or other agents intended to relieve stomach distress and typically given by dropper for infant colic and reflux.

group B strep (GBS) Obstetricians are aware that when a bacterium known as group B strep is colonizing a mother's vagina during pregnancy, her baby is more likely to develop an early infection with this bacterium after birth. Precautionary antibiotics are given to infected mothers during labor even though a scientific review finds no decrease in infant deaths from this practice, and a great number of other complications result.

H. pylori *Helicobacter pylori*. A bacterium that colonizes the stomach or small intestine in a portion of children and adults; it's often linked to chronic inflammation, sometimes leading to painful ulcer formation.

heme The iron-containing non-protein portion of hemoglobin, which is the oxygen-carrying compound of blood.

hemoglobin Consisting of heme units, the protein compound in red blood cells that carries oxygen and that's red when full of oxygen. A hemoglobin blood test will show whether the blood is too low in iron, referred to as iron deficiency anemia, which leads to a reduced ability to carry oxygen in the blood.

hiatal hernia Physical condition when a bit of stomach has pushed up (herniated) through the diaphragm. This elevates and weakens the sphincter between the esophagus and stomach and enlarges the opening in the diaphragm. Often blamed as a cause of reflux, its mere presence in a child should not call for any kind of treatment and, unless it is large, it is likely not the key cause of reflux.

hindmilk The later portions of breastmilk that come out of the breasts during a longer nursing or pumping session. It's higher in fat than the earlier foremilk. In actuality, two kinds of milk—foremilk and hindmilk—are not made; rather, it's a gradual transition from sugary milk to higher fat milk. These terms are simply used for descriptive purposes.

Hirschsprung's disease A congenital form of megacolon; a condition in which the nerves that control the muscle contractions responsible for moving stool through the colon are not completely formed as a fetus develops. This insufficiency may affect one small section of the colon or larger parts of the intestine.

histamine An immune system agent released in reaction to unwanted microbes in order to signal defensive immune system responses. In an allergic individual, histamine is released in excessive reaction to allergens, which leads to inflammatory immune system actions and undesirable symptoms in both upper airways and the intestines. bacteria ("pneumococcus") that cause several kinds of infections, such as pneumonia, meningitis, ear infections, sinus infections, and bloodstream infections.

human milk fortifier Premature infant formulas, generally cow milk-derived, specifically designed and promoted for addition to human milk to compensate for supposed need to boost protein or other nutrients in mother's milk or donor milk.

hydrolyzed Chemically broken down into smaller molecules.

hydrolyzed milk formula Promoted for formula-fed infants who are milk allergic; has proteins broken down into their amino acid building blocks, although the process is generally incomplete and some potentially allergy-producing intact proteins remain.

hygiene theory Theory to explain the development of allergies in young children, created from observations that children in more modern or sterile environments seem to develop more allergic tendencies. Refers to concept that children exposed to fewer and less variety of bacteria may have a greater propensity for developing allergies.

hypersensitivity Sensitivity reaction. A term sometimes used interchangeably with the terms food intolerance, food sensitivity, and allergy, especially relating to delayed-type allergies. It's an over-reaction by some inflammation- or hormone-regulatory agents in the body that produces unwanted symptoms in response to certain foods or other agents that most people do not react to.

hypothyroidism A disorder that occurs when not enough thyroid hormone is available. Thyroid hormone controls the rate of body processes. Some signs of hypothyroidism in a young infant are late birth or large size at birth, prolonged jaundice after birth, constipation, poor feeding, cold limbs, and a hoarse cry.

IBD *See* inflammatory bowel disease.

IBS *See* irritable bowel syndrome.

IgA antibodies A class of antibodies that help protect against invading organisms in the digestive tract and other mucous membrane tissues. Young infants are unable to develop good IgA responses, but IgA antibodies are secreted in high quantities in breastmilk, through which they provide immune protection against organisms invading via the nose and mouth in nursing children.

IgE antibodies A class of antibodies that function in protection against parasites and also cause allergic reactions to various agents in allergic people. They react quickly to the presence of allergens and induce histamine releases that prompt further inflammatory responses.

IgG antibodies A class of antibodies involved in a later phase of immune response to invading organisms. IgG is also often involved in intestinal responses to food allergens in delayed-type food sensitivity reactions. IgG antibodies cross mother's placenta to be stored in the infant's system and assist the infant in protection against many organisms the mother has immunity to, for about 6 to 9 months. Some IgG antibodies are also provided in breastmilk.

IgM antibodies A class of antibodies involved in early response of the immune system to invading organisms. IgM is also often involved in intestinal delayed-type food sensitivity responses.

immediate reaction Also known as type 1 hypersensitivity reaction or IgE reaction. Allergic reaction that begins minutes after exposure to an agent to which one is sensitized. An immediate-type food reaction that can occur shortly after eating or possibly just breathing the food, involves IgE antibodies, and that may produce hives; swelling of the lips, tongue, and throat; and difficulty breathing.

infectious diarrhea Term usually equated with gastroenteritis. Illness with frequent watery stools, possibly along with vomiting, as a result of intestinal infection. Rotavirus and norovirus are the most common sources of intestinal infection in children.

inflammation The process of immune system response to infection or other irritation. Tiny blood vessels become leaky so that white blood cells can leak out into the assaulted area to fight invading organisms and initiate other protective and healing responses. At times inflammation can become excessive and problematic. Allergic and sensitivity reactions involve unwanted and unneeded inflammatory responses that cause discomfort and damage tissues.

inflammatory bowel disease (IBD) A group of painful, chronic intestinal irritations generally involving diarrhea and ulceration of intestinal tissues, which leads to poor absorption of valuable nutrients. An inflammatory condition in the large and/or small intestine: chiefly, Crohn's disease or ulcerative colitis. Symptoms may come and go and can include weight loss, abdominal pain, gas, bloating, diarrhea, green stools, and rectal bleeding. The tendency toward developing an IBD may be hereditary, but many environmental factors are involved, such as early antibiotic drug exposure, early infant formula exposure, and non-avoidance of foods to which the digestive system is reacting. Although mainstream treatment is immune-blocking drugs and surgery, most IBD sufferers will go into remission on a diet free of dairy proteins, other tailored dietary modifications, flora restoration, and other gut healing measures. (Not to be confused with irritable bowel syndrome, IBS).

intolerance Food or chemical intolerance. The term can be used generally to include any sort of negative reactions to foods or chemicals in sensitive people, as sensitivity or hypersensitivity reaction. The term is also used in a stricter sense to refer to lactase enzyme deficiency (lactose intolerance); various other digestive enzyme deficiencies; or to gluten intolerance (celiac disease), a chronic inflammatory reaction to wheat and some other grains.

intussusception An odd folding of a piece of intestine inside itself that creates a dangerous intestinal blockage. May produce raspberry-colored poop with gel-like blood and mucus, likened to red currant jelly. Requires *immediate* medical attention.

inulin A specific kind of fiber found in many vegetables and some fruits. Inulin is found to be highly effective at feeding healthy flora. Extracted inulin is often used as a prebiotic supplement for promoting healthy flora.

iron deficiency anemia Reduced ability of the blood to carry oxygen to the tissues of the body due to inadequate iron. Iron is needed to form hemoglobin, the oxygen carrying portion of red blood cells. A blood test result of low hemoglobin indicates iron deficiency anemia.

irritable bowel syndrome (IBS) Chronic but fluctuating intestinal discomfort that may present with frequent diarrhea or may involve both diarrhea and constipation. It is a more vague diagnosis that is often made when no other causes for intestinal symptoms can be found. IBS has similar symptoms to IBD but typically with little inflammation or intestinal damage, and no bleeding. It can often be controlled with adaptive dietary measures. Stress and floral imbalance can increase episodes.

jaundice Yellow discoloration of the skin and eyes due to accumulation of bilirubin, a normal breakdown product of red blood cells that are in excess after birth. Jaundice is commonly seen in breastfed infants in the first days and weeks after birth. Because of slight possibility of brain damage if levels become excessively high, monitoring of bilirubin may be required. It can be treated with exposure of skin to blue or green light, or to sunlight.

kangaroo care A method of providing heightened physical contact with a newborn in order to provide body warmth and to neurologically and hormonally stimulate the infant to heighten regulation of breathing, digestion, heartbeat, and other functions. Especially of value for premature infants. Typically, the infant wears only a diaper and is held against the adult's bare chest, often between the mother's breasts to encourage thoughts of breastfeeding.

La Leche League, International (LLLI) An international organization of mothers dedicated to providing breastfeeding information and support to pregnant and nursing mothers. LLLI typically offers local monthly informative meetings and other modes of mother-to-mother support.

lactase The enzyme that digests the milk sugar lactose. Because lactose is only found in mammal milks, which are only intended for babies, it is usual for lactase enzyme production to wane after childhood. This natural condition in humans is commonly called lactase enzyme deficiency or lactose intolerance. Many people of Northern European descent have inherited genes for lactase enzyme persistence and tolerate lactose throughout most of their lifespan.

lactation The *making* and providing of milk through the mammary glands (breasts).

lactobacilli *Lactobacillus* is a genus, or group of bacteria, that make up a small but beneficial portion of normal intestinal (and vaginal) flora. They're found in great abundance in exclusively breastfed infant intestines and provide powerful immune protection. *Lactobacillus acidophilus*, *L. casei*, and *L. brevis* are example species of beneficial lactobacillus bacteria.

lactoferrin A breastmilk protein that binds with iron and supplies highly absorbable iron to the infant while protecting the iron from being available to feed unwanted bacteria. Provides great amount of immune protection to exclusively breastfed infants. Tiny amounts of lactoferrin are also found in tears and saliva and in other mammal milks.

lactose Sugar naturally found only in milks, such as breastmilk and cow milk. Present in many milk formulas and in other foods made from milk. It feeds beneficial flora and provides immune support when it is the predominant source of sugar.

lactose intolerance The lack of good lactase enzyme activity for lactose digestion typically in older children and adults because lactose is naturally only intended for babies. Many adults of Northern European descent maintain lactase enzyme persistence, easily digesting lactose for much of their adult lives.

lactulose An artificial sugar made from chemically altering lactose. Often prescribed for constipation in children, does not add sugar calories or raise blood sugar, and feeds beneficial flora.

large intestine Colon. Last portion of the digestive system, ending in the rectum. Water is absorbed from the colon, firming up the stool as it is stored until evacuation. The colon houses the majority of intestinal flora and absorbs vitamins made by these colonic bacteria.

latex *See* aloe vera latex.

leaky gut Impairments in the tightness and completeness of the cellular junctions along the walls of the intestines, which allows proteins and various other components to leak through the incomplete barrier and into the blood stream; the presence of uninvited proteins in the blood stream can cause allergic and immune reactions. Young infant intestines are naturally "leaky" for passing factors from mother's milk, but otherwise a leaky gut is a result of intestinal inflammatory damage.

leptin A hormone in breastmilk that helps baby gradually feel full and limit his milk intake to just the right amount.

lower esophageal sphincter A muscle ring between the esophagus and stomach. Intended to allow swallowed contents headed down the esophagus to enter into the stomach but prevent acid-drenched stomach contents from making their way back up.

lysozyme Found in saliva, tears, mucus, and breastmilk, it's an enzyme that provides protection from infection by breaking down the walls of bacteria.

manual disimpaction Use of a finger to gently coax out hard pellets of stool blocking a person's rectum.

meconium staining When meconium has passed into the amniotic fluid before baby is born. Although rather common, it's considered a sign that baby may have been under stress. There are concerns that, when staining is present, baby may aspirate some meconium into her lungs.

meconium The first stool of a newborn. Thick and greenish black, meconium is made up of shed skin and hair cells and other materials the infant filters out of the amniotic fluid as he regularly drinks the fluid and urinates the liquid portion back out.

megacolon An enlarged section of colon that. can be acquired when a child continually withholds stool, and a portion of the intestine becomes progressively stretched. The muscles in that section weaken, and the section of colon may even become paralyzed. Periods of total blockage may result and serious infection can occur above the obstruction.

meningitis A serious inflammation of the membranes covering the brain and spinal cord (the meninges), usually due to a viral, bacterial, or other infection, although there are several possible non-infectious causes. Consequences can be serious because of the proximity to the brain.

microbiome Person's entire makeup of microbial inhabitants. All bacteria, viruses, bacteriophages, and fungi found on or in a person's body, such as on their skin, in their sinuses and other orifices, and in their intestines.

microbiota Flora. The microbes that make up a microbiome.

milk oversupply A great abundance of breastmilk production that may slightly overwhelm a young nursing infant with a strong ejection of milk or that may cause symptoms of fussiness and green stools due to a high portion of foremilk and lactose consumption.

MRSA Methicillin-resistant *Staphylococcus aureus* is a form of staph bacteria that has developed resistance to a large group of standard antibiotics. MRSA is an increasing source of dangerous infection; once an infection danger mostly inside hospitals, community-acquired MRSA is widespread today.

NAP1 A very severe strain of *C. diff* that has become prominent and is affecting children as well as elderly people

necrotizing enterocolitis (NEC) A life-threatening intestinal condition that is almost entirely linked to formula feeding in premature infants; part of the intestinal lining becomes inflamed and dies off as acids build and secondary infection sets in.

NICU Neonatal intensive care unit, or intensive care nursery (ICN). Hospital unit specializing in the care of premature or ill newborns.

non-IgE reaction A hypersensitivity reaction that does not involve IgE antibodies and that is a delayed reaction. A non-IgE food reaction may begin 2 hours to 2 days, or occasionally 3 days, after the food exposure, and may involve many various immune system factors such as IgG, IgA, and IgM antibodies, T cells, and various cytokines.

norovirus Common viral gastrointestinal infection in babies and aged. Symptoms include vomiting and watery diarrhea. It's spread by contaminated food or from one infected individual to another. Spread is fecal-to-oral or possibly respiratory as viral particles are aerosolized above fresh vomit, for instance. Short-term immunity occurs after infection, but not permanent immunity.

NSAIDs Non-steroidal anti-inflammatory drugs, sold over-the-counter and also as prescriptions, and typically used for reduction of pain, inflammation, and fever. Ibuprofen (Advil, Motrin), naproxen, and aspirin are popular examples. They can cause damage to the stomach lining and cause bleeding. Fever reduction can prolong illness. Other dangerous but very rare side-effects occur.

oligosaccharides Fiber-like factors in breastmilk that feed health-promoting flora and help to prevent unwanted bacteria, viruses, and even parasites from gaining hold of the intestinal wall.

omega-3 fatty acid A class of fatty acids nutritionally important for maintaining nerves and other cells of the body. The three major types are alpha-linolenic acid (ALA), eicosapentaenoic acid (EPA), and docosahexaenoic acid (DHA). DHA and EPA come from breastmilk, fish oils, certain animal organs (seldom consumed today), krill, and algae, and are more readily used by the body. The body can also make these fatty acids from ALA, found in nut and seed sources, though infants and many others have poor conversion abilities.

opportunistic bacteria Bacteria that may reside for long periods of time, or permanently, among a person's flora, without detrimental infection, but that will take the opportunity to develop infection and illness when the immune system is impaired. Opportunistic bacteria may serve to keep even more serious bacteria in check.

oral rehydration Appropriate electrolyte fluids provided to baby by mouth (orally) in order to prevent dehydration during an illness where bodily fluids are being quickly lost via vomiting or diarrhea.

organic disorder An organic disorder is any condition in which there is a visible or measurable physical change in the body that reveals the existence of the disorder.

oxytocin Hormone released in response to close contact, especially skin-to-skin contact. Oxytocin improves immune system responses and promotes bonding and a sense of well-being.

patch test A longer acting kind of skin test than scratch testing, helpful in discovering some delayed-type hypersensitivity reactions that produce rashes. Potential allergens are planted across an area of the back and watched over days for the development of local reactions in the skin.

phototherapy Exposure to full spectrum light or specific light waves for therapeutic purposes. Visible blue and green light rays are especially helpful for promoting beneficial bilirubin breakdown in infants with excessive jaundice.

physiologic jaundice Mild to moderate jaundice seen commonly in newborns; should be considered normal and is thus referred to as physiologic jaundice, as a part of normal physiology. *See also* jaundice.

pneumococcal vaccine Pneumonia vaccine. Vaccination against many strains of *Streptococcus pneumoniae* bacteria ("pneumococcus") that cause several kinds of infections, such as pneumonia, meningitis, ear infections, sinus infections, and bloodstream infections.

pneumonia Inflammation of the lung, generally caused by bacterial or viral infection. It's a lower respiratory tract infection that causes difficulty breathing.

PPI drugs Proton pump inhibitors. A newer class of antacid drugs, such as omeprazole, Prevacid, or Prilosec. They reduce stomach acid secretion and are used to treat reflux, ulcers, and some other disorders. Prescribed commonly for infant reflux diagnoses without good evidence of benefits.

prebiotics Dietary or supplemental fiber substances that act as food for beneficial probiotic bacteria in the intestines and that improve their activity. Prebiotics are typically certain kinds of complex carbohydrates known as soluble fiber.

probiotics Specific strains of bacteria, such as members of the lactobacillus and bifidobacterium groups, and possibly fungi, that add to the quality of one's natural intestinal flora, potentially improving the overall health of an individual. Probiotic bacteria occur in yogurt and in other fermented foods as well. Probiotic supplements are available in powder, capsule, or liquid forms.

pyloric stenosis A thickening of the sphincter that controls emptying of the stomach into the small intestine. Thickening causes narrowing of the stomach exit and projectile vomiting. Most commonly found in young, formula-fed infants.

rectum The final portion of the large intestine, ending at the anus. Acts as storage for stool. As stool accumulates in rectum, nerve signals are sent that provide an urge to poop, or defecate. If pooping, or stooling does not occur, the stool may be returned up to the colon where more water will be absorbed before the intestine's next effort to have the stool evacuated.

reflux *See* gastroesophageal reflux.

respiratory infection Respiratory tract infection. Overgrowth of bacteria, a virus, or fungi in some portion of the respiratory tract—such as the sinuses, throat, or lungs—that causes illness and discomfort. Upper respiratory tract infections include an ear infection, sore throat, or a cold. Pneumonia is a lower respiratory tract infection affecting the lungs.

Reye syndrome A syndrome, or set of serious symptoms, blamed on the use of aspirin along with chicken pox or other viral disease. The existence of this syndrome has been debunked, although aspirin does have risks, including when used during viral infections.

rotavirus Virus that is the leading cause of severe diarrhea in infants and young children. Symptoms include vomiting and watery diarrhea. Spread by contaminated food or from one infected individual to another. Spread is fecal-to-oral or possibly respiratory as viral particles are aerosolized above fresh vomit, for instance. Some level of immunity can develop after a first exposure.

salmonella infection Bacterial illness that previously was known for food poisoning illness but has recently increased in incidence due to widespread antibiotic use, especially in young children. Salmonella may be a quiet part of flora, possibly obtained from visiting a doctor or hospital. Infection and diarrheal illness can occur when competitive bacteria are wiped out by antibiotic drugs, allowing tougher salmonella to take over.

sensitivity reaction *See* hypersensitivity reaction.

serotonin A hormone, or chemical messenger, chiefly found in the digestive tract. Serotonin receptors also occur in the brain and respond with pleasant emotions. Certain intestinal food reactions can cause altered serotonin in the brain, leading to altered or swinging moods.

SIDS *See* sudden infant death syndrome.

skin test Scratch test or patch test to look for allergic responses. Scratch tests involve dozens of tiny scratches in skin on the back and application of minute amounts of various substances that are suspected of causing immediate-type allergy. After 15 minutes or so, each individual scratch is observed for the presence of redness or swelling, indicating an allergic reaction. *See also* patch test.

small intestine Portion of the digestive tract from the stomach to the large intestine. Receives digestive juices, and most food digestion and nutrient absorption occur along the small intestine.

sorbitol A natural fruit sugar, especially high in prunes. Weakly digested and thus remains to draw water into the intestines, thereby loosening stools. Sometimes prescribed for baby constipation. Used in "sugar-free" candies.

species The biological classification name for a type of organism. Families of bacteria and other organisms are divided into genera and then into species. Microorganism names consist of their genus and species, such as *Lactobacillus acidophilus*. Species tend to represent a group of organisms that are capable of breeding with each other.

staph Common shortened name for bacteria of the genus *Staphylococci*, generally referring to an infection. Most species of *Staphylococci* are non-infecting. A staph infection is generally from the common infective species, *Staphylococcus aureus*.

Staphylococcus aureus Most commonly infectious strain of staph bacteria, recently growing in its infective rate and power both inside and outside of hospitals, most notoriously as MRSA, or Methicillin-resistant *S. aureus*.

stool transplants Insertion via enema of a rather large amount of stool from a very healthy individual into an individual that is quite ill with gastroenteritis, with the intention of replacing flora to cure individual. Procedure has a high cure rate for *C. difficile*.

strain A sub-variety of a species of microorganism. A species may be divided into many sub-types, or strains, just as dogs are divided into many breeds. Different strains, varieties, or breeds are theoretically able to breed with each other and produce offspring.

strep Common shortened name for bacteria of the genus *Streptococcus*, generally referring to an infection. Several species of *Streptococci* are known to be helpful flora and several other species can become infective when given the opportunity. Group B strep is a popular strep bacterium because it is tested for in late pregnancy and implicated in potentially infecting newborns. Streptococcus pneumoniae ("pneumococcus") strains are well known for their ability to cause several kinds of infections, such as pneumonia, meningitis, ear infections, sinus infections, "strep throat," skin, and bloodstream infections.

sudden infant death syndrome (SIDS) The sudden and unexplained death of an apparently healthy infant between one month and one year old. Many suffocation deaths were once lumped in with SIDS deaths, but increasing efforts are being made to distinguish between suffocation deaths and unexplained, SIDS deaths.

tape test Home test for existence of an intestinal worm infection. A piece of Scotch Tape is taped to itself to make a ring with the sticky side out. Place this sticky ring of tape in close to anus, just before bed time, and leave it there for the night. Bring the tape to doctor's office to be inspected under a microscope for the presence of worm eggs.

tongue-tie A tongue that is over-anchored to the bottom of the mouth, restricting its movement. It can prevent a baby from being able to efficiently obtain milk from mother's breast.

total parenteral nutrition (TPN) Provision of a full nutrition solution through a major blood vessel, rather than by mouth. TPN is often required for prematurely born infants and can cause liver damage and poses infection risks.

trans fat Hydrogenated vegetable oil. Oil that is unnaturally altered to remain solid at room temperature. Consumption of trans fats, typically found in pre-packaged foods and many restaurants, raises bad cholesterol (LDL), and increases risks of heart disease and cancer. One must read package ingredients in order to avoid these, as even a label stating zero grams per serving may contain nearly one half gram.

triclosan Ingredient used in many products labeled as antibacterial, including soaps, wipes, and hand sanitizers. Strongly suspected of being a hormone disruptor for both thyroid and estrogen, and a possible carcinogen.

type 1 diabetes A condition in which pancreatic cells that develop insulin—which manages blood sugar levels—are destroyed by an individual's own immune system. *See also* diabetes.

type 2 diabetes Once called adult-onset diabetes—now occurs at increasingly younger ages. In this insulin-resistant diabetes, blood sugar levels can become dangerously high as insulin loses its effectiveness. *See also* diabetes.

ulcerative colitis A type of inflammatory bowel disease (IBD) that affects only the colon and is associated with chronic abdominal pain and weight loss. Ulcers, or open sores, frequently develop throughout the colon, causing blood in the stools. *See also* inflammatory bowel disease.

villi Intestinal villi. Small finger-like projections that cover the walls of the small intestine where they increase the surface area and provide specialized cells for nutrient absorption.

villous atrophy Destruction of the villi, the tiny fingerlike projections that cover the walls of the small intestine. Damage to the villi interferes greatly with the absorption of nutrients. Commonly seen in celiac disease and other intestinal hypersensitivity reactions.

WHO World Health Organization. Coordinated by the United Nations, a worldwide organization that acts to promote the general health of the people of the world; campaigns specifically to boost nutrition and to reduce tobacco usage; and acts to monitor, prevent, and treat infectious diseases.

withholding of stool Especially common during toddlerhood, the chronic ignoring of the body's signals to pass stools and the purposeful holding-in of stools. Resultant constipation leads to painful stool passage and further desire to withhold. Sometimes withholding behavior is missed because loose stool from above a hard blockage area of stool will leak past the blockage and soil underpants or diaper.

Index

LINDA F. PALMER, D.C. After running a successful chiropractic practice focused on nutrition and women's health for over a decade, Palmer's life became transformed in 1995 as she was confronted not only with health challenges in her newborn son but also with a lack of useful advice from pediatric sources. As she delved into medical studies, she became amazed by large conflicts between the research findings and standard pediatric protocols. Her extensive literature reviews and consults with young families culminated in her writing *Baby Matters*. After an IPPY Award-winning 2nd ed., the 3rd ed. was temporarily released as *The Baby Bond*. After a print-run sell-out, *Baby Matters* is back. Palmer also co-authored *What Your Pediatrician Doesn't Know* with pediatrician Susan Markel.

Extensively documented, her healthy parenting books present the scientific evidence behind attachment parenting practices, supporting baby's immune system, and sparing drug usage. Palmer has instructed in physiology, pathology, and pediatric nutrition, lectured in breastfeeding, and has served as one of Mothering's "Ask The Experts" since 2001. She lives in San Diego with her son and physicist husband. You can find an assortment of infant health articles at her website, BabyReference.com, and her Facebook pages, The Baby Bond and Baby Poop.

SUSAN MARKEL, M.D., is a board-certified pediatrician who has a private consultative practice specializing in parent coaching and child health. A graduate of Tufts University School of Medicine in Boston, Dr. Markel became a fellow of the American Academy of Pediatrics in 1981, and an International Board Certified Lactation Consultant (IBCLC) in 1997. During her years in private pediatrics practice in central Connecticut, Dr. Markel was an assistant clinical professor of pediatrics at the University of Connecticut Health Center, teaching pediatric residents. For many years, she served as a medical liaison for the breastfeeding support organization La Leche League International.

Susan Markel and Linda Palmer first collaborated on producing Markel's well-received book: *What Your Pediatrician Doesn't Know Can Hurt Your Child*. For a private parenting and infant health telephone consultation, find Dr. Markel at AttachmentParentingDoctor.com.

1/17 ② 2/16